SCOTT
The Rhymer

SCOTT
The Rhymer

NANCY MOORE GOSLEE

THE UNIVERSITY PRESS OF KENTUCKY

Publication of this book was made possible in part
by a grant from the University of Tennessee
Better English Fund, established by John C. Hodges.

Copyright © 1988 by The University Press of Kentucky

Scholarly publisher for the Commonwealth,
serving Bellarmine College, Berea College, Centre
College of Kentucky, Eastern Kentucky University,
The Filson Club, Georgetown College, Kentucky
Historical Society, Kentucky State University,
Morehead State University, Murray State University,
Northern Kentucky University, Transylvania University,
University of Kentucky, University of Louisville,
and Western Kentucky University.

Editorial and Sales Offices: Lexington, Kentucky 40506-0336

Library of Congress Cataloging-in-Publication Data

Goslee, Nancy Moore, 1941-
  Scott the rhymer / Nancy Moore Goslee.

  p. cm.
  Bibliography: p.
  Includes index.
  ISBN 978-0-8131-5274-5
  1. Scott, Walter, Sir, 1771-1832—Poetic works. 2. Narrative
poetry, Scottish—History and criticism. 3. Scotland in literature.
4. Romanticism—Scotland. I. Title.
PR5343.P63G66   1988
821'.7—dc19   88-5513

This book is printed on acid-free paper meeting
the requirements of the American National Standard
for Permanence of Paper for Printed Library Materials.

∞

To my daughter
SUSAN

CONTENTS

Acknowledgments ix

Abbreviations x

Introduction 1

1. *The Lay of the Last Minstrel:*
Page and Book 18

2. *Marmion:* The Metaphor of Forgery 41

3. *The Lady of the Lake:*
Romance as Theme and Structure 67

4. *Rokeby:* "Fatal Art"
and the Redeemed Estate 95

5. *The Bridal of Triermain:* "Fragments
of . . . Rifted Stone" 129

6. *The Lord of the Isles:* History,
Scenery, and Fictions of Silence 155

7. *Harold the Dauntless:*
Plundering a Name 177

Conclusion 206

Notes 216

Index 243

ACKNOWLEDGMENTS

I WISH to express my thanks to the Pierpont Morgan Library for the use of the autograph manuscript (M451) and first printed edition (PML 44351) of *The Bridal of Triermain*, and to the staffs of the Morgan Library and the Houghton Library at Harvard University for their helpfulness. The University of Tennessee Graduate School Faculty Research Fund supported travel to the Scott conference in Aberdeen, and the John C. Hodges Fund for Better English of the University of Tennessee provided travel money to two other conferences, summer research grants, and an additional grant to assist in the publication of this book.

I wish also to thank the following journals and editors for permission to use material they have published in earlier form: *Texas Studies in Language and Literature* 17 (1975): 737-75, for "Romance as Theme and Structure in Scott's *The Lady of the Lake*"; *Scottish Literary Journal* 7 (1980): 85-96, for "*Marmion* and the Metaphor of Forgery"; *Scott and His Influence*, ed. J.H. Alexander and David Hewitt (Aberdeen: Association for Scottish Literary Studies, 1983), pp. 41-50, for " 'Letters in the Irish Tongue': Interpreting Ireland in Scott's *Rokeby*"; and *Romanticism and Feminism*, ed. Anne Mellor (Bloomington: Indiana University Press, 1988), pp. 115-36, for "Witch or Pawn: Women in Scott's Narrative Poetry."

ABBREVIATIONS

BT	The Bridal of Triermain
FQ	Fairie Queene
H	Harold the Dauntless
JL	Jerusalemme Liberata
L	The Lay of the Last Minstrel
LI	The Lord of the Isles
LL	The Lady of the Lake
Letters	The Letters of Sir Walter Scott
M	Marmion
Minstrelsy	Minstrelsy of the Scottish Border
OF	Orlando Furioso
PW	Scott's Poetical Works
R	Rokeby

INTRODUCTION

TO DISTINGUISH this book from much recent writing on his novels, *Scott the Poet* would make a satisfactory enough title—but a prosaic one. Further, its flat claim is too restricted, as if he were the only poet worthy of the name. Though readers in 1810, at the peak of his poetic reputation, might well have agreed upon such a claim, his absence from the modern canon of Romantic poets strongly refutes it. My aim is to recall his presence. Giving this book, and thus Scott, the title "Rhymer" recalls a specific element of his poetry, its closeness to the speech and song of oral tradition, and also a specific, half-legendary and half-mythical figure who offers a model for the poetry arising out of that tradition.

Like other serious medievalists of his time, Scott identified the thirteenth-century border minstrel Thomas of Ercildoun as the author of the Auchinleck Manuscript's romance *Sir Tristrem*. Like many less scholarly readers of romances, he also identified him as that Thomas the Rhymer who rides out of history to become the protagonist of his own romance, following the elfin queen to her alien paradise under the border country's Eildon Hills.[1] From his inclusion of the ballad *Thomas the Rhymer* in his *Minstrelsy of the Scottish Border*, Scott returned to the Rhymer again and again until the end of his life. As Ruth Eller and Judith Wilt have shown, this figure signified a deep poetic impulse that remained even after Scott's apparently thorough-going conversion to the novel and continued to shape its patterns.[2] More than the symbolic focus of an impulse or feeling, however, this questing, visionary protagonist who yet comments wryly upon his own art offers a model for analyzing the structural and thematic patterns of Scott's major narrative poems, those apparently naive but often skillfully ironic plays of hermeneutic perspective. My analysis of these patterns will begin with the genre of romance illustrated in the Rhymer's journey and will explore both the "mode" or mood of its created world and its formal structures.[3] As Thomas the Rhymer does in hs own ballad, moreover, this analysis will repeatedly move beyond the world of romance to consider its relationship to various "realities" beyond it. The first of these realities that provides a context for romance is the development of poetry from a communal oral tradition to the more solitary relationship with an audience achieved through writing and publishing, a relationship subject to the demands of written legal and historical evidence. The second is the larger, more violent development of Scottish and British history from feudal to modern cultures. The third is the contrast between the limited, passive roles of women in those actual historical cultures and their archetypal, powerful roles of elfin queen or elfin changeling in romance.

For modern readers, the elfin queen who leads the Rhymer into her enchanted world is apt to recall not the ballad or medieval romance, nor even Scott's publication of them in the *Minstrelsy*, but Keats's transformation of that source in *La Belle Dame Sans Merci*.[4] Still another reason, then, for alluding to Thomas the Rhymer as a model for Scott the poet is to confront and clarify Scott's relationships to the now better-known poets who were his contemporaries in the romantic period. Because Keats's ballad explores the power and the cost of visionary imagination, it powerfully exemplifies what M. H. Abrams, Northrop Frye, Harold Bloom, and others have called "high romanticism": poetry that claims an autonomous, constitutive power for the imagination, but then often recoils from its own heretically-divine creativity. In spite of such last-minute conformity, this poetry is characterized by religious, political, and aesthetic insubordination, by Promethean rebellion, and, often, by a Promethean isolation.[5] Furthermore, that autonomy of imagination also manifests itself in a richly metaphorical texture, in contrast to the often almost formulaic rapidity of Scott's poetry, close to its origins in the oral tradition. Recently, Jerome McGann and Marilyn Butler have argued that this "high" romanticism should not be the sole norm, because it excludes the realistic, ironic, and often politically and metaphysically conservative work of the novelists Austen and Scott, and because it only awkwardly and partially includes the realistic and ironic, if radical, poet Byron. Romanticism thus demands either a larger definition or an updating of Lovejoy's plurality of definitions.[6]

Stimulated by Lukacs's analysis of the way historical process acts out its struggles in the apparently passive Waverley hero, critics are already well-embarked on a revaluation of Scott's novels.[7] Until recently, this revaluation has directed itself toward the canon of the nineteenth-century novel and not, given its generic focus, toward the canon of romantic poetry. Further, although these political, social, and historical readings of the novels offer a valuable context for reading Scott's poems, their standards of realism offer a one-sided perspective upon the symbolic, even mythical, representations of historical conflict in the poems. Thus, McGann's and Butler's calls for including realism as well as visionary imagination in the romantic canon may pave the way for Scott's novels without doing so for the poems that are already closer to the works of high romanticism than to the novels.

A few critics have written well about Scott's poetry.[8] Three other recent critical developments, however, can help to clear a place for a wider reading of those critics and for a more extensive reevaluation of these poems. The first is a tendency within the criticism of Scott's novels. Since the studies of Alexander Welsh (1963), Francis Hart (1966), and Robert C. Gordon (1969), patterns of romance in the novels have appeared as valuable shaping structures instead of flaws in their realism. More recently Graham McMaster, Jane Millgate, Daniel Cottom, and Judith Wilt have returned to this approach. McMaster has noted repeated, obsessive mythic patterns; Millgate has traced the motif of the "dreaming boy" as an image of the poet-author from *Rokeby* through the early novels; Cottom argues that the uses of enchantment in the novels are ideological; and Wilt argues for the recurrence of the figure of Robin Hood embowered in the greenwood.[9] Seizing upon Northrop Frye's claim that the plot of the novel, in general, is one of kidnapped romance, Wilt shows neatly how the literal kidnapping of the Waverley heroes leads first to a kidnapping of their romantic dreams by realism, and then to a counter-kidnapping of realism, ultimately, by romance.[10] Even if it were only to illuminate this process for the novels, Scott's more overtly romancelike poems would bear further examination before all of their complex narrative techniques have been kidnapped by the novel critics, who tend to treat the poems like prophets more honored out of their romance world than in it.

The second critical development that should prepare readers for a greater receptiveness to these poems is the development of narrative theory. Because this development emerged in part from Vladimir Propp's morphology of folk tales and from Claude Levi-Strauss's studies of myth, and because even its most technical proponents have often sought, like Frye, to include the narratives of popular as well as high literature, it has tended to broaden critical attention from the high mimetic tradition of drama and the novel and to interest it in the genre of romance.[11] Far more specific application of modern theories of narrative to Scott's poetry can be developed than I have attempted here; one example is Graham McMaster's Levi-Straussian analysis of *The Lady of the Lake*.[12] Instead of applying specific structuralist techniques, I have drawn upon the suggestions offered by recent narrative theories for defining romance as a genre.

The third critical development that offers a context for reevaluating Scott's poems is of even broader applicability than narrative theory. Yet feminist theory, like narrative theory, has found a particularly important subject matter in the stereotypes or archetypes of romance. Again, Keats's *La Belle Dame* can clarify the problem—or confirm the mystery. As Gina Luria and Irene Tayler have argued, women in the poetry of the high romantics gain power as they recede toward the unknowable roles of a transcendent muse or of an often equally transcendent woman in a quest romance.[13] A recurrent problem in interpreting the poems of Blake, Coleridge, Keats, and Shelley that employ such figures is to decide whether the male protagonist's desire for the woman is a desire for an actual person, so that his imagination is the vehicle, or whether the desire for that personal relationship is only the vehicle for defining an infinite search for imaginative envisioning. Without concluding that both are vehicles for satisfying the writer's and the reader's impulse toward a sexually-motivated narrative closure,[14] we can still see that feminist questions about the status of women in visionary romance are closely related to questions about the structure and significance of romance narrative. Is Thomas the Rhymer's enthrallment by the elfin queen a master-plot or a mistress-plot? Is her world, like Keats's "melodious plot / Of beechen green," an otherworld in which nature, death, and transcendent imagination all struggle to find voice through the poet's song? Just as the genre of romance has not yet been disguised fully as realism, so the witch or enchantress in Scott's prototypical narrative has not yet been exiled to an attic, as have female protagonists in nineteenth-century women's novels.[15] Instead, she presides in her grotto, her bower, her lake, her underworld.

Yet, for all these claims, her power is limited in Scott's poems. To examine the ways in which he defines the plots and themes, the structures that establish the generic patterns of romance, and then relates them to the demands of realism, we should turn first to the *Minstrelsy* and to the place of *Thomas the Rhymer* in that collection. Working inductively through that example, we can then consider its relationship to more recent theories of romance.

In the first edition of the *Minstrelsy* (1802), Scott saw his task as transcribing, mostly from oral sources, the traditional ballads of his ancestors' border country. These he classified, according to his subtitle, as "historical and romantic ballads." Jane Millgate points out how, within each of these classifications, Scott moves from oral to editorial, romantic to historical, Scots to English as he encloses ballad in commentary.[16] Because I emphasize the historical and romantic classifications, my sense of this "mixture of modes" is somewhat more dialectical. At the end of his second volume, which included the romantic ballads, Scott also added a third section, titled "Imitations of the Ancient Ballads." These imitations included modern ballads by Scott himself and by friends. Even though he had added two rather freely-constructed new parts to the traditional ballad of the otherworld journey, Scott placed *Thomas the Rhymer* in his second category of traditional ballads and not in his "Imitations" section. Following the traditional ballad, he added a second part by piecing together extant fragments consisting of Thomas of Ercildoun's supposed prophecies. For the third part he himself avowedly extended the original narrative to include Thomas's final return to Elfland.[17] Among them these three parts of the ballad roughly represent his three larger divisions of the *Minstrelsy*. The original ballad (now part 1) exemplifies, or so his notes assert, Scott's category of romantic ballads. Though it does not exemplify the historical ballads, the prophecy (part 2) tests the relationship of poetic to factual, historical events. Finally, Scott's own newly-written third part draws upon both romantic and historical elements. Although Scott's definitions of historical and romantic in the first two parts of the *Minstrelsy* are only implicit, his use of these categories can further define the interplay between romance and history in the three parts of *Thomas the Rhymer*. In turn, this three-part ballad revision and the romance fragment Scott publishes with it will suggest a model for his own narrative poems.

The ballads Scott classifies as historical consist for the most part of the riding or raiding exploits of his ancestors and other border clansmen. Though many of the episodes are known only through the oral tradition, his editing apparatus reinforces whatever elements of documentary verifiability he can find. Some, like the Percy-Douglas conflicts in "Otterburn" or "Chevy Chase," describe characters and incidents known well beyond their native territory through historical and dramatic sources and through wide circulation of the ballads themselves.[18] Others describe local border heroes who are labeled as villains in contemporary reports from frustrated Elizabethan border marshals, reports that Scott cites in his notes. Still others, like "Sir Patrick Spens," are not set in the borders at all, and so cannot draw upon that cultural portrait Scott establishes through his introductions and notes. Scott attempts to supplement the cryptic narrative of that ballad, a spareness he saw as an erosion through time of a fuller original, by inserting specific details from Scottish relations with Europe.[19] Although these ballads follow the structures of oral tradition in their honoring of a certain kind of heroism, they are not incompatible with the standards of truth demanded by a written modern history, as Scott's editorial apparatus works carefully to show. They are often partisan in their narratives, but that partisanship is clearly shown (except when Scott shifts praiseworthy episodes from other clans to the Scotts). Moreover, they celebrate public events, even if the public community is often smaller than a nation. Finally, the two sides of the border so often transgressed are mirror images of one another, so that crossing the border involves no radical transformation of perspectives as it does in moving from a normal to a romance world. Scott's successive relocations of the action of "Katherine Janfarie" from the *Min-*

strelsy to *Marmion* illustrate this in a way that *Marmion* itself, though extremely historical, does not do because it is transformed by the romance pattern.[20]

None of these historical ballads turns upon supernatural or magical power; most describe a communal world of active violence in which women occasionally appear, but usually as victims or pawns in the acquisition of property. The "fires of feudal rage" Thomas Warton speaks of in Scott's epigraph to the *Minstrelsy* refer, in effect, to the feuding quarrels of clans and to the patriarchal feudalism that defined the clans. These fires are either warning beacons (the burning towers and haystacks) or the rage of their owners eager for retaliation, not the fires of romantic passion. Scott exploits precisely this ironic limiting of symbolism in canto 3 of *The Lay*, then startingly turns back to its traditional symbolism of passion.[21]

In the romantic ballads we find, not surprisingly, the fires of emotional and sexual passion. Yet here Scott's category of romance is broader. These groups fall into overlapping subgroups: some are romantic because they show passionate relationships, others because they include fantastic or supernatural events, and still others because they follow the plots of quest romance as a formal genre. The ballads in the romantic category that come closest to historical standards of verifiability are those that narrate tragic love affairs recalled through specific place names and family names, such as "The Douglas Tragedy" (*Minstrelsy*, 1803, 3:243-50) and "Lord Thomas and Fair Annie" (*Minstrelsy*, 1802, 2:104-10). All too clearly, such events are neither fantastic nor improbable. Overlapping this group is another in which the narratives turn upon supernatural episodes: ballads such as "Clerk Saunders" (*Minstrelsy*, 1802, 2:33-41) are included in both of these definitions of romantic, for the lover returns as a ghost. Overlapping this second group is a third in which the narratives follow the patterns of medieval romance as a genre and are probably derived from such romances. In "Kempion," for example, a questing knight fights a dragon and frees a lady—though in this fused, pre-Spenserian version of the Andromeda myth, the dragon *is* the lady and must be freed from her enchantment.[22] In the riding or raiding ballads, men usually ride out as a group to battle other men; most often in these romantic ballads, individual, solitary men encounter individual women and come under their spells, whether natural or supernatural. In the historical ballads the scene of the action is often the tower; in the romantic ballads it is often the isolated bower in the wilderness—surely symbolic of a shift from male to female focus.

The first part of the ballad *Thomas the Rhymer* shows aspects of all three of these definitions of romantic derived from the *Minstrelsy*'s arrangement. True, the love affair between Thomas and the elfin queen seems to involve more curiosity, both intellectual and sexual, than passionate emotional commitment. In the first or "ancient" part of the ballad its outcome is not one of tragic conflict but, for Thomas, almost a comic triumph. This part of the ballad concludes with his return to "earth" after seven years, but it stops short of dramatizing either that return or any emotional impact on him. Yet whether Thomas himself initiates his journey into fairyland by seducing the elf queen, as in the medieval romance, or whether she seduces him with a mere kiss, as in the ballad (*Minstrelsy*, 1802, 2:252; *PW*, 655), his journey is clearly supernatural.[23] Further, it is a paradigm for much medieval romance. As such, it also points toward Ariosto, Tasso, and Spenser. All of these models, medieval and Renaissance, find renewed life in Scott's own narratives. Because this generic continuity also forms the basis for modern theories of romance, the discussion that follows will focus more sharply upon the first part of the ballad than upon the second and third.

In his own narratives Scott uses the spatial patterns of romance suggested in *Thomas the Rhymer* but varied both by Renaissance romantic epic and Renaissance romantic comedy: the quester ventures into an isolated, enchanted ground, often suggesting mythic natural origins, in search of some recognition or transformation. The ballad of *The Rhymer* further defines, for true Thomas and for us, the nature of this enchanted ground. Just after he begins his journey with the "Queen of fair Elfland," she urges him to "abide and rest a little space, / and I will show you ferlies [marvelous visions] three." The first, "yon narrow road . . . thick beset with thorns and briers," is "the path of righteousness," after which, she adds wryly, "but few inquires." On the other hand, "that braid braid road / That lies across that lily leven," is "the path of wickedness." There is an alternative to these extremes, though, a "bonny road, / That winds about the fernie brae . . . That is the road to fair Elfland." In another version, the third road lies geographically as well as morally between the road to heaven and the one to hell. When their journey continues, even that "fernie" road, a pleasant path to wilderness, contains elements first of hell and then of heaven. They wade through darkness and blood, then come to an Edenic garden, complete with apple. Given this spatial plotting, we can begin to drawn upon the spatial and temporal patterns found in romance by modern theorists of the genre.

Within its horizontal pattern the progress of Thomas and the elf queen into the world of romance seems to demonstrate the "vertical perspectives" described by Northrop Frye. These perspectives "symbolize a contrast between two worlds, one above the level of ordinary experience, the other below it." Extending Frye's mapping of romance, Patricia Parker and Fredric Jameson both criticize that mapping as insufficiently temporal. Their revisions, tested against *Thomas the Rhymer*, will prove especially useful for analyzing both the temporal momentum of the plots in Scott's own narrative poems and their "negative hermeneutics," as Jameson calls it—their layers of different interpretive responses to different historical eras.[24] Because Parker's discussion combines the Christian eschatology of Revelation and Roland Barthes's partially linguistic structures of desire, it can be related to other theories of romance that link private motive to public motives or goals. These theories can also help us analyze the link between Thomas the Rhymer's discussions of his language and his art with the elfin queen and Scott's views of the relationship between the play of fiction and the truths of history. Because Jameson evaluates the usefulness of romance in different historical cultures, he too can be helpful in relating the function of minstrelsy and prophecy in *Thomas the Rhymer* to their usefulness in Scott's modern reassumption of the medieval minstrel's role. Jameson also points to redefinitions of truth and fiction, but places these in the context of changing socioeconomic factors.

If in the elfin queen's "ferlies," romance seems a space lying between the apocalyptic extremes of heaven and hell, Patricia Parker suggests that such extremes characteristically lie outside the narrative action. The romance itself, she argues, demonstrates a moment of hesitation or respite, an "erring" "before [its goal or object] is fully named or revealed." She differs from Frye, whose *Anatomy* is in many respects her point of departure, not only by defining a liminal or threshold space for romance, but by making that "space" part of a temporal as well as a spatial pattern. Frye later argues that the romance narrative characteristically shows a descent from the "idyllic" into the "demonic or night world" and then a return, a cycle that defines the quester's identity.[25] Working from a distinction between chivalric or quest romance and pastoral romance made by Humphrey Tonkin, Parker establishes the linear parallel between the search for a woman or a more obviously transcendent goal in quest romance and the search for salvation at the end of time in Christian eschatology or apocalypse. Within this linear, temporal pattern, the cyclic retreat into a greenwood or a bower, characteristic of Renaissance pastoral, takes place in a moment of lingering commitment to this world and its pleasures. The quester is half drawn toward fulfillment and half lingering still to desire it.[26]

Several other critics have defined romance as an intervenient, playful moment, an eddying or error that both delays and defines the discovery of its goal. The goal described by these critics, however, is not the apocalyptic revelation of salvation history but the revelation of a psychological identity both individual and communal. Following Henry James's definition of romance as "experience liberated . . . disengaged, disembroiled, disencumbered," John Pikoulis speaks of the genre's double psychological purpose. Like Frye's assertion that "the quest-romance is the search of the libido or desiring self for a fulfillment that will deliver it from the anxieties of reality but will still contain that reality," and like Gillian Beer's assertion that the romance "allows us to act out through stylized figures the radical impulses of human experience," Pikoulis's argument focuses upon romance's "concern with the problem of both public and private identity."[27] This concern arises through obsessive themes and motifs and is only approachable, he argues, through what James describes as "the beautiful circuit and subterfuge of our thought and desire."[28]

Although the Rhymer's journey to Elfland seems to illustrate Frye's pattern of a spatial cycle more than it illustrates Parker's model of a temporary delay in a progress toward apocalypse or salvation, those alternate routes remind us that his present journey is a playful interlude before more serious choices. They remind us also that such a framework of choice probably reflects the Christianizing of an earlier, pagan underworld journey.[29] Parker's mapping of romance can also guide us, as we shall see later, in placing Scott's romance narratives within a context of serious choices about larger patterns of history.

Because the problem of reporting Thomas's journey is built into his encounter with the elfin queen, the traditional first section of the ballad partially disarms external criticism both of its place in a larger, more orthodox pattern of history and of its truthfulness. When she first points out the "fernie" road to Elfland, the queen warns,

> . . . Thomas, ye maun hold your tongue,
>   Whatever ye may hear or see;
> For, if ye speak word in Elfyn land,
>   Ye'll ne'er get back to your ain countrie.

This prohibition, a variant of a common motif in ballads that describe such otherworld journeys,[30] obviously challenges a minstrel more than the average quester. Because his speech would exert a temporal, sequential pattern over the timeless spatial realm that she leads him to, he must willingly suspend its sequence for a short while or risk the more permanent suspension of remaining forever in the timeless "Elfin land."

Parker points out a relationship between speech and history developed by Augustine: "His model of temporality and of textuality was the form of the sentence, each syllable giving way in a successive, or syntagmatic, movement toward the 'rest' at its end. Language, for Augustine, is a sign of man's distance, or difference, from God, and his image of apocalypse is . . . a textual one—the time, prophesied in Isaiah, when the heavens, like the Scriptures, will be 'rolled together in a scroll'."[31] In Scott's edition of the ballad, then, the temporality of speech may seem alien to Elfland because by Augustine's analogy it would point toward the process of historical completion. The queen's threat also suggests that speaking within her realm might transform itself into participation in her country's dreaming fictions, as eating becomes participation in Hades' world of death for Persephone. If he violates her injunction and speaks, the threat of his world's temporality would result in the counter threat of his irreversible—hence in a way historical—departure from his "ain countrie" of historical time. This paradox or impasse represents, we might say, the dual nature of narrative and especially of romance: ongoing and delaying, sequential in its narrative syntax and yet metaphoric or substitutive in its playful erring. Thus the intermediate, "plastic" or "plasmatic" quality of fiction,[32] its elusive and transformative power, is challenged by the representative of a world that seems to offer just such a possibility—by the elf queen herself.

Her second challenge to Thomas's vocation suggests not that his speech will carry temporality and hence history into her atemporal world, but that the minstrel's historically "real" professional speech is a kind of fiction and hence unreal. Her challenge links the Persephone myth more clearly to the problem of whether the poet is an accurate reporter—or, if he isn't, to the problem of what his role might be. After they pass through the river of blood,

> . . . they come on to a garden green,
> And she pu'd an apple frae a tree—
> 'Take this for thy wages, true Thomas;
> It will give thee the tongue that can never lie.'

In a wonderful moment that both satirizes and yet affirms the importance of mediating fictions, the Rhymer makes his epithet "true" a partially ironic one:

> 'My tongue is my ain,' true Thomas said,
> 'A gudely gift ye wad gie to me!
> I neither dought to buy nor sell,
> At fair or tryst where I may be.
>
> 'I dought neither speak to prince or peer,
> Nor ask of grace from fair ladye.'

In claiming, "My tongue is my ain," Thomas both refuses her gift and asserts his power of speech in Elfland.[33] The ballad does not make clear whether Thomas successfully avoids this apple of discordant truth telling, or whether we inhabitants of that country should believe in any report of his journey. Who narrates his history is not clear, either. The apparently omniscient narrator, telling of Thomas's journey in third-person form, is exempt both from the assumed credibility of a first-person account and from the warnings against Thomas's reliability as a truth teller. Thus the status of the narrative lies, like Elfland, between judgmental extremes. In his own narratives, Scott cannot claim such exemption; instead, he constantly contextualizes his narrators, both within their narratives and outside them.

One further problem of interpretation lies beyond the teasing self-referentiality of Thomas's artistic debate with the elfin queen: the relationship of that debate to the sexual enthrallment that begins the minstrel's journey and that leads to his visionary prophecy. His claim in mid-journey to his own tongue, his own speech, his own narrative, seems both a rebellion of gender against his enthrallment and a rebellion of genre against the elfin queen's role as the presenter of visions. Yet the romance versions of Thomas's journey make Thomas's prophecies a parting gift from the elfin queen. In the *Minstrelsy*, Scott's transition into the prophecies that he has brought together as part 2 of the ballad is a carefully skeptical introduction; in part 2 Thomas himself, acknowledging no gift from the elf queen, speaks as prophet. This struggle over the parentage of vision and prophecy becomes a repeated motif in Scott's own poems.

In the traditional ballad's tension between Thomas's self-referential and rational assessments of his own art and his acceptance of the uncanny encounter with the elfin queen, we can see a complex attitude toward the criteria of reality and fiction. Scott's half-dismissive, half-fascinated framing of the ballad in his modern editorial apparatus creates a further historicizing context, as Millgate points out. Fredric Jameson's historicizing of Frye's theory of romance provides some suggestions both for Scott's interpretation of medieval and Renaissance romance elements in his own narrative poems and for our interpretation of Scott's choices. Frye's " 'positive' hermeneutic," Jameson argues, is a search for meaning "which tends to filter out historical differences." To define a mode or world of romance, Jameson argues, Frye's method should be corrected with a "negative hermeneutic": "A history of romance as a mode becomes possible . . . when we explore the substitute codes and new materials which, in the increasingly secularized and rationalized world that emerges from the collapse of feudalism, are pressed into service to replace the older magical categories of Otherness which have now becomes so many dead languages." Jameson has already argued for making relative instead of absolute the categories of Good and Evil Frye names as essential to romance oppositions: what a given culture calls Evil is what it fears as Other, or even what it fears as a competing force similar to itself and therefore needs to fight off. Any particular version of romance, then, is "a form of social praxis [or action], that is, a symbolic resolution to a concrete historical situation." Moreover, this symbolic resolution may itself incorporate older, "sedimented" value-structures drawn from earlier versions of the romance.[34] Both the idea of romance as a symbolic resolution and the idea of that resolution containing and transforming earlier resolutions will prove extremely useful for Scott's transformations of his traditional material.[35]

In Scott's poems, the transformation and use of magical codes to project a nostalgic harmony that is also heuristically prophetic is extremely important. One of the ways Scott accomplishes this transformation and projection is to shift, while still reporting their magic, from the incantatory, performative codes of his enchanters to the magical code of the poet, and especially of the writer. Describing poetry as magic seems at first glance so hackneyed an idea as to be a cliché. Yet we take such claims with great seriousness when we read the high romantics, and Scott intends this transformation of powers more seriously than he admits. His poems are riddled with metaphors, symbols, and signs of the rival magical powers of singing minstrel and of written text, of codes acceptable to writer and reader that evoke older magical conflict. Codes, scrolls, books, and documents are crucial to the transformation of his plots. Moreover, his conversion of sung narrative to printed document makes acceptable an older magic by transforming it to the modern poet's writing.

Scott's second and third parts of *Thomas the Rhymer* move toward direct confrontations with history. Working from Andro Hart's 1615 compilation of miscellaneous prophecies, Scott reinforces, if less explicitly than in romance versions, the folk-literary tradition that Thomas's sojourn in the timeless realm of fairyland has made him a visionary who can prophesy the future. Many fourteenth-century accounts report that the minstrel foretold the death of Alexander III even though Thomas was far distant from the scene. Yet all of the turning points in later Scottish history that Scott's Thomas tells to the historical Corspatrick, supposedly in that moment of Alexander's death in the thirteenth century, had of course taken place by the time Hart published his collection. Hart's final, redemptive prophecy of James VI's ascent to the throne of England is, as Scott points out, the revision of an earlier "prophecy" designed to create public acceptance of a regent from France (*Minstrelsy*, 1803, 4:103-8). The final stanza of Scott's revision of Hart, moreover, seems to look ahead to the United Kingdom's domination of the ocean in the Napoleonic wars. Scott's notes frame this record of prophecy with an inscription that distinguishes skeptically between past historical event, supposedly prophetic vision of the future, and manipulation of fictional prophecies of the future, apparently confirmed by past accuracy, to control the present. If the second part of *Thomas the Rhymer* begins by recalling the timeless romance world of Elfland, it ends almost by overcoming time through the manipulation of ongoing history in a complex backward and forward series of perspectives. Moreover, it suggests that Scott saw a range of possible relationships between historical narratives and present events, as well as a range of uses for the specialized techniques of dated-back prophecies. Hazlitt's jibe that Scott is *laudator tempores acti* can be turned to suggest that narration of the past can prophesy or shape in other ways our conceptions of the present.[36]

In the third part of *Thomas the Rhymer*, the one most thoroughly and admittedly Scott's own fiction, romance worlds and historical worlds confront each other both more explicitly and more gracefully than in the second part. In part 3 the Rhymer's brief return to earth includes his own narration of several central Arthurian romances. Yet his return to Elfland, led by a group of supernatural animals, is witnessed briefly by a Douglas—a historical border character, and one who figures in many of the traditional historical ballads Scott had collected for the *Minstrelsy*.

This synthesis leads to Scott's successful framing and fusion of historical and romantic narratives in *The Lay of the Last Minstrel*. Moreover, it also raises the complex question of how romance in all of Scott's longer "imitations," his "original" poems, is related to historical patterns.[37]

Except for an introductory discussion of *Harold the Dauntless*, which I will consider as volume 2 of *The Bridal of Triermain*, my analyses of these poems will consider them in the chronological order of their publication. This chronological order reveals no planned progress on Scott's part through various historical eras. It does, however, reveal a rather surprising alternation among the poems in the relationship of romance to history. Although all of his poems involve love stories and thus fit one definition of "romantic" developed in the *Minstrelsy*, Scott's poems alternate between narratives that turn upon major historical events and those that turn upon the typical events and patterns of romance, like those in the ballad of *Thomas the Rhymer*. *Marmion* (1808), *Rokeby* (1813), and *The Lord of the Isles* (1815) are in some sense almost epic versions of the "riding" ballads, for each either begins or ends with a major battle: Flodden, Marston Moor, and Bannockburn. Granted, *The Lay of the Last Minstrel* (1805) depicts the "riding" or "raiding" society of the border ballads most closely. Yet like *The Lady of the Lake*

(1810), *The Bridal of Triermain* (1813), and to some extent *Harold the Dauntless* (1817), its action turns upon the ambiguous powers of an enchantress or witch resembling the elfin queen.

In this second group, Scott follows much medieval and Renaissance romance that links the realm and practice of magic more often to women than to men, often associating such enchantresses or witches with the apprehension of nature as mystery, not as rational order. This pattern, of course, recalls far older mythic patterns and also points toward Jameson's hypothesis that romance emerges from an agricultural society's magical struggles with good and evil. As if Scott were alternately drawn to that mythic pattern and then repelled, he developed quite a different role for women in the first group of poems I mentioned above, those that are more historical. In these three narrative poems, women are typically part of the focus for struggle in the plots, but they do not possess the magical powers of enchantresses or nature goddesses. Instead, they are pawns. Although their passivity contrasts with the greater activity of the enchantresses, they too reinforce a similar archetypal or mythic connection between woman and nature. The heroines in *Marmion*, in *Rokeby*, and in *The Lord of the Isles* are focal, in most cases, because they are closely associated with landed property. "Local" might be the better word. In a cupidity apparently more financial than sexual, the women are desired by both heroes and villains for the land they have or will inherit; in the heroes, this desire is fused with romantic commitment. Although Scott treats this association of desirable women with desirable land from a historical and sociological point of view as part of his explorations of feudal and what he himself calls "patriarchal" society, the more mythic assumptions explored in some recent studies bring these women closer to the symbolic roles of the enchantresses in my first group of Scott's poems, those more closely associated with the romance opposition of knight and witch. In both cases the woman is alien, existing beyond the male protagonist's control or comprehension as does the wilderness of the natural world.[38]

In the second or romantic group, though, the women who are pawns are perhaps beyond comprehension, but not beyond control. Moreover, in two respects Scott's enchantresses differ from such classic enchantresses of romance as Malory's Vivien, or Keats's La Belle Dame, or Thomas the Rhymer's elf queen. In both respects, their differences move them closer to the heroines who are pawns of a patriarchal society. First, Scott's two most thoroughly developed enchantresses—the Lady of Buccleuch in *The Lay* and Guendolen in *The Bridal of Triermain*—owe their education in magic to their fathers. The Lady of Buccleuch also owes hers to her husband's paternal ancestor, Michael

Scott. Thus one myth of magical origins of power transforms—and tames—another, more matriarchal one. Second, in the plots of the poems, all of these enchantress figures are either vanquished, most often by a vanishing of their world, or become domesticated, relinquishing their magic. Both of these steps might be described as a kind of "naturalizing," except that the process seems to remove them from a nearly mythic wilderness to a cultural or social order.[39] Furthermore, their "fathering" by male magicians points back to the importance of the male poet, whether minstrel or writer, who chants or inscribes his magical codes and thus shapes the poem's world—even if in Scott's poems he is not usually, as in *Thomas the Rhymer*, the protagonist.

If the powers of these enchantresses become limited, those of the pawns sometimes increase with a symbolic resonance that recalls the magical transformations of romance. Several of the poems contain female protagonists who are changelings like those in Shakespeare's romantic comedies, women dressed as male minstrel pages. In one of these, the changeling is also the pawn whose property is in dispute. Yet these evocations of a different sort of romance from Thomas the Rhymer's journey into the elf queen's realm also illustrate an underlying geographic pattern in all of Scott's narratives, a pattern shared—as Frye notes—by medieval quest romances and Renaissance romantic comedy.

In the four "romantic" poems, the romantic comedy's pattern of a cyclic journey from court world into a green world or wilderness and return to court world also includes the romantic narrative pattern—both medieval and Renaissance—of the venture into an enchantress's bower or castle. In the poems grouped by their absence of powerful enchantresses, however, the "enchanted ground," to use Johnston's title, remains as a basis for the narrative whose plot is based upon historical events. Thus, even the poems in which enchantresses preside may be concerned with the realistic recognition of historical eras and problems. Similarly—or conversely—the apparently realistic narratives that describe women as pawns employ a structure of romance or "enchanted ground" in their spatial patterns and thus make use of romance to supplement and interpret their historical realism. No simple categorization of historical or romantic can work for these narrative poems.

Moving from a civilized, apparently idyllic world into a less controlled, more primitive world, these poems seek both to restore some values of that primitive world to the civilized one and to discover the powers and dangers of the analogous primitive world within the self of the protagonist. Though appropriate for the elf queen's three paths and though fascinating for Spenser and for Milton, Parker's pattern of romance as a temporal delay in a salvation history moving forward toward apocalypse seems at first glance wildly inappropriate for Scott's own narrative poems that focus realistically upon this world and for his sense of enlightenment gradualism in history.[40] Yet in this gradualism, as many critics have suggested, is an undercurrent of longing for the primitive and violent, or even for the ordered communal rituals of the past that changing patterns of belief and of society are inexorably destroying.[41] For Scott, then, romance in its temporal aspect might be defined as a wandering that holds back from the salvation of historical development through rational, progressive improvement—not a holding back from infinite, self-annihilating divine or transcendent eternity, but a delay of a moment, a few hours, a few days, in that ameliorating progress. That moment is objectively historical, because Scott searches for historical crises in which such tensions find expression. Yet it is also romantic as it protests the ongoing temporality and homogenizing of history.

In the poems, that sacrifice is often connected with a woman's relinquishing of magical power; that power, once alien from social control, returns to it in altered and male-dominated form. It is also connected with a shift from the incantatory speech or song of a minstrel to the inscription of writing. Given the definition of romance as a delay on the threshold of major, progressive change, we might speculate that the more spatial, time-transcending "new magic" of writing makes it more appropriate to the romance world than the progressive, sequential temporality of speech. That progressive quality is particularly evident in Scott's characteristic rapid narrative pace, the drive from one episode to the next instead of a Keatsian or Wordsworthian lingering over the implications of a single episode or scene. We move into and out of a romance world almost before we are aware of its implications. In fact, if implication is the characteristic narrative pattern for Ariosto, Spenser, or Milton, the opposite seems true for Scott.[42] Explication of his mysteries of plot and identity is never long delayed, given his exigencies of publishing; and his readers, even if they stay up all night reading his new poem, can finish it quickly and return to their normal lives and to their normal respect for enlightenment.[43] Yet many of the characteristics of the oral tradition, some of which Scott uses, seek to offset the temporality with a spatiality of repeated, parallel patterns in sound, image, and motif.[44] Moreover, the "normal" lives of his readers, like those of Darsie Latimer and Alan Fairford in *Redgauntlet*, are bound, fenced, by writing as the tool of civilization: as historical and legal documents that seek to verify past events and to order the events of the present into a social order larger and less personal than that once ordered by voice. Finally, as Scott himself is acutely aware, the custodians of the ordering by voice had in his own time become fewer and more isolated. Ironically, only writing like his own can preserve both the ballads and romances once sung, and the tensions of that transition from song to writing.

ONE

The Lay of the Last Minstrel

PAGE AND BOOK

THE BORDER LEGEND of the mischievous goblin-page Gilpin Horner is not the genesis of Scott's first fully original book, though he so claimed a quarter of a century later in his 1830 introduction to *The Lay* (*PW*, 52). Nor does that local goblin even appear in *The Lay* until the end of canto 2, almost a third of the way through the poem. Yet his first action is to open a book. He thus claims a role in opening Scott's own book for interpretation; and a part of that interpretation, in turn, leads to a discovery of the ambiguous power of reading. Granted, the book he opens is hardly an ordinary one. Just unearthed from the grave of the wizard Michael Scott, this "Mighty Book" of spells is needed by the recently widowed Lady of Buccleuch to defend her land and family. Though she is herself a witch, her own magic has faltered in the present crisis, and she has sent William of Deloraine, her most experienced fighter, to bring the wizard's book from his tomb in Melrose Abbey. That eerie, gothic quest, described in canto 2, has proved less dangerous than a random encounter almost at the end of his return journey: Baron Cranstoun, a son of the neighboring Kerr clan that had killed Deloraine's own chieftain, now strikes him down. Regretting his hastiness, but afraid of being found on Buccleuch land, the younger man returns home but leaves his page to help Deloraine. We have just learned that this page is somehow supernatural; but now we seem to see him become a goblin as we read—or, rather, as he reads.

When the goblin-page finds the "Mighty Book" brought from the wizard's grave, he ignores his task of attending to the knight's wounds. Bound with iron clasps, the book "would not yield to unchristen'd hand, / Till he smear'd the cover o'er / With the Borderer's curdled gore." This propitiatory offering opens the book to him, and because he, unlike Deloraine, can read, his world is transformed:

> . . . one short spell therein he read:
> It had much of glamour might;

> Could make a ladye seem a knight;
> The cobwebs on a dungeon wall
> Seem tapestry in lordly hall;
> A nut-shell seem a gilded barge,
> A sheeling seem a palace large,
> And youth seem age, and age seem youth:
> All was delusion, nought was truth.   [L, 3:9]

With their overcoming of the ruins of time and their suggestion of transsexual disguises, these lines recall elements of the border ballads that Scott had already published and that he would use again in his own narratives. Their transformation from peasant hut to chivalric castle suggests the upward social mobility—in his characters and in their author—as he turns from ballad to lay.[1] With its reflexive self-mockery of "all was delusion, nought was truth," these lines epitomize both a fascination with the magical transformations of romance and a critical self-mockery for succumbing to that fascination. That double attitude will characterize not only this poem but all of Scott's narrative poems that follow this one. Gilpin's opening of Michael Scott's book thus opens Walter Scott's own career of writing books of poetic fictions that exhibit a transforming "glamour" or—as the technique of such magic is described in stanza 11—"gramarye."

Although both words are medieval Scottish versions of "grammar," a skill often associated with magic by the illiterate, Scott and the ballad tradition he draws on distinguish the two. If "glamour" suggests a metaphoric or paradigmatic substitution of one appearance for another, "grammarye" is closer to its original meaning and suggests a grammar of performative utterance, a syntax for ordering the elements of language used by witches and magicians. Including the substitutions of glamour, this metonymic language of magical command becomes in Scott's repetition the linguistic basis or language of his narrative.[2] In that repetition, however, comes the framing recognition of historicity and skepticism.

For *The Lay* itself, this demonstration of the power of a book points to the major blocking element of the plot: the recently widowed Lady Buccleuch's plan to prevent her daughter's marriage into the neighboring family responsible for her husband's murder and to preserve the independence of her domain after her husband's death. Her initiative in sending for the book of magic is itself part of a pattern of actions that "make a lady seem a knight." The goblin's accidental discovery of the book points toward the chaos that such a contravening of sexual roles, or even such an assertion of intellectual power, leads to, and it also becomes the first step in a process of conservative correction. Thus, one main theme to be pursued here is the plight of the enchantress as intellectually aggressive woman.

Examined in more detail, Gilpin Horner's opening of Michael Scott's iron-bound book may be read to confirm these challenges both to genre and to gender. Smearing his book with blood, this anarchic goblin may represent both an author's imagination escaping all normal constraints[3] and a nightmare vision of the "ideal reader" attracted by such violence. Because the blood is that of the illiterate Deloraine, in some sense his wound marks a sacrifice to the "unchristian" anarchy of a culture dominated by writing. Such anarchy at both ends of the communicative process seems a vision particularly appropriate to mark the shift from singer and listeners to writer and readers, from mutual social definition to some more private, more alienated relationship. In this passage early in canto 3, a wariness enters the narrating minstrel's tone: if the goblin is unreliable either as implied author or as implied reader, the book itself—as written document—contributes to this explosive unreliability. It does so partly through its content, which declares, "All was delusion, nought was truth," but even more through its nature as document, not as voice. Randomly available to any reader who seizes it, the book is almost demoniacally free of the social constraints imposed upon the minstrel who performs traditional songs in the midst of his own society.

Two different but related challenges to "truth" appear in the *Lay*, not only shaping our perceptions of the inner narrative, but shaping the narrative itself. The first of these challenges is posed by the generic expectations arising from Scott's arrangement, even codification, of the ballads he heard, wrote down, and then published in the *Minstrelsy*. From its publication, critics have debated the problem of the *Lay's* genre.[4] If we follow Scott's lead and think of it as an expanded border ballad (*PW* 1830, 52), the problem is not fully solved, because Scott himself had divided his collection of authentic border ballads into historical and romantic categories. Taking place in circumstances and in a setting that would normally produce a more or less historical riding or raiding ballad, the events of the minstrel's narrative also include magical episodes from romantic ballads, folklore, and romance.[5] Gerard Genette's terms for framing narratives will prove useful here: the "diegetic" narrative is the primary story told (in contrast to a "mimetic" dramatization); a story told by a character in the diegetic narrative is "metadiegetic"; and a story framing the main or primary narrative is "extradiegetic."[6] Here Scott writes about a ragged, vagrant minstrel, displaced from his earlier career by the events of 1689. Although this narrative is not the most important nor the lengthiest, its presentation is the more direct and hence should be termed diegetic.

The lay that the minstrel himself sings describes events taking place about a century and a half earlier, a little after 1552 (see Scott's note 5, *PW*, 57); this innermost narrative is metadiegetic. Finally, the relatively few references Scott makes to his own role as narrator and also his notes constitute an extradiegetic frame, a level of commentary from the present time of writer and first readers. One might argue that Scott represents his courtly minstrel, the inner or metadiegetic narrator, as fusing the realism of the raiding ballad with the more fantastic elements of the courtly romance. Problems of generic classification thus enter the inner narrative, the minstrel's lay. They also enter, in turn, the representation of the diegetic framing narrative and of the briefer extradiegetic one.

Within the minstrel's lay, moreover, the different sorts of truth possible in the oral tradition and in cultures communicating by books are both represented. Minstrels who represent the oral tradition in its prime appear in canto 6, responding to their audiences with narratives that include some magic, yet are constrained in their values by the face-to-face encounters with their society. Michael Scott's book of magic, on the other hand, is the central image for a cluster of metaphors that illustrate writing's escape from social embedding and its definitions of a group's sense of truth; and yet writing also signifies the scientific, legal, and historical documentation necessary for a more modern sort of truth. Thus the tension between the frame narrators and their modes of presentation is repeated within the minstrel's metadiegetic narrative, his lay, and there it receives a symbolic resolution.

Although the riding ballad seems to dominate the genre of the minstrel's lay, these magical events and the romantic love plot place increasing strain upon the usual concerns of a riding ballad. Like the raider Walter of Deloraine, the raiding genre is intercepted. Ironically, the attempts of the Lady of Buccleuch to halt the developing love plot and to restore to her domain after her husband's death its normal cultural pattern of military activity—that is, of raiding—compel her to employ her magic. Once she does so, her own role has the potential power to generate a romance plot of the *Rhymer* or Renaissance sort, in which the enchantress presides over a magical castle or realm beyond the borders of ordinary life. This is a pattern that Scott will use with subtle skill in *The Lady of the Lake, The Lord of the Isles, The Bridal of Triermain*, and, with a kind of careless abandon, in *Harold the Dauntless*. In *The Lay of the Last Minstrel*, however, the lady's plot of enchantment does not generate a geographical mapping of an enchanted world, a retreat or purgatory from which the quester must return. Instead, as her plots fail, disrupted by a more benevolent if often more accidental gramarye than her own, the whole larger society described by the minstrel seems for a moment to enter an enchanted, peaceful state. Not only is the demonic transformed into the paradisal, but that sacred magical realm expands to fill the entire narrative space—cultural and geographical—described by the minstrel.

The outer, more realistic and harsh realm normally defined by geography then becomes defined by two enclosing levels of history: that of the ragged, homeless minstrel who tells the tale in a border castle now deprived of any real function, and beyond him that of the modern poet still further exiled from this central moment of peace. Yet both of these levels, although far more realistic because they contain no magic, nevertheless echo in a sort of distant resonance the Rhymer's pattern of romance as a mysterious plot organized by a presiding enchantress. Because we approach the minstrel's lay through them, these romance patterns, even if faint, begin to influence our perception of the plots and patterns in the *Lay* itself. Thus we should consider them first.

An outermost frame is more developed in the 1830 edition of the *Lay* than earlier, because in his introduction to that edition Scott develops his own role as minstrel. There he explains that "the lovely young Countess of Dalkieth, afterward Duchess of Buccleuch," had "enjoined on me as a task to compose a ballad on the subject" of Gilpin Horner (*PW*, 52). After marrying into the border family of the Scotts of Buccleuch, she had begun to investigate border legends, including that of the mischievous goblin. To judge from the evidence of Scott's letters in late 1802, her inspiration was not the source for the *Lay* but an auxiliary stream.[7] Yet his willingness to forget his own independent creativity is a tribute to her remembered charm. Although the 1805 poem is formally and feudally dedicated to her husband, then the head of the Scott clan, the countess acts as a sort of muse, enchanting the visitor into writing, and her early death in 1814 frames the poem in a still sharper awareness of death and time. As Mary Lascelles points out, "For Scott, the house of Buccleuch was an idea, and the reigning duke and duchess an embodiment of that idea."[8] Further, the Dalkieth estate at Bowhill included on its grounds the ruins of Newark Castle, the setting for the minstrel's narrative.[9] Thus the picturesque enclosure of the spatial setting corresponds to the temporal enclosures of the narrative.

At Newark, the relationship between the ancient minstrel and the late seventeenth-century Duchess of Buccleuch parallels that of Scott and his countess, but approaches a little more closely the romance pattern of a solitary knight entering an enchantress's isolated castle. Although the minstrel is no knight, he is a wandering refugee from a chivalric age:

> The last of all the Bards was he,
> Who sung of Border chivalry;
> ....
> Old times were changed, old manners gone;
> A stranger fill'd the Stuarts' throne[.]
>   [*L*, Introduction before canto 1]

In this "iron time" after 1689, his art both outlawed and outmoded, he must beg from peasants and is hesitant to enter the "embattled portal arch" and "ponderous grate" of Newark Castle. Yet although prompted by charity instead of mysterious spirits, the "iron door" opens to admit him into a sheltering and nurturing world. Within the "room of state" where the minstrel has been led to perform the music he has offered, he finds the duchess surrounded "with all her ladies," a little like Sir Launfal's mysterious queen in her "pavyloun."[10] This audience, both teasing and encouraging in its responses, makes of his performance both a trial and a regeneration.

The duchess and her ladies do not submit the minstrel to tests of physical valor or imprison him in Newark Castle through enchantment, but they do test his ability to confront the past and to be more than its passive prisoner. Through their challenge, he develops the confidence and ability to describe past romantic and military acts so that they may revitalize himself as well as his present audience. In an isolated castle empty of men, or at least of male aristocrats, he presents a narrative of an earlier castle bereft of its chieftain but working out its survival. Whether he represents traditional male, patriarchal values or female alternatives to them can best be shown through analysis of his lay. First, a closer analysis of the interplay between minstrel and audience will show his own trial by ordeal, even if it is a gentle ordeal in a welcomed performance. That performance, the self-conscious recreation of a nearly defunct oral tradition, reinforces the larger tension between romance and history as it demonstrates the tension between oral and written text.

The inhabitants of this castle, so surprisingly friendly to him, are precisely grounded in a historical identity that is personal, regional, and national and that thus calls forth and supports his own sense of a proud past. Not only a graceful allusion to the modern Harriet, Countess of Dalkieth, Scott's description of the seventeenth-century duchess recalls a tradition that she had helped to save his great-great-grandfather in 1715. Partly because of this personal association, Scott's references to the infamous Duke of Monmouth, to whom Anne of Buccleuch had been married in 1663, are "sympathetic."[11] Here the complex, pathetic, and nearly sordid details of Monmouth's life and of his marriage-for-property[12] are passed over for the focus that will link his widow both to the minstrel and to the earlier Lady of Buccleuch in the minstrel's narrative:

> For she had known adversity,
> Though born in such a high degree;
> In pride of power, in beauty's bloom,
> Had wept o'er Monmouth's bloody tomb!

By keeping the elegaic distance, moreover, Scott as the modern, early nineteenth-century narrator can associate Monmouth's destruction with the further destruction of the Stuart line.

Mentioned several lines earlier, it is recalled in the minstrel's explanation that he had once played his "ancient strain" for "King Charles the Good, / When he kept court in Holyrood." One of the most magical aspects of this castle seems to be its preservation of past courtliness and past political loyalties, values on which the minstrel has based his art. The analogues between past and present are so successful that they seem almost to cancel the intervening time. This synthesis is the work of his art, however, and it is gained in part through his encounter with his audience, the duchess, and her attendant women.

In the interludes between the recited portions of the minstrel's narrative, his coming to terms with his own losses and his facing of death lead to a somber dignity and power.[13] Yet this encounter is tempered by a range of other moods and themes associated with those moods. If the castle seems a magical shelter from the "cold . . . way" and the "iron time," it also stimulates his song's magical power to transform the singer. As he begins to listen to his own "measure wild," he is transformed from a figure "mark'd" by a "weary pace," a "timid mien, and reverend face," into an ecstatic and newly creative performer: his "faded eye . . . lighten'd up . . . / With all a poet's ecstasy," and "each blank, in faithless memory void, / The poet's glowing thought supplied."[14] This "glowing thought" resolves with a gentle mockery the debate between Bishop Percy and Joseph Ritson over whether minstrels were original composers or merely rote performers, and it offers an escape from challenges to the minstrel's presentation of historical, verifiable truth.[15] If this minstrel gains through his oral performance the poetic creativity Percy advocated, he defends himself against charges of improbability with a Ritson-like defense. Sensing a protest in his audience at the climax of the supernatural episode in which Deloraine lifts the book from the weirdly lit tomb of Michael Scott, he goes on: "I cannot tell how the truth may be; / I say the tale as 'twas said to me" (*L*, 2:22). Such an intervention, of course, reminds his audience and Scott's of the changing criteria for truth, and this alters our perception of the tale.

His next intervention, beginning at 2:29, is more like his loss of assurance at the end of the first canto because it is a more personal reminder of his age and lingering loss. Yet, perhaps because this time we hear the minstrel speak directly to his audience instead of hearing the modern narrator's report of his words through indirect discourse, as in the earlier interludes, this break in the narrative also forms part of a complex rhetorical turn on the process of "enchantment," a word he uses in 2:30. After he plans the assignation of "the Knight and Ladye fair" . . . under the hawthorn's boughs," he turns teasingly to his audience in stanza 29 and denies their narrative expectations. In stanza 30, his tone and his reason for that denial turn more personal and more serious:

> Alas! fair dames, your hopes are vain!
> My harp has lost the enchanting strain;
>   Its lightness would my age reprove:
> My hairs are grey, my limbs are old,
> My heart is dead, my veins are cold:
>   I may not, must not, sing of love.

More a traditionalist than a revolutionary in his attitude toward narrative decorum, Scott's narrator fears the incongruity between his own emotions and his story. Yet this plea for pity has begun with a courtly description of his audience as they eagerly wait for the "melting tale" he falsely announces in a series of romantic cliches verging on parody. Moreover, it immediately precedes the report of another manifestation of enchantment, the mysterious goblin who breaks into Cranstoun's life and into the narrative. One wonders if the minstrel is deliberately distracting his audience from its skepticism by evoking its emotional responses.

This possible link between the two kinds of enchantment seems confirmed when, in the interlude after the end of canto 2, a third kind of enchantment comes into play. As the minstrel's voice begins to fail, "Full slyly smiled the observant page, / And gave the wither'd hand of age / A goblet." The page and the "attending maidens [who] smiled to see / How long, how deep, how zealously," he drinks the wine, are laughing, if gently, at the inspiring vitality of the wine as it creates a new youth. In a wonderful interchange, the minstrel "look'd gaily back to them, and laugh'd"—as if to accept their genial manipulation of his mood—and then begins his third canto with an eloquent praise of love as the motivating energy of the human world. Not only is love "the dearest theme, / That ever warm'd a minstrel's dream," one that can "wake my heart to notes of flame," but

> Love rules the court, the camp, the grove,
> And men below, and saints above;
> For love is heaven, and heaven is love.   [*L*, 3:2]

Almost immediately, however, he skillfully distances these transcendent but somewhat sophistical sentiments by quietly attributing them to his romantic lead: "So thought Lord Cranstoun, as I ween, / While, pondering deep the tender scene, / He rode through Branksome's hawthorn green" (*L*, 3:3). In a further distancing, Cranstoun's lyrical meditations are set in the same ballad-like scene of "hawthorn green" as the earlier tableau of "Knight and Ladye." Thus, although gracefully accepting the artful management of his audience, the minstrel manages their emotional enthrallment by a distancing and exorcism of his own emotional and physical vulnerability.

If romantic love is the "dearest theme" of minstrels, their second main theme is surely war. During the interlude between cantos 3 and 4, as the minstrel completes his description of Branksome Castle preparing for an English attack, that theme develops a more personal meaning through the sympathetic questions of his "listening throng." When they ask, "Had he no friend, no daughter dear, . . . No son to be his father's stay . . . ?" he responds with two elegaic stanzas that contrast the Renaissance violence of the Teviot, shown in his narrative, to its present pastoral peace. At first described in universal terms, "human time" becomes the total, painful consciousness of all individual memories: Time,

> . . . though it change in ceaseless flow,
> Retains each grief, retains each crime
>   Its earliest course was doom'd to know;
> And, darker as it downward bears,
> Is stain'd with past and present tears.   [*L*, 4:2]

He turns them to his own part in that tidal estuary:

> Low as that tide has ebb'd with me,
> It still reflects to Memory's eye
> The hour my brave, my only boy
>   Fell by the side of great Dundee.   [*L*, 4:2]

The specific historical placing of his son's death at Killiecrankie in 1689 again illustrates both the repeated discontinuities of the Jacobite cause and its cost in the lives of men. Though the minstrel consoles himself by remembering his son's "death of fame . . . with conquering Graeme," the indefinite participle "conquering" is already cut off, in time and in meaning, by his almost unnoticed verb in the preceding lines: at Killiecrankie, "the volleying musket [from the supporters of William III] play'd / Against the bloody Highland blade." As the personal pain of an individual memory gives him the power to make real for his audience the tragic, cumulative force of that river of "human time," this interlude becomes universal. If the minstrel's memory of his narrative has gaps, into these gaps or rifts comes not only a playful creative invention, but individual emotion.

Although Barthes and Parker analyze the delaying tactics within a narrative as the "hermeneutic code" or the "erring" playfulness specific to romance, we can read the minstrel's pause here as a similar delaying, though outside his narrative, to avoid its completion. Thus these delays are errings at the next, or the diegetic, level of the narrative. When he completes his tale, the minstrel must leave this unexpected bower at Newark to continue his less playful wandering, even exile, as he moves toward death, and he must return to the consciousness of irreversible change in the political and personal continuity he has valued: a Stuart king, a Stuart leader, and his own son, all lost. Through the sympathetic questions of his audience, however, the break in his narrative flow becomes the recognition of time's flow. Unchanging and appearing inevitable, yet it is marked by the changes along the banks of the river Teviot and thus by a version of Jameson's "negative hermeneutic," or the registering of changes like those in an often-retold romance narrative. In Scott's romance narrative of the minstrel's stay at the castle, this delay in the time of his performance leads the minstrel through the irreversible desolation of personal memory to the more reversible and finally redemptive conversion of minstrel memory for public uses.

The two remaining interludes, also growing from the ladies' questions about the minstrel's personal situation, develop into more universal discussions of any minstrel's public function. Between cantos 4 and 5, the minstrel's digression, the ladies' comments, and in the first two stanzas of canto 5 his own response, all analyze the minstrel's uses of memory, particularly of a memory that preserves fame for the community. Between cantos 5 and 6 he defines the importance of patriotism or love of one's own geographical region and culture—a more specific kind of memory—not only for the individual minstrel who describes them but for every person who merits minstrel's praise as a means of fame.

At the end of canto 4 the minstrel concludes his narrative of preparation for the single combat between the English Musgrave and the Scottish Deloraine with a self-defense of his technical military knowledge reminiscent—though Scott surely did not know it—of the *Ion*.[16] This self-defense finds support in a full-scale subnarrative by the minstrel that anticipates both his main narrative's single combat and the skill of its narration. Against "full many minstrels" who argue for combat on horseback, he appeals to his own teacher, who not only "knew each ordinance and clause, / Of Black Lord Archibald's battle-laws" (*L*, 4:34), but defended his own knowledge by fighting for it, on foot: "He brook'd not, he, that scoffing tongue / Should tax his minstrelsy with wrong, / Or call his song untrue." After the rhapsode Ion appeals to Homer as authority for his knowledge, Socrates forces him to admit that the individual shipbuilder or general has more specific technical knowledge of his own field than does even the greatest of poets. In contrast, this "jovial Harper" who taught the narrating minstrel supports his authority with technical experience: he kills the scoffing rival minstrel. Scott's note wryly points out, as the minstrel protege does not, that this killing led to the accusation of murder, to the minstrel "roaring Willie's" capture, and to his execution.

Yet even such a radical affirmation of the minstrel's *techne* does not forestall some further questioning from the minstrel's audience about his truthfulness:

> With many a word of kindly cheer,
> In pity half and half sincere,
> Marvell'd the Duchess how so well
> His legendary song could tell
> Of ancient deeds, so long forgot.

Her voiced praise so reiterates his overcoming of "fickle Fame," "feuds, whose memory was not," and "ancient deeds so long forgot," that the duchess implies the impossibility of truthful, historical reporting even as she praises his overcoming that impossibility. Far more patronizing than the duchess's pitying praise, the narrator's further intervention at the end of the canto is clearly also self-mockery: he criticizes poets as a "simple race . . . [who] waste their toil / For the vain tribute of a smile." On one level the modern narrator seems more obtuse, more simple than his complex minstrel. On another level, that obtuse distance from the minstrel is also self-mockery, a tone surely confirmed by his note on roaring Willie. This reminder of a similar foolishness that binds minstrel and modern poet makes us suddenly recognize the writer, who has been almost transparent once we have moved within his main text, and reminds us that we have an active though distanced role as his readers.

When the minstrel "smiled, well-pleased" at this praise for his memory, he seems as straightforward, as "simple," as the narrator claims he is. His opening stanzas in the next canto, however, are remarkably complex and move well beyond the ballad tradition to examine the pathetic fallacy as it appears in pastoral elegy. In analyzing this convention of natural forces voicing their laments through a poet's song, he is of course describing a tradition that may have begun in an oral culture but has become an enormously sophisticated written one. Nature does, in a sense, mourn over a dead poet, the minstrel claims:

> Not that, in sooth, o'er mortal urn
> Those things inanimate can mourn;
> But that the stream, the wood, the gale,
> Is vocal with the plaintive wail
> Of those, who, else forgotten long,
> Liv'd in the poet's faithful song,
> And with the poet's parting breath,
> Whose memory feels a second death.

Sustained in a second life through the poet's voice, these human spirits momentarily move and speak through the landscape because, paradoxically, they are being silenced into nonexistence "with [his] parting breath." On the one hand, these lines make a skeptical assertion that the only immortality comes from the poet's or minstrel's own voice recalling the association of lover, hero, and king with hawthorn, battlefield, and "mountain's misty throne." On the other, the passage asserts that, even though deprived of his voice, these spirits find at least a brief voice of double mourning—for themselves and the poet—through the natural elements local to their earlier existence: they "liv'd . . . with the poet's parting breath." Through the poet's earlier associations of spirit and place, moreover, his audience may sense that voice for a longer time.

If immortality after death is the issue in these lines, the threat of death in life, a threat haunting both the minstrel and his audience, dominates the final interlude, the one between stanzas 5 and 6. Like the preceding interlude, this one develops the relationship between place, memory, and the individual self. When the minstrel's words conclude a requiem for the English Musgrave at the end of canto 5, his "harp's wild notes . . . The mimic march of death prolong." So effective is the minstrel's harp that his audience "bade him tell, / Why he . . . Should thus, with ill-rewarded toil, / Wander a poor and thankless soil," when his music could help him to a decent living in "the more generous Southern land." In asking him this, the ladies deny his art any real purpose beyond entertainment or emotional consolation; but the "aged Harper" takes strong offense at any attempt to separate words from music, as Thomas the Rhymer also did, or the song's content from its proper context: "my own, my native land!" Even less than hearing his harp ranked above "his flowing poesy" does he like the "scornful jeer [that] / Mispris'd the land he lov'd so dear." "Scornful jeer" is surely strong language to apply to his courtly and courteous audience, but this language takes on an almost prophetic privilege. The minstrel's defense of his words, at the beginning of canto 6, is appropriate both to oral and written poetry; it proceeds, however, from the close ties between performing minstrel and his immediate audience, to an analogous closeness between minstrel and location, culture and nation. The temporal heritage of the minstrel, and in turn of the modern poet, is preserved and validated in their spatial community.

The famous paean to patriotism thus criticizes his own—and Scott's—audience for insensitivity to the values arising from a communal oral tradition. His scorn of the "man, with soul so dead, / Who never to himself hath said, / This is my own, my native land!" extends to a warning of another kind of death:

> If such there breathe, go, mark him well;
> For him no Minstrel raptures swell;
> . . . .
>
> Despite . . . titles, power, and pelf,
> The wretch, concentred all in self,
> Living, shall forfeit fair renown,
> And, doubly dying, shall go down
> To the vile dust, from whence he sprung,
> Unwept, unhonour'd, and unsung. [L, 6:1]

Just as in his defense of a redefined pathetic fallacy a canto earlier, the singer calls the loss of "fair renown" a second death; and in both cases the medium of that renown is the minstrel's song. In canto 5, however, it is the loss of that medium that leads to silence and a second death. Here it is the loss of an earlier feeling. Without love for his own "native land," the "wretch" is "concentered all in self" and can merit no minstrel's celebration of other-directed moral values, of values that benefit his society.

Taken with this one, the first seven lines of the minstrel's next stanza seem to form a Wordsworthian explanation of the way love of nature leads to love of human society—the title and theme of Book 8 of *The Prelude*. Yet in contrast to Wordsworth's natural settings, Scott's natural locations are already socialized.[17] If "Caledonia, . . . land of brown heath and shaggy wood, / Land of the mountain and the flood," is "meet nurse for a poetic child," it is also, the minstrel says, the "land of my sires." When he asks "what mortal hand / Can e'er untie the filial band, / That knits me to thy rugged strand," he knits human paternity and natural maternity—or foster-maternity—into his parentage. Marked by more specific place names, the second part of stanza 2 also become a more personal lament for the minstrel's lost society. "Of all bereft," he turns to his "sole friends," the "woods and streams" of Yarrow, Ettrick, and Teviot: they will remain "even in extremity of ill." Because it is an archaic name, "Caledonia" has few political repercussions. Yet this personal lament is also political, if indirectly so, since the minstrel's losses have followed from the lost Stuart cause. If the minstrel does not directly name Scotland, that silence reverberates for the writer as well as for the singer.

The minstrel's outburst of nostalgic patriotism—nostalgic in the Odyssean sense as a profound longing for home—leads once more to a recognition that he is "forgotten and alone," denied by history the legitimate social and even political function that he has just defined. Yet he turns self-pity into mild poetic revenge, filling almost the entire sixth and final canto—often called superfluous by critics—with minstrels filling their traditional role:

> Not scorn'd like me, to Branksome Hall
> The Minstrels came at festive call;
> Trooping they came, from near and far,
> The jovial priests of mirth and war. [L, 6:3]

Finally, when he ends his song, he is able to maintain a microcosm of that traditional role. Given a "lowly bower" close beneath Newark Castle, he can himself help travelers with food and with his "tale of other days"; and in summer, when "the aged Harper's soul awoke!" with the rest of a resurgent nature and society, both "the rapt traveller" and hunters stop to hear his song. Instead of measuring relentless and tragically-burdened memories of change, the Yarrow "bore burden to the minstrel's song";[18] and the narrative of the minstrel is converted into the idyllic freedom that he represents at the end of his lay.

Through the minstrel's venturing into the dark castle, then, and through the testing of his emotions and values, he gains a renewed sense of dignity for himself and his vocation. When he first enters, the glittering circle of ladies within the castle is so unexpected that they seem the enthralling enchantresses of romance. In a sense they do charm him into charming them through his regenerative song. We cannot push these romance allusions too hard, since they are less explicit than many Scott will make in later poems; yet they greatly reinforce the transforming effect of minstrel and actual audience on one another during this oral performance. Paradoxically, much of the interplay between the minstrel and his castle of beautiful women leads toward what Alexander, following Jeffrey and perhaps also Schiller, calls the "sentimental" nature of the interludes.[19] To use the word in Schiller's sense, these passages are individuating, personal, and subjective in contrast to the more objective, balladlike presentation of the minstrel's narrative. In other words, the framing narrative dramatizes the flexibility of the oral tradition in action, but is itself an artifact of another sort altogether—that is, of Scott's writing. In turning to the minstrel's inner narrative, we find a more exact representation of traditional, naive, oral narratives and a simpler representation of traditional minstrels in unself-conscious action. Surprisingly, however, we also find a narrative in which writing and its metaphorical extension, the transforming magic of gramarye, play an active part. This activity also symbolically evaluates the outermost narrator as writer. Like the inner chamber of one of those transforming castles or grottos in romance, the innermost narrative abruptly conveys us to the bleak hillside, or to its equivalent, the skeptical realism of Scott the writer. To read the inner narrative in this way is not to reduce an alien, objectively historical cultural moment to an allegory or metaphor of a far more modern *Kunstler-Roman*. Instead, inner, metadiegetic narrative and outer, extradiegetic frame interpret writing across and through the dramatic, present voicing of the "last minstrel."

To speak of a "present voicing," however, raises further questions that should be considered before turning to that inner narrative. These questions pertain to the definitions of self and artist in three differing historical eras and may be phrased through the working out of a ratio: the minstrel performing in the communal, oral tradition is to the modern poet, writing in private and publishing for unknown readers, as the "pre-individual" self of the medieval period (Jameson, *Political Unconscious*, 113) is to the apparently individual, creative self of the romantic era, the self claimed by its poets. Yet it is more often the attributing of prior or ultimate value to presence and voice that, according to Derrida, leads to the belief in a transcendent self or subject. Moreover, in Abrams's and Bloom's definitions of high romanticism, the voice of the self's own prophetic imagination calls up, encounters, and merges with an objective world. Thus the romantic self believes in its own free speech, its own freedom through its own speech. Derrida's criticism of such logocentrism (a belief in the metaphysical reality incorporated in words such as *logos*) would, presumably, not distinguish between the medieval and the romantic poet on the basis of their metaphysics of presence. He would, however, criticize the romantic poet for privileging voice without recognizing his complicity in a culture of writing.[20]

To some extent, the deconstructionist skepticism of presence and voice in the romantic period aligns itself with the only partially Marxist analogy in which writing links the individual, private imagination to a distanced, absent, reading public—or, better, to a public for whom the author is absent.[21] It also aligns itself, curiously, with the far more common-sensical skepticism of Scott's enlightenment heritage.[22] The main conclusion to be drawn from these analogies and their criticisms is a skeptical one: neither Enlightenment or poststructuralist skepticism, on the one hand, nor romantic privileging of voice, on the other, will allow us to work out too neat a scheme for interpreting the relationship of minstrel to modern poet. Scott plays it both ways.

At the center of the minstrel's sung narrative is a figure whose struggles to control her world through both written and spoken magic are analogous to the problematic powers and limits of the imaginative self confronted by Scott and his minstrel. The early Renaissance Lady of Buccleuch deploys her magic to protect her family and border terrain after her husband has been killed. As the minstrel begins his lay, he contrasts the physical power of the waiting soldiers in the castle hall to the intellectual, visionary power of the lady in her isolated tower. His shudder of horror at the lady's solitary incantations asks protection for himself and for his audience who may explore such topics, not for other characters: "Jesu Maria, shield us well!" (*L*, 1:1).[23] Yet if the lady's incantatory magic is powerful in calling spirits from the vasty deep and having them answer her, the answer of river and mountain spirits to the lady is one that announces an ethical view opposing her own: "Till pride be quelled and love be free," she will receive no more help from them. The pride is her own, in her self, her art, and her immediate family; the love is her daughter's for Baron Cranstoun, a member of the family that has just killed her husband (in 1552; see Scott's note 5). Although the lady uses her magic to help her take on the male role of leadership her son is too young to assume, these nature spirits express what Carol Gilligan would call a more profoundly female vision: they urge a vital reconciliation instead of a killing revenge, a quelling of the lady's pride and a freeing of her daughter's love.[24] Instead of listening to those vocal presences, however, the lady continues her proud and individual challenge to romantic and domestic love. She also continues her usurpation of male power: in order to defend her view of family integrity, she sends for a book of spells buried in the grave of its author, the local but renowned male wizard whose name is also Scott. In another sense this further reliance on magic increases her resemblance to the witches or enchantresses of romance who may indeed have descended from fertility goddesses but who draw men away from the human, social, and domestic ordering of that fertility.[25]

Yet the questing or erring knight of romance in this narrative makes his journey away from the enchantress, and at her own request. Justly celebrated as an instance of Scott's power to describe both the border country and rapid physical action,[26] the eerie journey of this illiterate moss trooper (a raider who evades pursuit in trackless bogs or mosses) leads like the Rhymer's romance journey into a kind of otherworld. For William of Deloraine, Melrose Abbey is a world of death. His low-key heroism in the natural world's rough border country contrasts sharply with his fear as he and the abbot unearth the wizard's book. That unearthing seems a double violation of natural order. A "Mighty Book," as both its guardian monk and the narrating minstrel say, it will gain a Lazarus-like new life, but as an apparently anti-Christian sacred text or scripture. Earlier an assistant to the wizard, the monk has done penance, "yet all too little to atone / For knowing what should ne'er be known" (L, 2:5).

To reinforce the significance of the wizard's magic as an extremely powerful art, Scott has his minstrel describe the abbey's Gothic architecture as if it too is being redeemed from death: the lines move back from ruin to stony art to fantastic, originating impulse. His famous opening lines in the second canto are spoken to his late seventeenth-century audience but also to Scott's own early nineteenth-century one. For both, though not for Deloraine, the abbey was in ruins:

> If thou woulds't view fair Melrose aright,
> Go visit it by the pale moonlight
> . . . .
> Where buttress and buttress, alternately
> Seem fram'd of ebon and ivory;
> When silver edges the imagery,
> And the scrolls that teach thee to live and die[.]

Because this chiaroscuro of ruinous beauty, of death and life, does not clarify whether the "scrolls" are the stone ornaments with their sculpted narratives or are some remaining manuscripts, the entire building becomes a sacred text.[27] In stanza 11 the minstrel goes on to speculate about its origins through a more magical, less orthodox process that points toward the subversive power of the wizard's text:

> Thou woulds't have thought some fairy's hand
> 'Twixt poplars straight the ozier wand,
> In many a freakish knot had twin'd;

> Then fram'd a spell, when the work was done,
> And chang'd the willow-wreaths to stone.

Even if the "silver light" shows "many a prophet and many a saint" in the still unbroken windows seen by Deloraine, this context of magic and magical texts gives a strangely resonant irony to the image of St. Michael: "Full in the midst, his Cross of Red / Triumphant Michael brandished, / And trampled the Apostate's pride." The sign of the cross is triumphant, in part, one might speculate, because it also symbolizes the illiteracy—complete or partial—of an oral culture. Beneath the "bloody stain" cast by the red cross on the pavement is buried the wizard who is the namesake of St. Michael, but one whose "Book of Might" makes him an apostate not only by its content but by its inscription as writing.

The wizard's power, explains the monk who once shared it, can free the stony landscape of the natural world from its established patterns with a demonic energy nearly divine:

> Some of his skill he taught to me;
> And, Warrior, I could say to thee
> The words that cleft Eildon hills in three,
>   And bridled the Tweed with a curb of stone:
> But to speak them were a deadly sin[.]   [L, 2:13]

The godlike powers of its written spells become manifest only through speech. Yet whoever reads the book may speak the spells. Freed from the dead hand of their author, spells can be either reinterpreted or redirected against his original intentions. Recalling the wizard's intention that his book help the Scott family at time of need, the lady recalls his book to support her concept of family. Her mission to release the wizard's book thus points forward to the similar, if more playful, call from the most recent lady of the Scott clan that her early nineteenth-century retainer write a book about local magic. The chief whose death prompts that earlier Lady of Buccleuch to send for the wizard's book, moreover, is named Walter Scott: the poet's eponymous warrior ancestor has died, we might speculate, to make way for the powers of another Scott ancestor, the reputed wizard Michael Scott.

Within the narrative, however, those powers are denied to the Lady of Buccleuch. Instead, the malicious goblin Gilpin Horner suddenly enters Scott's book, seizes the wizard's book, and forces it to open. Thus forcing both the wizard's text and Scott's own text into disorder, the goblin seems an animate and demonic *aporia*. At the end of canto 2, we suddenly learn that Margaret of Buccleuch's unsuitable suitor Cranstoun is served by an "elvish dwarf." As the minstrel explains how the dwarf had entered the baron's service, we begin to see that his defining characteristic is to leap playfully and disruptively from one realm to another. When Cranstoun was hunting in Redesdale's remote glens,

> He heard a voice cry, "Lost! lost! lost!'
> And, like tennis-ball by racket toss'd,
>   A leap, of thirty feet and three,
> Made from the gorse this elfin shape.

There is a dry humor in the minstrel's description of Cranstoun's reaction, quite different from the Gothic horror prompted in Deloraine by the wizard's grave and book: "Lord Cranstoun was some whit dismay'd; / 'Tis said that five good miles he rade, / To rid him of his company." Yet the dwarf "was first at the castle door," and he eventually finds employment. Again, the minstrel drily comments: "Use lessens marvel, it is said." The dwarf's alertness and his devotion have served the baron well, "though small his pleasure to do good."

Taken alone, this "marvel" might seem only an image of anarchic violence or of the id and not a figure for some original imaginative energy or presence that breaks through the conventional patterns of understanding. Yet arising from the goblin's arbitrary acts is a pattern of relationships that confirms this second interpretation: a pattern that links page, book, and lady. The goblin's spontaneous substitution of himself for the "Mighty Book" requested by the lady arises from his own quick study of its gramarye, its magical text. Following the bloody encounter between Cranstoun and the returning Deloraine, the goblin discovers the book and reads "one short spell." This is just enough, evidently, for him to perfect the shape-changing skill of glamour, in which "all was delusion, nought was truth." Through the glamour of the written spell, he then enters the lady's castle and thus replaces the book's latent and ambiguous power with his own malicious and energetic presence.

In a further exchange, his presence is even more explicitly linked to the lady than is the wizard's book she waits for. In an apparently spontaneous maliciousness, the goblin disguises himself as a playmate and leads the lady's "fair young child," the heir of Branksome Hall, into the woods. There, after frightening the child with "his own elvish shape," he abandons him. A band of English invaders soon discovers him and holds him for ransom. When the aggressive boy declares his own identity first by fighting off their dogs and then by announcing that he is "the heir of bold Buccleuch" and can call up for his rescue "every Scott, from Esk to Tweed," the English reiterate his heritage: "I think our work is well begun, / When we have taken thy father's son" (st. 19). Meanwhile, the goblin takes on his appearance and his place in the Buccleuch family:

> Although the child was led away,
> In Branksome still he seem'd to stay,
> For so the Dwarf his part did play;
> And, in the shape of that young boy,
> He wrought the castle much annoy. [L, 3:21]

The socially-acceptable, masculine, and other-directed aggression shown by the real child is distorted by the goblin into a painful pinching and sudden outbursts of flame: his violence, like the lady's magic, is a violation of domestic peace because it dislocates acceptable roles. It is nevertheless the dark side of that society's socially-accepted violence. This connection is suggested by the minstrel's sequence of images at the end of canto 3: from the dwarf's small bonfires to Margaret's romantic musings on what she thinks is the evening star that "shakes its loose tresses on the night," to her recognition that the "star" is in fact the beacon blaze of war, the Scottish borderers announcing the arrival of the English and rallying support as far as Edinburgh.[28]

This conflagration ends the third canto, but in the interlude the theme of sons' problematic relationship to parents' values continues as the minstrel mourns his own son, killed at Killicrankie. In the fourth canto, because the disguised goblin's efforts to avoid detection by the lady lead to his temporary banishment from Branksome to another castle, that banishment makes both explicable and threatening from the lady's viewpoint the English forces' announcement that they possess her biological son. Yet the goblin is, in his rebelliousness and in his magic, a child of the witchlike lady. In replacing her biological son, the goblin frees her temporarily from the social chain that makes her only the mother of the new child-chieftain. And like her, he expresses an anarchic, disruptive individuality through a transforming magic.

Though shaking the fabric of society, however, this rebellion does not fully transform it. Instead, the wizard's "Mighty Book," left with Cranstoun when the dwarf enters the lady's castle, makes possible a larger change. Tutored by his now-returned goblin-page, Cranstoun uses the book's gramarye in canto 5 to enter Branksome in secrecy. Although the goblin hopes that Cranstoun's presence in the castle will lead to sexual anarchy, the lovers can control the fires of their own passion well enough to redirect both passion and magic.

Disguised as Deloraine, Cranstoun substitutes himself for the wounded mosstrooper in a formal single combat, fighting an English champion in order to free the lady's biological son. Structurally balancing his skirmish with Deloraine in canto 2, this second single combat makes reparation for the first by restoring the Buccleuch heir to his family. Cranstoun's disguise as a retainer of the Scott family, moreover, proves prophetic. When the actual Deloraine, "half-naked" and "ghastly," staggers into the lists, Cranstoun removes the borrowed helmet and reveals his own identity. Once the lady learns of his generous service, she reluctantly quells her pride and gives love its freedom, allowing him to marry her daughter. Thus his interpretation of the book's spells completes and reorders the exchanges, almost the metaphorical substitutions, made by the maliciously energetic goblin, and brings peace not only between the feuding Scottish border clans but even, temporarily, between Scots and English.

Unwilling to disturb this fragile peace, itself so nearly a kind of glamour or illusion in that normally violent society, both Cranstoun and the lady are discreet about the nature of their struggle. "Much of the story she did gain," the minstrel comments, his balanced lines including the pun that confirms the interchange in his own story between goblin energy and written speech: "How Cranstoun fought with Deloraine, / And of his page, and of the Book / Which from the wounded knight he took" (L, 5:27). Cranstoun, however, leaves "half his tale . . . unsaid"—the half concerning his own use of the book—as if narrating his own experiment with magic might commit the Baron too fully to its practice, or as if narrative itself is that commitment to magic.

Because the lady, too, "car'd not . . . to betray / Her mystic arts in view of day," their conversation after the formal combat is constrained. Yet she planned "ere midnight came, / Of that strange page the pride to tame, / From his foul hands the Book to save, / And send it back to Michael's grave" (L, 5:27). Her attribution of "pride" to the dwarf comes right after her own painful and public relinquishing of pride as her chastising nature spirits had demanded. She associates the goblin's expression of pride with the supplementary power of the book, but "pride" seems in both cases to be an independent self-assertion that makes use of the wizard's neutral spells. Her intention to return the book to the grave suggests that she is beginning to relinquish such independence for herself—or, at least, that she now sees her family's identity as defined more by loving alliance than by hostile self-assertion. The minstrel's careful rejection of the "false slander" of "some bards" who claim that the lady would not enter the chapel for her daughter's wedding confirms this turn from individual pride and imaginative energy toward a communal harnessing of that energy:

> . . . I trust right well
> She wrought not by forbidden spell;

> For mighty words and signs have power
> O'er sprites in planetary hour:
> Yet scarce I praise their venturous part,
> Who tamper with such dangerous art. [L, 6:5]

Instead, she stands by the altar and assents to the sacramental words of her daughter's wedding. Dwindled from magician into domestic mother of the bride,

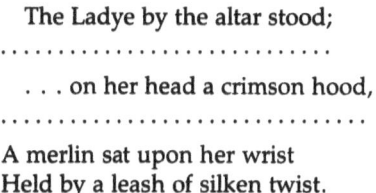

> The Ladye by the altar stood;
> ....
> ... on her head a crimson hood,
> ....
> A merlin sat upon her wrist
> Held by a leash of silken twist.

Both she and the hawk are hooded; its allusive name confirms it as the emblem of her present state of submission.

Yet her intention to leash not only her own magic words but the gramarye of Michael Scott's book meets, like all her attempts, a reverse that proves more socially generous in its twist. She is anxious to return the book to the wizard's grave. Instead, in an exchange that confirms the interdependence of goblin-page and book, the wizard leaves his grave, stalks through the wedding feast, and claims the still-malicious goblin as his own. When the shadowy figure says, "Gylbin, come!" the elvish page mutters, "Found! found! found!" and vanishes. Though apparently chastised, the goblin thus gains a paternal recognition and control, more than a total repression. With the dramatically if skeptically-described return of its author from the grave, moreover, the written text of Michael Scott seems to lose its threatening moral ambiguity and confirms the lovers' goal of an harmonious, cooperative, and social world. The wizard's presence and voice, even if reported on the weak evidence of a terrified crowd, validate his text.

Almost overlooked in this dramatic return from the dead, the book itself is apparently left behind when the wizard and goblin vanish together. If we look for further references to it in the minstrel's tale, we find instead another, more sublime vanishing of a book in the renewed presence of its creator. Through a pilgrimage to Melrose, the border clans try to quiet the restless soul of the wizard, and the minstrel's narrative concludes with a tribute to divine presence over text, the singing of the *Dies Irae*. In the face of an apocalyptic divine presence, "shrivelling like a parched scroll, / The flaming heavens together roll" (L, 6:31).[29] Although the minstrel advocates his own priority as present singer and preserver of a communal and traditional vision, however,

Scott as writer has the last word. He is now free to circulate his own individual, private text, doubly validated by wizard and minstrel. Yet because the minstrel's song has also shown not quite the interchangeability but the familial relationships of written text and goblin energy, he preserves his own anarchic originality of imagination and his own identity by defining his family origins. Like the dwarf goblin he becomes a son of the witchlike lady whose magic is chastised; and he writes for her, and for us, a book of magic that escapes the grave.

TWO

Marmion

THE METAPHOR OF FORGERY

PROBABLY THE MOST famous lines in *Marmion* come toward the end of the poem. In canto 6 that ambiguous hero recognizes not only that his rival de Wilton lives, but also that the forgery Marmion practiced to disgrace him has become public knowledge and will in turn disgrace Marmion. "O what a tangled web we weave," he says ruefully, "When first we practise to deceive" (*M*, 6:17). Though Marmion describes his own snarled pattern of plots, counterplots, and betrayals, his words also betray a significant metaphorical pattern in Scott's poem—a pattern of ambiguous metaphors for fictions that claim to escape the judgments of history. The most central of these metaphors is that of Marmion's "peculiar," "commercial," and unheroic crime of forgery;[1] but a well-knit web of other metaphors for fiction as well as dramatic uses of fiction in the plot extends its significance. Read literally, Marmion's forgery, as well as a series of prophecies, songs, and other written documents that involve possible deceit and reinterpretation, all make possible the complications and then the unwindings of the fictional narrative Scott spins out with such skill. Read metaphorically, they question the place of that narrative, one that evokes romance conventions and structures, within the already-inscribed, already public historical narrative of a stage of Scottish-English history culminating at Flodden. Each of these interpolations within the larger fictional narrative interrupts that narrative's creation of its own temporal flow by drawing attention to alternative truths and alternative times—different versions of the characters' pasts, different versions of the future, different relationships between private vision and public truth. Thus they both delay the main fictional narrative and point out its delay before the final judgment of that now-immutable final battle—a battle so painful in memory that Scottish chroniclers and historians did not want to name it.[2]

From its beginning *Marmion* confronts the tension between fiction and history more directly than does *The Lay of the Last Minstrel*. In *The*

Lay the actual writer could remain concealed behind the nostalgic and powerful figure of the traditional minstrel, and the minstrel then mediated between the magical fictions of the lay, presided over by Michael Scott's grave-breaking book and the skeptical readers of Scott's published book. In *Marmion*, Scott establishes himself in virtually all of his circumstantial presence of place, time, family, and friends as both narrator and writer. If the critical success of *The Lay* has made him capable of using the traditional minstrel's harp, it has raised demands that as a major poet he conform to public expectations of genre and abandon the local and playful voice of the border ballad tradition with its familiar histories and its romance traditions. In response to these demands, Scott prepares an eloquent defense of romance, both of its local errancy and of its illustrious tradition among British poets. This defense leads his readers to expect an inner narrative even more magical and romantic than the minstrel's lay; and yet the actual story is notoriously unromantic, even antiromantic in its closeness to the unheroic historical realities that lead up to Flodden, and above all in the commercial, not even physical, crimes of its protagonist.[3] Further, this realism extends to the situation of the women in the poem. Manipulative though some of them are, their roles seem far from that of the Rhymer's elfin queen or of the last minstrel's Lady of Buccleuch. Given no supernatural witchcraft, they appear to be pawns in Marmion's—and other men's—plotting for property. Scott's signals to his readers—to his immediate circle of friends addressed in the prefatory letters and also to his unknown readers—seem then a defensive maneuver to clear the ground not for the glamour or gramarye of romance itself, but for the private, if realistic, fiction that is only a "Tale," not a history, of Flodden Field.[4]

Yet the rhetorical excess in this maneuver should make us look more closely at both the structure of the main narrative and at the unchivalric nature of Marmion's crime—a crime that uses writing. That crime, committed in the past, does not itself form the main action of the poem, though the discovery of the crime comes as a result of that action. The main action, the English ambassador Marmion's journey to Edinburgh to make James IV a final offer of peace from Henry VIII, both evokes and denies the two genres of ballads in Scott's *Minstrelsy*. Although some of its most famous passages celebrate Marmion's riding north from Norham, the English envoy's task is not to raid, but to forestall the Scottish army's foray across the border. Yet in this emphasis upon history, the narrative seems to emerge from that subgenre of the *Minstrelsy*, the historical or riding ballads.

The narrative's denial of romance is more complex; denial precedes evocation and transformation. Aligning itself with Marmion's public purpose is his private quest for Clare, to bring about the marriage and the merger of properties prepared for by his forgery. Although this quest and the character it manifests are the very opposite of chivalric, both Scott's structuring of it and the characters' comments upon their journey evoke the quest romance as a shaping, normative model against which Marmion's unethical, exploitative behavior is judged. In this way the evocation of romance fiction defines the primarily realistic action. In another way, however, the clearest sign of that debasing of chivalry by opportunistic realism, Marmion's forgery, is a metaphor not only for the self-indulgence but for the opportunism involved in the writing of romance fictions, of documents that subvert the verifiability and the ethical responsibilities of history and law. Although the introductory epistles confront Scott's new fame as a writer through his friends' exhortations to direct his art more conventionally, they deny, by omission, his commercial success, a success that places even more pressure upon his need to evaluate the public purpose of his new poem. In spite of this denial, however, the pressure of that success manifests itself in his narrative. Marmion's forgery enacts Scott's own ambivalence toward the free inventions of his imagination in romantic narrative and toward their successful publication; it is thus a literary as well as a literal act.[5] Finally, however, the narrative structures of romance—delays that avoid and yet lead to revelation and to judgment—can correct the errors of Marmion's writing and thus confirm the value of those errant romance structures.

After first considering how the prefatory letters define romance and then define Scott himself as a writer of romances, we will turn to the narrative he presents through that persona. Next, Marmion's private quest for a bride, ironically contrasted to romance narrative, will show the interplay between romance roles and realistic roles for the women in the poem. A defining subgenre of this narrative strand, halting its flow to raise questions about its validity—and, in this case, to affirm a limited power for the woman—is the song. We will then consider the more public strand of Marmion's twofold quest, the embassy to James IV, as that converges upon historical events. Surrounding this journey and its public outcome is a series of prophecies, a disruptive subgenre that claims knowledge of future public events and, through that claim, tries to alter them. Both song and prophecy are the acts of poets—more exactly, of the "rude" bards, primitive seers, and minstrels from whom Scott develops his own self-concept as a northern and local poet. Though the activities of singer, prophet, and writing poet may be continuous, as Spenser and Milton claim them to be, in *Marmion* prophecy most often operates as a visual or visionary mode, and song as oral, musical performance. Together, they move toward the often brilliant pageantry of the written poem. In the final section of this chapter, subgenre and main narrative converge to consider the status and interpretation of written documents. Marmion's forgeries and Scott's fictions move toward the judgmental factualness of Flodden.

Recently, in response to Scott's contemporary critics and to the challenge of placing him among his contemporary romantic poets, his introductory verse epistles have garnered high praise for their Wordsworthian, yet more socialized, themes of the genesis of imagination through place. Their complexity of tone and their range of reference, always controlled by the writer's personal friendship for the "receivers" of his letters, have been well attested to.[6] In tracing Scott's definitions of romance, I will focus upon only two related elements of that complexity: his definition of himself as writer as well as singing minstrel, and his use of romance to connect local Scottish origins to larger British purposes.

In the framing epistles, Scott's references to the genre of romance are less direct than one might expect, and that very resistance to generic formulae is clearly part of their appeal. As J.H. Alexander points out, the most fully-developed and intense discussions of Scott's own art occur in the first, third, and fifth introductions; not surprisingly, these also contain the fullest range of allusions to romance.[7] From an indirect survey of characteristic romance episodes and plots in canto 1, he turns in canto 3 to an investigation of his own poem's local and national roots, as he himself has experienced them. In canto 5 romance allusions become a way to describe the more recent history of Edinburgh and to evaluate the relationship of present political reality to his own romance fictions.

In the letter preceding canto 1, the survey of romance occupies only the last third of the letter. Before it, a meditation on late autumn at his own Ashestiel leads into a far less local meditation. In these opening lines he frames a conflict between the role of national British poet, serious and skilled enough to support his country's highest military and political aims with epic or panegyric (canto 1 and later canto 5), and that of local Scottish minstrel, enjoying a more limited and casual play with words: he loves the "license" of a "desultory song" (canto 3) or (in 4) an "idle lay." A deliberately chosen loyalty to the Union and its culture conflicts with an earlier, intuitive loyalty to Scotland and to the border country. Parallel to this, though not yet clear to the reader, is Scott's decision to focus a narrative upon English characters and an English victory over Scotland, but to use an elegiac tone as he points the poem again and again toward the climactic battle. Within the narrative Marmion's forgery turns upon his framing of de Wilton for lack of loyalty to England. Forgery, then, points at several levels toward a possible betrayal of public, official loyalties by private desire and the fantasies of wish-fulfillment.

The privacy of that desire is less evident in the first epistle, however, than is his shift from the "bard-like mood" and "Gothic harp" with which he praises English heroes, to a loss of confidence only gradually restored by his friend Stewart Rose—"for few have read romance as well." His tribute to Rose's work on romances leads through earlier Arthurian episodes in Malory, through Spenser, Milton, and Dryden, and from there to his own lesser attempt "to break a feeble lance / In the fair fields of old romance." Both his allusions to several of Lancelot's encounters in the *Morte* and his own playful allegory of a newly-awakened "Genius" of romance, "Chivalry," delineate characteristic plots for romance. In neither case, however, does he raise explicitly the idea that he will use such plots as models for *Marmion*. He argues only that "the mightiest chiefs of British song / Scorned not such legends to prolong." With their own prolonging of narrative delay, these plots have overcome both the traditional high-cultural hierarchy of genres and the threat of time. Scott overcomes the difference between these illustrious predecessors and one who collects the milkmaid's "shrilling lay" or the "ancient shepherd's tale" (*PW*, 92) by referring to them as the chiefs of "song," who still hear the "legendary lay" and convey the "ancient minstrel strain." He also dramatizes that continuity with a miniature allegory of himself and Rose, editor and modern poet, participating in the endlessly repeated quest for romance. "Though dwindled sons of little men," Rose and Scott can remember the lofty names of the three earlier poets and can themselves become knights who "seek the moated castle's cell, / Where long through talisman and spell . . . Thy Genius, Chivalry, hath slept." When this figure emerges, awakened by "the harpings of the North," he will be surrounded by all the panoply of romance, from "Fay" to "dragon" to "wizard," to "errant maid on palfrey white." Although no specific enchantress receives the blame for imprisoning the "Genius," the train that accompanies his new foray includes personifications of the moral virtues missing both from the Lancelot whose ambiguous heroism foreshadows Marmion's and from Dryden's Restoration court, whose "niggard pay" and demand for "licentious . . . song" hints at the profanation of writing for money.[8] Romance gains new life, in part, through the moral choices that deploy the repeated motifs.

By the beginning of canto 3, Scott's narrative has included both an "errant maid" to be rescued and an erring woman now past both wandering and rescue; but its developing realism precludes the fays, dragons, and wizards he catalogues in the epistle to the first canto. Even the wizard-priest he places in the bleak landscapes of St. Mary's

Loch in the second epistle must be conjured into presence by a conscious act of the poet "to frame him fitting shape." Because it does not distinguish between oral and written modes, this visual, even sculptural, metaphor further develops the continuity of romance from minstrel to poet. Yet at the beginning of canto 3, Scott includes in his letter to William Erskine that friend's habitual criticism that the poet should not "ramble on through brake and maze, / With harpers rude of barbarous days."

More than in the second epistle, then, Scott must continue in the third to define and defend romance as a genre. He does so, however, not by confronting the "fitting shapes" of its sometimes fantastic personae, but by searching for the origins of that particular shaping impulse in the natural settings of his childhood. In one sense, he is naturalizing romance. Yet because the specific nature to which he ties these origins of romance is so volatile and energetic, it is no constraint, but rather the opposite. Furthermore, the strongest affirmation of this "viewless chain" or "secret power" between creative self and landscape follows Scott's rejection of the three "higher" genres he claims Erskine is urging upon him: elegy, epic, and tragedy. Although refusing a "task more meet for mightiest powers," Scott does not simply say that his meet task is to write romance. Instead, he redefines romance through memory, history, and place until that detailed and loving continuity can validate both "witches' spells" and "warriors' arms." Through his own history, he seems to move from the former to the latter, to "patriot battles, won of old / By Wallace wight and Bruce the bold." Yet even those battles are tied to his childhood "mimic ranks of war," to the pebbles and shells—natural objects—that served him for toy soldiers. Romance is play or fantasy, then, but fantasy that possesses both a history and a local habitation. Moreover, it is fantasy that will take written form, as his repeated references to "lines" begin to suggest in the preface to canto 3.

In the introduction to canto 5, however, this fusion—in which history validates romance and romance gives emotional meaning to history—seems to break apart again. Even though Scott describes Edinburgh through an elaborate comparison to Spenser's Britomart, the present political circumstances to which that comparison leads him compel him to "avert mine eyes, / Bodings, or true or false, to change, / For Fiction's fair romantic range." Already personified in his second stanza as "Caledonia's Queen," the Edinburgh Scott now enters is more beautiful and more open than it was before Flodden, or even in his own childhood. Like Britomart freed from her armor and her male disguise, the city at peace is "lovelier far / Than in that panoply of war" that had defended her since ancient times. Yet the shadow of the Napoleonic wars and possible invasion prompts him to turn back to a separate and controllable romance world, to the "fair romantic range" of fiction already mentioned, or to

> . . . tradition's dubious light,
> That hovers 'twixt the day and night:
> Dazzling alternately and dim,
> Her wavering lamp I'd rather trim,
> Knights, squires, and lovely dames to see,
> Creations of my fantasy,
> Than gaze abroad on reeky fen,
> And make of mists invading men.

Soldiers' fantasies are more dangerous than his, and less pleasant. Finally, because editors of past romances, such as his friend George Ellis, to whom this epistle is written, can "redeem" those romances from the past and can teach the harp of modern poets "a sound of the romantic strain," the practice of romance can "repair . . . Time's ravage."[9] Even if it cannot undo the damage of past wars, it can celebrate both the playfulness and the heroism of past cultures, from "Anglo-Norman" through Elizabethan. Scott's final model for his own art is not earlier sung or written narrative, however, but stained glass. As in *The Lay*, the Gothic cathedral is a model:

> . . . bold in thy applause,
> The Bard shall scorn pedantic laws;
> And, as the ancient art could stain
> Achievements on the storied pane,
> Irregularly trac'd and plann'd,
> But yet so glowing and so grand,—
> So shall [the Bard] strive . . . .

Though returning to his self-effacing claim that he prefers "tradition's dubious light," this image from Gothic pictorial art thus shows both greater confidence and greater emphasis on "story" than on the misty shapes of individual figures. With new confidence he will renew "field, feast, and combat . . . and loves and arms, and harper's glee, / And all the pomp of chivalry." Even within the narrative, a joyous art of "glee" and "pomp" offers an order quite different from the "pedantic laws" of neoclassical genres.

Scott's Christmas letter to Richard Heber that introduces canto 6 is less obviously about his own art. Yet his imagined dialogue with the classicist, like his earlier imagined debate with Erskine, playfully seeks to establish common ground between the established canon of great literature, in its "classic times," and his own "Christmas tale." A fully-developed gothic parable addressed to Heber playfully explores the idea that all books, even the most revered and solemn classics, contain and must ultimately release irrational, imaginative forces. In the vaults of a castle, he writes, "a mighty treasure buried lay, / Amass'd through rapine and through wrong," and guarded by a phantom huntsman. Struggling with him is "an aged necromantic priest" whose "words . . . make / The stubborn Demon groan and quake." To release the treasure, as Heber releases "literary wealth" through his books (l. 234), the Conjurer must "learn to tell / The very word that clench'd the spell" yet "scarce three letters has he won" (ll. 173 ff.). The treasure amassed "through rapine and through wrong" suggests not only the plot Marmion develops but also the guilt Scott may feel at his motives for writing and his fascination with such fictions or superstitions. Yet both may be redeemed, as he suggests to Heber, by the right words. In a sense the demon huntsman *is* the treasure, brought to our ordinary daylight world though not yet fully explained by the poet-necromancer's words.[10] This symbol of an illicit imaginative force, which is buried and must somehow be redeemed from the tomb, also appears as we shall see in the momentarily prophetic figure of the minstrel, buried alive but speaking still.

Within the narrative, Marmion's squire Fitz-Eustace is almost as well-read in romance as the friends to whom Scott writes these epistles. The judgments of Fitz-Eustace that emerge from his reading, described early in cantos 4 and 6, define clearly the typical actions of "loves and arms" in romance. Developing Scott's passing reference in canto 1 to an "errant maid" as a typical romance character, Fitz-Eustace draws particular attention to the role of women in the poem, a role both confirming and ironically denying romance stereotypes.

When Marmion and his attendants are riding through isolated woodlands on their way to Edinburgh, the squire looks around with enthusiasm. Their "pleasant path," he tells Marmion, is

> Such as where errant-knights might see
> Adventures of high chivalry;
> Might meet some damsel flying fast,
> With hair unbound, and looks aghast;
> And smooth and level course were here,
> In her defense to break a spear.

In "twilight nooks and dells," the squire goes on, her rescue and her reward of the rescuer would find an appropriate setting. No real heroine prompts these speculations in Fitz-Eustace. Rather, he is anxious to "show his lore" of romance, acquired from a "huge romantic tome" of "Caxton, or De Worde" (*M*, 4:4), and to distract Marmion from his brooding silence.[11] Each aspect of his romantic vision, however, is ironically fit to intensify Marmion's dark mood. The knight has just fought in an apparently ghostly single combat a rival he had earlier betrayed and believed dead. Instead of rescuing the woman for whom he and de Wilton had competed, Marmion is laying plans to remove Clare even from the nunnery where she had taken refuge from him, in order to marry her and gain her property. Finally, he has begun to worry about another nun he had seduced earlier and has just betrayed to ecclesiastical justice. Though he only imagines Constance's "hair unbound and looks aghast," the second canto has shown us just that, directly and powerfully. Far from rescuing her, he has been the means for her capture, her trial, and—although he does not yet know the outcome—for her condemnation to death. Thus his squire's chivalric dreams, even if stereotyped functions, become a precise measure of Marmion's own depravity.[12]

Fitz-Eustace's second allusion to romance, in 6:3, is less extended but equally well timed. Although Marmion has sent the abbess away and has claimed an ambiguous role as Clare's protector and escort, both of them are virtual prisoners at Douglas's castle of Tantallon while Marmion waits for a final resolution of his peace offer to James IV. Douglas has urged Clare to abandon her novice's gown for her own clothes, but the change, although intensifying her beauty, also intensifies her fear of Marmion's intentions. On the "lone" and "grim" ramparts of Tantallon, Fitz-Eustace suspends his target practice "on the gull and crow" to watch her

> . . . at distance, gliding slow,
>   And did by Mary swear
> Some love-lorn Fay she might have been,
> Or, in Romance, some spell-bound Queen;
> For ne'er, in work-day world, was seen
>   A form so witching fair.

For all its grimness, however, this castle leads to her release from Marmion's documentary spells. Her discovery first of de Wilton's armor and then of his apparent ghost standing beside it contributes to a resolution of the plot with all the convenient wish-fulfillment of romance. Like Marmion, she had believed that her preferred suitor, de Wilton, had died several years earlier in a judicial trial by combat. Forced to defend himself against Marmion's accusations of a treasonous correspondence, accusations backed by letters Marmion and his mistress Constance had forged, de Wilton is badly wounded and believed dead; his loss of the physical combat, moreover, publicly establishes his guilt. In fact he had gone into exile as a crusader, returned as a palmer, and in that disguise had become the guide for Marmion's journey into Scotland. After a mysterious knight defeats him during a secret midnight combat, Marmion recognizes the knight as de Wilton but believes he is a ghost, haunting him for his misdeeds. Now, in canto 6, another sort of *revenant* from the grave supports de Wilton's return to his true identity—and to life. Before her death, Constance had passed on to the abbess, who is traveling with Clare, Marmion, and the palmer, a packet of letters that prove both her own and Marmion's part in the earlier forgery. More appropriately than she realizes, the abbess passes them on to the palmer before Marmion sends her away. Armed with that evidence, de Wilton has persuaded Douglas to rearm and to rededicate him as knight. While standing vigil over his armor, he is found by Clare and reconciled with her. Flodden will be the more official and public reversal of his trial by combat, confirming his apparently supernatural elfin victory over Marmion at the hill-fort in canto 3. Fitz-Eustace's fictions of romance do not extend to the defictionalizing by which Clare is freed from bondage, but they prepare us for its fictionlike completeness.

Fitz-Eustace's response to Clare's almost visionary presence also epitomizes the dual nature of woman in romance, a duality anticipated in the ambiguity of the phrase "errant maid." Clare seems "spellbound" prisoner, but she is also "witching fair," spellbinding to those who see her. Similarly, even the women whose spellbinding by song and by forgery at first seems so successful are themselves prisoners by virtue of—or by vice of—their enthralling powers. Although Scott seems to turn in *Marmion* from the romance pattern in which a mysterious enchantress lures a male quester into an alien world, in fact he combines that pattern with the one Fitz-Eustace and Scott both allude to—that of the innocent damsel in distress. Both Malory and Spenser, of course, constantly show how difficult it is for the knight to distinguish between these two kinds of "errant maids." Scott, on the other hand, clearly distinguishes between them but begins, if very schematically, to show the common social constraints or prisons that force women into such extremes of gender definition.[13]

The clearest example of such a romance pattern used to define a social reality is that of Clare as the "damsel flying fast," in Fitz-Eustace's portrayal, or "errant Maid on Palfrey white," in Scott's own. When he first introduces her in canto 2, the narrator emphasizes not only Marmion's desire to possess her land, but her relatives' support of his claim: "Her kinsmen bade her give her hand / To one, who lov'd her for her land" (*M*, 2:5). This sort of pressure Scott will explore more fully and more tragically in *The Bride of Lammermoor*. To avoid it, Clare has fled to the convent of St. Hilda. Although we do not see this flight represented directly, we do see that it fails to end her wanderings; a whole band of nuns, as well as the abbess, become damsels in distress by being caught between the two hostile armies of England and Scotland. When James IV assigns Marmion to escort them back across the frontier to England and assigns Clare to be returned to her unsympathetic kinsmen, he sets the falcon, to use the poem's metaphor, to guard the chickens. Publicly, Marmion is their chivalric rescuer from the chaos of war; privately, he is the pursuer from whom Clare needs a rescuer.

Ironically, however, the physical assault or possession Clare fears is delayed by Marmion's stronger desire for economic possession: "Safer 'twas, he thought," to wait until kin and king "her slow consent had wrought." Marmion needs no emotional response to support his "flame," since "he long'd to stretch his wide command / O'er luckless Clara's ample land" (*M*, 5:28). The narrator goes on to argue that all physical or emotional desire had been directed to Constance: "If e'er he lov'd, 'twas her alone, / Who died within that vault of stone" beneath the abbey on Lindisfarne. At this point Marmion knows only that Constance has been imprisoned at his "command," not that she has been buried alive. Yet the emotional denial or starvation implicit in his planned relationship to Clare receives an ironic complement, a fuller definition, through his complicity in Constance's imprisonment and starvation. Almost every appearance of Clare has contrasted to our view of Constance: she is on board a ship with the wind blowing freely, she rides on horseback, or she paces the high seaward ramparts of Tantallon, ghostly but in the open air. Yet she too faces an imprisonment. If it is less obvious and less deadly, less full of Gothic horror than Constance's, it is insidious precisely because it is more commonplace. Her final "asylum" from "this barbarous lord," she says in 5:32, "is my own / Against the dreaded hour" of an unwanted marriage: "A low, a silent, and a lone, / Where kings have little power. / One victim is before me there," she concludes. Though she actually speaks of de Wilton preceding her in the grave, she seals her kinship with Constance.

Even though Scott carefully distinguishes between Marmion's physical desire for Constance and his economic desire for Clare, the traditional patterns of male "command" or domination tend to equate the two desires and to see one as the symbolic counterpart of the other.[14] Reinforcing Clare's romance role as the passive maiden in distress, this social and economic role increases her passivity so that she resembles her land. Like it, she is an object to be exploited. In her alienness, however, she shares none of the mythic or supernatural energies of a Circean nature goddess or of an elfin queen who haunts the Eildon Hills.

Nor are such elfin or Circean powers of supernatural naturalism possessed by Constance or by Lady Heron, the characters whose power with words is as enthralling as their physical attractiveness. Because of their skill with words, both of these women seem surrogates for the poet; but this analogy is troubling for two reasons. First, their roles either as surrogate or as muse make more explicit the ethical ambiguity of the poet's role as a writer of romance. Second, such a symbolic reading, though enriching the poem, tends to deny the more realistic social problems they face as characters within the poet's narratives, and thus to avoid the question of their responsibility for, or victimization by, these problems. Because the songs performed by Lady Heron and by Constance dramatize both the problematic function of poetry and the problematic role of women, this subgenre can help us evaluate the validity of these interpretations.

Like the prophecies to be considered later, these songs are public and dramatic. Their origin is not so much mysterious as anonymous, however; not attributed to superhuman agency but recognized as human and communal. Though the songs are heard in a few moments, they come closer through repeated form and repeated performance to becoming established texts. Interpretation occurs as the singer chooses song to match occasion and as the audience responds to the performance. With dramatic irony, both of the fully-presented songs become far more effective than the singer intended. Though in different ways, each is closely associated with one of the two morally-ambiguous antiheroines of the poem, "Young Lochinvar" with the historical and all too public Lady Heron and the untitled song with the fictional, private Constance de Beverly. At the opening of the poem, Marmion privately scorns "the harper's barbarous lay" that he hears at Norham, while publicly and politically praising it.[15] Later in the poem, however, he is forced to acknowledge the political power of the emotions provoked by song in both public and private spheres. The ethical problems raised by the songs thus do not turn upon the issue of truth and falsehood, as we will see that the prophecies do, but force us to consider another aspect of Marmion's forgery as a metaphor for romance fiction—the appeal of fiction as wish fulfillment. Thus, even if they interrupt the main romance narrative, they begin to interpret its fulfillment.

Though "Lochinvar," the song Lady Heron sings at the Scottish court, has given its name as eponym for a romantic hero, the song becomes through its dramatic context a more "barbarous lay" than those Marmion hears at Norham. For both Lady Heron and her song, based on an actual border ballad, belong properly at that border castle. Her presence at Holyrood in Edinburgh suggests a fusion of mythic and romance roles, of Circe and the elfin queen. This fusion is confirmed by her ballad, by its effect, and by her later return to Norham.

Even the factual accident of her name suggests flight into the wilderness. This metaphor is developed by Heron himself in canto 1: "No bird, whose feathers gaily flaunt, / Delights in cage to bide: / Norham is grim and grated close." He goes on to equate his absent wife to a falcon or a greyhound, but harder to leash than either; he has given up trying. Marmion indeed journeys through a wilderness before reaching the king, and his discovery of Lady Heron with the king in Holyrood resembles, though Scott does not explicitly point this out, a Guyon discovering the Circean Acrasia with her captive knight in Spenser's Bower of Bliss. Edinburgh is of course a larger, more urban settlement than Spenser's treacherous garden, and the castle belongs to Lady Heron only *de facto*; she has usurped, in Heron's words, "fair Queen Margaret's bower" (*M*, 1:17). Further, Marmion is no temperate Guyon. Yet these romance analogues in fact control the expectations of the characters as well as of the readers.

"Lochinvar," Lady Heron's song at Holyrood, is based on one of the romantic ballads in the *Minstrelsy*.[16] Like its sources, it contains no supernatural elements or quest-romance patterns; its romance is the promise of emotional and sexual fulfillment. When Marmion hears Lady Heron perform the song for James IV, its pounding rhythms and its wish-fulfillment pattern of escape generate a series of ironies that converts lyric interlude to dramatic action. Though the ballad's plot of an earlier lover returning to carry the bride away from a dreaded marriage will later prove roughly parallel to the plot of de Wilton rescuing Clare from Marmion,[17] the lawless yet heroic initiative of Lochinvar resembles Marmion's. When Marmion comes into the room, the lady smiles at him as if to acknowledge him as her rescuer; yet in doing so she breaks the spell of a more important resemblance. In singing to the king, she has urged him to become her Lochinvar, and he has succumbed. As she greets Marmion and in effect interrupts James's fantasies, he in turn rejects the attempt to preserve peace that Marmion's "parchment broad" contains. The "word" of the song, redirected toward Marmion with "smile" and "look," has destroyed the power of the written word he carries, and its false mood of triumphant conquest leads both to Marmion's defeat as peacemaker and later to James's fatal delay at Norham.

Though Lady Heron may be, as Scott's poetic text suggests, an official hostage to insure border peace (*M*, 5:10, but see Scott's notes 11 and 67), she has held the king hostage even in Holyrood. Later, word spreads that after James captures Norham, his army "inactive lay" while he "was dallying off the day / with Heron's wily dame" (*M*, 5:34). The narrator does not describe this return to Norham, but its mood, by implication, contrasts greatly with the "grim and grated" military readiness of the castle in canto 1. Paradoxically, her return fulfills

Heron's claim that, like a wild falcon, "she'll stoop when she has tir'd her wing" (*M*, 1:17). In making the pleasure-seeking Lady Heron a minstrel and her romantic escapist ballad the source of public irresponsibility, Scott displays the amoral power of poetry and the need for its comprehension and control, as his allusions to Dryden suggested in the introduction to canto 1. At the same time, he illuminates, if glancingly, the illicit but spacious maneuvering room Lady Heron creates in escaping from Norham's "grim and guarded" world of military priorities.

Both as a realistic and active antiheroine and as a figure standing for the poet, Constance plays a complex role in the poem. Her song, the second in the larger narrative, is less well-known than "Lochinvar," and the dramatic ironies it provides are part of the more wholly fictional web of Marmion's private affairs. That web is multifictional, for not only is Marmion Scott's invention, but Marmion's "tangled web" of intrigue has drawn Constance into it and made her, too, a spinner of fictions. Because the singer in canto 3 is Fitz-Eustace, her song is performed in a less calculated way than is Lady Heron's. Yet Constance's "favorite roundelay," even sung after her death, could scarcely be more pointed in its message to Marmion. From a blandly sentimental opening that describes lovers parted by fate, it becomes more violent and accusing: "Where shall the traitor rest, / He, the deceiver? / Who could win maiden's breast, / Ruin, and leave her?" (*M*, 3:10). Except for Marmion, the usual audience for earlier performances of her song and for this one as well has believed her to be Constant, a page boy and "our choicest minstrel." The slight shift in the form of her name draws attention to the network of betrayals in which she is both victim and agent.

In earlier performances, her song was a repeated favorite for all but Marmion. For him, it would have been a lyric warning against his betrayal of her—and perhaps also a goad to such betrayal. As we hear it for the first time in canto 3, we can watch Marmion's struggle between remorse for the betrayal she warned against and denial of responsibility for her fate. Yet because the palmer sonorously prophesies her death, he prompts Marmion's quasi-prophetic encounter with the elfin knight. The innkeeper has announced how a Scottish king, venturing into the ruins of a bronze age hill fort, long ago defeated an elfin knight and forced him to prophesy the future. Because Marmion too wants a prophecy, he rides out at midnight, only to encounter and be unhorsed by the disguised de Wilton. Constance's echoing song, then, leads directly to a partial redressing of Marmion's other major betrayal, his defeat of de Wilton in the judicial combat. It thus prophesies his "lost battle" in the hill fort. It also points beyond this "phantom" or fictional battle toward a rough pattern of his fate in the more actual battle of Flodden:

> . . . Borne down by the flying,
> Where mingles war's rattle
> With groans of the dying.
> . . . .
> Shame and dishonour sit
> By his grave ever;
> Blessing shall hallow it,
> Never, O never!

Physically, her threat comes close to fulfillment: the dying Marmion echoes it in canto 6. In a further irony, his body lies buried in an unmarked grave on the battlefield, whereas that of an Ettrick peasant is taken to his family vault. Her threat of such exposure, however, is not only a structural foreshadowing but a symbolic motif in which Scott again both censures and praises the art of poetry. For though the strongest agents of disciplined morality in the poem bury alive his amoral minstrel, her song still speaks, unrepressed, beyond that burial as a voice vengeful in intention but finally moral in effect.

Within the narrative both of these equivocal minstrels, Lady Heron and Constance, are the objects and provokers of illicit sexual desire. Lady Heron's song reinforces that desire against all public, formal loyalties; Constance's song attempts to control it, though she herself has evoked it, by enforcing a private loyalty. Linking imagination and sexuality, these figures are muselike guardians of forbidden powers whose exercise brings guilt, not only for the king and for Marmion, but for Scott himself. Scott's fascination with the imaginative power he partially condemns by its association with illicit sexuality appears in the realistic and personal introduction to Constance's song. Such a "wild and sad" air, he says, he has heard as highlanders work in the lowland harvest, "and deem'd it the lament of men / Who languish'd for their native glen; / And thought how sad would be such sound . . . Where heart-sick exiles, in the strain, / Recall'd fair Scotland's hills again" (*M*, 3:9). His political commitment to a unified Britain and his aesthetic commitment to a serious and celebratory poetry threaten with their discipline to exile him from the uncontrolled, spontaneous songs of "Scotland's hills." Thus in the epistle to this canto Scott quotes his friend Erskine as recommending classical models and British themes (ll. 33-42), but repeatedly claims his natural "impulse" lies in escapist fictions such as *Marmion*: "Though wild as cloud, as stream, as gale, / Flow forth, flow unrestrain'd, my Tale!" (ll. 241-42, repeating with slight variation ll. 21-22). The question raised with this impulse as with the sexual one is whether it is the impulse itself that deserves guilt or only its misuse if it betrays others.

In both of these songs, Scott has examined the ethical ambiguities in the use of such powerful arts to structure human desires into fictions that may, if acknowledged and interpreted, show a more profound truth. The issue becomes more acute as the art becomes more accessible to judgment, and it becomes more fixed and permanent as it is converted from visionary and oral to written form.

Yet if we read Constance's role solely in terms of its significance for the poet's art, we risk overlooking the more directly represented yet complex difficulties involved in her attempt to manipulate the social roles of gender. Although Constance appears directly only in canto 2, the recurrent references to her in cantos 1 and 3 describe her in two radically opposed sets of clothing, both of which disguise her true self—or, at least, the self she would like to be. Her nun's clothing, as "sister profess'd of Fontevraud" (*M*, 2:20) and her later disguise as a minstrel-page (*M*, 1:15) deny her sexuality, though in quite different ways. Both, also, play a role in generating romance plots shaped by the use of such disguise. Traceable to ballads and to Elizabethan romantic comedies, the girl's disguise as a page boy allows freedom to pursue a lover and, in Shakespeare's comedies, to educate him unwittingly both in love and in responsibility. Britomart, on Scott's mind in the epistle to canto 5, and her predecessors, those militant disguised heroines of Tasso and Ariosto, develop a similar role but a far more physically powerful and controlled one. Yet this romance convention, and particularly its optimistic ending, is countered by the more recent romance convention of the Gothic novel, and specifically by its recurrent and only superficially opposite characters, that of the rebellious escaped nun and the imprisoned woman. Neither the Elizabethan nor the modern Gothic romance roles reinforce the courtly medieval romance cherished by Marmion's squire. Instead, their odd fusion in this poem questions Fitz-Eustace's idealism.

Constance's career, to the extent that we know it, moves from convent to military campaign back to convent. We know nothing about her original reasons for becoming a nun, only that she, like Clare and the abbess, is of aristocratic origin: her name was Constance de Beverly (*M*, 2:20). Unlike the other two, however, she seems to have no family or wealth to define a social position both within and beyond the convent. The abbess, Scott tells us, "early took the veil and hood, / Ere upon life she cast a look, / Or knew the world that she forsook" (*M*, 2:3). Clare's situation is quite opposite, because she chooses the convent to forget the death of de Wilton and escape Marmion's suit.

Because Scott tells us nothing of Constance's motives for entering the convent, we thus find it difficult to judge her motives for leaving it. More than a novice, she stands condemned "for broken vows, and convent fled" (*M*, 2:30). She herself is savagely critical in retrospect, telling her inquisitors, "I left the convent and the veil" because "I listen'd to a traitor's tale" (*M*, 2:27). Marmion's "tale" is presumably the fiction that he will marry her. Yet there is a faint echo of Desdemona listening to Othello and hearing of a wider world, an echo consistent with Constance's choice of disguise upon escaping from the convent.

Because Scott denies her the dignity of an interior self to show her motivation for this crucial step, he also denies her full status as a heroine. In Gothic novels a nun who leaves the convent usually falls into one of two categories: either some clearly-defined villainy has forced her into the convent or, once in it, the nun has become depraved and thus villainous herself.[18] Remaining a nun leads either to passivity or to depravity. We see tendencies toward both of these in the abbess. Constance's later actions—her forgery and her attempts to poison Clare—make her a villain, but her escape and her cross dressing suggest a sympathetic impulse toward freedom—as if she, like the women forced into convents in Gothic novels, deserved a fuller development of the self in the world.

Yet her male clothing does not seem a means for escaping from the convent into a conventional, domestic female sexuality. Instead, though in pursuit of sexuality, it is both an escape from domestic morality and a means of asserting male power. In Shakespeare's romantic comedies, the pursued lover is ignorant of the heroine's cross dressing, which thus acts to test affection and to protect chastity until the barriers that bar marriage can be overcome. In *Marmion* Constance's freedom from social constraint, if it leads first to sexual fulfillment, is shortlived and finally illusory.[19] During her underground trial at Lindisfarne, she condemns her escape as a new kind of subservience: "For three long years I bow'd my pride, / A horse-boy in his train to ride" (*M*, 2:27). Her description of herself not as a minstrel-page but as a "horse-boy" obliquely but powerfully describes her sexual servitude to the "traitor" who has exploited the vulnerability of her disguise. His betrayal of her to the ecclesiastical authorities, finally, involves more than his hypocritical revelation that she has broken her vows. She has also, in her jealousy over Marmion's interest in Clare, hired a man to murder her rival—but Marmion has seen through her disguised plan and suborned the murderer, building such strong evidence against her that she is condemned to death.

With this second betrayal ends any lingering resemblance of Constance's role to Rosalind's or Viola's. Her idyllic Elizabethan romance is replaced by Gothic horror, by live burial within the vault that lies, in turn, within the convent walls. If this descent into the underworld at first seems to resemble the Rhymer's Orphic descent into the elf queen's realm, that parallel lingers only long enough to confirm Constance's lack of power. If we see her usurpation of the male roles of minstrel and writer as analogous to that practiced by the Lady of Buccleuch, her punishment for using her less literal magic is far more severe. Further, in spite of Poe's later examples, her punishment seems to return her to a radical version of the woman's situation.

Such imprisonment of women in Gothic novels has been interpreted in two apparently opposite ways: as a terrible extension and thus a criticism of the social constraints already placed upon all women and as a metaphor for the biological patterns of female space, to be confronted and accepted.[20] In the latter interpretation, this confrontation often leads to release, regeneration, and integration into adult society for the female protagonist.[21] In other words, the imprisonment seems a distorted form of an initiation rite like the older Eleusinian mysteries. Because Constance has already experienced a more direct, less symbolically anticipatory sexual initiation, this reading of the prison would for her become an ironic confirmation of her victimization by her own sexuality. If Scott's plot followed more conventional Gothic lines, that initiation would have become more obvious through the birth of a child. Here, because her letters eventually lead to Clare's ability to leave the convent and marry de Wilton, we might speculate that her difficulties somehow lead to a rebirth for Clare, into a womanhood exploited neither by her own sexuality nor by others' desire for her property. Constance's walled-up cell interprets Clare's imprisonment in the social constraints placed upon women not as owners but as bearers of property. Although Constance has tried to murder Clare, then, it is her own death that gives Clare a life beyond the convent. Thus her enforced exploration of vault and cell anticipates Clare's properly socialized sexuality, as the word "constancy" suggests. Within the narrative only the abbess, ironically, knows enough of both women's situations to make such an interpretation, and she is incapable of making it, at least consciously. She does, however, carry forward the written documents that link the women and thus allow the writing of a resolution.

A series of shifting romance analogues, then, defines the roles of the three important women in the poem. As these Gothic patterns of imprisonment end Constance's Elizabethan-romance escape, they recall the image of Lady Heron as a caged bird, reluctantly freed from Norham's grim towers by her husband. Like Constance, Lady Heron escapes that prison, and the prison of social convention, for a more romancelike role as a temptress dallying with history. Equally active, equally practiced in the use of song, and equally immoral, yet not equally punished, these two contrast sharply with the passive, silent, and moral Clare, whose only action is to flee into the convent. She is indeed Fitz-Eustace's "damsel flying fast," to be rescued by others and then rewarded by a marriage in which love and property interest fortunately coincide. Although this "romantic" outcome is central to the values of the poem, a larger version of the rhythm of dalliance leading to judgment that we see in the careers of the other two, less reputable women shapes a final version of romance in the poem, a version that submits romance to the judgment of history.

There is no *Dies Irae* sung at the end of *Marmion*, as there is in *The Lay*, to foreshadow the Last Judgment.[22] Yet from the secret underground trial of Constance in canto 2, a repeated pattern of trials alternates with a group of foreshadowing prophecies on the one hand, and a series of delays or dalliances on the other, until all are resolved—or, at least, concluded—in the battle of Flodden. This interweaving of prophecy, delay, and minor trials that culminates in a major judgment also weaves together the web of fictions spun by the characters and by the author. This judgment does not end time, but draws Scott's "tale" into it.

The fictional events of this poem, along with a few minor historical events, take place in a temporal space, largely undefined by the chroniclers, between the gathering of the English and Scottish armies and their commitment to battle from early August to early September 1513.[23] A later and fictional version of Henry VIII's embassies during the preceding spring which sought to delay war, Marmion's mission to the Scottish court at Holyrood is an attempt to increase that delay before battle, even to reconcile the two kingdoms and thus to avoid battle altogether. Although his public motivation is thus historically plausible, it cannot fully succeed without violating the immutable fact of the actual battle, the fact that confirms and judges Scott's fictions. Because of its public urgency, this mission seems quite unlike the more private wanderings or "errings" of the solitary knights in romance. Yet it becomes a way for Marmion to complete his own self-designed romance quest based on the fiction of de Wilton's treachery. Because Heron had taunted him at Norham about the delay in his planned marriage to Clare (*M*, 1:14), Marmion is the readier to dally with Lady Heron at Holyrood, thus angering the king, defeating his embassy of peace, and apparently ending—through Scott's fictional but realistic and detailed characterization—the delay before battle.

Viewed in this way, Marmion's often-criticized high route to Edinburgh (instead of the easier, more heavily used, coastal route) becomes an additional signal, on Scott's part, of this delaying or deferring of a judgment for the pleasures of dalliance along the way.[24] In this case the pleasures belong as much or more to Scott's readers, trained in the picturesque and the sublime of landscape, than to Marmion himself—his black mood is for us part of the scenery. Those scenes of isolation in cantos 3 and 4, however, enhance the process of self-discovery and self-judgment in Marmion himself and thus reinforce the parallel between his individual judgment and the larger historical pattern of revelation and judgment at Flodden.

The most dramatic episode in this process is Marmion's attempt to wrest the prophecy from the elf king at Gifford, an attempt that in effect becomes a second trial by combat. The visionary mode claimed by this and three other prophetic moments in the poem brings them into direct conflict with the standards of actual truth or validity demanded by public and chronicled history. Scott uses three of the episodes as foreshadowing devices to place his "Tale" in the context of historical events that lie ahead of it. As she is condemned to death on Lindisfarne, for example, Constance's prophetic raving in canto 2 anticipates both the dissolution of the monasteries and the picturesque ruin the abbey will then become. Though her prophecy is verbal, it leads to both pictorial effect and to historical fact. Making no attempt to explain the now obvious accuracy of her pronouncements, Scott allows our retrospective viewpoint to silence such questions. The two prophetic visions that point toward Flodden, however, as well as the more private episode of the elfin knight and his repeated prophecies, are carefully set within a framework of multiple viewpoints.

The first of the Flodden prophecies, the mysterious figure who appears in the church at Linlithgow to warn James IV against going to war, is tied to the poet's role as prophet not only by his suggestion of a power in words to convey profound truth, but also by the figure's appearance. He resembles a picture of the apostle John, whose gospel begins with the Word given human form. Moreover, Marmion hears of his appearance through the narration of the courtier and poet Sir David Lindesay, a witness to the figure's mysterious arrival and vanishing. Lindesay voices no direct skepticism about this appearance, though he remains discreetly silent about whether it was supernatural or human. Scott's presenting it through such indirect narration supports his own skeptical remarks in the notes and in the epistle to canto 6. There he writes:

> Such general superstition may
> Excuse for old Pitscottie say;

> Whose gossip history has given
> My song the messenger from Heaven,
> That warn'd, in Lithgow, Scotland's King[.]   [*M*, 6:204-8]

Here, however, it is Scott's "historical" sources who chronicle these unlikely breaks from present into future. As we turn back, then, to the figure warning James in Linlithgow, we see a reluctance to deny directly the validity of its existence, supported by the validity of its now-verified message. At the same time, we also see a continual focusing of these prophetic appearances from the conflicting claims of superstition or fact toward the middle ground of a fiction that "never affirmeth."

More directly presented in the narration, the second prophetic vision of Flodden—also derived from Scott's historical sources—is also more directly challenged.[25] As the abbess hands de Wilton the packet of papers that will clear his name, they are interrupted by "a vision" announcing the names of those to die at Flodden, but a second voice takes exception to de Wilton's inclusion in the summons. In the next canto de Wilton explains that the second voice was his (*M*, 6:8). His initiative is possible because of his skepticism: this "strange pageantry of hell," he tells Clare, "featly was some juggle play'd, / A tale of peace to teach." With this suspicion of human agency behind the hellish pageantry, he participates in the prophetic mode, acknowledging and using its powerful effect while remaining skeptical of its superhuman origin. In the introduction to canto 6 and in the notes, Scott shows his own skepticism of the prophecy reported in his sources; but the active skepticism of de Wilton enters and shapes the narrative. Its primary influence is not the revelation of the historical fact of Flodden, nor even its revelation of Scottish attempts to delay or forestall James's march on England, but its revelation of de Wilton's character in contrast to Marmion's, for his skeptical and active use of superstitious prophecy increases as Marmion's own skepticism decreases. And though de Wilton's most important manipulation of prophecy occurs earlier, in canto 3, the reader's suspicions about his role in Marmion's battle with the elfin knight are not confirmed until this moment, when he reveals both his identity and his character to Clare.

Undertaken to make the elfin knight speak prophetically, Marmion's midnight battle in the deserted hill fort is enormously important in the structure of the poem. Taking place almost at midpoem, it is the only physical encounter in the narrative between these private but central protagonists. Redressing the trial by combat that has taken place before the direct narrative begins, it is the private and fictional correlative to the public, historical battle of Flodden at the end of the poem. Its fictional nature is a complex one, however. In the most obvious sense, the encounter is more fictional than Flodden because the two characters who fight are both invented by Scott. Yet these two invented characters must themselves confront aspects of the episode that appear to be fictional from their point of view.

As de Wilton, disguised as a palmer, accuses Marmion indirectly of having murdered Constance, the landlord of the inn supports the palmer's visionary remark by citing a "hamlet legend" (*M*, 3:18). The legend is quasi-historical because it involves the Scottish king Alexander III and an elfin knight who appears as the English Edward I and who is compelled when defeated to reveal future Scottish victories. When Marmion rides out secretly to the hill fort, he too encounters a mysterious knight but can compel no prophecy from him, or rather no prophecy that he can recognize. Scott delays the full explanation of the encounter by using a series of limited viewpoints. In canto 3, the squire Fitz-Eustace wonders at Marmion's being "stirr'd by idle tale" when "he scarce received / For gospel what the church believed" (*M*, 3:30). Though he sees Marmion return with dirt on his armor, he knows only that the legend has enough substance to unhorse his master. In canto 4, Marmion confesses to Lindesay that he now believes the tale valid because his antagonist was the apparition of an enemy—de Wilton—whom he believes dead. Lindesay's comment steers a careful course between objective belief in the phantasm and a psychological explanation: such spirits cannot harm except "when guilt we meditate within, / Or harbour unrepented sin" (*M*, 4:22).[26] Not until canto 6, when de Wilton can make public the written history of Marmion's forgery—and when Scott can turn to the climactic battle of a more public written history—is the elfin knight's identity revealed as human. De Wilton has put the fiction of an "idle tale" to work by playing upon Marmion's guilt. His physical victory over Marmion is thus prepared for, and completed by, the power of manipulated fiction. That fiction, moreover, opposes and implicitly criticizes as a worse fiction the earlier trial by combat in which de Wilton's physical defeat seemed to announce a divine judgment that confirmed Marmion's accusations against him.

The identification of poet as prophet, and thus as claimant to a special knowledge or vision beyond that of ordinary facts, has been subject to ironic challenge at least since Plato's *Ion*. Here Scott presents the special knowledge but attributes its power not to its skeptically-viewed source but to the human longing for some intervening transcendent power, a longing that virtually creates a power with a kind of communal imagination.

Though he goes on in *The Lady of the Lake* to explore the psychology of prophetic trance, in *Marmion* Scott makes two of the prophetic visions appear mysteriously unmediated by human agency, and thus displaces the role of poet to interpreter or manipulator of these visions. Lindesay interprets the visions in Linlithgow; de Wilton interprets and uses the phantoms around the cross and the "hamlet legend" of the prophetic elfin knight.[27] In the second case, though casting himself as prophetic elf, he resists the role of his prototype, who is forced to prophesy as he is caught between the military prowess of the king and whatever supernatural power speaks through him. Instead, de Wilton controls his self-revelation to present a more active, human sort of prophecy. In a similar way Scott himself is an interpreter and a manipulator of our prophetic longings. He allows us to indulge them safely, for many of them can be validated by the later history he has the advantage of already knowing as past action—or, more easily if not more credibly, they can be validated by the fictions he writes to fulfill the "private" prophecies. Such a quasi-prophetic history is both easier and more reassuring than the "turn, or else" calls of Old Testament prophets or the visionary apocalyptics of Blake and Shelley.[28] Yet the very glibness of this "past-perfect" prophecy calls attention to Scott as the manipulator and raises in a more serious way the issue of the moral responsibility of fiction. Prophecy thus is metonymic of the poet's art—a source or cause standing for the effect and making us see it, but not the center or substance of that art as in the work of Scott's contemporaries.

Before the final testing at Flodden, a nearly apocalyptic turning point in the fortunes of Scotland, the Scottish king himself creates two separate delays in the action: one fictional and one historical. The first of these is his consignment of Marmion and the English nuns to Douglas's castle at Tantallon, to keep them out of the way of his army's southward march. Although one might again accuse Scott of a delay for the sake of a scenic route, this delay is no dalliance but a private trial for Marmion. Given no opportunity to testify in his own defense, he is condemned by the written evidence of his own forgeries, which the abbess, after receiving them from the condemned Constance, has handed to de Wilton, who then gave them to Douglas. The second delay is indeed a dalliance, but one that shapes the finality of historical event instead of deferring it. Although the king's delay at Norham with Lady Heron follows a romance pattern, it is in essence historical, and it leads him into a fatal version of the confrontation between armies he had already too blithely begun. As Scott moves closer to the actual events of that irreversible history, the irony of James's misplaced belief in the play of romance becomes clear.[29] So too however does Scott's own well-placed but always skeptically considered belief.

The battle itself draws romance into a confrontation with history, but it also tempts the protagonists of history to follow the norms of romance. When he sees the English army crossing the Till and thus vulnerable to a flank attack, James's final delay—again historically accurate—recalls his dalliance with Lady Heron and prompts Scott in a suddenly more partisan narrative voice to lament, "Why sits that champion of the dames / Inactive on his steed? . . . What 'vails the vain knight-errant's brand? . . . O for one hour of Wallace wight, / Or well-skill'd Bruce, to rule the fight" (*M*, 6:20). The king's self-deluding romanticism, both in this delay and in his insistence, a little later, in leading the main charge, contrasts with Marmion's cynical claim before the battle that "the pheasant is in the falcon's claw . . . Clare shall bide with me" (*M*, 6:22) and with his more laudable, yet equally practical attention to the whole army's strategy even as he is dying. Although both men, James the historical victim of romance and Marmion the fictional manipulator both of fiction and of fact, are at least partially redeemed by their physical heroism in battle, the historical battle itself, Scott suggests, enacts a kind of glorious death wish at the center of James's chivalric fantasies. Because he takes with him in that death most of a generation of Scottish aristocracy, Flodden indeed marks the end of the chivalric era James dreamed of fulfilling. That leveling conclusion, reflected in the historical confusion over locating the king's body among the battle's corpses, may have led to Scott's fictional exchange of Marmion and the Ettrick peasant in death.

As Marmion dies, he cannot hear the priest, for "A lady's voice was in his ear," singing Constance's prophetic song. Thus her voice speaks again from the vault to which he had betrayed her, just as it spoke through the letters that she had sent with the abbess, letters that exposed Marmion's and her own forgery. These letters, along with other "written" texts within the narrative, draw further attention to Scott's own minstrel song as forged document. Three of these groups of written documents are letters: the forged letters that originally frame de Wilton, the second packet of letters in which Marmion had instructed Constance, "our minstrel," to complete her forgery of the evidence against de Wilton, and the "parchment broad" of his diplomatic mission. The final written text is the ironic inscription on Marmion's Lichfield tomb. The preceding discussion has shown how the "parchment broad" of the peace proposal has been made ineffectual by the more elemental and volatile powers of song that are also the sources of Scott's poetic fictions. Now we see how Marmion's own writing, the packet of instructions for the forger, becomes the means for completing his downfall and for his redemption. Those letters were nearly buried with Constance at Lindisfarne. Like her song, however, they emerge from that grave to document her vengeance upon Marmion. That vengeance was necessary, moreover, because Marmion had buried too deeply the validity of his own love for her, love he acknowledges only as he hears her song, living after her, in canto 3. Finally, these letters that have survived her burial in the Lindisfarne vaults reveal his attempt to gain the "mighty treasure" of Clare's estates, treasure he tried to amass "through rapine and through wrong." The letters are thus a truer treasure, a kind of valid "literary wealth," to echo the terms of Scott's epistle to Heber.

We might well interpret the correction of the forged letters by the "true" ones as a condemnation of fiction altogether, and there is surely an element of self-censure for Scott in the symmetry of his plot. Beyond this, however, is a further interpretation suggested by the parallel between the second unforged set of letters and Scott's prefatory letters to his friends. Though they are aware of it to different degrees, both Marmion and Scott show a need to use writing and yet to confess and correct it. As the correction or chastising of Marmion proceeds through these analogues of poetic fiction, we have seen through the epistles that Scott's own confidence in the act of writing grows. Yet in this process Scott neither accepts Marmion's forgery nor in spite of powerful self-criticism rejects his own poetry as forgery. Instead, he explores the parallel in order to show their final difference. In making written documents both the frame and the device that constructs and collapses Marmion's "tangled web" of plotting, Scott forces us to judge both Marmion and the art apparently shared by character and author.

The parallels between Marmion and Scott are striking. Marmion uses his written fiction to gain land and increased social status, but the truth behind his forgery and the truth carried by song and prophecy betray his guilty antiromantic quest for Clare and his moral mission of peace. We can of course make a biographical case for Scott: he uses his poetic fictions for just such purposes and then projects his guilt at the representation of wish-fulfilling romance as serious work or heroic action worthy of such rewards by showing Marmion as disgraced forger redeemed only by heroic physical action. Yet there is more than physical courage and prowess on which to base Marmion's redemption. His attempts to keep his private corruption from tainting his public responsibilities resemble Scott's own attempts to separate invented fiction from actual history, then allowing history to judge the conclusion of this romance narrative.[30] Neither can succeed, however, until he can acknowledge fiction not only as literally untrue but as emotionally valid. Though Marmion's framing of de Wilton was forgery, his trial by fiction has taught him better. And through Marmion's narrative, Scott has learned that he need no longer fear placing his imaginative romance narratives on paper. They are not an irresponsible forgery, and his self-exposure as a framer of fictions is one assurance of a deeper honesty. Though the Ettrick peasant is carried off to be buried in Marmion's rich tomb, as if Scott still sees himself as a perpetrator of fraud, it would be fraud only if he were to become another sort of poet—classically epic or narrowly historical. Marmion's actual burial in the soil of Flodden beside the spring seems the commitment of one who now understands his own groundings in the valid fictions of his native tradition, but who can also cross the border, better than James at Flodden, to claim cousinship with the larger world of England's writers of romance.

THREE
The Lady of the Lake
ROMANCE AS THEME AND STRUCTURE

IN THE FIRST CANTO of Scott's *The Lady of the Lake*, the disguised King James V of Scotland has become lost while following a stag into the highlands near Loch Katrine. As he blows his bugle with the hope of calling up one of his attendants, a strange girl appears, rowing a skiff toward the shore. Cautiously "the Hunter left his stand, / And stood conceal'd amid the brake, / To view this Lady of the Lake" (*LL*, 1:17). From this epithet, sounding almost as if it were suggested by the rhyme and not occurring again in the narrative, comes the title of Scott's poem. From it, also, comes an emphasis upon the love plot that has led many readers to view Ellen Douglas, the girl who is so glancingly given this epithet, as the central character of the narrative. Edgar Johnson argues instead that "the struggle between clan and crown, not the tenuous love-story of Ellen Douglas and Malcolm Graeme, is the real theme of the poem" (*LL*, 1:348). Supporting this assessment, Jill Rubenstein has shown how Scott develops a symbolic dimension for individual characters to make them representative of this struggle; yet the character of the king, she observes, has an unfortunate tendency to frame his world as an eighteenth-century revival of medieval romance.[1] Her observation, however, points the way toward another reading of Scott's poem. Through his deliberate testing of the way romance as a genre may explore and even shape reality, Scott links the love plot more firmly to the theme of political conflict and at the same time resolves his own uneasiness about the writing of such romance.

Eighteenth-century revivals of medieval romance clearly shape Scott's ideas about the genre, but his debt to late eighteenth-century historicism is also strong enough to prevent any simple anachronism in the perspective of an early Renaissance king. Instead, the poem traces the meaning romance as a genre carries in at least three different historical periods: the medieval, the Renaissance, and his own. Though obviously close to eighteenth-century perspectives, the last of these moves beyond them to echo the Renaissance's self-conscious but confident celebration of the transforming powers of romance. As the title and the narrator's epithet suggest, medieval and particularly Arthurian romance sets up a pattern of expectation for the encounter between the disguised king and Ellen Douglas in the first canto. In the larger structure of the narrative, however, Scott uses not medieval but Renaissance forms of romance. Finally, the narrator as nineteenth-century minstrel searches for the psychological and historical roots of his romancer's art. Through his own self-portrait and, within the narrative, through the figures of bard, minstrel, and half-mythical, half-skeptical lady, he can test the function of romance in a context of historical change.[2]

This hermeneutic use of romance as a genre resolves some of the stresses placed upon Scott's use of that genre in the first two poems. Although the Lady of Buccleuch in *The Lay* is an enchantress with magic as real as the elf queen's, the structure of the minstrel's narrative is in many ways more like that of a riding ballad than of the Rhymer's romance. Although Clare is a pawn in Marmion's quest for property, the structure of that narrative resembles a romance quest into an otherworld until the delayings of romance end in the final judgment of unavoidable history at Flodden. In *The Lady of the Lake*, Ellen's role as enchantress and the narrative pattern of the king's journey into the highlands and back follow the pattern of romance presented by the first, traditional, part of Scott's ballad *Thomas the Rhymer*. Two facts seem to subvert this greater generic consistency: Ellen's lack of any literal magic and the king's historical identity. She is no real enchantress, though she may well become a real pawn; he is a real king, or attempts to become an actual ruler after his premature inheritance of the crown at the all too nonfictional Flodden. Yet because these two central characters delay both recognitions, the structures of romance can finally and confidently reshape history, both national events and the more local event of a woman's choice in marriage.

Scott's own act of generic choice is more disguised in this poem than in the first two, however. *The Lady of the Lake*, unlike *The Lay* and *Marmion*, seems scarcely concerned at all with the anxieties of writing. No book of magic, as in *The Lay*, or forged documents, as in *Marmion*, both impugn and celebrate the poet's transforming gramarye. The tension between historical chronicle or legal document and the modern writer's use of fiction vanishes gracefully and almost entirely. In the written poem, he confirms almost without guilt the role of speaking, singing, and naming—or the withholding of names—to represent an oral culture that nurtures romance. In the poems that will follow this one, that guilt remains absent from the two anonymous poems containing strong romance structure and strong enchantresses; it returns in the two poems more concerned with history and with the historical plight of actual women as pawns. Yet, as *The Lady of the Lake* illustrates, even if in a benign and playful way, the guilt is discovered in, and then denied to, the enchantresses in these romances.

Medieval romance in this poem appears through the double filter of Malory and James V, the latter both literary character and historical king. For these reasons it ultimately takes on greater social and historical consciousness than the typical courtly romance Erich Auerbach describes in *Mimesis*. Though Scott's poem still demonstrates much of that basic shape of "trial by adventure . . . to give the knight opportunity to prove himself," his knight also learns more of the "sociological and economic foundations" left unexplained in most romances;[3] by proving himself he thus improves his rule. This redirection of romance develops, however, out of an initial dichotomy between the actual, historical world of James V's kingdom and the more fantastic one of literary romance.

The poem's chronological setting in the early sixteenth century favors a certain consciousness of historical change among all of its characters. Postmedieval, Scotland is a world just entering the Renaissance. Posttribal, it has not yet established a strong central government.[4] The conflict between clan and crown represents James's efforts to establish such a government. The beginning of the poem, however, finds the disguised king seeking some temporary escape from this effort. After riding out of Stirling on the stag hunt, he quite consciously defines the highland world he stumbles into as a world of medieval romance. Thus it becomes a world doubly distanced from the reality of his political conflicts: first by time, and even more by the essentially fictional and magical nature of such romances. The narrator describes the landscape into which the hunted stag has led the king as "the scenery of a fairy dream" (*LL*, 1:12), in which the "mountains . . . like giants stand / To sentinel enchanted land." Almost as if overhearing these phrases, the king tells Ellen Douglas that "on the lake's romantic strand, / I found a fay in fairyland." When Ellen tells him a minstrel has foreseen the arrival of a "guest of fair degree,"

> The stranger smiled: ". . . to your home
> A destined errant-knight I come
> . . . .
> Doom'd, doubtless, for achievement bold." [*LL*, 1:24]

And they continue this bantering adoption of the roles of romance. Ellen invites him to enter her "enchanted hall" on an island in the lake and then, as he asks who she is,

> Turn'd all inquiry light away —
> "Weird Women we! by dale and down
> We dwell, afar from tower and town.
> ....
> On wandering knights our spells we cast."

Through this intelligent joy in acting out the gestures and style of medieval romance, Ellen and the king establish together a sort of mental romance geography in order both to escape and to explore in safety the less manageable terrain of Scottish politics and their personal consequences. In the urbane anonymity of these romance roles, each can challenge the other without revealing his or her identity. And each can play at belonging to a world subject more to imagination's controls than to those of history or politics.

Moving just beyond their consciousness of this rather general romance world is a more specific pattern of allusion to Arthurian romance, particularly Malory. Though the narrator makes this explicit only in calling Ellen the lady of the lake, he in fact parallels at several points Arthur's first encounter with the lady of the lake in the *Morte Darthur*. A stag hunt as a prelude, a magical lake and island presided over by a lady, a magic and mysterious sword, and the king's promise of a boon to the lady, all appear in both Malory and Scott. Yet as these parallels underscore the strangely magical nature of the world in which the king finds himself, they also recall the political problems shared by romance king and actual king alike.

In Malory, the series of episodes culminating in Arthur's first encounter with the lady of the lake begins with the threat of northern and western rebellion. Like the disguised James V, Arthur rides out hunting as a diversion from this and other serious problems. Earlier versions of the Arthurian material often begin with such hunts. Both *Geraint Son of Erbin* in the *Mabinogion* and *Erec and Enid*, Chretien's version of the same story, open as Arthur hunts a magical white stag. As Geoffrey Hartman notes, "The hunter lured by his prey behind nature into visionary experience" is a topos widespread in European literature.[5] Finding "a great hart afore him," Malory's Arthur "chaced the hart so long, that his horse had lost his breath & fell downe dead" (Caxton's Book 1, chap. xvii; Stansby, sig. F.1v). In his second encounter with a knight met on his hunt, Arthur breaks his sword and Merlin leads him to "a damosell going upon [a] lake." Within that lake a rock encloses "as faire a place [W: paleyce] as any is on earth," an "enchanted hall" like Ellen Douglas's. If he speaks "faire to her," Merlin tells Arthur, the "lady of the lake" will give him the sword "which the arm holdeth yonder above the water" (1, chap. xxiii; sig. G2).[6] When Arthur promises her a gift, she gives him permission to take the sword; it becomes, of course, both means and symbol of the providential magic hallowing his kingdom for a while.

In Scott's poem, too, the king has been troubled by rebellion. The stag hunt with which the actual narrative opens, often and justly praised for its evocation of vigorous, realistic action, recalls both Malory and his predecessors who describe near-magical hunts. When his lady of the lake, Ellen Douglas, leads the disguised king to an island lodge she calls an "enchanted hall," he is startled by a "clang of angry steel" as a heavy sword falls from its scabbard on the wall (*LL*, 1:27). Like Excalibur, it is said to be magical (*LL*, 2:15). The sword is not given to him directly; instead, though the king only suspects this, it belongs to his former guardian the Douglas. In his earlier attempts to shake off the power of his regents, the Douglas family, he has banished them, and they have found shelter with the highland clan of Roderick Dhu MacAlpine, into whose territory the king has stumbled. Thus the sword can come into his service only when the king ends Douglas's exile—as he does at the end of the poem.[7]

Aside from this, Scott abandons his specific allusions to Malory's characters and episodes after the first canto. In doing so, he also turns away from the structure of much medieval romance. As an attempt to trace Malory's lady of the lake through the *Morte Darthur* will show, she appears only intermittently and thus illustrates the highly episodic structure of that work and of the majority of its predecessors. Our assessment of the way Scott viewed that episodic structure of medieval romance is complicated, however, in several ways. First, we tend to impose our twentieth-century views of medieval romance structure upon his. Second, Scott's statements about the medieval examples of the genre, outside the statements or implications in his own poetry, tend to fluctuate in evaluation but to remain consistent in their description of a lack of controlling art. Third, he tends to disparage his own poems as he calls them "romances." Fourth, as we have already seen in earlier chapters, his own narrative patterns have developed in part from ballad forms of romance, far briefer and more tightly structured than other forms but retaining like the romances many of the narrative motifs and structures of mythic folklore.

Recent studies of medieval romance have shown an intricate form beneath their apparent chaos; particularly in the French prose romances, and in Malory, narrative strands "interlace" to form an ever-expanding set of relationships without clear climax or resolution.[8] Though both interest in romance and knowledge of its examples had increased enormously during the eighteenth century, critics had difficulty in finding adequate ways to describe its nonclassical structure without disparaging it. Although Hurd compared the structure of the *Fairie Queene* to a Gothic garden with its "separate . . . avenues" and their "common and concurrent center," criticism of the medieval romances continued to point to their episodic and fanciful formlessness, alternately praising their freedom from classical restraints and condemning their license.[9] When Scott includes in the *Minstrelsy* the "imperfect" romance version of *Thomas the Rhymer* as an appendix to the ballad version, he speculates upon the "great amusement" to be drawn from comparing "this ancient romance" with the ballad. Even though they are similar in "incident" and often in "expression," they are "as different in appearance as if the older tale had been regularly and systematically modernized by a poet of the present day."[10] Whether edited or not, the ballad points out a narrative order implicit, but obscure, in that romance; such an order is far more obscure in the complex interweaving of a whole cycle of romances like Malory's.

A more explicit characterization of unmodernized romances occurs in Scott's review of George Ellis's *Metrical Romances*. Writing for the *Edinburgh Review* in 1806, Scott describes the stories of these romances as "generally rambling and desultory, utterly incapable consequently of exciting the pleasure arising from a well-conducted plan, all the parts of which depend upon each other, and tend . . . to bring on the catastrophe." On the other hand, he goes on, "there is a sort of *keeping* in these ancient tales, which did not depend upon the minstrel's inclination, and from which he could not have departed. . . . this arose from his painting the manners of his own time as they passed before his eyes, and thus giving a truth and unity to the chivalrous events he relates, which the modern labourers in the vineyard of romance are utterly unable to imitate."[11] Scott also perceives in these earlier romances a "keeping" and "unity" that is not so much a neo-Aristotelean "well-conceived plan" as it is an inclusion of mythic narrative notifs.

In two later discussions of romance, both written after *The Lady of the Lake*, Scott continues this contrast between a "rambling" and a "well-conducted" plan, now identifying the latter with the epic. In his anonymous 1813 preface to *The Bridal of Triermain*, he tries to define romance in a way that would make it accessible to the modern poet: "According to the author's idea of Romantic Poetry as distinguished from Epic, the former comprehends a fictitious narrative, framed and combined at the pleasure of the writer; beginning and ending as he may judge best . . . . free from the technical rules of the Epee, and . . . subject only to those which good sense, good taste, and good morals apply to every species of poetry without exception" (*PW*, p. 586).[12] Here, however, Scott's purpose is primarily to defend the conscious, sophisticated freedom of the modern writer of romances, not to analyze the more naive freedom of the medieval singer and writer. In the preface he does not explore the sort of unity that the rules of "good sense" and "good taste" might imply.

His "Essay on Romance" discusses the evolutionary development of form in history. "There lies as wide a distinction between" romance and epic, Scott writes, "as between the rude mystery or morality of the middle ages, and the regular drama by which those were succeeded. Where the art and the ornaments of the poet chiefly attract our attention—where each part of the narrative bears a due proportion to the others, and the whole draws gradually to a final and satisfactory conclusion . . . the work must be termed an epic poem." On the other hand, "when a story languishes in tedious or minute details, and relies for the interest which it proposes to excite rather upon the wild excursion of an unbridled fancy that upon the skill of the poet . . . the author . . . is . . . no more than a humble romancer, and his works must rank amongst those rude ornaments of a dark age."[13] In this critical discussion Scott associates, though he does not equate, a lack of narrative pace and the lack of verisimilitude or plausibility: the "wild excursion of an unbridled fancy" is a poor substitute for the epic's coherent narrative form in appealing to the reader's interest.

This is a late view that may represent a hardening of Scott's views, yet it echoes his insistence while he writes *The Lady of the Lake* that his careless workmanship makes him, too, only a "humble romancer." Though he acknowledges criticisms of *Marmion* by promising to write out his next poem completely in prose before casting it into verse (*Letters*, 2:69), and though he spends more than two years turning over in his mind the possibility of a "Highland poem," the actual writing is as usual, he claims, quite rapid and directly in verse; he sends the early cantos to press before he completes his explicit plans for the later ones.[14] Self-effacingly, he describes the poem as "a grand romance ambling on all fours like the palfrey of Queen Guinevere" (*Letters*, 2:317). These partially-public statements about his craft are thus far less confident than his anonymously published description of the "free and unembarrassed" modern romancer in the *Triermain* introduction only a few years later.

His practice in *The Lady of the Lake*, however, may have contributed to that confidence, for the 1810 poem has in fact both a freedom from epic rules and a structure far tighter than either eighteenth- or twentieth-century critics have perceived in Malory and his predecessors; it shows, in particular, a clear climax and resolution. Ironically enough, then, according to the historically deterministic and heavily value-laden definitions of epic and romance in his encyclopedia article, Scott is writing "epic."

Before testing that sort of epic in *The Lady of the Lake*, however, we must consider more fully another form of medieval romance, the romantic ballad. As already pointed out, the elemental pattern of both the romance and the ballad forms of *Thomas the Rhymer* can also be found in the episodes of Arthurian narrative that include the lady of the lake: an enchantress lures a questing male figure through a natural wilderness to the edge of some ambiguously supernatural realm. In the Rhymer narratives, Thomas enters that realm and then returns. In the Arthurian episodes, Arthur encounters the realm early but enters it only as he hovers between life and death after the battle with Mordred. Of the four queens who preside over his final voyage, one is "King Arthurs sister, Morgan le fay," and another "Nimue, the chief Lady of the Lake."[15] In Scott's poem both Ellen and the king leave the highland world, so that the simpler circular pattern of the Rhymer's encounter with the elf queen and his journey into her realm becomes more complex. Graham McMaster argues that Ellen gains a strength like that of the lady of the lake from her association with a mysterious nature but loses strength and becomes vulnerable when she is drawn to Stirling and civilization.[16] Yet because that highland world represents for Ellen and the king both nature and the visionary powers of literary romance, Ellen's own literary, cultural consciousness of her mythic romance role as enchantress lends her archetypal power: she herself wields some of the codes that shape her existence. Nevertheless, the lady is assimilated into the civilization that had guided her in projecting her role as enchantress out into the natural world in the first place.

In a ballad sung by her family minstrel, Allan-Bane, Scott epitomizes this double role of the wilderness and of Ellen's role in it. Its cryptic and mysterious narrative shows, like *Thomas the Rymer*, all three modes of "romance" represented in the *Minstrelsy* ballads: romantic love, magic, and a plot that traces the errings of medieval romance, but far more tightly. A part of its conciseness comes from the unquestioning promptness with which its characters wield their magic.

Because their island refuge in the almost-magical Loch Katrine has been endangered by an outbreak in hostilities, Allan and Ellen withdraw in canto 4 to a still more remote cave. Like the lake, this cave is a traditional haunt of supernatural forces: "ill luck," the minstrel explains, "still haunts a fairy grot" (st. 11). Thus his intention in singing the ballad to Ellen is partly to cleanse the cave from such "ill luck" and partly to refocus Ellen's attention from worry over the warfare between king and clan. Dramatizing "ill luck," his ballad then counters it with a heroine's more powerful and more civilizing magic. The ballad parallels the larger Rhymer pattern, yet reverses its sexual roles. It also parallels and then anticipates the action of Scott's narrative by suggesting that a similar reversal can encourage Ellen in her own possible turning point from an ambiguous greenwood exile to an ambiguous courtly society.

The cave Allan describes in the ballad "Alice Brand" is at first merely a shelter for two aristocratic lovers, outlawed because their elopement has led to the slaying of the woman's brother. Thus they have violated civilization's laws and have retreated to nature. Yet the wood and the cave also define the supernatural realm of the "moody Elfin king, / Who woned within the hill" (st. 13). As the king complains, Lord Richard's axe despoils their sacred grove, and both exiles have worn, like foresters, "the fairies' fatal green." To punish them for this violation, the elf king calls up a "hideous dwarf" whom he confidently believes impervious to any human "cross or sign, . . . muttered word or ban," because the dwarf himself was once a "Christen'd man." His instructions to the dwarf would create in Lord Richard a static liminality like that of the knight so palely loitering in Keats's *La Belle Dame*:

> 'Lay on him the curse of the wither'd heart,
>   The curse of the sleepless eye;
> Till he wish and pray that his life would part,
>   Nor yet find leave to die.' (*LL*, 4:13)

When the dwarf Urgan encounters the lovers, his own sense of violation is far more personal and human than the elf king's sense of a profaned turf. Further, when he describes his own condition in "Fairyland," its marginality resembles the punishment he has been sent to mete out. He first denies the power of Richard's crossing himself, because his hand is stained with the murder of Alice's brother. Once conjured by the "bold" Alice's unstained hand, Urgan explains that he was "snatch'd away" to Fairyland in a doubly liminal moment. Wounded "between the night and day, / When the Fairy King has power," he hovered "'twixt life and death" until carried off to "the joyless Elfin bower" (4:15). That bleak realm only seems paradisal. Instead, though the sounds of "Fairy-land" are "merry" as its court rides out with its king, "all is glistening show," and "our inconstant shape, / [does] now like knight and lady seem, / And now like dwarf and ape" (15). This inconstant vacillation between a chivalric romance ideal and a subhuman level of behavior or experience seems neither playful nor creative to the dwarf. If Gilpin Horner cries, "Lost! lost! lost!" in the human world but enjoys practicing his strange gramarye in it, Urgan cries out that he is lost in the elf king's world of uncontrolled "glamour": ". . . wist I of a woman bold, / Who thrice my brow durst sign, / I might regain my mortal mold, / As fair a form as thine."

Interpretation of this glamour and its eventual stabilizing of meaning comes with Alice Brand's fearless signing of the cross:[17]

> She cross'd him thrice, that lady bold;
>   He rose beneath her hand

> The fairest knight on Scottish mold,
> Her brother, Ethert Brand!

As she completes his suspended, delayed narrative with her signs, he stands revealed with "as fair a form as [hers]." Yet by canceling out her lover's guilt for her brother's blood, Alice somehow cancels out even the lover's presence. She has not simply restored her brother from apparent death; she has, in the stanza's Promethean images, created him in her own image. The return to "Dunfermline grey" is "merrier" than life in the mysterious greenwood, but appropriately hazy. At the ballad's conclusion, the most dominant impression is that of Alice's control as a creative countermagician to the elfin king. Within her code or gramarye of civilization and Christian orthodoxy, she challenges both that "moody" king and, though less explicitly, her own God.

Although Allan-Bane sings the ballad to reassure Ellen that his mild and benevolent words can control the haunted cave where they hide, his song also seems designed to reassure her that she can achieve Alice's bold control of her destiny, and particularly of the fate of those she loves. Neither he nor Ellen comments directly on the relationship of this ballad-narrative to the roles from Arthurian romance that she and the king had played with earlier. Yet that deeper structure of allusion to those romance narratives can help to explain the significance of the ballad for the larger narrative of which Ellen is a part. If we turn back to the narrative function of the lady of the lake, of the elf queen in *Thomas the Rhymer*, or to the enchantress in *La Belle Dame*, we find powerful instances of the enchantress's magical control. Yet in all those narratives, the woman's enchanting power is allied to an alien nature, or to a visionary otherworld on the borders between nature and death—to the realm ruled in the ballad by the elfin king.

The contrast, even the reversal between those narratives and Allan's ballad suggests two points. First, her role as enchantress in the greenwood risks becoming mere "glistening show" because, in Allan's countermyth to Malory, the elf king rules that realm. It is not difficult to see an analogy to Roderick Dhu here; Allan's song argues for a deeper clash between the two than does even Ellen's aversion to his cruelty. It suggests in addition a mythic personifying of two values of nature: a nurturing fertility and an amoral violence. Her fate will not be the same as the mad Blanche of Devan's, whose subplot is a dark counterpoint to the ballad's lighter one. She is "a crazed and captive Lowland maid," explains the king's highland guide, "ta'en on the morn she was a bride, / When Roderick foray'd Devan side" and killed the resisting groom. Now, temporarily escaped, she seems to the king like a "lone heron [who] spreads his wing, / By twilight, o'er a haunted spring" (*LL*, 4:23).[18] Second, because of the ballad's plot, Ellen need not relinquish all power as she relinquishes the place and the role of an enchantress. Even though she will give up a magic grounded in nature, she can take on a magic that will work within civilization, subverting its codes of Christianity and patriarchy even while using them.

Ellen's first use of this power is not to employ a sign, but to make a substitution in the application of the narrative Allan-Bane has given her: this is a kind of hermeneutic glamour, a metaphoric delay in applying the concise ballad to her own suspended fate. Although it is indeed easy to interpret the elfin king as Roderick, lover and brother are more difficult to identify, just as they are in the original ballad. Conventions of the happy ending lead to the assumption that when all three ballad characters return to Dumfermline, the brother will either vanish into the new powers of Alice Brand, of which he seems a projection, or—more prosaically—that he will go his own way and leave the lovers alone. Yet the brother seems to replace the lover in that moment of rebirth and recognition. Just as Allan finishes his song, "up started"—to use the ballad's phrase for its half-underworld elfin characters—the disguised King James V returned explicitly as a lover. Ellen even sends Allan to "conjure" his guide, so startled is she that Fitz-James had passed through the highland scouts. When she refuses his offer to be transplanted to Stirling (*LL*, 4:17), she explains that the "noble youth" she loves cannot be supplanted in her heart: she substitutes Malcolm for him. In one sense, the king moves from lover to brother.[19] In another sense, as Ruth Eller argues, Malcolm's relationship to her is so mild as to be brotherly, so that the more dangerous subterranean forces of sexuality are charmed away:[20] Urgan's apelike nature vanishes, replaced by a mirror image or sibling of self.

If that civilizing sign of the cross represents the possibility for Ellen's control of personal relationships, it also stands for the king's civilizing rule over the clan, countering the burning cross that has placed clan values above personal or national relationships. Ellen's power will be purely personal and domestic; the king, by usurping a Renaissance version of Alice Brand's countermagic, can enact an Arthurian romance plot strengthened with a Renaissance rationality or even rationalizing of form. The king himself playfully develops and seriously puts to use some of these rationalizations, as we have seen him do from his first encounter with Ellen. Yet he is also put to use by Scott, to become in this narrative, like Arthur in earlier romances, an heuristic model for kingship or for other leadership.[21]

As the somewhat evolutionary scheme of his comparison between romance and epic suggests, Scott is in many ways praising a Renaissance ideal of significant literary form as much as he is the epic. *The Lady of the Lake* reflects his interest in this Renaissance ideal in two primary ways. First, the benevolent yet challenging confrontation of the sovereign with the lady of the lake reappears, after Malory, in several Renaissance works as a focus for the interplay between political fact and romance fiction. Her Renaissance appearances gather together two of the recurrent themes in Scott's narrative: building an image of political unity and validating romance as a way to accomplish it. And second, the structure Scott gives his narrative demonstrates the fusing of these themes. In its complex, subordinated unity of form and its traditional motifs it resembles those Elizabethan comedies based on pastoral and medieval romance.

One place in which Scott could find not only descriptions of these Renaissance appearances of the lady of the lake but also an awareness of their significance is Thomas Warton's *Observations on the Fairy Queen of Spenser*. Just as Hurd looked to the *Fairie Queene* to help him define "gothic form," Warton attempts in both the *Observations* (1754) and the *History of English Poetry* (1774-81) to reevaluate medieval romance and its relation to Renaissance imitators. In the *Observations* Warton sees the appearances of the lady of the lake in the Renaissance as an index for the continuing popularity of Arthurian romance. The entertainment at Kenilworth in 1575, a lyric response to it in Spenser's *Shepheardes Calender*, and Ben Jonson's *Speeches at Prince Henry's Barriers* all indicate for Warton that this figure from Arthurian myth was familiar enough to summon up with her an image of that ideal kingdom.[22] Yet as Warton and his Renaissance sources show, ladies of the lake reflect highly divergent attitudes toward romance as a genre capable of serious meaning.

Probably the most important appearance of the lady of the lake in the Renaissance is the one at Kenilworth. By 1821 his writing of the novel *Kenilworth* had of course shown Scott's familiarity with both the poetry and the politics of that occasion; but as early as 1803, his introduction to a ballad in the *Minstrelsy of the Scottish Border* refers directly to one of the main eyewitness accounts of the festivities, Robert Laneham's *Letter*.[23]

In the pageantry that welcomed Elizabeth to Kenilworth, the queen's encounter with a resident lady of the lake provoked an unscheduled debate over sovereignty, a debate in which romantic myth is punctured by historical actuality, then—later in the festivities—restored to include that actuality more gracefully.[24] According to Laneham, "her highness . . . rode into the inner gate next the base coourt of the Castl: where the Lady of the Lake (famous in King Arthurz book) with too Nymphs waiting vppon her, . . . attending her highness coming: from the midst of the Pool, whear, vpon a moouable Iland, bright blazing with torches, she, floting to land, met her Maiesty."[25] She told the queen "hoow shee had kept this Lake sins king Arthurz days, and now . . . thought it both office and duetie . . . to discouer her and her estate: offering vp the same, her Lake and poouer therein, with promise of repayre vnto the Coourt." But Elizabeth answered, apparently with some asperity: "We had thought indeed the Lake had been oours, and doo you call it yourz now? Wel, we will herein common more with yoo heer-after" (p. 7). This contest of sovereignty shows Elizabeth's readiness to see all pageantry as a game concealing yet conveying political meaning. It also suggests her readiness to see herself and the fictive lady of the lake as simultaneously mythical and actual figures. Both in tone and in event, the episode parallels Scott's poem. Though Scott's James V ostensibly holds sovereignty over Loch Katrine, he learns—through his pose as a knight of romance and his encounter with a lady of the lake—how that power is threatened by the willingness of Clan Alpine to shelter the Douglasses and to read his hunting of the stag as a more serious pursuit of the highlanders. As James consciously usurps the role of Arthur, he allies himself with a British cultural tradition developed primarily by the English, and thus he will raise the question of whether his "Sassenach" or lowland control over the highlands foreshadows English control over Scotland.[26]

When Scott has James usurp—or rather preempt—the role of the later Elizabeth, however, the Scottish king also threatens Ellen's sovereignty. Building on Elizabeth's first encounter with the lady of the lake, in which the lady in the "Pool" seems almost to reflect the queen, the Kenilworth entertainment went on to recognize and to exploit the complexities of gender involved in their allusions. Paralleling both Malory and Scott, the pageantry of Elizabeth's second encounter with Kenilworth's lady of the lake followed a stag hunt. To honor and flatter her, the anxious planners of the entertainment cast the queen as both romance hero and magically chaste maiden, asking her to free the lady from the lake that had been her sanctuary from a vengeful knight. The lady, explains Gascoigne, "coulde never bee delivered but by the presence of a better maide than hir selfe."[27] At two levels of romance fiction, then, the queen could reassert her challenged sovereignty. In Scott's poem, too, the king reveals a "better" self to free Ellen from a threatened marriage to Roderick Dhu—and thus at the same time to free his kingdom from rebellion. Before this, however, Ellen must repudiate his oblique offer of an illicit "bower" in Stirling and assert her personal and social reality as a "better maide" than his romance fantasies of her had seemed to permit.

In the April eclogue of Spenser's *Shepheardes Calender*, an appearance Warton links to the Kenilworth entertainment (p. 39), Spenser's editor, E.K., indignantly glosses the world of pastoral romance Spenser has constructed: "Ladys of the Lake," he writes, "be

Nymphes." "For it was an old opinion amongst the Auncient Heathen, that of every spring and fountain was a goddesse the Souereigne. Which opinion stucke in the myndes of men not manye yeares sithence, by means of certain fine fablers and loud lyers, such as were the Authors of King Arthure the great and such like, who tell many an unlawful leasing of the Lady's of the Lake, that is, the Nymphes."[28] E.K. seems to attribute this piece of fabling to what he sees as an irrelevant double meaning of "nymph" in Greek—"well water, or otherwise a Spouse or Bryde." In his unwillingness to see a range of meanings in the fictions of either medieval romance or classical myth his attitude contrasts sharply with that shared by both Elizabeth and her entertainers at Kenilworth. The fate of the ladies of the lake at E.K.'s hands seems to anticipate the more general fate of romance until writers such as Warton and later Scott began to search again for the more serious significance of its images, themes, and forms.

Like these Renaissance appearances of the lady of the lake, Scott's poem develops the theme of testing and building political unity through the iconography of Arthurian romance. His poem gives further shape to this theme through a structure resembling that of Elizabethan romance comedies in its formal unity and in its theme of social unity. In these comedies, as in Scott's poem, the dramatic action builds toward a climax within a romance world or "green world" of forest or field. There disguise and distance from normal patterns of civilization permit first a release from their restraints and then a rebuilding and unifying of the whole society.[29]

In Scott's poem the king rides into a greenwood world that seems to respond to the playful mood of his stag hunt. His disguise, the forester's simple clothes of Lincoln green, links him to several conventional roles in Elizabethan comedy, as well as to the "fairy" world so jealously guarded in the ballad of "Alice Brand." McMaster suggests that the king's green clothes are lowland dress that shows his alienation from nature, whereas the mixed colors of the highlanders' tartans allow them to blend in with the heather and then to rise, in canto 5, like the Cadmoi (pp. 19-20)—or like Urgan. To pursue this point on a realistic level, we would need to know when deforestation occurred in the Trossachs; Scott seems to describe a forested Renaissance landscape, in which green would be an appropriate camouflage (*LL*, 1:2) and not the more fully deforested heath of Scott's and his reader's own time.[30] On a more figural level, however, the Lincoln green is indeed a cultural artifact, but an artifact symbolizing an entry into or a blending with nature, as the elfin king protests in the ballad. It also represents escape from a specific social rank. As M.C. Bradbrook notes, "in romance and ballads" and in comedies based on those sources, "disguise is a proof and almost a badge of the lover," particularly of noble lovers who must test relationships without the lure of their rank. And second, "the ruler in disguise" frequently unmasks truths about himself and his society.[31] Beneath his disguise, the king eventually undergoes a kind of metamorphosis roughly similar to Prince Hal's—from a hunter of entertainment, playing at forester and knight-errant, through a recognition of the chaotic possibilities in romance, to a ruler testing the nature of his sovereignty. This change comes about through an ironic reversal in the nature of his hunt. In a structure similar to Scott's ballad-imitation of "The Wild Huntsman," though in a far less "gothic" mood,[32] the hunter becomes the hunted and receives an enforced education. Through this education and its attendant unmaskings, the king can eventually bring about a romance comedy resolution.

Triggering this reversal of the hunt are two forces: the political context of the king's affairs preceding the narrative and the political consciousness developed in it by two bardic and prophetic figures who represent the conflicting highland and lowland cultures. These forces also ensure that the eventual romance comedy resolution is not simply an escape from history. Because the historical James V earlier trapped the border chieftains through false hospitality, the highlanders in Scott's poem fear his hunt is simply a pretext for a similar move against them, again war concealed by play.[33] And as they then prepare for war, the lowlanders respond in kind—not realizing that their absent king has innocently started the chain reaction. Meanwhile, the disguised king encounters at Ellen's lake the Douglas's exiled minstrel Allan-Bane, a minor prophet who seems to guess, though privately, James's identity. With "his reverend brow" claiming from "the rising sun . . . a sparkle of inspiring flame" (*LL*, 2:4), the minstrel urges the king to make the hospitality he has just received his model for a more gracious kind of sovereignty than he has shown so far. Before this politic advice can take effect, however, a second prophet sets in motion the more radical education of the reversed hunt. A series of animal sacrifices made by Brian the Hermit, prophet of Roderick's MacAlpine clan, leads to his conditional prophecy for the outcome of their rebellion: "Which spills the foremost foeman's life, / That party conquers in the strife!" (*LL*, 4:6). This inhospitable prophecy begins the hunting down of the lowland stranger, still unrecognized as their ultimate antagonist, the king, to make a third sacrifice in the clan's pursuit of victory. Instead, the king is forced to revise his assumptions: escape from civilization into romance has proved to be a journey into an anarchy he must learn to control on two levels—the personal and the political.[34]

On his arrival at Loch Katrine, the king had distinguished between the "greenwood" of the idealized romance landscape he playfully envisions before him, in which "each bewilder'd stranger" is called "to friendly feast, and lighted hall" (*LL*, 1:15-16) and "these wilds" in which he "may meet with Highland plunderers." Though his encounter with the lady of the lake continues the conscious, amused role playing characteristic both of Elizabethan masques like those at Kenilworth and the romance comedies, he undergoes a kind of off-stage change during the two cantos in which Scott develops the character of Roderick Dhu and his clan. As a result the king's reurn in canto 4 to "rescue" his lady of the lake from the highlands mixes romance with political reality far less shrewdly than Elizabeth did at Kenilworth: for the moment he seems to believe that their game of chivalric romance can continue in a fictional world isolated from the real one. A psychological violence, an emotional anarchy, distorts his use of romance from its earlier literary and playful means of ordering conflict to a pretext for escaping it more thoroughly. When Ellen frankly and yet tactfully refuses his offer of a "lovely bower" in Stirling (*LL*, 4:17), she turns this mood of private anarchy aside. Yet just as in the king's earlier dream, when "he sought her yielded hand to clasp, / And a cold gauntlet met his grasp" (*LL*, 1:34), his attempt to clasp Ellen leads him into a more dangerous embrace with Roderick Dhu and thus with a more public and political form of anarchy. "No maiden's hand is round thee thrown," warns the narrator. At the end of his struggle with Roderick, the injured and desperate king "may now unclasp / The fainting Chief's relaxing grasp; / Unwounded from the dreadful close, / But breathless" (*LL*, 5:16). And the horse meant for Ellen, a "fairer freight," carries Roderick instead to Stirling.

Because the king had already given way to disorder, his savage embrace with Roderick is one of near equals. Led by his temporarily excessive belief in romance fictions, the king undergoes before his encounter with Roderick a kind of metamorphosis made explicit through his identification as hunted stag. When his guide leads the king toward ambush, the mad woman Blanche of Devan, who has been the victim of highland cruelty, also becomes its prophet. She sings first of her own capture in words that sound a thematic warning to the romance-fascinated king: "woe betide the fairy dream! / I only waked to sob and scream" (*LL*, 4:22). Recognizing his lowland voice and clothes, in a second and saner ballad she warns him of "the toils . . . pitch'd, and the stakes . . . set" for "a stag, a stag of ten, / Bearing its branches sturdily."[35] Though the narrator emphasizes the king's killing of his treacherous guide by calling him "lion" and "falcon," the king himself echoes the metaphor of the hunted stag to criticize his own foolishness at venturing into such dangerous territory. Brought to recognize the change in himself and in his situation through Blanche's songs, he can begin to reassert some contol over both.

Yet though the king appears at first less civilized, it is, ironically, Roderick's chivalrous behavior that completes the transformation from the hunting down of an unknowing victim to their almost ceremonial duel at the stream bordering the highlands. The king and the reader half expect Roderick to be an archetypal romance opponent, an embodiment of those dark anarchic forces suggested by his name (Dhu: black), his "shadowy plume . . . and brow of gloom" (*LL*, 4:27), and his reputation (*LL*, 5:5). Scott modifies these suggestions, however, both by the political and economic realities Roderick explains to the king before revealing his identity[36] and by the wildly chivalric gesture with which he accompanies that revelation. Calling up his forces from their places of ambush, "as if the yawning hill to heaven / A subterranean host had given" (*LL*, 5:9), he casts off the role of anonymous guide: "And, Saxon,—I am Roderick Dhu!" When the king meets this challenge by his readiness to fight, however, Roderick dismisses his men in order to prove both his pledge of hospitality as guide out of the highlands and his own physical courage in single combat on their border. He confronts the king, then, not only as an image of anarchy, but as a mirror of virtues the king must claim for himself: courage, hospitality, responsibility for his people.

Significantly, the king does not reveal his identity to Roderick—or the reader— until he has fully rejected the role of knight-errant for that of magician-romancer, a Prospero figure who can convert romance to the more generous, more tolerant, and more ordered form of romance comedy. This more tolerant order begins to display itself at the ford just before the duel, as the disguised king offers the mercy of "James at Stirling." Unable to accept even the warning of his own prophet, Roderick insists on avenging his clansman, the false guide already killed by the king. In the duel, however, his "wild rage" is "foil'd . . . by steady skill";[37] and the larger battle of which this encounter was to be but the precursor is controlled by an even more skillful art. While Roderick lies wounded in a prison-cell at Stirling, the lowland forces pursue the highlanders into the Trossachs. The two armies are evenly matched in their mutual destructiveness, yet when they reach Loch Katrine and face each other in "elemental rage," the king's herald arrives with a "milk-white flag," to announce that both rebel leaders are imprisoned at Stirling. Thus the clash of lowland and highland forces ends abruptly at the king's command, its heroic but misguided violence reduced to a kind of futile ceremony. Emphasizing still further this shaping of events through "steady skill," Scott distances the battle through narrative point of view. We do not learn of it until Allan-Bane casts the events he has witnessed earlier into a song that allows Roderick to die "as if" his "free spirit . . . soar'd from battle fray" instead of his prison at Stirling (*LL*, 6:14). The sovereign's control is thus a kind of minstrel's art, and as Allan tells of the halted battle, he sees that Roderick is dead and halts his song. If the primitive splendor of Roderick's land and his ethic begins to recede like the battle into the distance of a minstrel's lay, the king no longer sees that world as a romance fiction, free from the burden of political and social truth. Instead his duel with Roderick, ironically one of the most romancelike elements in the poem, has forced him to grasp control of green world and gray world alike. His control, however, increasingly expresses itself by applying the forms of romance to both worlds. As the king manages the concluding scene at "gray" Stirling, moreover, he does not reject romance but uses it with deliberate skill to establish a more benevolent sovereignty. Through that skill, Stirling becomes an enchanted castle, where disguises prove to have hidden only good.[38]

To complete his transformation from knight-errant to a sovereign who stands beyond and controls his realm, the king reveals his own identity—to Ellen and to the reader—at the same time that he reveals his restoration of the Douglasses to their place in the kingdom.[39] Playing upon the romance mood, he sets up "a thronging scene of figures bright" who seem to Ellen like those that "fancy frames" in the clouds at sunset: "Aerial knights and fairy dames" (*LL*, 6:26). When he continues to wear his "cap and plume" while all others are uncovered, Ellen can see through his disguise to recognize him as the king. He explains to Ellen that "when disguised I stray / In life's more low but happier way . . . Thus watch I o'er insulted laws, / Thus learn to right the injured cause" (*LL*, 6:28). His more private comment to her indicates, however, that this purpose has been earned by the end of the poem; the romance king has worked his way toward the more responsible but still playful historical king. By ending the exile of the Douglasses, he completes both public and private aspects of the plot. The judgment of "council" and "laws," he announces, has resolved the politically ambiguous place of his family between highland and lowland. Thus Douglas's sword, which like an unwieldy Excalibur nearly struck the king at the lake, now becomes his agent and a symbol of provisional unity. Second, he resolves the ambiguous place of Ellen in the love plot by prompting his lady of the lake to claim her boon from him.[40]

Though the two strongest figures in the poem, the king and Roderick, have been rivals for her as well as for sovereignty, the old romance pattern of victorious knight winning fair lady is deflected here. Even though Scott violates historical fact in reconciling the king with the Douglas family, he is evidently not willing to do the same for royal marriages. More important to the internal logic of the poem, however, the king's process of stepping back from knight-errant to ruler becomes complete as Malcolm Graeme, once the king's ward, now becomes his surrogate in this wedding masque of royal order. In the song that Malcolm uses to attract Ellen's attention, he uses images associated with the king: "I wish I were as I have been, / Hunting the hart in forest green" (*LL*, 6:24). So close is the association, in fact, that the song is mistakenly attributed to him.[41] Characteristically, the king arranges Malcolm's freedom and marriage to Ellen—a boon she is too shy to demand—by a teasing disguise of his own intentions. Promising "fetters and warders for the Graeme," James throws his own chain of gold around Malcolm's neck, then "gently drew the glittering band, / And laid the clasp on Ellen's hand." His gesture reflects no narrow restraint, however, but a larger order: as final image of the narrative, the "glittering band" of the king's chain unites the blond hunter in the highlands who has been a lowland prisoner with the dark lowlander who has been a highland exile. Their union promises in turn a society unified through love into a "glittering ring" reflecting the king's new sovereignty. That ring is, of course, neither history nor prophecy but an heuristic image, an ideal for the woman's sovereignty over the realm of the lake, which is her self's mysterious otherness, and for the king's sovereignty over a unified realm that Scott himself still hopes to create. The ring also suggests the satisfying circularity of a narrative now made complete by an uncovering and a naming, but by no more radical apocalypse. Because Scott has so idealized the king through his education in the snares and fulfillments of romance, he has deferred a more realistic confrontation with the historical James V, with still further instability in his kingdom, and with that more tragic lady of the lake, his daughter Mary Stuart.[42]

In his later *Triermain* introduction, Scott will claim freedom from the dominance of epic and history by abandoning the field of "sublime" poetry to the epic poets of the past who combined the "naked truth" of history with imaginative genius. "The political struggles and convulsions which influence the fate of kingdoms," he writes, interest the modern reader less than simpler accounts of the fates of individuals. Analogously, as romance is made up of these simpler, more private narratives, it is also an exercise in the poet's individual freedom: "In a word, the author is absolute master of his country and its inhabitants" (*PW*, 586). Yet Scott does not ignore "the political struggles and convulsions that influence the fate of kingdoms" in *The Lady of the Lake*. Instead, like the king at Stirling, he uses romance as a way of approaching and ultimately exerting some imaginative control over such struggles. In the course of the narrative, the king moves from a private, individual version of romance and of himself, through a confrontation with political and personal anarchy, toward the more comprehensive order of romance comedy. In the poem as a whole, Scott's narrator undergoes an experience similar to the king's, a journey into territories he does not control. Beginning with doubts about his own ability to waken the "Harp of the North" and to find an audience, the modern minstrel confronts through the portraits of the two earlier bardic figures the anarchic sources of imaginative energy that threaten the ordering power of his art and yet cannot be excluded from it. Through that experience he can become more an "absolute master"; he too can enlarge and redefine his sovereignty. If that sovereignty does not include all of history in some totally visionary transformation, it nevertheless will offer a validated model for coming to terms with historical process.[43]

To the extent that the narrator's quest is to discover and make use of the sources of his power, he shares a theme common to many narratives of the romantic period. In "The Internalization of the Quest Romance," Harold Bloom's description of that quest by the major romantic poets sounds in some respects very similar to Scott's *Triermain* introduction: "The movement of quest-romance, before its internalization by the High Romantics, was from nature to redeemed nature, the sanction of its redemption being the gift of some external spiritual authority, sometimes magical. The Romantic movement is from nature to the imagination's freedom (sometimes a reluctant freedom): and the imagination's freedom is frequently purgatorial, redemptive in direction, but destructive of the social self."[44] Furthermore, these two stages of romance seem analogous to the narrative and the narrating parts of Scott's poem. The main narrative resembles the pre-romantic quest, but in a secularized form: the external, almost magical authority of the lady of the lake grants the king first a delusive, then a more realistic authority to manage his kingdom through romance. That management is itself, of course, Scott's own heuristic romance fiction. In this perspective the objective, external "facts" that the high romantic poets redeem are most often those of "nature." For Scott, they are most often society and history,[45] and their redemption comes through the perfecting images and plots of Renaissance romance comedy. Through the achievement of a "reluctant freedom" of imagination, moreover, the narrator's framing stanzas resemble the internalized quest-romance of Bloom's high romantics. In *The Lady of the Lake*, however, that freedom does not destroy but redeems the social self.

By pointing to the redemptive patterns in both traditional and internalized versions of the romance, Bloom's passage is enormously useful. By suggesting that the "external spiritual authority" is internalized as the free agency of the imagination, his passage also points to the mysterious visionary women who, like the lady of the lake, may be instructress and muse. Tracing such a pattern in *Lady of the Lake* requires a clearer discussion of the way its narrative moves between society and nature. Implicitly Bloom's pattern is the linear one of salvation-history;

it is also a circular one of exile from, and return to, the redeemed nature of Eden. The fallen nature of that exile is also an alien history that must find shape through one or the other of these patterns. The medieval quester or the Elizabethan exiles find themselves in a nature that is alien enough to open itself and themselves to a sometimes magical, sometimes supernatural, revelation. That revelation can then redeem the society to which they return.

If we look at the narrator of *The Lady of the Lake* as a quester, we find that his role is far less dramatized than that of the wandering last minstrel who finds both shelter and inspiration in Newark Castle. As the modern narrator begins his poem, he describes his relationship with past minstrels and with past cultures through images of a natural decay that intervenes, like historical process, between himself and the harp he struggles to use:

> Harp of the North! that mouldering long hast hung
>   On the witch-elm that shades Saint Fillan's spring,
> And down the fitful breeze thy numbers flung,
>   Till envious ivy did around thee cling,
> Muffling with verdant ringlet every string
> . . . .
> Not thus, in ancient days of Caledon,
>   Was thy voice mute amid the festal crowd.

Saint Fillan, as Scott wrote gleefully in his notes to the *Minstrelsy*, could himself write texts by the light of his magically-glowing left hand.[46] Even the memory of that supernatural story is naturalized in this passage: first the breeze, and then the silencing ivy, have replaced that earlier magic. At the beginning of the poem, then, the recognition of change is destructive rather than therapeutic. Although the narrator goes on after these lines to use the vocabulary of inspiration, no correspondence between the natural breeze and his own mind develops to explain the sources of his imagination. He urges the Harp, an "Enchantress," to "wake again," and describes it as a "magic maze" possessed of a "wizard note." Through the image of the harp as an "Enchantress," he points toward the characteristic romantic tension between woman as muse and as independent character; he also recalls the association of imagination with an illicit sexuality, or simply with an active female sexuality, in *Marmion*. Yet the narrator does not directly confront an otherworldly woman who can act as muse, offering "the gift of external spiritual authority." He is not, like Thomas the Rhymer, both minstrel and quester. All of his metaphors for the harp emphasize his passivity before the instrument, a passivity even more troubling to the modern narrator than to the two bards who suffer within the narrative from the same dominating irrationalities of imagination. For the narrator at poem's opening, then, imagination and the continuing process of history both seem forces beyond his control.

If we look within his narrative, we find these roles of minstrel and quester sharply divided. The major quester is clearly the king. Like Thomas the Rhymer, the king can wield romance in politic ways. Moreover, he learns how to do so through his confrontation with the human, but imaginatively powerful, lady of the lake. If the king's discoveries about the dangers either of overromanticizing an alien culture or of treating it as too primitive are part of the modern narrator's discoveries for his modern readers, the sources for the narrator's authority are less clear than are the king's. He cannot, like the king, lay claim to a sovereign if still unrealized political authority. Instead, though the king's control of romance offers a powerful analogue for the poet's, the latter's authority is also defined—and in some ways limited—through two surrogates for the modern poet, the minstrel Allan-Bane and the highland prophet Brian the Hermit.

Like the narrator at the opening of the poem, these two seem at times helpless before the uncontrollable sources of their own art. Both of these figures also suffer from a recognition of political and social change beyond their control. Both of these figures go on, however, to demonstrate a poetic power in society. Furthermore, their power depends upon the demythologizing of Ellen, upon the usurping or limiting of her symbolic role as a nature goddess presiding like the elf queen over an ambiguous wilderness. What is remarkable about this poem, however, is that Ellen has laid claim to that role only in play, and yields it with grace. She herself, in fact, shares the narrator's most skeptical, psychological, and rationalist attitudes toward imagination and inspiration.

To develop his portraits of the minstrel Allan-Bane and of the prophet Brian the Hermit, the narrator first explores their passivity before these forces and then suggests that these forces are causes or conditions that, though troubling, may lead to positive and even benevolent effects.[47] As in *The Lay* and *Marmion*, however—and even more clearly in the later *Bridal of Triermain*—these forces must be associated now not with female but with male parentage.

The first of Scott's analogues of the poet, the minstrel Allan-Bane, begins a public definition of his vocation by deliberately claiming a prophetic transcendence for his art. He does so in order to impress upon the departing king his vision of a hospitality that will embrace even exiles (*LL*, 2:3). Lost after his hunt, the king has received hospitality from apparent strangers, though he begins to realize that among them are the Douglasses whom he has himself sent into exile. Allan-

Bane, recognizing in turn the knight of Snowdon's courtly origin, if not yet his full identity, urges him to return the hospitality he has received. The minstrel cannot maintain such careful, political control of his art, however, when Ellen asks him to praise the "high heroic pride" of Malcolm Graeme. By choosing the subject for his song, she indirectly asserts her commitment neither to the just-departed knight of Snowdon nor to Roderick Dhu. She thus departs for the moment from the role of wilderness enchantress that she has played with the king. Nor is her role quite that of a muse for Allan-Bane. Instead, she deliberately turns to the realistic social role she hopes will lie ahead of her and appeals to her retainer to define her domestic role in marriage.

Yet Allan-Bane struggles and fails "three times" to "wake" the appropriate music:

> Alas! than mine a mightier hand
> Has tuned my harp, my strings has spann'd!
> I touch the chords of joy, but low
> And mournful answer notes of woe. . . .

Wishing that the "dirge's deep prophetic tone" were "mine alone," he alludes to a tradition that "this harp . . . can thus its master's fate foretell." Twice before, the harp has transformed his intentions, and with sounds "disobedient to my call, / Wail'd loud." Most disturbing for Ellen is his haunting memory of the last time that "mightier hand" had seized his harp—on "the eve thy sainted mother died" (*LL*, 2:8). Now, as then, the dissonant sounds of the harp challenge the hope of a conventional domesticity and motherhood in the society where the Douglasses belong. These "sounds," Allan-Bane says in counter-metaphor, "come . . . appalling me who gave them birth." If again "mishap and woe" follow for the Douglasses, the minstrel offers to destroy both himself and the harp—as if the harp not only announces disaster but is the medium that actually conveys it. Although this account of inspiration begins by sounding like that ironically proposed by Socrates in the *Ion*, in which the poet or rhapsode is only a vessel through which something divine may speak, it ends with a more clearly negative image than Plato's—that of the minstrel's need to sacrifice himself to control the "mightier hand" that seizes control both of his song and of events themselves.

Skeptically labeling his apprehension the "fears of age," Ellen offers Allan-Bane an explanation based on associative psychology: the "unbidden notes" are "confusedly bound in memories' ties, / Entangling, as they rush along, / The war-march with the funeral song" (*LL*, 2:9). Though denying the more terrifying claims made earlier for the "mightier hand" of a transcendent inspiration, her theory reveals inadvertently how the "mightier hand" of political events has disordered his music. "All melodies to thee are known," Ellen reminds him, "that harp has rung, or pipe has blown, / In lowland vale or highland glen." In the present disharmony between the two cultures his music has drawn upon, that music must jar. Here Ellen herself is the lucid, rational debunker of myth. Her associationist, rationalist response that the disorder is only in the minstrel's mind thus affirms her promise of conventional motherhood against his mothering of a monstrous, because destructive, inspiration. Both Ellen and Allan, then, assert life-giving domestic values against the harp's prophecy of violence, exile and death, though Allan appears more pessimistic about their ability to prevail.

Instead of continuing to argue with him directly, Ellen playfully chooses another subject for his harp. In response to his longing "to see [her] grace . . . Scotland's court, [her] rightful place," she plays further with her role as a kind of queen or goddess of the wilderness. Crowning herself with a coronet of "blue hare-bells," she teasingly appoints Allan to sing now the praises of her wilderness suitor Roderick. To Allan, she plays almost impiously with the death he already fears. Naming Roderick with a smile, she mockingly both reveals and challenges his black and sacrilegious rule, like that of the elfin king, over "this western wild":

> The Saxon scourge, Clan-Alpine's pride,
> The terror of Loch Lomond's side,
> Would, at my suit, thou know'st, delay
> A Lennox foray—for a day. [LL, 2:11]

Allan's fuller response to this playful role comes two cantos later in his ballad of "Alice Brand." As we have seen, the ballad meets Allan's astute intentions for its heuristic role, but in singing it he neither claims nor is claimed by a prophetic inspiration beyond his control. Positive as his ballad is for Ellen, however, we may also read his substitution of an elfin king for the Rhymer's elfin queen not only as an image for Roderick but as a new, male parentage for the deeper, liminal or subliminal sources of his own art—and for Scott's.

An even more explicit pattern of male parentage for poetic vision appears in the poem's other analogue for the modern poet. The narrator, whose passive attitude before the "Harp of the North" is recalled in Allan's meditation and Ellen's phrasing, must learn whether some more active and controlling role is possible for his own and for Allan's art. He comes to such knowledge by following still further the problem of "unbidden notes" and their escape from the sovereignty of the bard's will and reason. Brian the Hermit represents the extreme point of the narrator's psychological journey toward anarchy, as Roderick does for the king's more literal one.

As a bardic figure whose central role is prophetic speech instead of intermittently prophetic music, Brian is even more than Allan-Bane an analogue for the narrator as poet. In fact, his prophecy of the coming battle appears not in human or divine form, but in letters, "characters of living flame!" The closeness of the analogy, however, emphasizes disconcertingly the primitive violence through which he invokes "prophetic dream" and through which it, in turn, seizes and dominates him: those characters are "not spoke in words, nor blazed in scroll, / But borne and branded on my soul" (*LL*, 4:6). As prophet for his clan, Brian seems to be the vehicle both for expressing and for continuing the primitive violence of its culture; "prophetic dream," and thus the imaginative vision of the later poet as well, seem forces of disordered energy. Yet if such prophecy is dismissed as the product of its culture alone, its energy is lost to the modern poet.[48]

More closely examined, however, the relationship between the prophet and his society offers an instructive pattern for the modern narrator who is alienated from his audience. For Brian's prophecy springs from a radical alienation from his own society. This alienation is accounted for in terms that neither deny such supernatural inspiration as the "mightier hand" of Allan's fears nor rely exclusively upon it. The latter explanation would make "prophetic dream" the product of a "creed outworn," and thus, again, inaccessible to the narrator. Instead, he cites as "strange tales" an account of Brian's engendering that places the child "beyond nature's law" because he is "bred / Between the living and the dead" (*LL*, 4:6), conceived as his mother keeps unexplained vigil in a "dreary glen, / Where scatter'd lay the bones of men, / In some forgotten battle slain." Whether Brian's illegitimacy is indeed "beyond nature's law," like Merlin's in Geoffrey's *Historia*, or merely beyond society's law, the narrator does not say.[49]

On the one hand, a naive or mythic interpretation of his conception "between the living and the dead" makes him a liminal figure like Ethert Brand in Allan-Bane's ballad that follows his prophecy in canto 4, and like Ethert an unwilling mediator between the human world and an ambiguously supernatural one. His supernatural fathering seems to make both himself and his inspiration either "fiend-begotten" (*LL*, 4:15) or divine. On the other hand, the narrator suggests that it is the psychological effect of this apparent inheritance upon the child, "a moody and heartbroken boy, / Estranged from sympathy and joy," that makes him into a prophet exercising freedom of imagination:

> Bearing each taunt which careless tongue
> On his mysterious lineage flung[.]
> ....
> ... frantic, he as truth received
> What of his birth the crowd believed,
> And sought, in mist and meteor fire,
> To meet and know his Phantom Sire! [*LL*, 3:6]

The narrator's conclusion to this genetic account of prophecy redefines Brian's search as a projection of his imagination and thus confirms the more psychological and skeptical view of imagination voiced by Ellen in canto 2: "Thus the lone Seer, from mankind hurl'd, / Shaped forth a disembodied world."

Yet the disembodied world, shaped though it may be from his individual needs, nonetheless converts the scene of his conception to the visionary scene of accurate prophecies: "Far on the future battle-heath / His eye beheld the ranks of death" (*LL*, 3:7). His alienation and suffering lead to a means of serving his mother's clan. Yet ironically, the specific prophecy induced by a ritual isolation in canto 4 also becomes a means of establishing the king's ordering sovereignty over the clan. Urged by the "dread extremity" of the clan's situation, Brian presides over "an augury" called the Taghairm practiced only by the clan's "sires" in such extremity. Stretching the "reeking hides" of a slaughtered white bull beside a cataract, he "waits prophetic dream" (*LL*, 4:4-5). His dream is a conditional prophecy that itself suggests a sort of ritual sacrifice: "which spills the foremost foeman's life, / That party conquers in the strife!" Immediately reaching beyond its obvious incentive to valor in battle, Roderick proposes "a surer victim . . . self-offer'd to the auspicious blow"—a lowland "spy" who is already being led astray by his apparent guide. The spy is the king, returning with the merely private mission of bringing Ellen back to Stirling; but first Ellen's warning at the cave where he has found her, then Blanche of Devan's song of the hunt set for a stag (*LL*, 4:25) alert him to his guide's treachery, and he kills the highlander. His second guide out of the wilderness proves to be Roderick himself, ready—he believes—to spill first blood, but to do so only on the chivalrous terms of single combat at the ford marking the border between lowland and highland territory. As we have seen, the king defeats him and thus cripples his leaderless clan in the later battle. Through this series of reversals, Brian's prophecy comes true. Thus, however private and anarchic its beginnings, prophecy in the romance narrative proves accurate and capable of ordering and is thus an heuristic model for the narrator.

The model Brian's prophecy offers for the engendering, or better, for the gendering of imagination is a far more radical model than Allan-

Bane's. The latter's elfin king only indirectly usurps sovereignty over a supernaturalized nature and its glamour from ladies of the lake and other such enchantresses. Brian's belief in his "Phantom Sire" claims more directly the masculine nature of his inspiration. Because his search for knowledge of that "mysterious lineage" has led not only through tribal magic but also through monasteries' "sable-letter'd page" and through all he can read of "magic, cabala, and spells" (*LL*, 3:6), it recalls the book of Michael Scott and that wizard's ultimate control over the Lady of Buccleuch. The killing of the white bull whose skin becomes almost a mantle for his prophecy converts his myth to an appropriate ritual. Brian's myth, ironically, protects his mother by emphasizing her powerless receptivity. With further irony the more obviously powerless Blanche of Devan, whose victimization is not at all supernatural, becomes the interpreter of his prophecy for the king who will fulfill it.

In the end, the narrator must incorporate the positive strengths of both male analogues. If Ellen's role as enchantress, a fiction even within the fictional narrative, is partially demythologized, she nevertheless remains closely associated with the poet's characteristic art. Like the prophet, the modern poet must convert personal alienation into public truth; and, like the minstrel romancer, he must direct that truth toward an ordered and harmonious world, a romance comedy world that will include "all melodies . . . of lowland vale or highland glen." He is not able simply to transcend history and return miraculously to the "festal crowd" of "fair dames and crested chiefs" who would once have been both subject and audience for his minstrel's song. Yet he can speak as Brian does, out of the recognition of loss; he can build, within the fictional world of his poem, the recognition of anarchy in historical process and in imagination. In that recognition, which is both his own and that of the characters he draws from an earlier age, he may achieve a continuity of attitude that is a partial transcendence of change; and he may build a romance fiction that does not deny but accommodates those anarchic forces as an uneasy starting point.

This continuing awareness allows the narrator to return his borrowed harp with an affirmation both of his own success and of the harp's harmony with the natural setting. Given such continuity, natural and historical process is less threatening: "Harp of the North, farewell! the hills grow dark, / . . . the fountain lending, / And the wild breeze, thy wilder minstrelsy; / Thy numbers sweet with nature's vespers blending." Though after this passage he returns to the role of alienated "last minstrel," he need no longer fear the "censure sharp" of those who "may idly cavil at an idle lay." The redemptive social vision worked out in his narrative is both a private consolation in his "secret woes" and an image for eventual reconciliation,[50] for a sovereignty of educated romance vision not only in the country of his mind but in that actual landscape of nature and history. The harp now responds harmoniously to both "mountain breezes" and "seraph . . . fire" (p. 273). Through their encounters with the gently challenging lady of the lake, presiding figure over the fluid, reflective world of romance, both king and poet have achieved a new sovereignty in their own countries. Finally and paradoxically, however, Ellen's dual role both as the lady of the lake who symbolizes romantic imagination and as the smiling skeptic of its transcendent power, becomes her gift to the king and above all to the poet. In this way Ellen triumphs over both her demythologizing and her domestication.

FOUR

Rokeby

"FATAL ART" AND THE REDEEMED ESTATE

IN *English Bards and Scotch Reviewers*, first published in 1809, Byron satirizes both of Scott's narratives then in print. Claiming with gleeful cacophony that "lays of minstrels . . . / On half-strung harps whine mournful to the blast," his criticism of *The Lay* skips as lightly as the "goblin brats" he mocks in Scott's poem. His attack on *Marmion* proved more savage. Criticizing Murray's prepublication agreement to pay "half-a-crown per line" for "a stale romance," Byron chides Scott for "descend[ing] to trade": only "sere" bays and faded laurel are the reward "of prostituted Muse and hireling bard!" (ll. 175-82).[1] In *Rokeby* one of several minstrel figures within that complex narrative expresses an anguished assessment that seems to intensify Byron's accusation:

> . . . shuddering, [Edmund] thought upon his glee,
> When prank'd in garb of minstrelsy.
> 'O, be the fatal art accurst,'
> He cried, 'that moved my folly first;
> Till, bribed by bandits' base applause,
> I burst through God's and Nature's laws! [*R*, 6:5]

On the surface Scott's quarrel with Byron was made up in the summer that *Rokeby* took shape.[2] Beneath the surface—and Edmund speaks these lines while having returned to the bandits' cave on the Greta's cliffs—the problems Byron so broadly satirizes through his charges of "prostituted Muse," "stale romance," and "hireling bard" continue to trouble and to challenge Scott. It would be too simple to claim in Scott's defense that, far from prostituting his muse, he has taken Byron's chastising voice for his inspiration. As we have seen, Scott's concerns about the validity and social purpose of fiction play a significant role in shaping *Marmion*, and a similar fascination with the responsible linking of romance and history structures both that poem and the more serene *Lady of the Lake*. Yet Byron's satiric phrases, coupled with Edmund's self-condemning rhetoric, can help us analyze *Rokeby*'s complex, multiple definitions of a poet's responsibility for property, for an estate's—and by extension even a nation's—stability. Though he is most clearly its "hireling bard," Edmund is not the most central character in *Rokeby*, nor is he even its sole minstrel, for he shares that role with two other young men. All three of these share within the poem Scott's task of restoring "stale romance" to life. This task is both primary and secondary in the poem. Reinterpreting the physically heroic, yet misguided past action of an older generation of male protagonists, a past retold through inscription and scroll, the minstrels also reinterpret history; that reinterpretation is itself a primary action. Thus "hireling bard" and "stale romance" are both redeemed.

Neither in the romance patterns of the past nor in the bardic arts of the present is there a muse like Thomas the Rhymer's elf queen. In contrast to *The Lay* and *The Lady of the Lake*, no visionary enchantress leads the hero or minstrel into a visionary, paradisal world. Instead, the only major female character in the poem is more often a victim of the estate she will inherit. She acts at times as a minstrel, and, more often and more conventionally, as an inspirational object to the three young men who play at minstrel to court her. Yet, as the marriageable heiress to Rokeby, she is inevitably a pawn in the plots and desires of others. Although she herself is enchanting to the young men, it is her land that enchants several of the older ones, and their plotting aims for the possession of land through a forced marriage. This plot stands at the center of the poem *Rokeby*, as the estate Rokeby stands at the center of the poem's geography. Scott's "prostituted Muse" might then be reinterpreted here, and later in *The Lord of the Isles*, as a muse concerned with the realistic social consequences of women as pawns in the struggle for place.

Although Matilda is more realistically limited by her property than mythically in control of her realm, both the "hireling bard" Edmund and Scott himself claim such a mythic, even esemplastic, power of building domains. Edmund's remorse in the robbers' cave is as acute as if he had achieved some powerful Promethean magic of the sort celebrated by Blake and Shelley and remade the world to his own design: his "fatal art" has caused or enabled him to "burst through God's and Nature's laws." Yet his Prometheanism is clearly more conservative and guilt ridden than theirs. Further, his rhetoric is more cosmic than his actual crime: through the distracting charm of his singing, he has helped to destroy the largest manor house in the neighborhood. Yet because Rokeby was a Royalist house and embodied a tradition of stable property and its feudal loyalties, the robbery and burning of this Yorkshire estate symbolize one effect of the civil war between Royalist and Puritan during which the poem is set.

This undoing of estates by poetry is strikingly opposite to Scott's own process in writing *Rokeby*. Planned to celebrate the house's history and thus to claim that history for the present owner, his friend John Morritt, the narrative will also, he noted wryly, pay for his own new estate, Abbotsford (see *Letters*, 3:30; 40; 68; and 88). "I . . . must call in the aid of Amphion and his harp," he wrote Mrs. Clephane on 18 January 1812, "not indeed to found a city, but if I can rear a cottage it will be very fair for a modern lyre" (68). A little later, on 4 May, he wrote to the same family that he had been working out "a romantic subject and . . . nearer to that of *Marmion* than any of the other attempts I have made" (3:116). Not only is the morally ambiguous Bertram similar to the earlier ambiguous Marmion, but Scott linked that ambiguity to his own role as hireling bard. In the next sentence he wrote, "But my cottage is rising."

Although lightly and ironically phrased in the letter, this relationship between a poet's Amphion-like creativity and his social responsibility is important not only for the origin of *Rokeby* but for the formal development of plot and theme worked out in it. Critics have been either awed or irritated at the poem's intricate plot; Kroeber's complaint that Scott should really have written it as a novel is only one of the most recent.[3] Again, however, the poet seems a step ahead of his critics. The more successful his publishing of poems after *The Lay*, the more aware he becomes of the tension between minstrel's song and writer's published documents. In fact, he organizes the structure of *Rokeby* through just such a distinction. The most important plot line, that of the Mortham family, Scott develops most fully in cantos 2, 4, and 6. As if to reinforce its historicity, he supports the unfolding of this family's story with a series of inscriptions or written documents; yet the story itself follows a romance archetype. In cantos 1, 3, and 5, on the other hand, the younger generation of the poem plays at minstrel to escape from the pressures of its own political situation. Yet their songs develop models for interpreting the specific events of history into more universal significance.

Although he disclaims any larger significance for this family narrative, it possesses both particular historical and a larger generic response. Scott's headnote to the poem announces a private "Fictitious Narrative . . . without any purpose of combining the Fable with the Military or Political Events of the Civil War" (*PW*, 313). Yet the "private" characters of the Mortham family and of families from the adjoining estates, the Wycliffes and the Rokebys, show a complex range of attitudes toward the civil war and its crucial issues. Furthermore, this "fable" of a private family and its relationships closely follows the regenerative patterns of Alexandrian and late Shakespearean romance, with its promises of social reconciliation as well as individual rebirth. Far from invalidating the indirect but still powerful "combination" of private and public events, this generic revision of romance suggests an heuristic model or solution for the religious and political problems not only of seventeenth-century England but also of Regency Britain.

Critics have seen Scott's choice of geographical and historical setting—Yorkshire in the civil war—as the poet's deracination. Scott himself blamed the poem's failure to surpass the enormous sales of its predecessors upon his turn from the primitive song of a "patriarchal" Scotland to what George Ellis called "the sober annals of . . . seventeenth-century" England.[4] That choice also sets the scene for a more extreme example of a theme already seen in the Scottish poems: the uprooting and dislocating of a society. True, the society in *Rokeby* is far less coherent as a cultural group than the borderers of *The Lay* or the "primitive Highlanders" of *The Lady of the Lake*, both of whom are to some extent "living in a simple and patriarchal state" (*PW*, 1830, 380). Thus the nature of its lost coherence and the nostalgia for its restoration both appear less strong. *Rokeby*'s society is, instead, a neighborhood defined not by geographical or cultural isolation but instead by confluence: first, the confluence of the Greta and Tees Rivers and second, the convergence of historical forces upon that strategic juncture. Its characters are relatively sophisticated, their "manners founded upon those peculiar habits of thinking or acting . . . produced by the progress of society" (*PW*, 380). Less easily separated from modern audience or modern minstrel than Scott's earlier characters, they are also less easily separated from other such neighborhoods of their own time, torn by civil war. As a result *Rokeby* develops in sharp contrast to *Marmion* and to *The Lady of the Lake*. In those earlier poems, one central, sophisticated figure is both victim and spinner of romance fictions. *Rokeby*, on the other hand, describes a "period of public confusion" in which entirely too many characters find themselves with the education and the imagination to create their own plots, whether of private romance or private enterprise.

To judge from the letters, Scott's choice of geographical location for his poem preceded his choice of historical setting (3:30, 10 December 1811; 3:40, 20 December 1811). Once he had chosen Rokeby, the nearby battle of Marston Moor would offer a dramatic historical moment. Although logical, this choice posed difficulties arising from the complexity of the larger conflict of values in the English civil war. Karl Kroeber has charged that Scott's problem is not the choice of milieu but its development: "*Rokeby* gives us the sense of real historical forces at work, . . . [yet] Scott makes us conscious of the artificiality, the sensationalism of the personal exploits he recounts."[5] In contrast to Scott's earlier poems and to the novels soon to follow, Kroeber argues, *Rokeby* presents characters who show neither strong convictions nor much knowledge about the political and religious quarrels going on around them. According to G.E. Aylmer, however, "There is a sense in which the war consisted of a large number of local and even personal conflicts coming together on a national scale. It involved the settling of many private and family feuds, very much of the kind . . . found in the sixteenth century; it was in this narrower sense a war of cliques and factions, arising from the nature of family ties and from the system of clientage and patronage."[6] Scott's poem demonstrates and criticizes these feuds. The "public confusion" of the war's course up to 1644 and of the battle itself becomes a prologue for the local ambitions and loyalties shown by many of his fictional characters. These local ambitions and loyalties in the poem frequently recognize, filter, and distort, as they seek to exploit, the larger clash of values. Furthermore, the most apparently extreme of these clashes points toward a reading of seventeenth-century history as a paradigm for early nineteenth-century religious and political conflicts, specifically that between Irish and English.[7]

The historical battle of Marston Moor, fought on 3 July 1644, makes an effective prelude for this chaotic situation. Marking the first clear parliamentary victory and the beginning of Cromwell's rise to prominence, it was a notable turning point in the war. Yet, ironically, the turning point of the battle itself was notoriously unclear for those on the field. As Scott's lengthy notes explain, almost all of the generals on both sides left the field thinking they had been defeated. When his fictional narrative opens, a member of Fairfax's parliamentary army brings "tidings from the host" to a fellow parliamentary supporter who holds the stronghold of Barnard Castle. Bertram reports, in an extended epic simile, that "the eddying tides of conflict wheel'd / Ambiguous," until Prince Rupert's arrival; and then, "in tumult lost, / Our leaders fell, our ranks were lost. . . ." Though Bertram reports a new "rumor" that Cromwell "has redeem'd the day" (R, 1:19), not until the end of the second canto does Oswald learn finally that "brave Cromwell turn'd the doubtful tide" (R, 2:31).

Preempting any direct account by the narrator, Bertram's analysis of motivation in the two armies concisely reviews the bases of political and religious conflict and cynically dismisses their validity:

> "On either side loud clamours ring,
> 'God and the Cause!'—'God and the King!'
> Right England all, they rush'd to blows
> With nought to win, and all to lose.
> I would have laugh'd—but lack'd the time—
> To see, in phrenesy sublime,
> How the fierce zealots fought and bled

> For king or state, as humour led;
> Some for a dream of public good,
> Some for church-tippet, gown, and hood,
> Draining their veins, in death to claim
> A patriot's or a martyr's name." [R, 1:12]

Denied leadership in the parliamentary forces because "I could not cant of creed or prayer," Bertram dismisses those leaders as "sour fanatics." Moreover, each is a "superstitious fool" for seeking "El Dorados in the sky!" Seeking earthly profit, earthly gold—and earthly "name" and "fame" rivaling those of the Spanish conquistadors—is, he claims, a more valuable and more honest goal.

Oswald, too, though he had earlier "glozed upon the cause / Of Commons, Covenants and Laws, / And Church Reform'd," is forced "beneath grim Bertram's sneering look" to admit a more practical and selfish interest in the battle. Though he greets the news of the battle's loss with "assumed despondence," he awaits the second part of Bertram's narrative with "troubled joy." In the narrator's significant metaphor, Bertram has finally "forc'd the embarrass'd host to buy, / By query close, direct reply," taunting him, "What reck'st thou of the Cause divine, / If Mortham's wealth and lands be thine?" (R, 1:15). An ironic interplay between the alliances of friendship and the disintegrating forces of politics and private profit shape this climactic section of Bertram's story. Seeing the "kindred banner" of his neighbor Rokeby on the opposite, Royalist side, Mortham tells Bertram before the battle: "Thus . . . will friends divide!" Yet the friend to whom he tells this is preparing to shoot him from behind in order to seize a part of the fortune they had gathered together as fellow buccaneers. In his later narration Bertram's metaphors of a turning tide, though commonplace at least since Shakespeare's Brutus, recall the violent ocean origin of Mortham's pirate treasure. Finally, Bertram acknowledges the continued divisiveness, almost an entropic fragmentation, of the bonds of friendship, when he refuses Oswald's hospitality. In his native village, he explains, an "ancient sculptor's art" shows "an outlaw's image" in the stone, and a legend records the vulnerability of even that "giant . . . hunter" to "brother's treachery" (R, 1:20). That image, so haunting to Bertram, foreshadows his death, though a redemptive death, on the stone paving of Eglinton Abbey.[8]

This dark portrayal of friendships destroyed for increasingly worse motives associates the historical context of Marston Moor and the civil war not with clear heroism but with futile chaos. In *Marmion* Scott describes the battle of Flodden Field in a similar way, at least in the careless preliminaries that led to the Scottish defeat. Yet there Scott uses a clearly-defined military heroism partially to redeem both James

IV and the English Marmion. Thus the narrative purpose of the battle is that of a tragic recognition, even if one tinged with irony. As the earlier poem moves toward a definite historical moment and toward its narrative resolution, the two truths reinforce one another, the historical battle acting as an apocalyptic, uncovering conclusion to the dalliances of romance. In *The Lady of the Lake* the historical James V is treated more freely, but that freedom is a preparation, through the playful recognitions of romance, for the history that lies ahead of him beyond the end of the poem. In *Rokeby* the definite historical moment at the beginning of the poem is itself an indefinite and chaotic one. Although the poem's fictional villains plan to conclude their plots through that chaos, even the emergence of a decisive parliamentary victory does not avoid delays. Through their difficulties and through the dalliance of the younger generation, the poem moves through further chaos to a more benevolent resolution, one that is symbolically historical: its disinterment of the past leads to the possibility of an evolutionary, not revolutionary, change in society.

In two important ways Scott's use of history in *Rokeby* is closer to that in *The Lay* than to that in the other earlier poems. First, both poems depict the effects of political turmoil in a relatively small neighborhood of gentry or lesser aristocracy. This geographical pattern, which modifies Scott's use of a journey into a green world characteristic of much romance, leads toward the second similarity between the two poems, a tripartite temporal perspective. In *The Lay* the processes of historical change appear more through the contrasts of the two framing narrators to the inner narrative than in the main narrative itself. In *Rokeby* this tripartite pattern is more a matter of allusion and interpretation than of explicit narrative structure. The religious and political conflict of 1644 is further analyzed by references back to Elizabeth I's campaign in Ireland and analogues forward to the English-Irish tensions in Scott's own time. Within the main narrative, the process of historical change is clearly signaled through the chaos caused by new money in that landowning society. The negotiable power of money or "treasure" in the poem is not that of city merchants financing the Parliament's cause and eventually building the Whig faction, but the more exotic gold and jewels Mortham and Bertram have plundered from the Spanish main. Yet it has a similar destabilizing effect on conservative society. Thus the treasure must be found, redirected, and even redefined, in order to restore the manorial families and the ruined abbey to a version, perhaps only a vestige, of their traditional function.

Through the confluence of its two rivers—the Greta and the Tees—the geographical setting of *Rokeby* also reflects the confluence of other, primitive sources of energy and power that challenge the architectural and social order of its neighborhood. In addition to the specific events of the civil war, three different primitive and exotic milieux influence the setting through their offstage but powerful cultural patterns. The most spatially vast and spatially distanced of these is the world-ranging seascape of piracy; but the primitive culture of Ireland and the upstream scenes and values of Bertram's border country of Redesdale also act as sources for images of sublimity that reinforce the local sublimity of the river gorges. In *The Lady of the Lake* and in *Marmion*, the principal character travels beyond familiar borders into a more primitive and violent realm. In *Rokeby* the characters recall such journeys but travel only in the primitive gaps or ravines between their own neighboring estates or households.

Significantly, Scott associates both Bertram and Edmund, his lawless fighter and his lawless bard, with a geographic region and a society further upstream, both geographically and temporally, from the junction of the Greta and Tees. To move upstream is, in effect, to move back toward social origins, to structures more tribal and primitive than those around Rokeby. A glance at a topographical map of northeast England shows how the upland mass of the northern Pennines continues from Stanmore, just west of the poem's central neighborhood, north through Northumberland to the Scottish border.[8] Thus Bertram's border village of Risingham in Redesdale, near Otterburn, has ties both to Rokeby and to the violent border warfare shown in *The Lay*:

> In Redesdale his youth had heard
> Each art her wily dalesmen dared,
> When Rooken-edge, and Redswair high,
> To bugle rung and bloodhound's cry,
> Announcing Jedwood-axe and spear,
> And Lid'sdale riders in the rear.
> [R, 3:2; see also Scott's note 26, PW]

His superstition, grown from "many a tale / Of wonder in his native dale" (R, 2:11), and the giant sculpted form of the Risingham outlaw suggest a kind of upstream potentiality for energy, as do the puzzling lines in which he recalls "the dawning of [his] youth . . . over Redesdale," a youth whose uncontrolled energy the Dalesmen saw as an omen of danger, "as bodeful as [the borderers'] beacon-flame" (R, 6:21).

Though Edmund of Winston, the "hireling bard" whose self-condemnation opened this chapter, is a local boy from "Winston's bowers," a little downstream from the junction of Greta and Tees, one of his songs also points to the Pennine uplands and to the Scottish borders beyond. In canto 3 he catches the attention of the robbers and ends their "mutinous debate" by a final song that fuses local geography and less local legend: the name of the song's protagonist, Allan-a-Dale, echoes the nearby place name of Allandale and also recalls the minstrel who belonged, by tradition, to Robin Hood's outlaws. The outlaw of his song is made local by references to Richmond, to the "rere-cross on Stanmore," and to border lords like Ravensworth and Dacre.[9]

Scott's pirates emerge not only from the historical sources attested to in his notes but also from a long literary tradition ranging from Greek and Elizabethan romance to more recent *sturm und drang* portrayals of robbers—on land or sea—as noble outlaws.[10] These influences raise conflicting expectations for the way in which their patterns of violence can be integrated into, or will reform, the existing society. Typically, the romance pattern leads through threats of external violence to the restoration of lovers, of lost children, and of society, whereas the *sturm-und-drang* pattern begins to question such conservative order. In *Rokeby* the piracy in which Bertram and Mortham have spent so many years serves at least three purposes: to comment upon the all-too-analogous society at home; to develop both in the characters and in the readers a sense of emotional extremes freely enacted; and to develop the symbolic motif of buried treasure, which will reveal an answer to the conflict between definitions of the pirate in Renaissance romance and of robbers in German romanticism.

In the first of these purposes, the continual violence of the buccaneers becomes more than exotic color when we read it as analogous to the English civil war. Explaining his return to England, Bertram remarks tellingly, "Civil discord gave the call, / And made my trade the trade of all" (*R*, 1:18). Although Bertram himself regards his buccaneering as English warfare against Spain, his cynical term "trade" also descries the amorality of that "civil discord." Through his contrast of Bertram with the somewhat similar Mortham, Scott further analyzes the motivations of these two buccaneers-turned-Puritans and suggests that those motives may be more general.

Bertram goes on to explain that the pirates are not completely amoral, since they have a code for dividing their treasure and thus for ensuring both a temporary loyalty and a recurrent heroism (*R*, 1:21; 3:23). Yet the character building encouraged by such a society leads to an ambiguous heroism. Although critics have noted the presence of the morally ambiguous hero in this poem as in *Marmion*, some have seen Bertram as that hero and others, Mortham. Because Scott had been reading the first two cantos of *Childe Harold*, Byron's wandering protagonist may have intensified the portrait of a remorseful Mortham, haunted by a mysterious past crime (see *Letters*, 3:114). Scott himself, to judge from his letters, was delighted by his "Caravaggio sketch" of the outlaw Bertram; Peter Thorslev correctly identifies Mortham and Bertram as variants of the same ambiguous role.[11] Scott seems to overload the poem with the fashionable rebel he and Byron had developed, as if Mortham and Bertram, like Scott and Byron, are rivals for this dubious crown. In fact, however, this doubling is dramatically justified. The two figures react against one another in a complex psychological clash of temperaments that becomes almost a paradigm for the clash of temperaments among the Puritan factions of the civil war.

At first Mortham and Bertram do seem to be duplicates, the follower Bertram modeling his self-annihilating violence on that of his remorseful leader Mortham. Because in the early cantos neither Bertram nor the reader knew Mortham's reasons for remorse, his contagious attitude seems a kind of existential given, a defiant and stylized Byronic protest against man's condition in an absurd world. A distinction soon emerges, however, based in part on the narrator's persistently Miltonic description of Bertram and in part on Bertram's changed attitude toward Mortham's new religious intensity.

Like Milton describing Satan, Scott first emphasizes Bertram's physical and psychological "scorn" of the world's limits, then the selfish misdirection of his abilities. A "scorching clime" has darkened his "eye of flame" that "mock'd at pain, and knew not woe" (R, 1:8). If his sang-froid is "worse than apathy," yet "even now," he goes on,

> . . . by conscience unrestrain'd,
> Clogg'd by gross vice, by slaughter stain'd,
> Still knew his daring soul to soar,
> And mastery o'er the mind he bore. [R, 1:9-10]

Bertram himself gives a similar description of Mortham: "a moody man . . . Desperate and dark." Mortham differs only in the inward nature of the adversity he suffers and in the resulting pattern of motivation, self-annihilation, and not "lust for gold." So long as they are involved in the same desperate enterprises, Bertram admires Mortham. The latter's self-description in his autobiographical "scroll" to Matilda suggests their affinity, using the same word, *frantic*, to describe his death-seeking acts (R, 4:23).

Yet their different motivations gradually drive them apart. Though "foremost he fought in every broil," gaining Bertram's admiration, Mortham "scornful turn'd him from the spoil . . . Preaching . . . Of mercy and humanity" (R, 3:22-23). As Mortham finds a new consolation in religion, however, Bertram, "no superstituous fool" in his self-description, cannot share Mortham's feelings. The latter's "doubts, horrors, superstitious fears" are prompted by "wily priests," Bertram claims, who "damn'd each freeborn deed and thought" (R, 1:17). Denzil in canto 3 confirms Bertram's description that Mortham's religion has brought him little relief. Although he was "In youth . . . a lusty reveller[,] . . . since return'd from over sea, / A sullen and a silent mood / Hath numb'd the current of his blood" (R, 3:21). As a result, not only are the two estranged, but Bertram's license becomes more extreme in the face of Mortham's sobriety (R, 1:17). Together the two of them suggest two forces acting, and often conflicting, in the Puritan revolution: rigorous law, restraint, and inhibition opposed by violent, undirected energy. Scott here shows little of the sympathy he will show the covenanters a few years later, but he does develop the same technique of using an array of characters to portray an array of the single characteristics of a movement.

Yet if Mortham is haunted by his own past, Bertram is now, in cantos 2 and 3, haunted by Mortham. Although influenced by the tales of wonder he heard as a child, Bertram is even more deeply influenced by stories that "seamen love to hear and tell / Of portent, prodigy, and spell" (R, 2:11), and in particular by the practice of killing "a slave, or prisoner" to guard buried treasure. Believing he has seen Mortham's ghost haunting his family tomb, Bertram feels increased guilt at Mortham's murder. Thus he too becomes "a moody man . . . desperate and dark." For both figures, then, piracy has brought a freely-exercised release in physical violence, but the physical violence has been intensified by a self-directed emotional violence. There is a strange echo here, as in several of Scott's poems, of Wordsworth's then-unpublished play *The Borderers*, in which Wordsworth's character Oswald argues for a completion of self through guilt.[12]

Already, then, the literal buried treasure Bertram has helped Mortham win and now wants for himself begins to stand for buried aspects of the self and its past. As in *The Lay* and *Marmion*, this burial leads to the disinterment and interpretation of documents that prove ironically redemptive: Michael Scott's "mighty Book" and Constance's papers that, surviving her, reveal Marmion's forgeries. More exact interpretation of this treasure comes later in the poem, as the various "scrolls" containing Mortham's history are read and interpreted. Before that interpretation comes a change in the primitive off-stage milieux influencing present action: from piracy, concentrated almost entirely in the first three cantos, to Ireland, concentrated in the last three.

Toward the end of *Rokeby*, a subordinate villain unsnarls its intricate plot by explaining that Redmond O'Neale, the exiled grandson of an Irish chieftain and penniless foster child of Sir Richard Rokeby, is the long-missing son of Rokeby's neighbor Mortham. Years before, when the child's grandfather had sent him from Ireland back to Yorkshire, the Stainmoor outlaw Denzil had stabbed Redmond's escort and stolen "a reliquary and a chain . . . of massive gold." On the chain were hung "gilt tablets . . . with letters in the Irish tongue," letters that Denzil had learned to "spell . . . by the book, / When some sojourn in Erin's land / Of their wild speech had given command, / But darkling was the sense." Because he has just overheard Mortham's part of the story, Denzil "now . . . can interpret well / Each syllable the tablets tell" (*R*, 6:13). The outlaw's quick study of Irish seems scarcely more probable than his miraculous discovery of Redmond's identity. Yet because romances always discover their lost children through such tokens, the familiar literary pattern compels our acceptance of both. By making these tokens Irish and by making Redmond half an O'Neill, Scott evokes a country almost as remote as "the seacost of Bohemia" in *The Winter's Tale*. Yet as he uses an archetypal romance plot to draw together the very different cultures of seventeenth-century Ireland and England, Scott also teaches his readers how to "spell . . . by [his] book" a more realistic interpretation of that cultural clash. Analogous to the simultaneous quarrels within the English civil war, it also reflects the political and religious quarrels between England and Ireland in his own time. Furthermore, those inscribed tokens conclude a series of allusions to writing in the poem that begin to resolve significant questions about the political and social responsibility of a modern, publishing minstrel whose audience is far wider than a single clan or court. Interpreting these "letters in the Irish tongue" leads toward the analysis of the poem's structure to be considered in the second part of this chapter: an analysis of Scott's alternation between cantos on minstrelsy and cantos on writing and decoding the Mortham family romance. In pointing toward the unity of the poem, these Irish allusions also offer a way to understand the political and cultural union that it proposes as an imaginative, yet serious model.

Friends with whom Scott discussed the poem felt the still-remaining power of those historical forces so strongly that they feared bias in the poem's nineteenth-century audience.[13] Reassuring them, Scott writes: "I shall keep off peoples kibes if I can for my plan though laid during the civil wars has little to do with the politics of either party" (*Letters*, 3:88). To judge from R.L. Edgeworth's response, Scott's careful footwork succeeds. "You have most dextrously avoided all the perils of controversy religious or political," Edgeworth writes. "Rokeby's loyalty must charm / all times & all parties." As an Anglo-Irish landholder, Edgeworth surely feared perils already current in his own time: most specifically, the controversy over Catholic emancipation that accompanied the union of England with Ireland in 1800. Another Irishman, Henry Boyd, also praises Scott's reconciling historical vision: "Rokeby came out at a very seasonable Time, if, as every one here admires it, the character and sentiments could prevail upon us of this Island to harmonize with one another."[14] Although one might argue that Scott's choice of location drew him willy-nilly into the historical context of Marston Moor in 1644, he is under no such necessity to include Redmond O'Neill and his Irish heritage. Their presence, then, suggests no simple avoidance of political or religious controversy. Instead, Scott dextrously calls up and reconciles such controversy, both in past and present, through his own and his characters' use of sympathetic elements in Irish culture and of poetic romance.

The Irish society described in the second half of the poem seems scarcely less alien than that of the half-outlawed buccaneers described in its first half. Both seem to be exotic, violent cultures, and yet in spite of geographic distance both, as already noted, show too close an analogy to a Yorkshire in civil war (*R*, 1:18). Adventurous Elizabethans had, in fact, combined buccaneering and Irish expeditions.[15] As Scott turns from buccaneers to Irish local color, however, he turns from a degenerate version of modern society to a more nurturing, if more primitive, society. Its portrayal, touched with nostalgia, modulates toward the romantic conclusion of the Mortham romance. Its two most important figures—the warrior chieftain and the bard who inspires his deeds—reinforce Scott's concern with the relationship between historic action and its poetic interpretation. In looking more closely at his specific uses of Irish historical and cultural background, however, the reader is caught between irritation at his apparent inaccuracy and admiration at his gloriously evocative, yet politically neutral, treatment.

In canto 4, the narrator's tone is almost epic as he ties his fictional protagonist Redmond to one of Ireland's greatest heroes: "Who has not heard how brave O'Neale . . . To fiery Essex gave the foil, / And reign'd a prince on Ulster's soil?" (*R*, 4:6). Even though a rebel, Hugh O'Neill can be safely admired, not only for his victory at the Blackwater in 1598 but also for his voluntary "flight" into exile in 1607, removing his threat to English supremacy.[16] When Mortham and Rokeby escape after the battle at Blackwater to Turlough O'Neill's "mountain-hold, . . . Slieve-Donard's cliffs and woods," Scott also follows the Elizabethan descriptions of the way Ulster chieftains lived.[17]

In developing his Irish Samaritan, however, Scott turns from historical although indirect allusions to Hugh as "brave O'Neale" and focuses instead on a less precisely historical figure: his elected heir or Tanist. Taking advantage of the uncertainty inherent in this mode of succession, Scott invents his own Tanist.[18] Thus his Turlough, who rescues Rokeby and Mortham, is free to be more generous than the historical O'Neills, though able to share their patriotic glory. Scott's fictional Tanist also allows him to elide nearly twenty years, in order to connect the Irish rebel heroism of 1598 with its rebirth in Redmond's loyal heroism of 1644. Even if one grants that Rokeby and Mortham were still young enough to be active fighters at Marston Moor—for they would now be in their sixties—Mortham's elopement with Edith O'Neill, daughter of the fictional Turlough, and Redmond's birth remain a problem. This chronological flexibility, however, allows Scott to avoid divisive discussion of the O'Neills' defeat and the first plantations in Ulster.

Even more important, it allows him to avoid mentioning another heroic but more red-handed O'Neill, Hugh's nephew Owen Roe, returned from Spanish exile to help lead the Catholics' uprising in 1641.[19] Because Redmond's grandfather had apparently sent him back to Yorkshire well before this second rebellion, Scott can ignore its greater religious divisiveness and mob violence. Instead of describing any specific religious or political problems, the retainer who brings Redmond to Yorkshire speaks in an Ossianic and universalized lament:

> For Turlough's days of joy are done;
> And other lords have seized his land,
> And faint and feeble is his hand;
> And all the glory of Tyrone
> Is like a morning vapour flown.   [R, 4:8]

Again, drawing upon his Elizabethan sources, Scott makes the primitively-dressed figure who brings this message not only a dramatic symbol of an ancient culture (R, 4:8), but of a dying one: for "hid beneath his mantle wide, / A mortal wound was in his side" (R, 4:9). The long mantle criticized by Spenser as "fit house for an outlaw, . . . meet bed for a rebel" (R, n. 42), can no longer hide the destruction of the wandering life that made it functional. Paradoxically, the abruptness of this figure's death and thus Scott's portrayal of "all the glory of Tyrone" largely through Redmond's childhood memories allows the child, as if still sheltered by the mantle, to sustain a cultural, imaginative inheritance both more romantic and more immediate than an exact, historical treatment would allow. Redmond becomes both Tanist and *fileadh*, or bard, for that culture; and its focus on the bard gives new life to his English heritage as well.

For the Irish society that so intrigues Scott, as it did even the censorious Elizabethans he was reading, ranked hereditary bard and fighting man as mutually important. "These Irishe Bards," Spenser explains, celebrate "whom so ever they fynde to bee most . . . dangerous and desperate in all partes of disobedyance, and rebellious disposition," thus threatening the Tudor ideal of a centralized government.[20] Redmond, however, recalls a significantly more civilizing vision of the bard's power:

> I've seen a ring of rugged kerne,
> With aspects shaggy, wild, and stern,
> Enchanted by the master's lay,
> Linger around the livelong day,
> ....
> Obedient to the bard's control. [R, 5:10]

As Redmond laments this lost culture controlled by the bard, he himself becomes bardic. His lament, however, is far from the specific, bitter diatribe against the "remorseless tyranny" of "the Saxon nation" and its "illegal and extra-judicial proceeding" that Scott's sources attribute to a seventeenth-century "family-Olamnh to the O'Neills of Clannaboy."[21] Instead, like the dying protector who brought him to Rokeby, Redmond uses a universalized, Ossianic vocabulary and tone to evoke emotional assent, not political dissent (R, 5:10). As Scott steers between the views of conquering and conquered bards, Spenser and the "Filea of O'Neill," he surely muses over whether the bardic tribal minstrel must appear in modern, Anglicized society as outlaw or rebel. Both his own search for a literary living and his readings in more modern attitudes toward traditional Irish culture, however, pointed toward a possible resolution of this sharp break between tribal bard and publishing, profit-making writer.

In his *Dryden*, completed in 1808, Scott mentions Howard's *The Committee*, the Restoration play from which he draws Oswald's plot to sequester Rokeby's estate and force Matilda's marriage to his son. The play also contains, however, an important group of Irish characters, both romantic and comic, who eventually win out over their Puritan rivals.[22] In his life of Swift, finally published in 1814, Scott describes with sympathy Swift's championing of Irish independence. He writes Matthew Weld Hartsonge, the Irish poet who helped him with research for the Swift edition: "I have been shaping a Tale of the Civil Wars, in which an Irishman makes a conspicuous character. . . . with all of this national interest, I am delighted with every anecdote of Irish manners and antiquities."[23]

Irish interest in their own "manners and antiquities" had grown intense during the late eighteenth century, as literary and political nationalism influenced one another. From 1781 a series of Irish harp festivals, some sponsored by Wolfe Tone and the United Irishmen, attempted to recreate the heroic culture for which the bard had been custodian.[24] In 1786, Joseph Cooper Walker published his *Historical Memoirs of the Irish Bards*, which included the politically-focused lament of the O'Neills' bard quoted earlier; although Scott quotes extensively from Walker in his notes (47, 53, 55), he only summarizes that passage.

Three years later Charlotte Brooke's *Reliques of Irish Poetry* urged a "cordial union" between "the British muse" and her "elder sister in this isle."[25] After the political union in 1800, several Anglo-Irish novelists borrowed her family metaphor to dramatize the encounter of bardic, Catholic Irish culture and Ascendency proprietors. Sidney Owenson's *Wild Irish Girl* (1806) concludes "with hope [that] this family alliance be . . . prophetically typical of a national unity of interest and affections."[26] In Charles Maturin's *Milesian Chief* (1812), the unpremeditated dissonance of a family harper prophesies that the Irish hero's union with the English heiress to his lost estates is as doomed as his cultural and political rebellion.[27]

Although Scott pursues a similar metaphor both in the birth of Redmond and in his eventual marriage to Matilda, his seventeenth-century setting avoids a direct confrontation with the more recent manifestations of these problems for Scott's audience: the 1798 rebellion, the partially corrupt union vote of 1800, and the attempts since that time to gain Catholic emancipation. A look at almost any issue of the *Quarterly Review* or *Edinburgh Review* shows the constant public debate, rising to a crescendo with the establishment of the Regency in 1811.[28] Scott's choice of an Irish Catholic loyal to his own cultural heritage and also to the English king—for he fights alongside his foster father Rokeby—must surely be read in this context.[29]

Although the main reviews make no comment upon the immediate political and religious relevance of this Irish material, an additional review of sorts, one that went through at least five editions in 1813, points up its contemporary significance. John Roby's *Jokeby, a Burlesque on Rokeby* converts Redmond O'Neal to Terence O'Rourke, wielding a shillelagh—and exiled from Ireland because his grandfather has gone bankrupt and has run out of potatoes.[30] His transformation of Rokeby and Mortham, however, is less comical and more topical: instead of serving in Essex's army to fight the Irish rebellion of 1598, they leave their usual vocation as London thieves to help "brave O'Rourke" store "pike and weapons" in Erin's "rebellion hot"—a clear allusion to the rebels' method of arming in 1798.[31] Reading Scott correctly as a sympathetic advocate of Irish culture, Roby parodies that sympathy by interpreting it as support of political and military revolution.

Even more important than its inclusion of recent political events, however, is *Jokeby*'s omission of Scott's answer to these events. Shamelessly borrowing whole lines of their songs, Roby parodies all of Scott's would-be minstrels and all but one of their songs. He also omits Redmond's response to it, a light-hearted description of possible roles for minstrels. To understand the importance of that song and response, we must look at the minstrels whose roles, although seeming merely nostalgic, begin to shape their songs and Scott's poem toward a more realistic purpose.

Like Allan-a-Dale in Edmund's song, Scott seems continually to lure us away from the central locations of his poem to the more primitive, often violent scenes of the borders, of piracy, and of Ireland. Yet as the modulation from piracy to Irish semipastoral suggests, he has organized the poem with great care. Controlling this centrifugal tendency and converting it to a centripetal one is a carefully-organized symbolic alternation between internal and external scenes within the neighborhood of Rokeby. The internal scenes move from Barnard Castle (canto 1) to the robbers' cave (canto 3) to Rokeby (canto 5) and, in canto 6, back to the cave and to the half-indoor ruins of Egliston Abbey. Only Mortham of the major houses is omitted from this list; an external scene before its tomb (canto 2) strikingly confirms its inability to house the living. Shaping still further this Spenserian alternation of forest and castle is a modulation in tone already seen in the change from piracy to Ireland. After the underworld allusions of the first three cantos, culminating in the cave of canto 3, an Edenic outdoor setting in canto 4 signals a lightening tone that increases in spite of the intensified overt violence of cantos 5 and 6. It becomes clearest in the contrast of the second cave scene with the first.

Following to some extent the alternation between interior and exterior settings is the significant alternation already referred to between minstrelsy and the complex unwindings of the Mortham family "history." Though the description of Wilfrid in the last ten stanzas of canto 1 appears at first to lessen the dark tension of the preceding interview between Bertram and Oswald in Barnard Castle, it introduces a motif that eventually controls that tension. In canto 3 the introduction of Edmund in the robbers' cave again begins a series of interludes to lessen tension both for the outlaws and for the readers. Yet his similarity to Bertram begins to suggest a more central symbolic role. Brief references to minstrelsy in canto 4 lead up to the complex role playing of canto 5, in which all of the younger characters, as if reliving the past of the Rokeby estates, pretend to be minstrels. Because Edmund's songs make way for Bertram's invasion of the manor house at Rokeby, this minstrelsy seems disastrous. Yet Edmund's change of heart, originating in Rokeby Hall, leads to a second cave scene in canto 6. There Bertram reforms as well. There, too, Edmund discovers the "scrolls" that make Redmond's earlier minstrel pleas for British unity prophetic of the symbolic political reconciliation brought about through the discovery of his identity.

Not surprisingly, although the content of the minstrels' songs frequently questions the relationship between hall and heath, all of these episodes that test the morality and the power of minstrelsy are set "in hall." In contrast, the episodes that explore the Mortham family's history through secondary narratives usually place the reading or retelling of these intradiegetic narratives outdoors. Most of these episodes occur in cantos 2, 4, and 6. Through this alternation Scott first suggests an association between a civilizing culture and his art of minstrelsy and a parallel association between greenwood and the romance plots. He then asks, implicitly, whether the minstrels shape the Mortham plot as part of their art or whether it is more objectively "real," more valid a history, than they, who stand within it, can offer. Because the embedded Mortham-narratives involve writing, however, he also raises his recurrent question of the competing validity of oral and written art.

In the first canto, Scott's description of Wilfrid as a pallid and ineffectual minstrel scarcely leads the reader to suspect a strong view of that art—either negative or positive—later in the poem. Through the symmetrical arrangement of the stanzas, Scott condemns him both by contrast and by comparison with his father. In the first stanza, the external landscape bathed in clouded moonlight changes "as a guilty dream, / When conscience, with remorse and fear, / Goads sleeping fancy's wild career." This dream, the vehicle in several following similes, then becomes the tenor. Both characters find themselves in the heightened emotional and imaginative states often symbolized by the moon; but Scott contrasts Wilfrid's usual physical passivity to his father's usual activity at seizing events. As Oswald waits for results from the plotting he later (R, 6:31) calls his "arts," his "emotions" are like the clouds "in wild and strange confusion driven" (R, 1:2, 4). In the last ten stanzas of the canto, Wilfrid's emotions build toward expression in a song to the same moon, though he longs to see it in more "serene" mood. Although Wilfrid has "vainly . . . loved" the kind but uninterested Matilda and has courted her forlornly through his music, his father urges him "to . . . love and woo the . . . heir of Rokeby's knight" in order to further Oswald's own plots—to consolidate his own estate with the adjoining one of Rokeby.

Through Oswald's interview with Bertram, we know that the obvious moral guilt of the father's action has in turn goaded his "Fancy" into action. In Wilfrid's case, however, Fancy has led to the moral guilt that both father and an almost gratuitously censorious narrator impute to him. Though the narrator praises his "minstrel's skill," in which Wilfrid "caught / The art unteachable, untaught" (R, 1:26), he condemns the intuitive and emotional basis of that art with a series of striking images. A far more savage temptress than the flirtatious but kind Matilda, Fancy is a Circean manipulator. In "some wild and lone retreat," she "flung her high spells around his seat," and "gave" him "her opiates . . . to flow / Which he who tastes can ne'er forego . . . , / Till, to the Visionary, seem / Her daydreams truth, and truth a dream" (R, 1:30). A momentarily gentler irony recalls that much of this portrait can be taken as an exaggerated self-portrait: ". . . such a mind / Is soft, contemplative, and kind."[32] Yet the final simile through which Scott portrays his allegorized Spenserian temptress Fancy is even more critical:

> . . . like the bat of Indian brakes,
> Her pinions fan the wound she makes,
> And soothing thus the dreamer's pain,
> She drinks the life-blood from the vein.   [R, 1:32]

In the first image Fancy feeds the poet, not with honeydew or "the milk of Paradise" that inspire the prophetic, even godlike poet in *Kubla Khan*, but with the opiates that Coleridge claims apologetically as partial cause for his own flawed vision. Worse yet, in the second image she becomes a vampire and tastes in her turn.[33] Although Scott's more obvious meaning is that the "life-blood" she takes is the last vestige of common sense and the capacity to act, he also suggests that she drains the visionary capability she gave earlier, as it becomes lost in its own excesses and incapacity for expression. Because he works through simile and personification, he protects Matilda, the actual object of Wilfrid's fantasies, from the mythic role of a temptress defined by misogyny. Yet through the personifications, he explores with much of the same ambiguity the motifs shown in *Thomas the Rhymer*. Instead of allowing Wilfrid to move fully into the visionary landscape with the seductive and perhaps demonic Fancy, Scott keeps him in a world marginally more like ours, so that he faces not a single awakening from dream, as in the greater romantic lyric, but a constant and awkward series of awakenings and new escapes. If his song seems to recognize the "sullen dye" of "a world of war and woe," its second stanza returns to a "serene," "fairy" vision of paradisal love; thus as his father breaks in upon his reveries at the end of the canto, he is once again shocked from dream.[34]

Yet although Scott severely, if sympathetically, criticizes the inaction caused by Wilfrid's thralldom to Fancy, an active, direct use of "the minstrel's magic power" (R, 1:32) threatens in cantos 3 through 5 to prove even more morally culpable. Like Wilfrid, Edmund of Winston owes much of his impulse toward art to unrequited love; but like Wilfrid's father Oswald he practices his art in civil chaos.

At first hearing, his three songs in this canto present an ideal of glamorous freedom "beneath the greenwood bough" (R, 3:19), confirming the robbers in their rebellion from society. The "reckless glee" of his songs thus forms a sharp contrast to "remorse's bitter agony," which he suppresses "with dauntless air, / As one victorious o'er Despair" (R, 3:15). Unlike Wilfrid's more subjective lyrics, then, his art is a public performance in sharp and nearly tragic contrast to his more private feelings. These feelings are not fully private, however, but find enough visual expression in his face and "in his wild notes" for Bertram to find an echo of himself.

Furthermore, his songs themselves show a range of attitudes toward life in the greenwood. The first two show a "glamour" almost in the Scottish sense of the word, a mysterious and nearly otherworldly attraction too eerie to be comfortable. Although all three share the same plot of a would-be robber-bridegroom wooing a girl away from civilization, the first song ends ambiguously, the second ends sadly, and only the third—a more historical than magical ballad—ends with a successful elopement.

In the first song, it is the girl who offers to "roam with Edmund" in the green world of "Greta woods." Surprisingly, he counters her romantic, Spenserian pastoral fantasy of reigning as "summer queen" with his darker vision. The "riddle" he frames (R, 3.16) moves beyond the world of outlawry to that of some natural energy or force, or even to the liminal powers of an elf king. A ranger's "blast is heard at merry morn, / And mine at dead of night"; and "when the beetle sounds his hum, / My comrades take the spear." Finally, he denies his name in an assertion less of legal safety than of myth:

> Maiden! a nameless life I lead,
>   A nameless death I'll die;
> The fiend, whose lantern lights the mead,
>   Were better mate than I!

By telling the girl of his need to forget "what once we were, . . . Nor think what we are now," he implies a very human remorse and suggests that the mythic reverberations of his song are another form of escape from that remorse. Turning back to his refrain, he annihilates all memory of human association to a green thought in a green shade: "Brignal banks are fresh and fair."

His second song shows the fragmentation of an idyllic greenwood world as a pair of lovers parts. Appropriately, the dominant rhetorical figure in the first stanza is an ironic synecdoche that stands not for a larger whole but for just such a fragmentation:

> A weary lot is thine, fair maid,
>   A weary lot is thine!
> To pull the thorn thy brow to braid,
>   And press the rue for wine!
> A lightsome eye, a soldier's mien,
>   A feather of the blue,
> A doublet of the Lincoln green,—
>   No more of me ye knew,
>   My love!
>   No more of me ye knew! [R, 3:28]

Fragments of the natural world must be her clothing and consolation for the remembered fragments of the lover's presence. Here with great effectiveness Scott turns his characteristic style of separate, cumulative parallel grammatical phrases to symbolic purpose.[35] In the second stanza, the speaker's prophecy of the condition for his return contrasts even more strongly with the timelessness of the green world shown in the first song: "The rose," now "budding fair, . . . shall bloom in winter snow, / Ere we two meet again." His hyperbole suggests not only the impossibility of their own meeting again, but also the impossibility of preserving any "garlands" for a "summer queen" in a natural and wintry world. Like such a garland, the lover vanishes; like Cupid leaving Psyche, he has remained more unknown and mysterious than simple concealment of his outlawed state warrants. What inner self, Scott seems to ask, may always remain hidden to the one who loves?[36]

Edmund's third song is also a "riddle" of vocation. Because this song is more specific, it suits the "merry men" far better than do the first two. Yet its parallel negative identifications point beyond the outlaw's freedom from social restraints to a freedom from all limits on his identity. Again, the outlaw in Edmund's song seems a limitless natural, almost supernatural, force: "Allan-a-Dale has no faggot for burning, / Allan-a-Dale has no furrow for turning, / Allan-a-Dale has no fleece for the spinning." When he comes wooing and the mother asks "of his household and home," he replies, "Though the castle of Richmond stand fair on the hill, / My hall . . . shows gallanter still; / 'Tis the blue vault of heaven, with its crescent so pale." In powerfully compressed metaphor, this elemental imagery affects the narrator's description of the parents: "The father was steel, and the mother was stone." Yet their rigidity cannot counter the outlaw's limitless, undefined energy, reflected through the verbal energy of his minstrel's magic, and his "craft" draws the girl away: "She fled to the forest to hear a love-tale" (R, 3:30). Because he is a minstrel, Allan-a-Dale seems the objectified version of Edmund; yet it is worth noting that this wooing, the only successful one of the three songs, conveys its success to us through a turn from lyric lament to rushing dactylic narrative. Further, because the girl has no voice or perspective, and because she disappears not only from her parents' house but from our view as well, much of the haunting tension in the first two songs between the two views of the greenwood, paradisal and nearly demonic, finds release here. In all three of these poems, the male speaker plays an alienating yet enchanting role similar to that which the narrator attributes to Wilfrid's Circe-like Fancy. Yet neither outlaw protagonist nor outlaw singer condemns this escape from rational, civilizing limits.

In canto 5, the public persona called upon in "Allan-a-Dale" dominates all of Edmund's songs, but his songs are neither the only ones, nor the most effective. If the function of his songs in the robbers' cave was to silence "mutinous debate" and keep peace, here their function is to keep a false peace while those outlaws break into Rokeby. The three young people who represent the great households of the neighborhood, however, are also testing their skills at minstrelsy as an ideal. Through most of canto 5, it is Edmund who imposes his carefully calculated fantasy of an "ancient English" minstrel "in mode of olden time" (R, 15) upon his audience. His songs seem to shape the canto with his "melodious plot," to borrow a pun from Keats: the first two are dramatically off-stage (R, 8, 9), the next two center stage (R, 18, 20), and the last (R, 27) yielding the stage, though now unwillingly, to the dark figure of Bertram. Yet the members of his audience, if fascinated by this concrete enactment of their fantasies of minstrelsy, gradually transform Edmund's public performance from falsity toward a new integrity.

We have already examined one cause of their willingness to believe such fantasies: Redmond's Irish history. The narrator's partial account of his childhood in canto 4 prepares us for Redmond's almost Wordsworthian memory of the Irish "Filea" when he hears Edmund's petitioning songs from beyond the gate: "At [the filea's] minstrel-string / My heart from infancy would spring" (R, 5:10). His memories of "the bard's control" over a "stern" group of clansmen and of the bard's honored place in Irish culture are associated with his own place in the scene. As he stood

> . . . by Owen Lysagh's knee
> (The Filea of O'Neale was he,
> A blind and bearded man, whose eld
> Was sacred as a prophet's held),

Redmond could "feel each . . . change of soul" worked by the bard. Because of the bard's cultural as well as personal importance, Redmond's memory turns to a lament for the loss of his country—a loss in which his own banishment from the bard's circle represents the whole culture's and in which "mantling brambles hide" the hearth of Clandeboy where the minstrel sang. Though the meter does not change to show a formal song in these lines (R, 5:10), his speaking from memory has for the moment recreated Owen's circle. Redmond, "in rougher strain, / Would sing of war and warriors slain." The two of them would then triumph over "Old England's bards," "Scotland's vaunted Hawthornden," and even "M'Curtin's harp . . . silenced on Iernian shore." It is Wilfrid's song and Redmond's response that the parody *Jokeby* so conspicuously ignores, since together they propose a positive, not satirical, solution to Irish-English tensions in 1812. In his answer Redmond has effectively redefined both his role in Scott's poem and Scott's own role in writing an "English" poem. Instead of regionally limited songs, he suggests songs that draw upon separate regions and national cultures to create a unified Britain; and Redmond, with combined sensibilities of responsible minstrel and active, loyal fighter, fuses the virtues abused in Wilfrid's and Edmund's earlier portrayals of minstrels.

This vision of future musical, cultural harmony as a model for political harmony moves ahead of the poem's plot, just as it moves ahead of the history Scott writes about most directly here. Before its achievement, the manor house of Rokeby, symbolic of an older order, comes to destruction. Both as an estate and as a building, Rokeby represents a near-desperate continuity with a feudal past: though "the fortress [had been] turn'd to peaceful Hall" (5:3), the civil war has prompted a partial restoration. Yet the restoration only makes more obvious the intractability of time and of these troubled times. "Dismantled . . . and desolate," the hall seems in the moonlight through its "lattic'd oriels" a "Gothic vault," a "funeral cave" (R, 4). As in *Marmion* Scott's sense of looking back in time through the spaces of ruins leads him not only to the full realization of a culture in its prime, but to its anticipations of decay.[37] All its banners lost at Marston Moor, the hall now shows in the moonlight only a few suits of armor, "cumbrous of size, uncouth to sight, / And useless in the modern fight." Yet although the scene seems indeed a funeral of medieval culture, that culture, like the suits of armor and the individual heroism they suggest, looms larger in this nostalgic perspective. And through the musical expression of nostalgia, which Edmund comes to exploit and ends by succumbing to, this "Gothic vault," like the robbers' cave in cantos 3 and 6, is transformed into a place of creativity and new birth. The rebirth pointed to most directly in Matilda's song is the transformation of a feudalism based upon land and buildings to one based on an almost spiritual "constancy":

> Let our halls and towers decay,
> ....
> We but share our Monarch's lot
> ....
> Still in death, defeat, and woe,
>   Ours be loyalty unshaken!
> Let Constancy abide,—
>   Constancy's the gift of heaven. [24]

Much of the effect of her song for the larger audience of the published poem lies in its anticipation of the irreversibility of Stuart exile after 1688, but her song's effect upon Edmund is to make real the feudal and Cavalier loyalties he had been pretending to advocate through his songs.

Edmund's first song, an incantatory advertisement sung outside the gate, draws some power from the hammer-stroke simplicity that corresponds to his knocks on the door. Yet its full effect comes from the ironic contrast of the song to its purpose. Claiming that his "strength" and "art" lie not on the battlefield but with "the peaceful minstrel-string," he then pleads, "Take the weary harper in!" Instead, the inhabitants are taken in by the song.

Once inside, Edmund distracts his audience with dreams "of olden time" (R, 15). Directed ironically at his own life and at Matilda, as well as to the nostalgia of the larger group, the first of his songs inside the house both analyzes and criticizes the dreams of minstrels. In childhood he says, "To musing prone, / I wooed my solitary joy, / My harp alone!" (R, 18). Later, as the speaker in the song gains the attention of a "baron's daughter" and inspires a "presumptuous hope," this implicitly sexual attitude is redirected. Yet after the thwarting of that hope he returns solipsistically to "the spell that lull'd me first, / My harp alone." Like the vampire Fancy that tortures Wilfrid, the harp both tortures and consoles through its dangerous isolation from all other values and commitments.

Yet this overly consoling harp is only the obverse, the dark side, of the elevated "inspiration" that prompts Edmund to sing the song. For surprisingly, the narrator's description of Edmund as he prepares to sing is less ironic than Edmund's own description of his singer:

> All [his] expression base was gone
> When waked the guest his minstrel tone;
> It fled at inspiration's call,
> As erst the demon fled from Saul.
> More noble glance he cast around,
> More free-drawn breath inspired the sound,

> His pulse beat bolder and more high,
> In all the pride of minstrelsy! [R, 17]

Though the effect lasts only as long as "the lay" itself, afterward allowing "the talent, with him born, / To be a common curse and scorn," its inspiration is therapeutic, banishing the demon of his lower self and converting him from Saul to David. Through the biblical allusion, Scott points toward a far more positive source of Edmund's "inspiration" than he has suggested before, one that would offset the charges of Wilfrid's "opiate"-like irrationality in canto 1. Edmund's self-critical song also offers a controlling consciousness to hedge around that inspiration.

Yet that consciousness quickly turns to a dangerous pride in its own complex control of multiple audiences. The lively anapests and loyalist sentiments of the third song, which ends with "a pledge to fair England, her church, and her crown," seem to demonstrate its loyalty to a cause beyond itself. Yet because Edmund's actual case is quite other than the one he overtly celebrates, the effect of this artistic prostitution is to increase "the hireling bard's" self-absorption in his minstrelsy: "The conscious pride of art / Had steel'd him in his treacherous part." Again, at the end of the stanza, the narrator comments, "What against pity arms his heart?— / It is the conscious pride of art" (R, 22). Here consciousness is anything but redemptive.

With one further twist of irony, Edmund is pulled out of this powerfully amoral concentration upon "his own successful skill" by Matilda's resemblance to a figure in the literary romance he, like Wilfrid, had constructed for himself. She appears "a princess fair," needing the help of "a destined hero's conquering sword" to be "to her rightful realm restored" (R, 5:25). For a moment Edmund finds himself in a romantic paradise. Like Adam dreaming, in the Miltonic image Keats repeatedly uses, he "awoke and found" his dream "truth."

Through the discovery of this sudden correlative reality, his dreams urge him to become a hero by a conquering word—by a final song that will warn his audience of Bertram's arrival. Yet in spite of his attempt to preserve the paradise, its Satan already lurks in the shadows. Edmund's final song, designed now not to signal Bertram but to "wear away the time" (R, 5:26), converts the biblical analogue of Adam's dream to a Gothic conjuring. By exploiting the situation of a "friar of orders gray" forced to "shrive" a woman who is then apparently murdered, Edmund suggests a developing parallel between the friar's situation and his own. Both possess powers beyond themselves, and both find themselves using their powers in morally ambiguous situations. Before meeting Matilda, Edmund was of course a volunteer among the robbers; now he opposes the action he has begun. In contrast, the friar in his ballad has apparently been forced into abetting a murderer who possesses a strong sense of ritual, but no sense of morality. If the monk had denied the sacrament of confession, it is not clear whether he could have saved the woman's life, and he would have risked endangering her soul. The murderer threatens that if the monk does not "shrive her free," her parting spirit will "fling all its guilt on thee" (R, 5:27). By excluding the Friar's state of mind entirely, Edmund's ballad does not allow us to see his anxious awareness of the moral dilemma; he is literally and psychologically blindfolded. Thus, almost paradoxically, his friar seems more an accomplice than does the similar character in either of the sources Scott notes. In its last two stanzas the ballad turns to the external, dramatic evidence for the murderer's state of mind:

> He looks pale as clay, and strives to pray,
> If he hears the convent bell.
> . . . .
> If he meet a Friar of orders grey,
> He droops and turns aside.

In a final justification of Edmund's external point of view, any semblance of that friar who was forced to participate in his crime also becomes an avenging demon: the outward image is fully sufficient for such haunting.

If we pursue the analogy between friar and minstrel, then Edmund has announced his own future as such an avenging or guardian demon. Events immediately following his song, however, convert this image of the friar into one of Gothic malevolence in the tradition of *The Monk* or *The Italian*. When the song ends, Matilda cries out, "Harper! methinks thy magic lays . . . can goblins raise!" She claims that her "fancy can discern . . . a visage stern . . . A human form distinct and clear"—but she then discovers its reality (R, 5:28). As Bertram seems to step out of the song, Edmund's delaying tactics have only increased the dramatic effect of his arrival. Yet, whether or not we assume Bertram overhears the song, it points toward his eventual similarity not to the Gothic villain but, like Edmund, to the avenging friar—or to a more active figure, a romantic hero, redeeming himself by countering the evil he had once countenanced.

In canto 6, no minstrel sings; but Edmund's retrospective analysis of his role at Rokeby makes the minstrel's calling a crucial part of the poem's conclusion. Furthermore, because the complicated narratives he tells in this canto are based on written scrolls and build toward the meaning of Redmond's tokens, inscribed "in the Irish tongue," the tension between song and document becomes stronger and must be resolved in a more modern definition of the minstrel's role. If this theme emerges from Edmund's guilt at the misuse of his gift, the responsive echo that his guilt finds in Bertram develops a means of expiation.

Scott's opening focus in canto 6 upon the yet unnamed Edmund's "solitary form . . . Gliding by crag and copsewood green" (*R*, 6:3) and entering the robbers' cave sounds strikingly like the description of Bertram in canto 3. As "lower and lower he descends" toward the cave, the narrator reads his face as he read Bertram's in canto 1:

> That stripling shape, that cheek so pale,
> Combine to tell a rueful tale,
> Of powers misused, of passion's force,
> Of guilt, of grief, and of remorse! [*R*, 6:3]

Yet the narrator's account of this satanic descent "lower and lower" is not only external but extraneous, since Edmund's own self-condemnation goes on to challenge the danger of interpreting superficial appearances and of creating fictions. If the narrator's perspective is like Milton's Uriel viewing "Satan disfigur'd" on Mount Niphates, Edmund is a far more repentant Satan. Among the cave's "masks and disguises grim'd with mud," he sees his own "peasant-dress . . . doff'd to assume that quaint disguise; / And, shudd'ring, thought upon his glee, / When prank'd in garb of minstrelsy."

Now repentant, he goes on to describe his errors in the lines quoted at the beginning of this chapter, lines more metaphysical in phrasing than any yet used in the poem:

> 'O, be the fatal art accurst,'
> He cried, 'that moved my folly first;
> Till, bribed by bandits' base applause,
> I burst through God's and Nature's laws!' [*R*, 6:5]

In painful contrast to his memory "of comrades' cheer, / That general laugh . . . as I rehearsed my treacherous part," he now sees himself as "murderer," responsible for the death of those comrades. He also holds himself responsible for the burning of Rokeby, though his final song was recognized belatedly as a warning and led through Matilda's intervention to his own safety. Thus, he has violated the divine law against killing and the human law against challenging the social establishment, represented by Rokeby and its family. In an exact and literal reading, the line is concerned with the moral effect of his "fatal art." Its phrasing also, however, as I suggested at the beginning of the chapter, points toward the terrors and the possibilities of the visionary imagination as Shelley, Blake, and Coleridge describe them. The satanic and Promethean energy of Edmund's "fatal art" seems capable of redefining both the moral and the physical shape of the universe, as Coleridge's poet in "Kubla Khan" would build both dome and cave with his music. Appropriately, as in Coleridge's poem, Edmund's largest, most radical claim for his art is fenced around both by more conventional judgments and by circumstances now past. Edmund on the surface wholly condemns his "folly," though the splendor of his language recalls the exhilaration of his earlier power and his "conscious pride of art." Edmund does not explicitly claim the power of building for his art, though Scott has jokingly done so; but through his repentance and Bertram's, the ruins of Rokeby and Egliston can house new life for their neighborhood.

Here, as in canto 5, his art calls up a concrete figure of its own anarchy: the recalling of his ambiguous powers conjures up Bertram once more. Through a series of oral and written narratives, however, his repentance aids Bertram's own, harnessing the demonic energies of that giant figure to the services of a purged art. The steel casket Edmund unearths from the cave and the narratives he recounts to Bertram contain written messages that demand interpretation and that complete the links forged earlier in the poem between the Mortham family history and writing. In a self-critical exploration of imagination, minstrelsy and song have dominated cantos 1, 3, and 5. Written inscriptions or documents suggest in cantos 2, 4, and 6 a more certain, historical basis to set against fantasy and imagination. Yet the completed story of the Mortham family is an almost archetypally pure romance. Moreover, the discovery of its "romance" ending is made by the minstrel Edmund. One might argue that Scott has simply given up the "real" world of historical event and retreated into popular formula. Instead, however, it seems clear that the minstrel's songs, at first delaying escapes from the more realistic demands of history, have taught us to read history's narratives not as isolated facts but as romantic or mythic patterns, which point in this larger narrative beyond death—of the individual, or of the limited, written word—into rebirth. Edgar Johnson is surely right to see Mortham's narrative as a version of *Othello* and of its romance extension, *The Winter's Tale*.[38] In *The Lady of the Lake* Scott modifies the pattern of Shakespeare's middle romantic comedies, a venture from history as reality into the green world of romance and then a return, by showing that the "green world" holds historical realities to be controlled by acknowledging and using romance forms. In *Rokeby* he uses the pattern of the late romances to reshape the writings of an apparent history, though a private family history, toward romance, and the minstrels are crucial agents in this process. The minstrels and their romances are in one sense, however, only intermediaries who allow the history of one age to be reinterpreted as a paradigm or "epitome," to use Sidney's word, for a later age. Finally, the more visionary minstrels, Edmund and Wilfrid, along with the more flamboyant satanic hero Bertram become victims not of the vampire Imagination but of the vampire History. They provide the imaginative lifeblood for the rebirth of Redmond not only as political minstrel but as political model for an active landowner.

The imagistic pattern through which Scott works out this story begins in canto 3 with the raw materials—the sensationalistic cliches, in fact—of Gothic romance and pirate adventure story. Thinking that he has killed Mortham in battle, Bertram sets out with Wilfrid to seize his former companion's treasure. The "form" that shadows him and then disappears behind the Mortham family tomb he believes to be Mortham's ghost, guarding the "hoard" of his "Indian wealth" as "skeleton and Skull" guarded the pirate hoards of "Raleigh, Frobisher, or Drake." In this setting Mortham's name begins to seem a pun on "mort" or "death." His estate, as well, seems so neglected that the family tomb is its appropriate focus: the "huge boughs" of "two mighty elms"

> . . . in arches bent
> Above a massive monument,
> Carved o'er in ancient Gothic wise,
> With many a scutcheon and device. [R, 2:17]

This landscape echoes a typical mourning picture of the time. As Bertram stands "pondering" beside it, he is unable to interpret the heraldic signs that tell the history of the Mortham family in quasi-hieroglyphics because he is unable to interpret as a living being the "warlike form" that suddenly reappears from behind it. Whispering to Wilfrid, "Tell thou none that Mortham lives," Mortham delays his physical return to public life until his family history, like the signs on his family tomb, can be read and interpreted.

The first stage of this interpretation is quite literally a reading. Describing Mortham's "despondence" to Wilfrid and Redmond in canto 4, Matilda explains that before going into battle he has left in her charge a "treasure huge of gems and gold" and "this disjointed dismal scroll, / That tells the secret of his soul" (R, 4:18). Without realizing it, Matilda has become the object both of Oswald's desire for treasure as land and Bertram's desire for treasure as cash. Yet because Bertram and Guy Denzil overhear her reading from Mortham's scroll, her reading becomes a means of redirecting these corrupted motivations—and, ultimately, of redefining the Mortham treasure from disoriented pirate wealth to human relationships. When this happens, the guilt attached to storytelling as buried treasure in *Marmion* and the guilt attached to seeking land and money may in part be assuaged.

Earlier in canto 4 the narrator's extended introduction of Redmond has apparently set the scene only for Matilda's problem in choosing between her two suitors. Because their rivalry in love leads so well into the Othello-like jealousy described in Mortham's narrative, we temporarily forget to match the two ten-stanza narratives, the first explaining Redmond's arrival on the scene as an Irish foundling (R, 4:6-15) and the second chronicling the loss of Mortham's child after the misguided killing of his wife (R, 4:19-28). As we learn from his scroll, Mortham's tragedy is both a literal and psychological example of Aristotle's *hamartia*, of a "shaft mis-aimed" (R, 4:21). Intending to kill his wife's apparent suitor, he also kills his wife; his intentions are misguided because the stranger is in fact his wife's brother newly arrived from Ireland. Because Mortham's narrative is emotionally disjointed and because it continues to conceal the Irish origins of his wife, however, even Matilda's reading does not complete the interpretation of his story from tragedy into romance. The narrator, too, has concealed some crucial aspects of Redmond's history earlier in the canto because he stays within the limited knowledge of Rokeby, Matilda, and Redmond himself.

Not until canto 6, when Edmund descends into the robbers' cave and unearths the mysterious casket, are these narratives drawn together. Framing the narratives, that setting becomes a place of creative origins like one of Shelley's "caves of Poesy," converting a tangle of false and true oral narratives and of false and true scrolls into a reborn truth. Seen as a Miltonic hell in canto 3, the cave itself now recalls for Edmund, the narrator suggests, the final toast drunk there by the bandits: "To Rokeby treasure-vaults!" And yet, he recalls, "They found in Rokeby vaults their doom, / A bloody death, a burning tomb!" As he digs up the casket with the "chain and reliquaire of gold," this cave becomes a treasure vault. Its most important treasure, however, is not the gold but what the gold tablets, and the Marmion-like web of fictions Edmund recounts, go on to reveal.

No less than four written messages, three of them "scrolls" and the fourth the gilt tablets in the casket, play significant parts in Edmund's complicated narrative to Bertram. Edmund is not the only one to use the biblical-sounding "scroll" or the equally biblical-sounding "tablets." The effect of this repeated vocabulary is to intensify the burden of truth placed upon these pieces of writing, to emphasize difficulties of exegesis, and finally to point, with their directionality, toward a kind of resurrection.[39] The first and fourth of these, in the order of Edmund's narrative to Bertram, are false documents prepared by Oswald's "arts";

the second and third reveal newly-recognized truths. A false story told at the beginning of Edmund's sequence of narratives, before he explains the "scrolls," involves Edmund in its toils but also foreshadows the final truth to emerge: Denzil has unscrupulously claimed the young minstrel as his son in order to leave him as hostage with Oswald and thus gain his own freedom. To bring about the "gentle restraint" that would persuade Rokeby to accept Wilfrid as a son-in-law, Oswald then "school'd" this false father and son in a "well-forg'd" tale to show that Rokeby had broken parole and must be more closely imprisoned. Yet no sooner is the "fatal charge" of that tale "scroll'd and sign'd" and Rokeby thrown into chains, than "in midst of Wycliffe's well-feign'd rage, / A scroll was offer'd by a page," who explains that a "muffled horseman" has left it.

With the arrival of this true scroll countering his false one, Oswald's "mimic passion . . . was turn'd to actual agony." Seeing his own elaborate plots and their supporting fictions begin to collapse, he enunciates Scott's nearly apocalyptic theme of rebirth through prophetic art: "As in the pageants of the stage, / The dead awake in this wild age, . . . Mortham has 'scaped!"[40] Mortham's letter, left by the mysterious horseman, works this archetypal pattern even more deliberately: "Though dead, thy victim lives to thee." In his own scroll, however, Mortham threatens to reveal that he is still alive and ready to reclaim his lands from Wycliffe only if the latter—whom he believes an Iago to his wife-murdering Othello years before—does not reveal the fate of Mortham's missing son. Thus he withholds one official rebirth—his own—for, he now hopes, another—his son's.

Although Oswald claims ignorance, Denzil explains that he possesses the evidence and has hidden it in the cave where his robbers have been living. That evidence, too, is written. Along with a gold chain, the casket unearthed by Edmund contains, as Denzil explains, "gilt tablets . . . With letters in the Irish tongue." Yet like the readers of Scott's narrative, Denzil could not interpret the words until he had overheard Matilda read Mortham's history in canto 4. "And now," he tells Oswald, "I can interpret well . . . / Each syllable the tablets tell." Knowledge of this written truth, however, generates still further falsity: to deceive Mortham about the fate of his son, now prisoner of war in Barnard Castle, Wycliffe writes still another false "scroll," implying that the missing child is "o'er the main." To control Denzil he sends Edmund, the man Denzil has falsely claimed as his son, both to deliver the second false scroll to Mortham (R, 6:26) and to find in the cave written evidence for Denzil's story about the true son.

Because Edmund as minstrel confronts a renewed sense of his responsibility as poet, these final attempts at false evidence fail, and the true documents he finds in the cave redefine the Mortham family history: from the heraldic inscriptions on the family tomb, through Mortham's own confused autobiographical scroll and his letter of threatened rebirth, to the final discovery of the casket and its tablets identifying Redmond O'Neale as his lost son.

Although thematically significant, however, Edmund's conversion is not fully sufficient to stop Wycliffe's final intention either of executing Redmond and Rokeby for supposedly breaking their parole or of using that threat to force a marriage between Matilda and his son. All of these problems of interpreting scrolls, tablets, and other written texts come to a dramatic crisis in the ironically appropriate setting of the monastic ruins of Egliston. There Scott's devious villain Oswald Wycliffe seems to act out a Protestant and Puritan morality play that parodies the work of the reformer John Wycliffe, who was in fact a native of the same neighborhood.[41] Because these written evidences of Mortham family history demand independent translation but reinforce family history—and are completed by Edmund, outcast of moral culture—they are alien neither to Puritan nor to traditional attitudes toward religious texts. Yet Scott's Wycliffe seems to view them as open to his own radical, self-aggrandizing interpretation, as he prepares to behead O'Neale and Rokeby almost on the altar of a church already desecrated by the "sacrilegious crime" of Puritan forces (R, 27). Now, among those ruins of "the Civil fury of the time," "Where once the priest, of grace divine, / Dealt to his flock the mystic sign; / There stood the block display'd." The dramatic entrance of the reformed and redemptive Bertram halts this new sacrilege without returning it to "mystic sign" and allows the true written history to triumph in its romancelike plot of rebirth.

Even if prepared for by his encounter with Edmund in the robbers' cave, Bertram's arrival seems a sacrifice of character development to narrative closure. In a sense it is, but so are Wilfrid's and Edmund's roles. All three are sacrificed to, or absorbed into, the reestablished life of Redmond and the renewed civilization he has come to represent. Because Bertram is the most active physical force in the poem, everyone's agent of power or energy, and because Scott repeatedly describes him as gigantic, it is tempting to consider him as a kind of "giant form" like one of Blake's four zoas, a force of imaginative or libidinal energy breaking out in rebellion. As a character, however, he is less single than such Blakean forces. The anguished division with which he views his own role as outlaw ties him both to Marmion, in the earlier poem, and to Mortham and Edmund within this one.

Two pairings of names reinforce this almost Blakean contrariety of opposition fused into a new union. Mortham, as already suggested, sounds like *mort*, or death, and he indeed seems to have been living in an almost deathlike state. Rhyming with Mortham, Bertram's name suggests "birth," as does the name of his own birthplace, Risingham. As we have seen, by trying to kill Mortham he acts as a catalyst for a series of events that bring about the rebirth of Mortham himself and of his family. It is important to note, however, that this ironic contravening of intentions does not last: for Bertram, like Mortham, undergoes a sort of conversion. The pressures toward this conversion are several: his new knowledge of Denzil's and Oswald's intended treachery toward Mortham—to which he responds as if only he, Bertram, had the right to attack his alter ego; his sympathy for Edmund, as if the minstrel's expression of remorse allows him to recognize his own; and a fatalistic but highly individual sense of approaching death. In a single stanza, Scott modulates from satanic to sorrowful images as Bertram recognizes how his allegiances have been twisted (R, 6:19). Although this recognition comes under the pressure of that already-experienced sense of approaching fate, it seems almost as if the recognition is the fate. It is as if his own vitality has gone to the reborn Mortham and his family, and he must himself die.

His final appearance fulfills this fate: "Through the Gothic arch there sprung / A horseman arm'd, at headlong speed— / Sable his cloak, his plume, his steed." Like a figure of doom, of final judgment, whose "tread / Hath wak'd the dwelling of the dead," he takes advantage of surprise to kill Wycliffe but is then killed himself. Ironically, his attempt to kill Mortham at Marston Moor had prevented father and son from meeting in battle (R, 2:25). Now his dying, finally, saves Redmond for reconciliation with his father. Thus Redmond, falling heir to the Mortham fortunes, also falls heir to Bertram's active physical energies.

He also falls heir to the artistic strengths of the two other minstrels. In a moment of great dignity, Wilfrid fulfills his earlier prophecy and dies at the Eglinton altar, in order to yield Matilda to Redmond, her other cousin. He also, in effect, yields his romantic sensibilities to be remembered and incorporated in their relationship, his weakness transformed by Redmond's greater energy and stronger, more militant cultural imagination. Although Edmund's yielding the bays—or the harp—to Redmond involves no such specific sacrifice, his vigorous but misused minstrel's art has offered a model of what that art might accomplish. After his discovery of the gilt tablets that prove Redmond's identity through their Irish engraving, he has no further role in the poem; he does not even appear in its final scene at the abbey. If we follow Ruth Eller's suggestion that Scott repeatedly gives his "poetic" characters who represent the active imagination names beginning with "E," then Edmund is undoubtedly the focus of this poem's commentary upon imagination.[42] That focus, however, is absorbed by the end of the poem into Scott's ideal fusion of action and imagination, of minstrel and his landholder and patron, the revised Edmund whose name becomes Redmond.

In another sense we might argue that as the genre of romance fulfills its demands for regeneration and reconciliation through that astounding sequence of scrolls and tablets, the oral tradition of a courtly minstrelsy in great houses, exiled and outlawed in canto 3 and falsely represented in canto 5, can itself find regeneration only through writing. Edmund's unearthing of the gilt tablets becomes, through Scott's own writing, a final step in the admittedly nostalgic and ambiguous rebirth of the power of minstrelsy. Finally, this country house poem, though less gemlike in execution than Marvell's "Upon Appleton House," uses its now-historical seventeenth-century setting to offer a similar model of order through the microcosm of a local estate. Nor does the conservatism of Morritt or of Scott himself as guardians of their estates stand in the way of his radically unifying vision for his own time, a vision that linked Fairfax's followers to those of the king, but also links, for his own time, Irish Catholic to Puritan to Anglican. The very nostalgic conventionality of his poem's conclusion softens but cannot quite hide this hope.

FIVE

The Bridal of Triermain
"FRAGMENTS OF . . . RIFTED STONE"

SCOTT'S DECISION to publish *Harold the Dauntless* in 1817 not as a separate poem but as the second volume of the still-anonymous *Bridal of Triermain* establishes more than a material bond between the two poems. Each of Scott's other poems first appeared in a magnificent four hundred- to five hundred-page quarto volume. In contrast, the volumes first of *Triermain* in 1813 and then of *Triermain* and *Harold* in 1817 are octavos, and each contains only about two hundred pages.[1] Almost pocket size, the lightweight volumes seem more appropriate for an individual, private reading. Lockhart conjectures that in this less-expensive format they may have been intended to rival Byron's romances, which were selling so effectively in octavo editions.[2]

A further physical resemblance between the two volumes also points toward a rivalry with Byron. When Scott published *Harold the Dauntless* as the companion to *The Bridal*, he arranged to have the later poem printed on an additional supply of the paper used for the earlier one. Watermarked 1812, that paper could only prove that *Harold* was printed no earlier than that. Yet through its use, Scott implies that it was written no later and thus that it was uninfluenced even by the first two cantos of Byron's *Childe Harold*, much less by the third. Offering manuscript evidence for a later date of composition, James Hillhouse thus argues for Scott's desire to claim priority for his *Harold*.[3] Another interpretation of the choice of paper is that it emphasized the pairing of Scott's two anonymous poems. If the first was intended as a light-hearted imitation of Scott himself, the second might be considered a similarly playful tribute to that other current master of poetic romance, Byron. Thus the 1812 printer's paper and the early 1817 publication date of *Harold the Dauntless* enclose a poetic career that Scott first parodies and then analyzes sympathetically and seriously in his poem.

At first glance the narratives in these two volumes seem anything but serious. Critics have generally found them as lightweight as their bindings.[4] Far shorter than Scott's other narrative poems, they blithely ignore the detailed historical context so important in those poems. Anchored neither by the major historical battles shown in *Marmion, Rokeby*, and the intervening *Lord of the Isles*, nor by the details of sixteenth-century clan violence shown in *The Lay* and *The Lady of the Lake*, these two poems are free to drift or wander through more overtly romantic milieux and episodes. In the anonymous introduction to *The Bridal*, a prefatory essay that remains in the 1817 two-volume edition, Scott and Erskine claim that the genre of romance is not concerned with the public, epic events that shape a nation's history but with the private crises of individuals within domestic relationships. We have already seen that Scott makes a similar claim in the almost simultaneously-published *Rokeby*, and that there it proved only partially true. In its intricate plot, the local family crises come to symbolize the larger political and religious conflict within which they are so carefully placed. The other distinction between epic and romance developed in the *Triermain* preface applies even less well to *Rokeby*. Within the private sphere the author is free to use any "supernatural machinery" he wishes, following not the standards of probability or realism but his own "pleasure." If an empirically-based history has taken over from epic the terrain of retelling a nation's public past, fantasy may still reign in the narration of private crises and their resolutions. Yet in *Rokeby* the only fantasy, the only elements of the supernatural, are located within the troubled minds of realistically-developed, if domestically-focused, characters.

In the two anonymous poems, on the other hand, fantasy and supernatural episodes appear not only in the minds of the characters but in the outward narratives of their actions. Although in *Triermain* the outer narrative acts, as in the *Lay*, to provide a distancing frame for the fantasy of the inner narratives, both its inner narratives and the main narrative of *Harold the Dauntless* are full of glamour and gramarye. So far, then, these poems fit the preface's definitions of romance. Its distinction between public and private, however, is more difficult to apply. The outer, modern narrative of *The Bridal* is indeed a "private" story, the courtship of a Regency heiress by a professional and poor soldier. Yet as we move inward and back in time, the narrative becomes both more fantastic and more public in its subject matter. The soldier, Arthur, tells two interlocking stories to charm his heiress into eloping with him. The first of these, set in the early fourteenth century, describes a border knight, Sir Roland de Vaux of Triermain, who neglects his usual border warfare for the private quest of a woman seen only in his dreams. To interpret his dream, Sir Roland consults a bard. The bard's narrative explains that the woman is the daughter of King Arthur and an enchantress and has herself been enchanted for five hundred years. Even if King Arthur's dalliance is in some sense a private affair, this poem as well as larger treatments of the Arthurian material insists upon the relationship, often tragic, between public and private commitments. The narrative of *Harold the Dauntless* takes up a major historical conflict, the conversion of the Danelaw to Christianity, but refuses to treat it either in ancient epic-historical terms or modern empirical-historical terms. Instead, romance moves outward and uses that rough framework of outer historical conflict for its own development. Both of these poems celebrate their "freedom" from epic as a genre and from history as a criterion of truth. Both, too, use the subject matter and the narrative techniques of ancient romance in order to explore, at first playfully but ultimately with some seriousness, the fantasies held within modern, subjective selves. Finally, because of their very lack of historical development, they are able to focus more closely, through the symbolic structures of romance, upon the inner, individual change from a subjectively indulgent self to a socially disciplined one.

Although their neomedieval verse form and medieval subject matter made both poems easily recognizable as Scott imitations,[5] the framework of their presentation to the public carefully distances them from specific authorial origin as well as from specific historical contexts. Both poems remained anonymous until 1819.[6] Further, in a striking departure from Scott's usual practice, no antiquarian notes frame the main narrative with modern, historically-conscious commentary: *Triermain* has only seven notes, those unusually brief, and *Harold* has none. Neither poem has even the brief preface or "advertisement" that places each of the other long poems in a precise historical and geographical setting. True, the poems are not quite orphaned from all origins. In the 1813 Preface to *The Bridal*, an anonymous persona looks back to his earlier fragment published in the 1809 *Annual Register*, though the persona is less developed and certainly less comic than the *Register*'s Caleb Quotem.[7] The same anonymous author later announces himself on the title page of *Harold the Dauntless* (1817, vol. 2) as "The Author of *The Bridal of Triermain*."

Even though the geographical settings of the two poems are not elaborated upon in prefatory material, they are complementary. The poems share symmetrical northern English locations, *Triermain* in Cumberland and *Harold* further east in Durham. Close to the Scottish borders, these locations of course resemble those of Scott's longer narrative poems. At first reading *Harold* also seems to complement *Triermain* in the use of primitive literary and cultural models, drawing upon Scandinavian saga to balance the earlier poem's use of originally Celtic Arthurian romance. The more specific settings of the two poems, however, resemble one another in a way that points beyond complementarity toward an underlying unity both of place and of genre. For their critical episodes, both poems dramatize the protagonist's solitary testing in a magical castle inhabited by witches or enchantresses.

Medieval castles have scarcely been absent from Scott's other major narrative poems. Like Spenser, he deploys them to establish an alternating and often ironic contrast between nature and culture. Yet Scott usually calls his castles by their own historically resonant names and places them in the actual flow of their strategic geography and history both before and after the events of the narrative.[8] In *The Bridal* and *Harold*, however, Scott follows Spenser more closely. He turns from actual to visionary castles, and from epic or chronicle history to a more direct use of medieval and Renaissance romance. In the first four poems and in *The Lord of the Isles*, the narrative patterns of romance are displaced into, or enclosed within, more realistic modes of representation. In this pair of poems, there is scarcely any displacement from the archetypal, external quest romance. Although that narrative action is directly presented, however, its encounters in magical castles are, as in many medieval narratives, symbolic confrontations. In both *Triermain* and *Harold*, questers enter castles that seem to be visionary extensions of their desire to find them and that confront both questers and readers with the challenge of interpreting the alien figures encountered there as part of the darker mythologies of their own minds.

These poems suggest two dominant thematic interpretations of the visionary castle and its inhabitants, both of which emerge from traditional interpretations of the motif in medieval romance. Each of these represents a different kind of internalization. One of these is suggested by an addition Scott evidently made in proof to *The Bridal*. At the beginning of canto 3 he added several lines of the ballad fragment, "Child Roland to the Dark Tower came."[9] Inevitably, the fragment makes us think of *King Lear* and of the confrontations resulting from Edgar's feigned and Lear's real madness: the dark tower becomes an internalized bedlam.

Both in *Harold* and in *The Bridal*, the magical castle also suggests another range of symbolic meaning, a tradition in the medieval iconography of the *hortus conclusus* as well as in the verbal, yet spatializing allegory of the *Roman de la Rose*. This tradition also appears in Spenser and Tasso, as well as Thomas the Rhymer. If the darkness, the blood, and then the paradisal garden of Elfland in some sense represent the elf queen herself and her entrancing, alienating sexual power, the castles of these two romances may also symbolize the female body. Scott makes use of no explicit allegory but rather of the psychological patterns that lie behind the mixture of fascination and terror in such a metaphor.

One way to link these two readings is to note that in both poems the consciousness of the male protagonist, though enclosed in and imaged by the castle, becomes vulnerable to some magical power associated with enchantresses or witches. Here Jill Rubenstein's suggestion that *The Bridal of Triermain* is a trial of imagination becomes particularly significant.[10] Entangled in this trial, however, is that fundamental problem of how we and the protagonists of the poems read or place the power of enchantment. Are those enchantresses inhabitants, if still unrecognized ones, of his mind? Are they manifestations of the forces of nature, seen as a sexual "other"? Or are the enchantresses as real as the questers but made unreal by the quester's alienating mythology? Freed by his anonymity from the responsibilities of an exact historical setting and from his usual restrained depiction of creativity, Scott can explore more directly the seductions of romance as a genre as well as the questions of gender and authority in matters of imagination. To explore these seductions ourselves, we should turn first to *The Bridal of Triermain*.

In spite of the lightness with which it wears its historicism, *The Bridal of Triermain* is indeed, as Jill Rubenstein argues, carefully structured to differentiate the three historical eras of its enclosed narratives. Each successive hero in time—King Arthur, Sir Roland, the modern Arthur—must struggle harder to realize his imaginative vision. Though in a more inward, subjective way than is usual for his poetry, the poem illustrates Scott's characteristic theme of gradual amelioration or progress in history. Yet though the trials of imagination are indeed central, they cannot be neatly linked to a sequence of improvement in the heroes through time. As Rubenstein argues, Sir Roland de Vaux of Triermain develops through his adventure in the castle of St. John not only a fierce faith in the making real of imaginative vision, but a steadfast and honorable character. Both characteristics show progress over those of King Arthur, whose adventures of five hundred years earlier form the narrative told to Sir Roland and lead to the improvement of his character. Because the modern Arthur narrates both of these stories to the woman he loves, his own imagination is brilliantly evident, and it is probably fair to assume that he recognizes the moral difference between his two protagonists. Yet a similar perceptiveness also belonged to *Rokeby*'s Edmund and was no guarantee, until the end of the poem, of his moral amelioration and his capacity, as a minstrel, to ameliorate the lives of others. Rubenstein suggests that Sir Roland de Vaux's world, the middle era between the two more corrupt worlds of the early medieval King Arthur and the modern soldier Arthur, illustrates Scott's characteristic pattern of amelioration. Before we grant the progressive, improving nature of Roland's, then the modern Arthur's imagination, we must look more closely at the intertwined development of these three chronologically different narratives and their varying effects on the audiences each is intended for. Not only do these effects vary from one part of a narrative to another, as the outer, diegetic narrative breaks in on its intra-and metadiegetic levels; but the completion and interpretation of one narrative sometimes makes its audience reconsider an already-completed narrative. This process of rereading is a process of hermeneutic interpreting that moves toward allegorizing. If we look at the narratives in this way, we can see not only that the protagonists move away from a mythic toward a more self-conscious perception,[11] but also that this process ties the problems of moral choice to the need to interpret art.

One of the most astonishing influences of this narrative interdependence is the modern narrator's accomplishment of his purpose—charming an heiress to elope with him—before he has completed his story of Sir Roland and, even more surprisingly, before he has proved its morality. If designed to reassure her that her choice was not irresponsible, his completed narrative does indeed serve that function—but we must keep in mind that it was the earlier Arthurian narrative that the bard Lyulph tells Roland, and not Roland's own more moral quest for the king's enchanted daughter, that shaped her choice to elope. We learn about that choice in the introduction to canto 3; and not until that canto does the new husband begin his narrative of Roland's actual journey to the enchanted castle where his dream-woman sleeps. Although the serious social consequences of elopement appear fully in Jane Austen's novels,[12] the wonderful fantasy of the romance episodes in *Triermain* seems to have persuaded both Scott's fictional modern heiress Lucy and his modern readers to overlook such difficulties. In spite of Morritt's and Lady Louisa Stuart's warnings that some readers would resent the modern Arthur's criticism of aristocratic society as trivial, most critics praised the poem's moral delicacy.[13] Presumably, they were affected by the completion of Sir Roland's tale in canto 3—or else they considered all three narratives as belonging to the realm of romance where such things freely occur.

How, then, should we understand Lucy's response to the earlier stages of her suitor's narrative? By examining more fully the steps backward into myth and then forward into the demythologizing of its enchantresses, we may understand more clearly her enthrallment by her Arthur-author's narrative imagination—and possibly her recognition and freedom from it.

After the 1813 Preface, celebrating the avoidance of public history and its epic battles, the poem opens in the present with the modern narrator, the soldier Arthur, charming the heiress Lucy through his storytelling. Drawing her away from the elegant Regency country house and its "lofty dome," evidence of a society with which he cannot compete directly, this author draws his Lucy into the privacy of a wooded part of the estate and there begins his inner narratives. His addresses to Lucy form an eight-stanza introduction before canto 1, where his first narrative begins. That story, set roughly five hundred years earlier, introduces Sir Roland, whose historical milieu in the medieval border country is briefly but specifically indicated. Such a place, and even such a knight, did exist in fact,[14] and Arthur refers realistically to Roland's border forays "against the Scot" (*BT*, 1:2) and to the "frost-fog grey, / That like a silvery crape was spread / Round Skiddaw's dim and distant head" (*BT*, 1:3).

His narrative, however, is modeled not on the riding or raiding ballads but on those Scott calls "romantic." Roland's visionary desires reach beyond real places. Content with no actual woman, he is haunted by a visionary figure, a Diana-like huntress. As if to suggest the anomaly of such a haunting among moss troopers, even his minstrels hear only their own notes and not her strange music. Both the visionary woman and the mysterious harp note that announces her appearance manifest themselves only to Roland. To mediate between the historical and the visionary, Scott's modern soldier narrator employs two intermediate narrators. More accurately, Sir Roland employs them both, recognizing their potentiality for receiving and interpreting vision: he sends his trustiest page to ask a "sage of power" for his interpretation of the vision.

Roland's instructions to the page include, like a recitation of his credentials, a realistic and yet symbolically evocative history of how the page entered his service. Rescued by Roland

>   . . . from the sack of Hermitage,
>   When that dark castle, tower, and spire,
>   Rose to the skies a pile of fire,
>   And redden'd all the Nine-Stane Hill,   [*BT*, 1:6]

the page is reborn from that place of death and is thus the readier to hear the sage Lyulph's strange description of a castle that ambiguously combines life and death. Lyulph, Sir Roland tells him, is descended from "Druid sires, / And British bards," those believed to have built Nine-stane Hill and "Mayburgh's mound and stones of power," past which the page rides to find him. Thus the sage "the characters can trace, / Graven deep in elder time / Upon Helvellyn's cliffs sublime; / Sign and sigil well doth he know." Interpretation of these ambiguous signs in the natural landscape becomes increasingly important as a basis for interpreting the narratives that follow, for both nature and the half-natural enchantresses are alienated others that the male protagonists—questing knights or author—must interpret.

After the page finds Lyulph "on the fragment of a rock, / Struck from its base by lightning" (*BT*, 1:8), the sage tells his Arthurian tale, a metadiegetic narrative now twice removed from the direct or diegetic level of Scott's own narrative. It begins in stanza 10 of canto 1 and continues without interruption by either audience until canto 2, stanza 27. Scott—or his soldier-narrator Arthur—avoids representing one further enclosure by having us hear Lyulph's tale as the page hears it, not as he retells it to Sir Roland; thus Lyulph's commentary interprets his narrative, but the page has no such role.

From his lightning-struck fragment of rock, Lyulph introduces his tale with an image that links his immediate place in the landscape to his powers to interpret "sign and sigil," which lie on the border between natural and conventional symbols. The image also foreshadows the ambiguous nature of the castle he will describe. He explains that his "rhyme" must begin "far distant 'mid the wrecks of time," for "bard and sage" have "handed [it] down from Merlin's age." Husserl's term "sedimentation" is perhaps too gentle an image for the violence done to this narrative through its successive interpretations, but the geological basis of that critical metaphor corresponds to Lyulph's awareness of the hermeneutic process working through time. It also points toward our growing awareness of the equally hermeneutic process of interpreting nature as art, or interpreting art as nature—a problem posed repeatedly by all levels of the poem.[15] Yet when Lyulph explains that the visionary woman Roland has seen is indeed mortal but has lived "five hundred years and one," we are jolted into considering the continuity of a story through time in a new, more literal way. The Arthurian narrative he begins to tell contains an almost infinite sedimenting of such interpretations, yet Lyulph holds open the possibility of a small earthquake.

Appropriately enough, Lyulph begins with the king's name and with a highly conventional romance motif: Arthur's yearning to escape his queen's bowers for "vent'rous quest . . . by wood or river." What is unconventional about this narrative is Arthur's active role in the quest and in the confrontation with a mysterious enchantress. Except for a few youthful battles, for the intermittent encounters with the lady of the lake, and for the fateful liaison with his half sister, the king's role in most of the Arthurian material is that of a legislator and then a ruler over the court from which other questing knights ride out.[16] When this Arthur rides out into the "desert wild," Lyulph has not yet placed him within that known career; but the king places himself, rather startlingly, in the role of an imitator of traditional romance models. His state of mind resembling that of Scott's James V in *The Lady of the Lake*, he "journey'd like errant-knight" (*BT*, 1:10) and saw the wilderness "with such romantic ruin piled," as a "theatre by Nature's hand / For feat of high adventure plann'd." Unlike James, however, he wanders from simile into myth, untested by historical reality. In the isolated Vale of St. John he finds a mysterious, silent castle. Like Launfal and other knights crossing into some fairy realm, he is led by a "band of damsels fair" to their enchantress queen. Once inside the castle, he finds himself ironically, if happily, enclosed in another bower.[17]

In canto 1 the queen's seductions appear entirely natural. She uses the same human beguilements Guinevere uses on Lancelot (*BT*, 2:15), and she is entirely successful. Scott's multiple audiences, too, seem charmed into silence by the natural inevitability of this relationship. There is no sharp narrative break between the formal divisions of canto 1 and canto 2, where we might expect responses from the page listening to Lyulph's tale, perhaps from Roland listening to the page's report of that tale, or from Lucy listening to the modern Arthur's. By refusing to describe the mutual seduction of King Arthur and the enchantress Guendolen in detail, and instead calling it a "common tale," Lyulph offers a distinctly moral commentary. Yet by linking Arthur's "gliding" first into "folly" and then into "sin" with the way time "glides away" as he lingers at the castle, the sage slides over the moral problems his various audiences, known and unknown to him, might well consider.

In canto 2, when the mysterious queen fears that the king's "hour of waking" from his infatuation is "near," she must turn to her supernatural powers. These powers connect her to an earlier world of myth: the bard Lyulph describes her as a sort of demi-nature goddess, supernatural though closely connected to the processes of an external natural world, "wood or river." Although Guendolen's "mother was of human birth," "her sire[,] a Genie of the earth," presided over courtship and fertility rituals until the coming of Christianity.

> Now, deep in Wastdale solitude,
> The downfall of his rights he rued,
> And, born of his resentment heir,
> He train'd to guile that lady fair,
> To sink in slothful sin and shame
> The champions of the Christian name.   [*BT*, 2:3]

Though he has lost territory to Christianity, the resentful genie has neither vanished, like Plutarch's gods at the birth of Christ, nor lost all power; the "guile" he teaches his daughter is described in stanza 4 as "her sire's soft arts the soul to tame." As stanza 3 describes Guendolen's practice of those arts, it slides, like the transition between cantos, from natural seduction to magical snare. It also glides, however, from a naively realistic acceptance of the existence both of the genie and his daughter to a subtly stated questioning of their actuality:

> Well skill'd to keep vain thoughts alive,
> And all to promise, naught to give;
> The timid youth had hope in store,
> The bold and pressing gain'd no more.
> As wilder'd children leave their home
> After the rainbow's arch to roam,
> Her lovers barter'd fair esteem,
> Faith, fame, and honour, for a dream.   [*BT*, 2:3]

The last six of these lines were added later to the manuscript, as Scott recognizes and reinforces his theme.[18] As the high romantics recognized, visionary desire, or visionary imagination, threatens to become not a means of redemption but of torture.

Characteristically, however, Scott gives the visionary woman a motivation. Thus, even though her explicit if mythological family history would seem to make her more obviously malevolent than Keats's and Shelley's similar elusive, visionary women, its very explicitness makes her less mysterious and more human. Further, it makes her failure to use her magic understandable. She promptly forgets "each rule her father gave, / Sunk from a princess to a slave." As in *The Lay* the lady has learned her magical skills from her father and thus does not draw her powers only from an originally female source in a fecund but alien nature. Scott's careful fathering of those mythic powers drawn from nature divides and thus controls the fusion of female and natural otherness so weirdly present in the powers of Thomas the Rhymer's queen of Elfland. Because of this weakening, Guendolen can keep Arthur, as Meleager captures Guinevere, only for a summer.[19] This is long enough to insure her own fertility (*BT*, 2:6-7) but not to confirm her divinity. Instead of continuing as a receding goal for the dreamer and luring him to destruction as the dream woman in Shelley's *Alastor* will do only a year later, she herself becomes the pursuer who must seek to maintain her summer's dream of fulfillment, to keep the father of her expected child.

Only as the king actually leaves, having broken from her natural charms, does Guendolen remember enough of her magical art to set a trap. Yet her use of magic clarifies neither her powers nor Arthur's power to resist them. Like Comus, or like his reputed mother Circe, she offers him a "cup of gold," a "draught / Which Genii love." To share the parting ritual, she drinks first. When the unsuspicious Arthur "lifted the cup," however, a "drop escaped the goblet's brink" and, "intense as liquid fire from hell," burned his horse so severely that its leap carried the king out of the vale (*BT*, 2:10). If Guendolen's ability to drink this fiery potion seems to confirm her own supernatural powers, Arthur's avoidance of it is less a moral or perceptual victory than a comic accident.

His judgment of the whole episode, like the audience's judgment, is made even more difficult by his retrospective view. When he "back on the fatal castle gazed,"

> Nor tower nor donjon could he spy,
> Darkening against the morning sky;
> But, on the spot where once they frown'd,
> The lonely streamlet brawl'd around
> A tufted knoll, where dimly shone
> Fragments of rock and rifted stone.   [BT, 2.10]

The only evidence remaining of the episode, says the narrator Lyulph, is "the dint / Where" the horse's "hoofs lighted on the flint," after the drink fell on its neck. This "the peasant still can show." As landscape enfolds both castle and narrative, the story becomes an euhemeristic folktale, the reading of improbable story from natural oddity. If Arthur had tasted the genie's drink, he might have been drawn permanently into Guendolen's Circe-like realm of enchantment and might himself have disappeared with the castle, folded into a liminal elf realm within, yet beyond, nature. On the other hand, the drink might simply have killed the king, preventing both his return and the fulfillment of his fantasy of a dallying escape into nature. As it is, he returns and follows the whole career told by the "history" of Geoffrey of Monmouth and the romances of later writers: giants captured, twelve battles won, and an almost perfect kingdom established. In contrast to Keats's knight or the newly prophetic Thomas the Rhymer, Arthur seems not to have put on the enchantress's supernatural knowledge with her sexual power. Though it carries suggestions of myth, his idyll seems a dreamlike dalliance without consequences, a subromance within the more realistic yet traditional romance world of Arthur's court.

Again with no intervention from any later listener or narrator, Lyulph skips fifteen years or more to focus in stanza 11 of canto 2 on the arrival of Arthur's hitherto unknown daughter at his Penrith court. Though one might expect the child of such a union to exercise her inherited magic and to pursue further the genie's vengeance against Christian culture, she pursues instead vengeance against Arthur's desertion of her mother. More aware of her mother as wronged mortal than as wrongdoing enchantress—a view more justifed by outcome than by her mother's intention—she turns the summer tournament meant to marry her off into an exposure of the decadence of Arthur's court. In contrast to her mother's earlier career as a receding visionary object, Gyneth and her new wealth become entirely too present. Abandoning their earlier commitments, all but three knights fight for her and for the two kingdoms Arthur promises with her. The sordidness of their motives is rewarded by the violence of their deaths. Though Arthur has given Gyneth his "leading-staff" to stop the tournament before it changes into such violence, she refuses to stop the slaughter and to restore the apparent order Arthur would have preserved in his court and in himself. Her destructive use of his phallic staff forms an appropriate revenge against Arthur's apparent seduction and abandonment of her mother.

Yet Gyneth does not complete her bloody quest for a husband among "the bravest, proved and tried." Instead, male magic intervenes with a claim to retaliate against her "mother's art." Arthur first uses this phrase in stanza 22, in response to her charge of "the faithlessness of men." In stanza 26 an angry Merlin arrives to avenge his nephew's death in the melee and repeats the charge: "Thy mother's art / Warp'd thine unsuspicious heart." Although Gyneth uses no magic but her beauty and her potential wealth, she now becomes the victim, or at least the object, of Merlin's own more powerful art. Even in his arrival on the scene, Arthur's enchanter usurps the powers of her mother's line:

> . . . rent by sudden throes,
> Yawn'd in mid lists the quaking earth,
> And from the gulf, tremendous birth!
> The form of Merlin rose!   [*BT*, 25]

Reborn from the earth, he has no use for women's powers of fertility; claiming the earth himself, he also denies the power of the "genie of the earth" who taught Guendolen her arts. Triply imprisoned by Merlin's spell—in sleep, in an enchanted chair, and in the mysterious castle hidden in the "Vale of Saint John," where she had come from—Gyneth is condemned to endure a more passive version of her mother's career.

Two slightly differing interpretations of this punishment are given at the end of the canto, one Christian and explicitly antifeminist, the second returning to the mythic pattern behind the romance to continue her guilt. Merlin states the first:

> Long endurance of thy slumber
> Well may teach the world to number
> All their woes from Gyneth's pride,
> When the Red Cross champions died.   [*BT*, 2:26]

Because she has caused Arthur's knights to kill each other in a most unChristian acting out of their greed, Merlin makes her an Eve causing a second fall—"All their woes—." Even if it does recall her genie-grandfather's antagonism to Christianity, Merlin's condemnation is surely an elegaic whitewashing of the knights' behavior. Her pride, moreover, mirrors Arthur's own. Claiming acknowledgment as his daughter, she plays upon his own too-easy buying-off of her claims, so that the anarchic violence she creates is only too appropriate a dowry.

The second interpretation recalls the genie's intentions even more fully, yet returns sympathy to the prisoner. Completing his narrative to the page, Lyulph explains that Gyneth "still . . . bears her weird alone, / In the Valley of Saint John." As a visionary image she has even more power than did her mother to draw knights astray: "Her semblance oft will seem, / Mingling in a champion's dream, / Of her weary lot to 'plain, / And crave his aid to burst her chain." Her imprisonment creates a trial of solitary, not social, bravery for the knights who are led either by her dream or by "her wondrous tale" to search for her:

> Most have sought in vain the glen,
> Tower nor castle could they ken;
> Not at every time or tide,
> Nor by every eye descried.
> Fast and vigil must be borne,
> Many a night in watching worn,
> Ere an eye of mortal powers
> Can discern those magic towers. [*BT*, 2:28]

Among those who see the castle, many are deterred by the "dismal threat / Graved upon the gloomy gate." Finally, "few have braved the yawning door, / And those few return'd no more." As her story is gradually forgotten, Lyulph implies, her power to haunt dreams is also lessened, and thus "well nigh lost is Gyneth's lot" (st. 28). Her very existence seems dependent upon the active imagination of narrator and dreamer.

The simile in Lyulph's final lines, however, suggests that, even though her sleep is deathlike, she will not vanish altogether but will be reborn in some apocalyptic moment: "Sound her sleep as in the tomb, / Till waken'd by the trump of doom!" If Arthur's dalliance with her mother made that castle the scene of a typical "erring" in quest romance, his return to Carlisle does not represent the same sort of entrance into history shown by the ends of *Marmion, The Lady of the Lake,* or even *Rokeby*. Arthur does, however, enter the known "history" of his romance career, and Gyneth's arrival is, like Merlin's, a gap in the expected surface of Geoffrey's or Malory's narrative. When Merlin's magic suspends her intervention, he defers her active quest for identity and selfhood, but sets in motion the dream visions and quests of the knights who may waken her into it. Whether her awakening will lead to a further errant dallying, or whether her sleep will last until the end of time, depends upon the next, enclosing narrative.

To consider the active realization of the knights' dreams also implies a complex assessment of the functions of romance as a genre. With its "yawning door," the terrifying castle in the mysterious vale resembles a Lawrence-like nightmare of the absorbing, consuming womb, seen as alien, annihilating, tomblike. Once realized as an actual person and not as a vision, Gyneth in part shares the castle's role as a physical trap that threatens the separate consciousness, even existence of the male questers. Yet she is in part freed from this role because in her sleep she too seems a virginal victim. Like the lady in *Comus*, imprisoned in her chair, she is immobilized. In sharp contrast to Comus, Merlin is trying to freeze, not to release, the natural fertility she represents. In greater fairness to Merlin, we might say that he is trying to reassert control over the lust and avarice that Gyneth has called out in the court. Daughter of a nature deity and a Circe, Gyneth has herself been a Comus, turning Arthur's ordered tournament into a brutal antimasque; but with Merlin's greater powers, she becomes the helpless lady.

Bruno Bettelheim argues that the spell cast over the Sleeping Beauty is a necessary period of narcissism in puberty, for emotional development to catch up to physical maturity. He suggests that the old woman, the evil fairy, represents the feared yet necessary aspects of physical maturity for women.[20] In this version, however, Merlin's sleep punishes Gyneth for not denying the witchcraft of natural fertility and process. She must become a victim in order to be saved from her own maternal sources of power. In some sense, too, her purging from enchantment represents a purging of the women in Arthur's court, whose bowers have distorted the social structures of male chivalry or at least of military alliance.

Even though Lyulph's story explores mythic levels, then, neither the middle scene at Arthur's Penrith tournament nor the two descriptions of the mysterious castle in the wilderness represent a socially or historically primitive culture. Instead, individual primitiveness breaks through the weakened, even decadent cultural forms meant to contain it, as in the tournament. Moreover, those cultural forms do not directly express any specific, historically-existent culture, though they contain traces or sediments of many because they are a schematized version of medieval Arthurian romance literature. These traces or layers were themselves culturally determined during various stages of the medieval period, but through so many times and places that the result seems a sophisticated artifact, though not a self-conscious one. Even though Lyulph's tale is set five hundred years earlier than his own time, it seems to include the interpretations and cultural values of that chain of bards and sages who have retold it until he received it. Paradoxically, although Lyulph and Roland at this point in the poem stand at the end of this narrative tradition, Roland's more realistically portrayed thirteenth-century castle seems rougher and bleaker—more primitive—than Arthur's more literary and idealized one.

Because of this interpretive tradition, it is doubly interesting that the modern Arthur ends Lyulph's tale without, for the moment, returning to its effect on the page or on Sir Roland. Instead, he fears interruption from another audience, the "trifling throng" of "courtly inmates" who finally begin to emerge from the country house at noon (canto 2, stanzas 1-3 of epilogue). To escape fully from them, he tells Lucy, "There is but one resistless spell—" to elope with him to Scotland:

> 'Twere hard to name, in minstrel phrase,
> A landaulet and four blood-bays,
> But bards agree this wizard band
> Can but be bound in Northern land.
>   [*BT*, 2: epilogue 7]

Most surprising is that, in the gap between his eight persuasive stanzas at the end of canto 2 and the six introductory stanzas of canto 3, Lucy evidently agrees to his proposal; for in canto 3 they walk in the highlands, under Ben Cruach, and he moralizes the beauty of the landscape: "Since . . . thine Arthur call'd thee wife, / Such seems the prospect of his life" (*BT*, 3). At her request he goes on to complete Sir Roland's story and to moralize it as well. The persuasive power of that moralizing, however, comes after Lucy's decision to elope and not before.

How does the listening Lucy, the modern heiress for whom all these stories are told, interpret them? Her own speech, her acceptance of his proposal to elope, apparently comes in the gap between cantos 2 and 3, if at all; we do not read it. In what we do read, she is a nearly speechless audience for Arthur: he must interpret her physical gestures, and he uses that interpretation to claim assent. His most skillful art, of course, is his Renaissance claim that he has no art but is only a simple soldier. His "conjuring wand" is a staff "of English oak," to swat away "some phantom, fashionably thin, / With limb of lath" (*BT*, 2: epilogue 1). Because of her silence, she resembles the sleeping Gyneth. Because of her role as financial pawn for contending suitors, she also resembles Gyneth at the king's court; but her role is far more passive. As a result it is difficult to tell what further interpretations she may make. In response to Arthur's narratives, Lucy may see herself at the end of canto 2 as a newly-awakened sleeping beauty, freed from

Gyneth's "weird," from a life so trivial that it has seemed a kind of sleep to her—or she may be lulled asleep, charmed by this ambitious minstrel of whom we know little except his rather cynical portrayal of the king for whom he is named.

Because the modern Arthur's narrating of Lyulph's tale and his social satire at the end of canto 2 are successful in persuading Lucy to elope with him to Scotland, he seems to anticipate his own character Sir Roland and to free her from enchantment. He has not yet shown, however, a clear moral sensibility in his own actions any more than in King Arthur's or—up to this point—in Roland's. Both an enchanter, like Merlin, and a knight, like those fighting for Gyneth's dower, he carries her from the greedy competition of a court to the highland wilderness where he narrates canto 3. Her name Lucy may be evidence of her clear sight in recognizing Arthur's potential good character, or may be ironic evidence that she lacks it.

With its concomitant attributes of honesty and faithfulness, Arthur's rough military role leads well into the more historically-specific portrayal of Sir Roland in canto 3 and makes more persuasive our tendency and Lucy's to identify Arthur with the increasingly moral aspects of Sir Roland's character. Those increasingly moral aspects, however, emerge neither from the rough border-ballad style of the first stanza of canto 3, nor from the romance-ballad fragment Arthur places just before it: "'Childe Roland to the dark tower came!'" Instead, it develops through the use of Renaissance romance structures drawn both from the matter of Charlemagne, in which the French Roland is the central hero, and from that of Arthur—from Ariosto and Tasso, and from Spenser. The mental, imaginative quest of Sir Roland is thus an allegorizing and analyzing of earlier myth and of medieval romance.

Even the earlier Arthurian story is grounded, if not in specific and realistic cultural patterns, in the specific cliffs, valleys, and rocks of the Lake Country. The "Druid" or megalithic stones seem only slightly transformed from natural formations and seem to have endured almost as long as natural stones. The mysterious castle, first appearing to Arthur in the glare of sunset, disappears into "fragments of rock and rifted stone." These meditations on stones that are margins between the cultural and natural resemble the narrator's interpretation of the uncompleted sheepfold in Wordsworth's earlier *Michael*. Yet here Scott, or rather his narrator Arthur, makes the gap between natural rock and imaginative vision a teasing and ironic one. Furthermore, the narrative in canto 2 is not built up, like the sheepfold, from normal tasks that bind the human to the natural. In contrast to Wordsworth's Grasmere shepherd, Scott's border knight Sir Roland is engaged in a task that alienates him from his normal functions in the landscape: he searches for a magically sleeping princess who has haunted his own dreams. The earlier Arthur may have searched for adventure in nature, but that nature glided seamlessly, unobtrusively, into myth about nature and into romance built upon such myth. For the more realistic Roland, the castle at first appears as an evanescent overlay, a projection of "wild illusions . . . which fancy had conceived": moonlight, mist, and even a meteor's light allow him to convert the crags temporarily and teasingly to "grey turrets." Once, dreaming in a cave, Roland wakes to the sound of a tolling bell and later seems to hear an answer to his trumpet call. In the *Chanson de Roland*, the dying hero waits in terrible isolation for Charlemagne's, or any, answer to his trumpet call, but their failure to answer means only the tragic, realistic fact that they have moved out of hearing, not that they are illusory. Here, the English Roland waits in a self-imposed and essentially playful solitude, attempting to find responsive human life in the "pile of granite fragments" before him, just as Lyulph called his narrative up from the "wrecks" of previous versions through time.

Both the modern Arthur who narrates his story and the thirteenth-century border knight describe this search for an elusive castle as a struggle to suspend disbelief, to believe that a transient illusion possesses, and will reveal, a more enduring reality. Roland's own analysis of what he fears is only a deception employs categories, drawn from folklore or myth, that recall the earlier Arthur's actual experience: " 'Am I then / Fool'd by the enemies of men, / Like a poor hind, whose homeward way / Is haunted by malicious fay?' " (*BT*, 3:13). Although his phrase "enemies of man" may use "man" generically and thus may refer to a pagan demon who assaults all Christians, his conjecture about a "malicious fay" also recalls the hostility to female power already shown in Lyulph's Arthurian romance and the seductions employed by the genie's daughter, not against all Christians, but against Christian knights. Thus his frustration at this difference between wished-for illusion and stubborn nature also includes a fear that his masculinity and his socially defined ways of expressing that male power in chivalric aggression may be limited; he may become a "poor hind."

As if to protest against such fears, he throws his battle-axe, stained with "Scottish gore," at the cliffs. When the small landslide caused by his axe reveals a "winding stair" with "moss'd and fractured steps," that outward aggression is apparently rewarded. The symbolism suggests that his vision comes both through sexual and through military aggressiveness.[21] The winding stair also suggests a meditative ascent into the solitary self, as in Herbert and Yeats. Thus the castle does not simply appear for him; after his gesture of external aggression, he commits himself to an ascent within himself. Only after he commits himself to ascending these stairs does he see the "Castle of Saint John" before him. Instead of employing Scott's usual precise spatial perspectives, this stage of his journey is vividly detailed but not clearly related to the larger scene of the valley; the journey cuts him off from the outside, natural world.

Although the Vale of Saint John and its geological formation called the Castle Rock do exist,[22] it is tempting to hear in Scott's and Arthur's repeated use of "Saint John" an allusion both to the gospel writer celebrating the creative power of the Word and to the writer of Revelation describing his scrolls and seals. For just at this point in the narrative, as the skepticism so clearly evoked must be suspended, Sir Roland confronts a series of written texts and an increasingly allegorical series of episodes. In this way Arthur's modern listeners and Scott's modern readers can follow his steps and thus accept his journey. Such a following builds interpretation into the narrative. Patricia Parker argues that romance is an "erring" or wandering that simultaneously points toward apocalyptic salvation and delays leaving the pleasures of the world. Lyulph's tale of King Arthur shows far more pleasurable delay than it does an impulse toward transcendence. The alternative transcendence of male and female magic, of Merlin's and Guendolen's enthrallments, compete with one another but only tacitly with Christian versions of immortality. As Roland enters the castle, however, his more purposeful quest includes interpretive conventions as part of its rational, allegorical structure. Although it does not move toward a final apocalypse at the end of history, it does move toward a judgment of romance as a genre and toward a more sophisticated and self-conscious use of the genre. This may indeed be a kind of amelioration or progress in the genre, or it may be a loss of belief in the naive wholeness of the romance world.

The first of these occurs in the "stern inscription" over the gate. Written "in shapeless characters of yore," it is still clear enough in its warnings both to quester and to reader. Any warrior whose quest has reached that point can no longer depend upon his patience and strength, because the castle has magical origins. Because of these explicitly stated origins, the reader too is warned not to enter the fictional castle as if it were real. For

> Never mortal builder's hand
> This enduring fabric plann'd;
> Sign and sigil, word of power,
> From the earth raised keep and tower   [BT, 3.16]

Thebes, Troy, and Milton's Pandemonium were raised by music; the pleasure dome and caves of ice might be built, says Coleridge's speaker in "Kubla Khan," if he could revive the damsel's "symphony and song."

The castle's inscription of natural and human texts repeats Roland's phrase about Lyulph's powers as interpreter—"Sign and sigil well doth he know"—but converts interpretation to performance. Ironically, the gap between creation and interpretation is widened. Here aesthetic appreciation is permitted both adventuring knight and adventuring reader, but further commitment discouraged, as if magic—or a powerful, constitutive, imaginative art—were a property or power only of "ancient days" and not available to a modern reader.

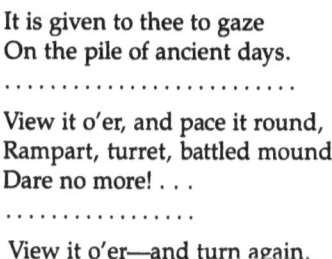

> It is given to thee to gaze
> On the pile of ancient days.
> ....
>
> View it o'er, and pace it round,
> Rampart, turret, battled mound.
> Dare no more! . . .
> ....
>
> View it o'er—and turn again.

This appeal to a limited antiquarian tourism would of course hardly deter the questers who have reached so far through "strength and fortitude," nor does it stop Sir Roland. Announcing, "I mock these words of awe," he pushes through the gate with his own "strong" if "mortal" hand, restoring the unreflexive action of the primary fiction and also the promise that later readers can enter that fiction. Yet he also anticipates Scott's recurrent, ambivalent symbolism of the hand in the novels, particularly in *The Fair Maid of Perth*, where it expresses both imaginative creativity and brute strength.[23] Thus the ambiguous nature of Roland's discovery of the castle—through both aggression and introspection—continues.

Like the earlier Arthur, Sir Roland finds the castle full of beautiful women. Yet the ones he encounters are more highly organized than Guendolen and her court, their doubly spatial pattern reinforcing the separate temptations they offer. As he moves onward from one hall to another, he is accosted by "maidens" from the four major continents. Those from Africa test his fear; from America, his avarice; from Asia, his sensuality; from Europe, his ambition or pride. Only the third group uses sexual temptation as its theme; but all four groups, scantily clad and seductive, encourage the same association between sexual possession and the possession of power over other objects and people. Roland, unlike Arthur's knights earlier, resists both levels of temptation. Because each group congratulates him and finds release as he overcomes their temptation, the women are not themselves malicious enchantresses but serve some larger, mysterious scheme that is ultimately benevolent for the virtuous knight. The women of Dahomey, for example, are both comic and sympathetic in their delight at escaping after five hundred years from "this cold glen" and its "pallid sun" (*BT*, 3:24). Their racial and geographical distribution universalizes the temptations and increases the significance of Roland's resistance.

This universality is chronological, as well, for the tempting women also foreshadow the colonial adventure and exploitations that in later history will replace border warfare. The Americans' chorus, offering the gold from Peruvian mines, sings that if the wealth they offer "were all our mountains bore, / We should ne'er in future story / Read, Peru, thy banished glory!"[24] Although Roland's temptation by ambition resembles Satan's offer of the kingdoms and his temptation of wealth might be seen as the temptation to turn stones to bread, neither parallel is close and no larger Christological pattern emerges—except the pattern of temptation itself as a path to moral and spiritual development. Much of the mood and setting comes from Alcina's castle in Ariosto, Armida's bower in Tasso, and Acrasia's bower, modeled after them, in Spenser. A closer look at these Renaissance models shows the skill with which Scott uses them, even in the reduced scale of this poem.[25]

In Ariosto, Tasso, and Spenser, the castle and garden are on an island, approached by boat. That model also appears in *The Lady of the Lake*; in this poem Scott's castle is in the middle of a mountain torrent, and Roland must also cross a moat. *Triermain* follows with only a slight increase in modesty Rogero's temptation in *Orlando Furioso*, that of Rinaldo's rescuers in *Jerusalemme Liberata*, and Guyon's temptation in *The Fairie Queene*.[26] Ariosto separates well and fountain from the castle, in the setting of the latter using direct instead of symbolic sexual description. The Renaissance theme of art counterfeiting the natural, which runs through all three earlier texts, also appears in Scott's narrative both before and after the specific temptations: in 3:19 and 3:37. Spenser makes this theme more explicit by having no castle, only a garden in which the enchantress Acrasia works her artifice. In all four, fountain and paradisal garden form a narrative and symbolic overture to sexual temptation. Although Edgar Johnson criticizes Scott's poem for lacking the lush sensuality of the earlier writers, we should keep in mind the modern frame tale: the rhythm of suspended desire has been subverted by Arthur's earlier persuasiveness.[27] Because of that success, however, the role of the woman changes.

At the center of these enclosures, the goal of Scott's knight differs from those of Ariosto, Tasso, and Spenser. In Ariosto and Tasso, the delinquent heroes Rogero and Rinaldo must be rescued from their sensual bondage in Alcina's and Armida's arms. In Spenser, the hero Guyon and his guardian palmer take the more dignified narrative roles that correspond to Rinaldo's rescuers, Charles and Ubaldo, in Tasso's narrative. The knight in Acrasia's lap, though eventually named when he is freed, remains only a function of the garden: his name is Verdant (*FQ*, 2:12.82). Roland's attempt is closest to Guyon's, for he is a rescuer. Yet he rescues not a preceding male quester victimized by an enchantress, but a younger, less guilty version of the enchantress herself.

With great precision Scott uses these analogues to earlier Renaissance romantic epics to recall Gyneth's parentage and to distinguish her from her mother. Rogero has adopted "wanton, womanish behavior . . . An Atys or Adonis for to be / Unto Alcina" (*OF*, 163-64); Rinaldo's "sword, that many a pagan stout had shent, / Bewrapt with flowers hung idly by his side" (*JL*, 16:30); Verdant has cast aside his sword. Although Scott's poem echoes these lines closely, they do not describe Roland. Instead, the lines (*BT*, 2:1) come from Lyulph's tale, the first narrative, and they describe King Arthur. Even more dramatically than Spenser shifts the balance of Tasso's narrative by making his main protagonist the rescuer instead of the victim, Scott shifts the balance of these sources by dividing them into two parts. Thus Rogero, Rinaldo, and Verdant are models for Arthur, and, even more strikingly, the Circean enchantresses Alcina, Armida, and Acrasia are models for Guendolen. In all four cases, these dominant enchantresses unman their lovers by embowering them in passive enjoyment. The sword hanging unused is both an abandonment of social responsibility and evidence of their impotence in the personal, if not the physical relationship.

Far less effective than the other three, Scott's Guendolen is also more sympathetic. As we saw, Arthur eventually decides to rescue himself, and she even spills the Circean cup that might have enchained him more permanently. Alcina, Armida, and Acrasia are indeed conquered, but only with superior magic beyond the power of their passive victims. Even with that superior magic, only Spenser's Acrasia is firmly conquered. She is caught like Venus in a net, her transformation of men to wild beasts reversed, and temperance triumphs to close the book. When Ariosto's Rogero puts on a magic ring of reason brought him by a protector, he sees "Alcina's foul disgraces and enormity" (p. 167) and "from this missapen hag . . . stole away" (p. 169); others, without the ring, may continue to be tempted. Tasso's Armida, deserted by Rinaldo, calls up an array of hellish magic and prepares to intervene against him in the Crusade. As she does so, her castle proves a model for Scott's:

> A shadow blacker than the mirkest night
> Environed all the place. . . .
> ....
> And all the palace vanish'd was and gone,
> Not of so great a work was left one stone.
>
> LXIX
>
> As oft the clouds from shapes of castles great
> Amid the air, that little time do last,
> But are dissolved by wind or Titan's heat,
> Or like vain dreams soon made and sooner pass'd;
> The palace vanish'd so, nor in his seat
>   Left aught but rocks and crags by kind there plac'd. . . .

All this sounds remarkably like Guendolen's vanishing castle, though Scott and Tasso probably shared Celtic and later medieval sources for this motif.[28] Armida's exit, however, is triumphantly in control and quite unlike Guendolen and Gyneth's entrapment in their own castle. The stanza above concludes "She in her coach, which two old serpents drew, / Sat down, and as she us'd away she flew." She is a scatheless Medea.

Though these Renaissance parallels surely make Guendolen's career as an enchantress seem less terrifying than those of the Renaissance Circes, they nevertheless make firmer the association of female sexuality, demonic enchantment, and a dangerously contagious, yet isolated and antisocial domesticity. If remote from normal society, the bower is feminizing for the heroes. Also, since these parallels with Ariosto, Tasso, and Spenser become far clearer in the third canto of *The Bridal*, we not only share the modern Arthur's tendency to interpret Roland's quest allegorically, but we also reread or recall the earlier Arthurian story of the first two cantos in a different way. In this retrospective process Guendolen's significance, if not her actions, seems more terrifying, and thus the need for Gyneth's purgation seems stronger. Through this network of allusions both to the preceding Renaissance poems and to the preceding parts of this one, Gyneth is trapped in a kind of sedimented, hermeneutic guilt.

Just as the elemental functions of romance heroes—those of errant dallier and of rescuer—are split between Arthur and Roland, so the function of witch and passive "damsel" to be "from danger freed," to use Fitz-Eustace's bookish phrase from *Marmion* (*M*, 4:4), are split between Guendolen and Gyneth, between mother and daughter. This generational distinction between the female figures should remind us of *The Lay*, in which the Lady of Buccleuch relinquishes her powers of witchcraft to make way for her daughter's conventional domesticity, and of *The Lady of the Lake*, in which Ellen relinquishes her role as "weird" woman presiding over her water-surrounded "castle" in the wilderness for a less magical and more conventional role in court. In *Marmion* the enthrallments link sexual desire not to the engendering of literal magic, but of literary magic. Yet a similar split occurs between the threatening powers of sexual and imaginative energy and the passive, acceptable object of desire-for-ownership between Constance and Clare. In *Rokeby*, as we have seen, male desire for ownership seems to dominate, and there is no weird woman who threatens to seize control. Scott's letter to Ballantyne of May-June 1812 (*Letters*, 3:112) amusingly debates whether he should give Matilda a mother: "Decency requires she should have one but she is . . . likely to be in my way." More accurately, it is what we might call the indecency of the older woman as witch or enchantress that tends to get in the way of appropriate, decent domestication. In 1812 that figure manifests herself very directly, but only in the anonymous poem he is writing at the same time—in *Triermain*, not in *Rokeby*.

Through contrast with the now more moralistic and more misogynist reading of the Arthurian narrative and through his return to analogues of *Comus* and "The Sleeping Beauty," Scott works out Gyneth's purification. Roland, a somewhat more charming Guyon, brushes off all temptation. Purified by this testing, he finds the sleeping Gyneth also purified by her long sleep: "Doubt, and anger, and dismay, / From her brow had pass'd away" (*BT*, 3:37). No longer the Circean enchantress whose refusal to use the warder created brute chaos in the tournament, she releases the warder into Roland's hands as she wakes up. As mentioned earlier, she now resembles the lady in *Comus*, temporary victim of a son of Circe:

> That form of maiden loveliness,
> 'Twixt childhood and 'twixt youth,
> That ivory chair, that silvan dress,
> . . . express
> Of Lyulph's tale the truth.

Like Milton's lady, she seems far younger than all the Circean arguments or the furor at the tournaments had led us to expect. Though a pun only in French, the ivory chair in which her life has been suspended seems almost to symbolize the suspended processes of her own sexual development. That suspension redeems her from being condemned as an enchantress.

Further, Roland's trials have made him wary of holding her in thrall. Instead of the earlier bluff, forthright egotism that we might have expected from him, he plays neither Comus nor even the gently aggressive prince in tales of the sleeping beauty:

> Motionless a while he stands,
> Folds his arms and clasps his hands,
> Trembling in his fitful joy,
> Doubtful how he should destroy
>   Long-enduring spell;
> Doubtful, too, when slowly rise
> Dark-fringed lids of Gyneth's eyes,
>   What these eyes shall tell.

At first reading the elided grammar of the line suggests that Gyneth wakes up, given the freedom to do so. Yet in a sense his hesitation does lead to that result. In his willingness to wait for her response, he reaches out "gently" to grasp her hand and kiss her. As he does so, "the warder" that had been in her hand "leaves his grasp." Neither the newly educated Sir Roland nor Gyneth, then, keeps that power over male aggression that was in Arthur's hands civic rule and in Gyneth's became, in both Arthur's and Merlin's view, "her mother's art." As Roland inadvertently parallels Prospero's breaking of his wand, the last magic of the poem becomes a release from magic. When "the warder leaves his grasp,"

> Lightning flashes, rolls the thunder!
> Gyneth startles from her sleep,
> Totters tower, and trembles keep,
>   Burst the castle-walls asunder!
> Fierce and frequent were the shocks,—
>   Melt the magic halls away;
> But beneath their mystic rocks,
> In the arms of bold De Vaux,
>   Safe the princess lay.
> Safe and free from magic power,
> Blushing like the rose's flower
>   Opening to the day. . . .

With that earthquake the magic castle seems to withdraw itself from any single interpretation, any single imagining of its existence and of the quest narrative it has generated. The earthquake shocks through which the castle disappears into the natural scene, leaving only "fragments of rock and rifted stone," is not quite an apocalypse announcing the end of time, nor—as in *Marmion* and *Rokeby*—is it the inevitable, wrenching return to known historical event. It is, however, the end of Roland's errantry and Gyneth's suspended life as unconscious object of others' dreams. Although the phrase "beneath their mystic rocks" suggests for a moment that both Roland and Gyneth have been swallowed up into the magic castle, Arthur's conclusion places them firmly in this world, far less haunted than the medieval grail questers or Keats's wan knight left waking on the cold hill's side. Arthur wraps up his fiction with a flurry of conventional phrases, as if afraid to confront their entrance into ordinary time too closely:

> Our lovers, briefly be it said,
> Wedded as lovers wont to wed,
>   When tale or play is o'er;
> Lived long and blest, loved fond and true,
> And saw a numerous race renew
>   The honours that they bore.

"Safe and free from magic power," Gyneth apparently retains none of her mother's art. One could say, in an extension of Virginia Woolf's thesis, that even though she was trapped in that castle, unconscious for five centuries, she had a room and a power of her own. Now this second generation enchantress has neither. The image of the castle, Arthur tells Lucy, still occasionally haunts a lost traveler. Yet he attributes the power of making it more than illusion to the male quester, not to the in-house female magician: "Never man since brave De Vaux / The charmed portal won." Thus the menacing power of an independent female imagination or an independent, aggressive female sexuality is redefined. The first now becomes the creation of a male moral and aesthetic criterion so compelling that Roland has in a sense realized his own fantasy by finding Gyneth; and the second becomes a passive blossoming out of sleeping innocence. Because the narrator Arthur has shown Roland's increasing sensitivity, however, he thus finally shows that he himself merits the heiress he had earlier persuaded to elope. The "evening breeze" that "comes chill" over the mountains is perhaps a reminder of the complexities the modern pair will face once free of the magic of story telling: "Fearless of the slippery way," Arthur tells Lucy, she will be "safe" as she "hangs on Arthur's arm." If he has wrested control of the romance world and its narratives from the female enchantresses once immanent within it, he has also told "some moral truth in fiction's veil." Moving from mythic medieval versions of romance to border history transformed into Renaissance allegory, he redefines, with increasing self-consciousness, two functions of romance as persuasive rhetoric. The very isolation in which we last see the modern lovers emphasizes the interpersonal nature of this persuasion but also its lack of communal context. Apparently the magical fictions of romance must be more thoroughly made safe—or suppressed—when only individuals, not society, stand against them. Thus the anonymous narrator's 1813 "Introduction," excusing romance as allowable within the private affairs of individuals, contains a tension and a qualification not evident until Arthur's story is complete.

SIX

The Lord of the Isles
HISTORY, SCENERY, AND FICTIONS OF SILENCE

CRITICS OF *The Lord of the Isles*, Scott's sixth major narrative poem, have long argued that the poem is dangerously split in focus. Against the largely historical treatment of Robert the Bruce, the fictional portrayal of a thwarted romance between two of his followers has appeared both frivolous and strained.[1] Increasing the uneasiness of "the minstrel's strain" or song is a split between fact and fiction in the narrative representation of Scott's characteristic minstrel figure—a woman disguised with minstrel's clothes and harp. She alo pretends to be mute and thus seems doubly powerless to shape events. In another split between fact and fiction, the middle cantos of the poem seem to rely on the factual descriptions of a guidebook to the Hebrides, yet that description is essential to Scott's use of romance within history. His imagination finds a new mode of narrative speech just where his minstrel appears to have been silenced: in the bleak sublimity of Loch Corriskin on Skye. In that silence he frames a confrontation with nature and history that validates his own song. His female minstrel finds a use for her weakness: it educates the poem's heroes in loyalty and humane responsibility, and it educates Scott's readers in both the mythic and the sociopolitical aspects of woman's ambiguous identification with land.

Like *Marmion* and *Rokeby*, *The Lord of the Isles* splices its fictional narrative into history through a major battle. Because Scott presents the battle dramatically and uses it to conclude his narrative, the resemblance of the new poem to *Marmion* is much stronger than to *Rokeby*, but that resemblance defines in turn some striking differences. Like *Marmion*, *The Lord of the Isles* ends with a battle of overwhelming significance in Scottish history, toward which the delays and wanderings of Scott's fictional narrative move as toward an inevitable, revealing moment. At Flodden the revealing moment is fatal for so many of the Scots that it seems finished and conclusive, a day of wrath at the end of an era of historical promise. At the historically earlier Bannockburn, on the other hand, the moment reveals a new beginning—if not the actual beginning of Scottish independence, its renewal through a king whose line will extend for four centuries. Thus in both poems the dilatory space for romance lies in the indeterminate moments between earlier known events and this culminating battle. Yet instead of *Marmion*'s strongly ironic tension between a few days or weeks of delay and Scottish defeat, this poem must work with long years of wandering, some documented and some not, before the wished-for and well-plotted decisiveness of Bannockburn. Moreover, the romantic elements already present in the near-contemporary chronicle of Bruce's guerilla warfare usurp the free play of Scott's fictional narrative. As in *The Lady of the Lake*, the king becomes the questing hero of romance early in the narrative and thus rivals the younger hero whose function should be that of pursuing lover. Yet in the later poem both romance hero and romantic hero are already shaped far more fully both by historical fact and by the romantic myths that had accrued around them.

Lord Hailes, whose *Annals* gave Scott a recent and skeptically rationalist account of Bruce to balance the fourteenth-century chroniclers, was acutely aware of the problems involved in altering a received public narrative of a national hero. Immediately after reinterpreting a crucial episode in Bruce's history, Hailes concedes that his audience may reject it: "For there are some facts which may be termed *the landmarks of history*, by which men have been wont to conduct themselves. He who removes them, or endeavors to place them in a different point of view, is considered by all parties as a pragmatical and dangerous innovator."[2] In his brief headnote to *The Lord of the Isles*, Scott approves such innovative reinterpretation of the traditional stories that have established themselves as "landmarks." In addition to Barbour, the late fourteenth-century chronicler whose *Bruce* combines contemporary evidence with romance motifs, the authority for Scott's own poem is "the venerable Lord Hailes." The modern historian, Scott goes on, is "as well entitled to be called the restorer of Scottish history, as Bruce the restorer of Scottish monarchy" (*PW*, 411). If a modern historian can wield new facts to destroy the emotionally laden "landmarks" of traditional national narrative, yet "restore" a nobler version of Bruce, Scott himself takes the factual but sublimely evocative geographical landmarks of the west coast and the Hebrides for navigation points to shape his own narrative restoration of Bruce's history.

In spite of his support for Hailes's skeptical demythologizing of Bruce, however, Scott places within the gaps of the historian's account a narrative of episodes drawn both from Barbour's *Bruce* and from his own imagination; and though it begins and ends in historical fact, this narrative forms a romance. No account of Bruce's 1308 return to the west coast of Scotland from Irish exile includes a journey to Skye and back, like the one Scott describes so fully in the middle cantos of his poem. Because Bruce's wanderings during this period before he lands at Carrick are not fully traced either in Scott's own sources or in more modern ones,[3] his interpretation does not violate known facts.

Yet through Scott's supplement, Bruce can begin to purge himself and the history of Scotland from the taint of irresponsible, violent rebellion against established government. By taking Bruce to Skye, Scott evokes an implicit but powerful analogy between this founder of the Stuart line and the descendant who tried to restore it in 1745. Working from the analogy, he can then educate Bruce toward an ideal of kingship that corrects the tainted idealism of the Jacobites.

Through the publication of *Waverley* in 1814, Scott had made dramatically clear the problems posed for and by the Jacobites who followed Prince Charles Edward in 1745: how to define loyalty and to evaluate violent rebellion. At first glance that problem appears less obvious for Bruce and his followers, who seem "shapes of epic grandeur" like Achilles or, better, Aeneas.[4] Yet that very heroism already accepted by Scott's audience has another, darker side that presents a further problem for the writer. In her discussion of *Redgauntlet*, Judith Wilt argues for a recurrent, troubling motif posed in the novels: that of the red-handed king whose power comes through some initial violence and thus continues to corrupt. From Robert the Bruce, a sense of historical guilt extends all the way to Scott's fictional portrayal of an even later Stuart attempt at usurpation than the one in 1745. She says, however, that Scott never takes up the problem at its source, in Bruce's actions.[5] Not in the novels—but in this poem he is well aware of it. Further, his allusive use of setting provides the basis for precisely the analogy with the last Stuarts that Wilt points to in *Redgauntlet*.

Not surprisingly, Lord Hailes's meditation on the "landmarks of history" follows his analysis of the single event that raises the greatest problem in evaluating Bruce's character: his violent and sacrilegious killing of Red Comyn, the heir of the English-supported Balliol and thus Bruce's rival for the Scottish crown, at the Dumfries altar. In the traditional Scottish version, Comyn had betrayed to Edward I Bruce's plans for rebellion. When Comyn denied that betrayal, Bruce stabbed him. Noting that the English account is understandably far less favorable to Bruce and less critical of their candidate Comyn, Hailes goes on to offer a third reading of the evidence. In his version both Bruce and Comyn appear less calculating and less morally guilty: "a hasty quarrel between two proud-spirited rivals" draws Bruce into the murder and thus into the immediate assertion of his claim to the Scottish crown. After this unplanned slaughter, Hailes argues, "the only alternative left for Bruce was to be a fugitive or a king." From "necessity and despair," then, not wily foresight, he begins the long and determined struggle through which he acquires a Promethean heroism and becomes worthy of his goal—the ruler of an independent Scotland. Both Hailes's skepticism of the chroniclers and his theory that neither betrayal nor premeditation was involved is supported by modern historical analysis.[6]

Even in this poem, so thoroughly focused on Bruce, Scott does not represent the Comyn killing directly. Instead, he presents a crucial later stage in which we can see the fugitive grow into a quester for kingship. After a confrontation with Comyn's allies during which each side struggles to recall the killing in order to define its own moral ground, Bruce turns northward and enters the geography of quest romance. Scott's original title for his poem, "The Nameless Glen," points to his use of Skye as a turning point in the typical circular journey of romance. Starting before the poem's beginning, Bruce follows a roughly circular path, his identity changing with his location. A baron at Carrick before his rebellion, he returns from Irish exile to become a hunted fugitive along the west coast, then retakes Carrick and becomes a victorious king at Bannockburn—the triumphant conclusion to the poem as well. All this is history. Scott's fictional addition, the trip north to Skye and then south again in cantos 3 and 4, forms an extra loop, almost an epicycle, of this larger circle. Framing the two cantos that describe this wilderness foray to Skye are two pairs of cantos that ostensibly describe more civilized realms. Set at Ardtornish Castle on the Sound of Mull, the first two cantos balance the last two. In the last two, the action turns from convent and castle on Arran, to park and castle at Carrick, and finally to the field of Bannockburn below Stirling Castle.

In its escape from documented history and from civilization, the wilderness journey between these cantos is both fictional and romancelike. At Ardtornish, elaborate preparations for the wedding of the Lord of the Isles and Edith of Lorn, meant to link two families who supported Balliol, are violently broken off when Bruce's storm-driven boat takes shelter at the castle. Motivated by patriotism, the laws of hospitality, and a desire to break off his wedding, the reluctant bridegroom MacDonald joins Bruce. In canto 3 the two sail northwest to the isolated Loch Scavaig beneath the Cuillin peaks on Skye. There they find Edith of Lorn, MacDonald's rejected fiancee, who has also come from the broken wedding celebration at Ardtornish and has disguised herself as the silent minstrel mentioned earlier. Their return south in canto 4 lies slightly to the west of their route north, between the islands of Canna and Rhum, then down the west side of Mull, past Staffa and Iona. Performing a prophecy fulfilling portage across the Kintyre peninsula to Arran, they and their supporters then cross to Carrick on the mainland coast.[7] Although Bruce's arrival there is a fictional addition, Ardtornish Castle did indeed belong to the Lord of the Isles, who changed allegiance and became Bruce's ally.[8] Once his forces cross the Kintyre peninsula and reach Arran in the middle of canto 4, the broad spatial pattern of the narrative has reentered the places documented in Bruce's history.

Confusingly, this supplementary romance narrative at the center of the poem contains two heroes. One is Bruce himself, crowned earlier at Scone but in quest of his kingdom and of the character to rule it. The other, his new ally Ronald MacDonald of the Isles, shares the same political quest and refuses to perform the role of romantic hero for Edith of Lorn. In the narrative logic of their journey into the wilderness on Skye, Edith might seem, like Ellen Douglas, to play the role of wilderness enchantress, an elfin queen who will either bewitch the male questers into dalliance or endow them with gifts for their nation building. Scott does indeed use these romance patterns, echoing his earlier poems and the romantic ballads of the *Minstrelsy*; yet he reworks them within the compelling limits of Bruce's specific public history and of the more generic, gender-based history of a woman in Edith's situation. Conventional, almost mythic narrative has created landmarks for his portrayal of the king; the conventional patterns of marriage mark women like Edith by the land and thus the wealth and alliances that they convey but that they are themselves nearly powerless to control.

By looking more closely at the landscape in which Bruce located his delay from the constraints and fulfillments of history, we can see that it, too, is marked by associations for Scott and for his readers. Those markings, moreover, reveal an interplay between romance and realistic political event that should guide our interpretation of Scott's fourteenth-century narrative.

As critics have complained, this fictional supplement to history does indeed allow Scott space to describe the mountains and sea lochs of Skye and to describe them more eloquently and emotionally than had earlier guidebooks.[9] More important, that setting also allows him to respond to themes that had fascinated the two most illustrious writers who had preceded him on that journey to the Hebrides and especially to Skye—Boswell and Johnson. In the summer of 1814, Scott paid his second visit to the Hebrides, to look once again at the setting for his partially-completed poem. With its focus on earlier times, the completed poem does not mention Johnson and Boswell directly; yet Scott's various accounts of this section of the trip show repeated references to these predecessors. Of Dunvegan on Skye, for example, Scott writes, "Dr. Johnson . . . has stamped his memory on this remote place."[10] Often, Scott's fascination with landscapes unmarked by any human presence recalls Johnson's similar, more oppressed, awareness of such emptiness.[11] Yet another of Johnson's paradoxical "stamps" upon these Hebridean landscapes for later travelers who read him is his denial that oral tradition can sustain itself past a generation; only writing, he insists, can inscribe a culture's values with any permanence. This protest is explored in the unusual silence of Scott's minstrel.

Boswell's journal also stamps its shape upon Scott's poem. Both eighteenth-century writers of course describe their circular journey from the civilization of Edinburgh north, then west from Inverness to the remote wilderness of the highlands and the Hebrides, and finally south to civilization at Auchinleck. Although factual, their journey follows a characteristic pattern of romance. Yet Boswell's journal, unlike Johnson's, contains within its center—their visit to Skye—the narrative of another journey, twenty years earlier. This journey, the escape of Prince Charles Edward across Skye in 1746, also completes the melancholy circle of his failed invasion, from his landing at Moidart in 1745 to his departure a year later, almost from the same spot.[12] A comparison of Boswell's Hebridean journey to Scott's Hebridean poem will show not only their structural resemblances but also a thematic relationship between the histories each entwines with romance patterns. Through this allusive relationship, Scott can answer the first and third of the criticisms I mentioned earlier—the split between public history and private romantic fiction and the split between his ongoing narrative and the bleak, apparently static, descriptions of Skye. Finally, through his response to Johnson's attack upon the oral tradition, Scott can answer the second of these criticisms, that of the silenced, feminized minstrel who seems to represent a loss of power. His answer to that criticism, however, raises that less traditional question posed by feminist readings of romantic poetry: whether to interpret the woman's role symbolically—as a visionary projection, a muse for the male poet or an alien nature-goddess—or realistically. Given Johnson's dour pronouncements on women preaching, any realistic interpretation should consider not only the fourteenth-century social context but also, if briefly, the early nineteenth-century one in which Scott responds to Johnson.

Although the parallel between Bruce's west coast wanderings and those of Charles Edward may at first seem surprising, even J.M. Barrow's modern history of Bruce titles one chapter "The King Over the Water"—a phrase usually applied to the exiled Stuarts.[13] The arguments for interpreting the poem through this analogy to a later historical event rest upon the chronology of its composition—an external element—and upon striking internal parallels. Although Scott waited to complete the poem until he had revisited its scenes in the summer of

1814, he had also delayed its completion in order to write *Rokeby* and *Waverley*.¹⁴ In the 1813 poem, Scott used Elizabethan and seventeenth-century patterns of religious and social conflict to suggest analogies with present conflicts; he was experimenting, then, with historical analogy. In the novel his complex portrait of Bonnie Prince Charlie ends at Clifton. Although Fergus MacIvor as his surrogate is executed at Carlisle, the prince lives on, less pursued in Scott's narrative than in fact. The Baron of Bradwardine tells Waverley about Culloden only briefly, and Waverley tells Fergus, on the morning of his death, of the prince's escape from the battle. The details of that escape are described only as "that remarkable history, so far as it had then transpired."¹⁵ Scott's final focus in *Waverley* is upon English and Scottish union. Yet his writing of the novel, followed so closely by his journey to the Hebrides, surely prompted some thinking about the parallels between Charles Edward and Bruce, both exiled princes who return to claim the Scottish throne—and upon their significance for modern readers who claim, like Waverley, to have relinquished romance for history.

The parallels between the two princes are most striking not in their identity but in their mirror image differences, transformations worthy of a Levi-Strauss. Although each exile claims he is the legitimate heir, Bruce claims only the throne of Scotland, and succeeds. Charles, claiming the thrones of both England and Scotland, fails in his attempt and yet lives on, like Bruce, as symbol of national or at least cultural definition. Each begins his campaign on the west coast and draws support from its most independent and westernmost clans; each, too, is opposed by the dominant clan of Argyll, which retains its English allegiance. Yet Bruce, both Norman and Gaelic in descent, succeeds in unifying most Scots; and Charles Edward, unable like Bruce to claim lowland loyalties and unable to overcome newer religious differences, fails. Scott's analysis of the latter's failure in the just-completed *Waverley* is detailed and realistic as it transforms the structure and presuppositions of romance. His method in the poem is more symbolic and allusive, almost emblematic, as it draws both Bruce's history and that of his Stuart descendant into romance.

Ironically, after Charles Edward's inadequate leadership and abandonment of the field at Culloden, the final stage of his retreat—his journey across Skye as a fugitive—completes a partial redemption of his character. One of the important shapers of this redeemed image of the prince is the romancelike narrative in Boswell's *Journal of a Tour to the Hebrides*. If one reads the 1785 first edition, the importance of Boswell's tracing "the Wanderer's" journey to Skye emerges on the title page. Along with mention of Johnson, the volume includes "an authentick account of The Distresses and Escapes of the Grandson of King James II, in the Year 1746."¹⁶ As Pottle's edition of the original journal shows, and as Boswell himself notes at the beginning of the "authentick" account in his published edition, he expanded his notebook version of about two pages "from what I was told by others personally concerned, and from a paper of information which Raasay was so good as to send me, at my desire."[17] The result is more than an "abstract," as Boswell calls it; the narrative itself occupies eighteen pages, and Boswell's further reflections on the problem of loyalty and legitimacy, another three pages.

Boswell's decision to expand Flora MacDonald's narrative and to include all of the episodes of 1745 at this point in the journal, also shapes the structure of the published journal in a way that points toward the structure of Scott's poem. Even though the final pattern of the published journal may have resulted from Boswell's poor estimates of typeface and raw copy,[18] the result is to place these narratives of "the Wanderer's" escape almost exactly at the center of the book. The prince's journey across Skye is embedded in the longer journey of Boswell and Johnson to the north and back. In turn, their pilgrimage is inspired by the cultural consequences of the prince's larger and unsuccessful journey southward: they want to witness a traditional society before it is irrevocably changed. Boswell's inner narrative, then, occupies the same position as Bruce's journey to Skye in *The Lord of the Isles*.

Although Bruce and Ronald do not cross all of Skye, going only to Loch Scavaig, the Cuillins, and Loch Corriskin, that savage landscape also formed a backdrop for the later prince's departure from Skye. "M'Kinnon's country" and the cave where McKinnon's lady served him an alfresco meal are near Elgol, across Loch Scavaig from the Cuillins;[19] small boats only slightly more seaworthy than the Laird's boat that took Charles southeast to the mainland for his further escape to France now leave from the same spot to take tourists across Loch Scavaig to the base of Loch Corriskin. While waiting for the boat, they can follow sheep tracks across the heather to "Prince Charles's Cave." Scott's journal of his visit shows no mention of that local tradition, perhaps because Boswell or his informants do not place it very specifically.

The most romancelike element in both of these circular journeys is the crucial role of the woman as helper of the weakened hero. Both the prince's rescue by Flora MacDonald and Bruce's and Ronald's rescue by Edith take place on Skye, and both involve cross dressing. In Boswell's narrative it is the rescued—the Prince—who wears a transsexual disguise; in Scott's fictional narrative, it is the rescuer, Edith. Although both disguises contribute successfully to those rescues, they differ sharply in their more immediate freedom for the wearer. At one point the prince wears male clothing, yet he is lowered in rank because he acts as Flora's male servant. His woman's disguise would seem to threaten even further his identity as a male hero, in order to save his life. Yet if we follow Sandra Gilbert's recent suggestion, such cross dressing may lead, as it does for Hercules, to a larger identity as a cultural hero.[20] Gilbert argues that for male writers in the twentieth century, men dressed in women's clothing only seem to lose power in such cross dressing, but in fact gain it; they do not take on the weaker social roles of the women they temporarily resemble, but gain their concealed sexual power. In Boswell's narrative Charles Edward's male identity is confirmed not only through mythic misrule but through comic realism. When the prince crosses a stream, he raises his dress so high that Kingsburgh warns him, "It might make a discovery."[21] Oddly enough, this realism heightens an essential, romantic heroism, just as Falstaff's claim that he has recognized Prince Hal as his buckram-dressed attacker points toward that prince's later apotheosis. Finally, however, even with Boswell's comic revelations, the threat to his prince is not quite resolved by the constant recognitions and professions of loyalty he encounters, nor by his successful escape—for it is an escape, not a conquest. His preparation through this humbling leads only to his transfiguring in legend, not to his own ultimate growth of character—and even this legend leads many of those fascinated with it, like Boswell and Scott, to recognize its ambiguity.

This legendary ambiguity also contrasts sharply with the romantic conventionality through which Edith travels for weeks with Bruce and Ronald. Unidentified as a woman, she is—even more outrageously—unrecognized by her former fiance. Reading the situation literally and realistically, at least one reviewer was scandalized by what he saw as impropriety.[22] In *Marmion*, of course, a similar woman disguised as a page does act improperly with the knight she attends, but Scott suffers no censure, both because the relationship is not dramatized in the present action of the poem and because Constance and Marmion suffer more than censure themselves. In this poem the earlier relationship between Edith and Ronald is treated realistically, though a part of that realism involves the effect of romantic circumstances upon the characters. From canto 3 on, this realism is modified, but not fully transformed, by the roles of women in two different romance conventions—the medieval quest, suggested in part by her green clothing, and Elizabethan comedy, suggested by her male's clothing. The specific nature of her disguise as minstrel adds still further complexity to this use of romance conventions.

In canto 1 her foster mother gently chides Edith for the "cold demeanor" that seems so inappropriate to the wedding clothes she already wears. Telling Edith first to look at the islands stretching out of sight and then at the mainland, "where many a tower / Owns thy bold brother's feudal power" (*LI*, 1:8), Morag reminds her how "auspicious" the morning is that will unite "the daughter of high Lorn" with "the heir of mighty Somerled": whoever "hears the tale" of this marriage will celebrate, in effect, its convenient alliance of land and politics. Only adding to this appropriateness is "Fame's heroic tale" (*LI*, 1:10) of Ronald's military success. Such feudal trumpeting has often seemed a weakness of the poem,[23] yet here it functions dramatically. For although Edith, betrothed to him since childhood by family arrangement, is prepared to love him by those "lays" of his "achievement," Ronald has not been equally prepared for her. After they meet—a meeting described only indirectly in the space of five lines—his response is "cold delay" (*LI*, 1:11). Although arranged marriages of this sort often enough led to indifference on both sides,[24] Edith's readiness to love leaves her doubly vulnerable. Subject to others' arrangements and others' more active lives, she is a willing pawn in the arrangements for the marriage. Yet because she wants the marriage to be more than an arrangement, she is an emotional victim. Although the early betrothal and the vast landscapes involved in the negotiations are characteristic of the medieval period, Edith's poignant demand for love—though surely not unknown earlier—also reflects the growing emphasis placed upon woman's sentiments and the frequent conflict of such sentiments with the economics of the marriage market in the late eighteenth and early nineteenth centuries.[25]

With Bruce's storm-driven arrival and then his recognition, the realism of larger political conflicts and actual historical characters breaks in upon the realism of Edith's typical characterization. His warders have already affirmed that they will welcome any distressed traveler, even if he had "aided . . . the murderous strife / When Comyn fell beneath the knife / Of that fell homicide The Bruce" (*LI*, 1:27). First defending the still anonymous Bruce by the laws of hospitality, Ronald defends him even more hotly when the English king's representative de Argentine claims possession of the rebel against that crown: a "long suppress'd . . . spark" of nationalism inspires him. Yet Scott has skilfully woven personal, nonhistorical motivation into this change of heart.[26] Earlier in the turmoil, the woman traveling with Bruce has revealed herself as his sister and thus as the woman responsible, if unknowingly, for Ronald's coldness toward Edith. When he speaks to Isabel, his language eclipses the place of Edith—his possessives, even his term "bride," are addressed confusedly to both women (*LI*, 2:19). Further, once Lorn sees that Ronald and his Islesmen are no longer his allies against Bruce but now the king's supporters, he threatens to marry Edith to another, more reliable ally—and he also reveals how unfeelingly he had pressed for the earlier marriage in spite of seeing Ronald's obvious indifference:

> Was't not enough to Ronald's bower
> I brought thee, like a paramour,
> Or bond-maid at her master's gate,
> His careless cold approach to wait? [*LI*, 2:25]

Though he objects most directly to her lack of pride in begging for mercy toward Bruce, Lorn's words offer her little basis for self-integrity of any sort. Her vanishing, then her reappearance, disguised and silent, in a near wasteland are only the outward correlatives of what her status has become at the end of this scene.

Her choice of a minstrel's disguise makes a further ironic protest against her situation. Even before the action of the poem begins, Edith has listened to the minstrels who celebrate Ronald's heroism and who then celebrate the aptness of their alliance. During the first two cantos, the minstrels at Ardtornish have distinguished themselves by their readiness to sing the socially appropriate, if emotionally inappropriate, aubades for her wedding day. In canto 2, Lorn supplies a "lay" for the resident minstrel Ferrand that represents Comyn's murder in terms so insulting to Bruce that the king virtually reveals himself to correct his own history. Echoing the "hireling bard" motif of Edmund's self-criticism in *Rokeby*, he warns his fierier brother Edward not "to chafe thee for a menial's song." Sardonically, he praises the minstrel who has "framed . . . thy strains / To praise the hand that pays thy pains" (*LI*, 2:14). Although Bruce has not been fully disguised, his clothing is more that of a refugee than of a king, and the minstrel's song draws out his identity as Comyn's killer and as a rebel fighter, but not yet as one worthy of the crown he has claimed. With the belated arrival of the abbot in *LI*, 2:21, that killing is debated more directly than through the minstrel's accounts. In the first two cantos, then, Scott the modern minstrel has made his predecessors the scapegoats for his own fictional recreation of history. Edith's disguise of a voiceless minstrel seems an effective criticism of the politically compromised art she has just heard.

Yet her role as disguised minstrel on Skye enables Bruce to work toward the kingship that will be fully confirmed, undisguised, at Bannockburn. Effective for others, however, her silent minstrelsy is not a disguise that lends her strength, as does Flora MacDonald's disguise of Bonnie Prince Charles. Instead, her weakness becomes a way to teach others to regulate their strength.

One reason for her failure to gain male strength through her disguise is that Scott reshapes and relocates episodes from Barbour's *Bruce* to draw out their resemblance to medieval romance. As he does so, he modifies the freedom of male cross dressing available to the heroines of Elizabethan comedy with a more conventional, even archetypal woman's role from romance. For Edith, however, the role of the elfin queen or wilderness enchantress carries no radically transforming gramarye. Instead, it emphasizes—yet, paradoxically, in a constructive way—her passivity as object.

In Barbour's chronicle an heroic, isolated encounter with treacherous huntsmen occurs during Bruce's wanderings between his landing at Carrick and his eventual seizing of Carrick Castle; it is one of a group of such episodes.[27] Scott moves the episode to Skye and changes the slaughtered sheep of the hostile huntsmen, intended as bait for the hungry guerilla fighter, to the very stag the king had himself been hunting. When he places the episode beside a remote lake and adds the mysterious figure of the disguised woman, transforming Barbour's "howswyff" who helps Bruce after the ambush, Scott clearly returns to the Arthurian allusions of *The Lady of the Lake*. Once again he signals entry into a romance world through a royal quest for a stag. Once again, too, that quest leads beyond ordinary experience to reveal a confirmation of kingship. Because Scott moves the episode earlier, before Bruce's landing on the mainland at Carrick, he also makes it a preparatory, initiatory passage to a far swifter seizure of Carrick than Barbour and later historians chronicle.

In that preparation the disguised Edith by no means thinks of herself as a nearly supernatural lady of the lake. With her "cap and cloak of velvet green" (*LI*, 3:22), she wears the fairies' clothing so jealously guarded by the elfin king in "Alice Brand," the minstrel's ballad in *The Lady of the Lake*. She thus shares with the elfin world and with traditional ladies of the lake that border-figure role of mediating between the natural and the supernatural. Because of her male disguise, however, she does not assume the sexual power of a Circean fertility goddess, or even of a Guendolen in *The Bridal of Triermain*. Unlike the ladies of the lake, she is also a border figure between the sexes. As Ronald later recalls, the men who brought her to Skye and who plan to ambush Bruce call her "Amadine . . . (In Gaelic 'tis the Changeling)" (*LI*, 5:18). Since they are her brother's allies, these men half-consciously recognize her disguised sexual identity. More consciously, they allude to the tradition that the fairies steal human children and leave behind their own "changelings." In canto 4 Edward Bruce only half-jokingly claims that his "elfin page" must have set the mysterious beacon on Carrick's shore that signals his brother's forces to land. Thus they do not quite believe her a male, nor does she possess, except associatively or iconically, the powers of a Nimue or a Morgan le Fay. Instead, she preserves only the half-natural, half-supernatural otherness of both changeling and enchantress.

Yet she does function as a guardian spirit. Though she gives neither sword nor the gift of prophecy, she protects the hero from ambush by warning him with an inarticulate cry. The help that Edith as minstrel page offers Bruce and MacDonald in the camp on Skye and at two other crucial points—in the assault at Carrick and finally at the battle of Bannockburn—emerges not through any strength she gains or is freer to exercise in masculine disguise, nor even through the sort of cool-headed, articulate, and yet ladylike manner apparently shown by Flora MacDonald, but through the double weaknesses of womanhood and muteness. Unlike the militant Britomart or the highly articulate Rosalind, she reveals in her apparent androgyny only a passivity. Yet her passivity awakens others, literally on Skye and more figuratively elsewhere, to the possibilities of tenderer emotions and attitudes than those normally shown in war. Her disguise works, then, not to make her more masculine but to make her companions recognize more domestically feminine and thus more compassionate human values in themselves.

In this romancelike delay within history, Edith's complex role also works to educate Bruce and MacDonald in a complex pattern of loyalties that makes the ethics of honoring vows in personal relationships a model for political allegiance. Here again, Boswell's narrative of 1746 plays a significant role. After his account of the prince's escape across Skye, Boswell meditates in his 1785 *Journal* on the way his private emotions might have drawn him into rebelling against his public and established loyalties to a unified, Hanoverian Britain. In those three pages, he praises the Highlanders' "fidelity and generous attachment, which, however enormous the judgment may be, are honourable for the heart"; but he goes on reluctantly to agree with the judgments of Blackstone and Paley that long-settled governments acquire a virtue that may be inconsistent with their usurping origins. "I myself," Boswell goes on, would not have rebelled against Charles I, for example, "though fully persuaded that the House of Stuart had originally no right to the crown of *Scotland*; for that *Baliol*, and not *Bruce*, was the lawful heir" (1785 *Journal*, 243). With an ironic twist, the Bruce and Stuart line is converted in time from a group of aggressive usurpers to established claimants. Thus their model of an orderly, established government supports the Hanoverians, not their own direct descendant. The irony emerges partly because Boswell retracted his "kind of *liking* for Jacobitism" in the original, unpublished journal.[28] Clearly, the historical typology I propose for Scott's poem, in which a modern Scottish recalling of Bruce fulfills and corrects the failure of the last Stuart of his line, is a typology already used by Boswell and thus familiar to Scott.

In the poem Scott only lightly touches upon Bruce's own awkward conflict of loyalties: though he had sworn feudal loyalty to an English overlord and to the English-sponsored Scottish king, he held far deeper loyalty to his own ambition for an independent Scotland.[29] Instead,

Scott first focuses upon the most obvious conflict between the Bruce and the Balliol factions, Bruce's killing of Balliol's heir Comyn. Then, through the accidental encounter of those two factions at Ardtornish, he turns to focus upon two analogous dilemmas of loyalty, public and private, faced by the virtually independent Lord of the Isles. When the minstrel Ferrand voices Lorn's version of the Comyn murder, Bruce partially corrects it. This exchange describes only the physical encounter between Bruce and Lorn at Dumfries after the killing: each now accuses the other of cowardice.

When the abbot arrives, he becomes the judge in a kind of trial, hearing first Lorn's reminders of Bruce's papal excommunication, then Ronald's and Dunvegan's reminders of English injustice to Wallace and others "for guarding well his father's land" (*LI*, 2:26). In the king's speech of self-defense to the abbot, Scott follows Hailes's portrayal of Bruce acting in a flash of temper, but preserves that "landmark" of the traditional narrative, Comyn's treachery in betraying Scottish plans for rebellion to the English: "No selfish vengeance dealt the blow, / For Comyn died his country's foe." Although emphasizing the rashness of his and his supporters' response to this perception of disloyalty, Bruce also makes unclear who is responsible for the actual killing. Though he struck the first "blow," he goes on to say, "Nor blame I friends whose ill-timed speed / Fulfill'd my soon-repented deed" (*LI*, 2:29).[30] Accepting responsibility for his own violence, he nonetheless argues that it was violence prompted by earlier violence: "I only blame my own wild ire, / By Scotland's wrongs incensed to fire." His metaphor sums up the dramatic pattern of imagery that has worked through the whole of canto 2, in which literal fire and darkness seem contagious, spreading to the wild eyes and to the drawn "brands" of the two factions. The same light then spreads to the abbot as he unwillingly prophesies Bruce's success with a power that "burns, . . maddens, . . constrains!" and forces him to bless the king (*LI*, 2:30-31).[31] Bruce's skillful presentation makes his disloyalty to England one pledge of his loyalty to a Scotland that does not properly exist in feudal vows, but in an ideal pattern for the future. The abbot's conclusion directs us beyond the establishing of that loyalty to its almost mythic fulfillment: "In distant ages, sire to son / Shall tell thy tale of freedom won, / And teach his infants, in the use / Of earliest speech, to falter Bruce."

Meanwhile, the problem of transforming violent impulse into a pattern of honorable relationships and contracts is explored through the semifictional character of the Lord of the Isles. At Ardtornish Castle, MacDonald's wedding to Edith of Lorn was to unite him to the English or Balliol faction among the highlanders. Bruce's accidental arrival at Ardtornish, however, leads to the fiery quarrel in which Ronald's own duties as a host, his love for Bruce's sister, and his recalling of Wallace all prompt him to swear allegiance to this royal claimant. In historical accounts Bruce forces this Lord of the Isles, Angus Oig MacDonald, to give up the English-allied "daughter of MacDougal of Lorn" whom he had already married for a new wife with a more appropriate political loyalty.[32] In Scott's poem the interrupted wedding leads for MacDonald to a testing and to an eventual reconciliation of affection and honor. Encouraged by Bruce, this honoring of vows becomes a model that replaces the threat of anarchy in Bruce's rebellion against England and his murder of Comyn.

The reconciliation between MacDonald and Edith is made easier—far too easy, according to some critics[33]—by Isabel Bruce's decision to join a convent. Her reasons, however, reinforce the theme of an honoring of vows to control potential violence. Bruce's sister—in these specifics reinvented by Scott—rejects MacDonald both because her loyalty has turned to the church and because his loyalty, she argues, must be to his betrothed bride. Although the historical Bruce had at least three sisters, and one of them was in fact named Isabel, all were already married.[34] Scott's Isabel, though drawn to Ronald, refuses him in part for her higher loyalty to the church and in part, one senses, out of fear that she will lose him as she has lost her brother Nigel (*LI*, 4:15-24).[35] Chivalric war games, the scene in which she first met Ronald (*LI*, 4:25), when turned to reality demand too high a cost. Her withdrawal to the convent reiterates the submerged criticism of violence in canto 2, shown through its images of flame, and earlier in canto 4, shown through the human abuses of power that have marked the Hebrides' landscapes (stanzas 8 and 9).

Almost wholly fictional, Isabel becomes more an ideal than an alternative or rival for Edith. Or better, their mutual self-sacrifice for one another develops an ideal of ethical behavior within the narrow constraints of their dependence. Isabel declares she will not accept Ronald unless Edith willingly gives him up. Overhearing, Edith anonymously returns the ring (*LI*, 4:27, 5:2-4). This mutual idealism clears the ground for a hierarchy of loyalties in which the protective sentiment Ronald shows for the disguised Edith has time to educate itself into a love less romantic than his attraction to Isabel, but more socially stable. Once Isabel's decision is made, Ronald must gradually forget the chivalric dreams prompted by his first meeting her at a tournament and turn to the actual responsibilities and loyalties in which chivalric display must be based.

Of the three episodes in which the changeling minstrel-page acts almost as a supernatural guardian for Bruce's cause, the first—on Skye—establishes a link with romance guardians like the ladies of the lake. The second most clearly shows her vulnerability and the way that vulnerability becomes a test of character for the men she encounters.

When Edward Bruce sends the page "Amadine" ashore as an advance scout before their landing at Carrick, he explains the double advantage presented by the physically frail and apparently mute boy:

> Noteless his presence, sharp his sense,
> His imperfection his defence.
> If seen, none can his errand guess;
> If ta'en, his words no tale express. [*LI*, 5:10]

Ironically, the "imperfection" is not of tongue but of phallus; and because Edith is not in fact physically mute but is physically weak, she requires enormous courage to resist the pressures to make her talk once she is captured. Passive as it is, however, that resistance both creates the delay needed by Bruce's forces and intensifies the sympathetic bond growing between her and MacDonald. Isabel continues to educate her brother in the task of honoring vows as a positive, if sometimes painful, way to stabilize and unify society. He in turn can educate Ronald, made more susceptible to tenderness by his guardianship of the nearly helpless page. Because Ronald has grown fond of the young minstrel-page who joined their forces on Skye, he can eventually accept the undisguised Edith as person more than as political pawn. Because Scott's Bruce also eventually supports the betrothal vows, he develops a higher morality than the historical king who separates the actual Lord of the Isles from his already-married wife.

Yet if the literary Bruce seems capable of moral education, that education by the two women is not really put to the test. As Scott points out, "King Robert's eye / Might have some glance of policy"; for his military campaign had destroyed Edith's brother, and now

> Ample, through exile, death, and flight,
> O'er tower and land was Edith's right;
> This ample right o'er tower and land
> Were safe in Ronald's faithful hand. [*LI*, 6:7]

So much for "Edith's right"; in reassuming her woman's clothing at the end of the poem, she reassumes her role as pawn, a happy one even though she loses "ample right o'er tower and land." Scott's repetition neatly and deliberately confirms the irony. Nevertheless, this move in the game follows her own and now Ronald's affections; and loyalty to the more individual moral responsibilities of family and religion reinforces the large political loyalties of Bruce's kingship.

The wavering hero's attraction to the sister of his leader, the sister's final turn to a convent, and the hero's return to his first, less dramatic emotional commitment strongly resemble the sequence of emotional and political alliances in *Waverley*. Even the use of a double for the royal prince, a double who draws off and is criticized for a dehumanizing violence, is similar: Bruce's brother Edward, though an actual historical character, parallels Fergus MacIvor in this role. In *Waverley* the vows of loyalty taken by Fergus and later the vow that Flora will take in the convent are in part ennobling and yet tragically divisive; the deceitful means used to force Waverley into the Jacobite camp criticizes these vows. In the poem MacDonald's honoring of his vows and Bruce's encouragement for his doing so become a pledge of stability to offset Bruce's earlier lawlessness in the Comyn murder. Thus the parallel between Charles Edward and Bruce becomes a contrast between distorting and constructive loyalties, and it finally offers the hope of a positive national myth that will still have applicability.

Given the detailed realism of *Waverley* and the still schematic qualification of legend in *The Lord of the Isles*, it is all the more striking that Scott pauses to note the irony in Edith's victory. In some sense it acknowledges his dissatisfaction that Ronald's character cannot in the scope of the poem develop as fully as Waverley's and that his reversion to Edith seems less convincing than Edward's to Rose. In another sense, however, it acknowledges his repeated and skillful manipulation of stereotypes in the poem to explore the place and the choices of women.

Because Scott's ironic tone makes clear his sympathy with Edith's powerlessness as a woman, we can argue that the most unusual form of her passivity in the poem, her voiceless minstrelsy, is also carefully thought out. To understand this silence, we must consider Edith's minstrel role from both of the perspectives that have guided the interpretation of women's roles in romantic poetry: the mythic or projective, and the realistic. From the first perspective, her qualities as a woman symbolize aspects of the male poet's art: she may represent the whole of his art or some aspect of it, particularly its transcendent, possibly otherworldly inspiration. It may also represent qualities alien to male consciousness—the natural or the supernatural beyond rational control. Her sexual oppositeness may bring a grace or a troubling alien vision, or her weakness may represent some weakness in the male author's art. From the second perspective, Edith's choice to disguise herself as a mute minstrel may comment further upon her social status as a woman—and even upon the alienating or subordinating assumptions of the first perspective.

We have seen that in several of his earlier poems, Scott shows anxiety about the writing down and publishing of romances based on oral tradition. In writing and publishing the poet loses touch with the minstrel's traditional audience and becomes subject to the criteria of written documents such as histories or law cases. In this poem the anxiety about verifying narrative against historical criteria is intensified by an anxiety about verifying its fictions against natural fact. Both anxieties turn upon the sources of Scott's art in oral tradition, and both impose themselves upon the author's surrogate within the poem, the silenced minstrel. This anxiety may well arise from the success of his novel, clearly a written form and also closer in its developed details to the factual verifiability of history. Yet it may well have become more acute as he recalled Johnson's thunderous voice in the quarrels over Ossian.

In his *Journey to the Western Islands* and in conversations with his Scottish hosts recorded by Boswell, Johnson's hostility to Macpherson's claims that his Ossianic poems were genuine relics of an oral tradition was only part of his hostility to any oral tradition. Not only was "the bard . . . a barbarian among barbarians," but "One generation of ignorance effaces the whole series of unwritten history. . . . memory, once interrupted, is not to be recalled. Written learning is a fixed luminary which, after the cloud that had hidden it is passed away, is again bright in its proper station. Tradition is but a meteor, which, if once it falls, cannot be rekindled." Although Johnson had clearly formulated these premises before arriving in Scotland, his attempts to discover remnants of an oral tradition soon confirmed them. One speaker distinguishes carefully between bard and *senachi*, "poet and historian of the house"; a second informant tells him that a single person customarily filled both roles; and a third agrees with the first but says "that neither bard nor *senachi* had existed for some centuries." The islanders' inability to give a true history of their bardic tradition and of its relation to history epitomizes for Johnson the unreliability of oral transmission. The Ossianic poems could not have been transformed as wholes, he reaffirms. Only "Caledonian bigotry" in Macpherson's audience supports the claim of their accuracy.[36]

Both in his 1806 *Edinburgh Review* article and in his 1831 notes to an edition of Boswell's journal, Scott agrees with Johnson's skepticism about the Ossianic poems, yet he strongly challenges Johnson's assertions about a total silencing of the oral tradition: "A nation, the government of which was patriarchal, and therefore dependent upon genealogical tradition—with whom poetry was a separate and hereditary profession, and whose language is a dialect of the ancient Celtic, must necessarily have possessed much original legendary poetry."[37] He even cites Barbour's *Bruce* to show that Ossianic stories were current in the fourteenth century. According to Barbour, Lorn described Bruce's vigorous defense of his men as equal to that of "Gaul the son of Morni [defending] his tribe against the rage of Fingal."[38] Lorn of course praises himself even more by making himself analogous to Fingal, the Ossianic hero. As he repeats this undoubtedly oral tradition, Barbour himself becomes an Ossian, the next generation's bard mourning his dead heroes.[39] Because his loyalties lie not with Lorn but with Bruce, Barbour may implicitly criticize Lorn for appropriating an heroic model more rightly the property of Bruce; yet the Celtic sources would more rightly have been the property of Lorn than of the only half Gaelic Bruce.

In *The Lord of the Isles*, a poem set in the landscapes Macpherson claimed were Ossianic, Scott avoids even Barbour's claim that his historical protagonists knew these legends or myths. Furthermore, in the willed silence of his minstrel, Scott also seems to accept Johnson's larger criticism of the oral tradition. One might argue that Edith's refusal to speak or sing neatly avoids the linguistic and cultural divisiveness that fractures Scottish nationalism, a divisiveness Scott shows so powerfully in *Waverley*. By her silent presence, Gaelic, English, and French speakers are united. A more central argument, though one not inconsistent with this one, reevaluates the convergence of historical and romantic patterns of narrative suggested earlier.

As we have seen, Bruce's journey to Loch Corriskin on Skye, Scott's fictional supplement to historical accounts, follows in many ways a typical romance pattern. In a pattern of this sort, the quester or wanderer confronts in the wilderness forces that are present, though seen less clearly, in the civilized world. Through the focus of Scott's descriptions, however, Bruce also confronts the bleak sublimity of a natural world that is permanent but indifferent to human desire. The minstrel's silence makes clearer this alien world's visual domination, its immutable resistance to any human speech that might impose fictions upon it or derive myths from it:

> ... rarely human eye has known
> A scene so stern as that dread lake,
>   With its dark ledge of barren stone.
> Seems that primeval earthquake's sway
> Hath rent a strange and shatter'd way
>   Through the rude bosom of the hill,
> And that each naked precipice,
> Sable ravine and dark abyss,
>   Tells of this outrage still.
> The wildest glen, but this, can show
> Some touch of nature's genial glow;
> ....
> But here ...
> ....
>   ... all is rocks at random thrown.   [*LI*, 3:14]

The narrator's metaphors attempt to humanize the landscape even as he describes its alienness: his figures suggest its almost sexual victimization by some still more sublime and remote power. Thus the most fictional part of the poem, in its origin and in its romance retreat from social reality, becomes a medium for confronting king and poet alike with an ultimate and humbling natural limit.[40]

Before encountering the minstrel, Bruce encounters this stark landscape and, with Ronald's help, attempts like the narrator to humanize it through an alternate pattern of description. Ronald explains that, although the bards attach some mythic significance to the mountains, naming them "Coolins . . . from old Cuchullin," more often they counter the hostility of nature with their own playfulness: "our islesmen's fancy frames, / For scenes, so stern, fantastic names" (*LI*, 3:16). Bruce's interpretation is more in keeping with that sternness: "May . . . these mighty cliffs . . . not mark a Monarch's fate,— . . . his soul a rock, his heart a waste! / O'er hope and love and fear aloft / High rears his crowned head—" (*LI*, 3:17). Bleak as this self-portrait is, it represents both his victory over the wrath that killed Comyn and his acknowledgment of that victory's cost. None of these attempts to humanize the landscape can fully overcome its alien grandeur. Instead, its otherness remains, defiant of modifying speech. The silent minstrel, spotted beside the lake just after Bruce has spoken, becomes an iconic mediator. She evokes the fictionality of romance narratives to suggest that the otherness of nature has always been represented in romance, though it has always offered some mysterious, tenuous promise of human relationship. In her green clothes she promises the fictional, yet heuristic fertility of such a dream. Further, as the narrative continues, the minstrel-page will also mediate between the granite isolation Bruce has adopted and the humanness of emotional bonds directed by responsible loyalty. Both mediations point toward the kingdom Bruce must build.

At the end of the poem, as if this grounding in the granitelike facts of natural existence has given its characters and his own art a new endurance and a new grandeur, Scott approaches the most historically validated part of his poem—Bruce's victory at Bannockburn against Edward II—through a fictional claim of minstrel speech. When Edith, still in disguise as the silent minstrel, thinks she sees the Scottish army waver for lack of reserves, she inspires a rabble of camp retainers to follow her into battle—and she does so by breaking into speech. Because this apparent miracle inspires both the retainers and the main army, Scott's poem makes her words responsible for completing the victory. For the third time in his romantic fiction, Edith has intervened to save the cause of Bruce and of independence. Several nearly contemporary chroniclers in fact describe a charge of camp followers at a crucial moment;[41] Scott adds only his minstrel as doubly fictitious cause. Thus, within the narrative Edith becomes a bard like those figures of Celtic tradition who sang to lead armies into battle, by having been a false one—both untrained and silent—earlier.[42] As narrating minstrel Scott defines an analogous role for himself: he invents or transforms the causes that came before his historical event while not transforming the outcome already recorded by historians.

This carefully circumscribed, even playfully ironic claim of the minstrel to motivate massive political and military events both as they happen and as they become history seems an answer to his critical precursor in the Hebrides, Samuel Johnson. The moment of speech that ends his minstrel's silence moves into his own written song and through it claims a diachronic continuity moving from oral tradition toward written history. His own poem, to become a visual and static printed book, begins to resemble that permanent "fixed luminary" Johnson opposes to the meteors of oral tradition. Yet its mode as song and speech, a mode expressed within the poem by the minstrel's fictional miracle, holds that permanence open to the fluid inventiveness of an individual imagination. To subvert Johnson's antithetical metaphors, we might call Scott's poem neither a fixed star nor a falling meteor, but a planet wandering further from or closer to some historically verifiable or permanent truth. As in *Marmion*, his fictional narrative has wandered closer in its closing stages to the apocalyptic reality of a transforming historical battle. Yet even the battle, in this poem, seems open to the playful possibility of fictional intervention—in part, surely, because the historical outcome is itself so wish-fulfilling for the Scottish writer and his Scottish audience.

Another way to describe Scott's resolution of this conflict between history's written truth and minstrel's spoken or sung fiction is to recall that the minstrel's silence within the poem became evident before the starkly sublime permanence of the Cuillins on Skye. Already seen as a kind of magnificent but absolute limit to human aspiration, these peaks also seem analogous to the empirically verified facts of history, before which a modern minstrel must at first fall silent in despair of changing them. The very permanence of these actual mountains, however, ultimately provides a way for Scott to validate his fusion of history and fiction. His subtle shaping of fourteenth-century nation building to show a public pattern of loyalties grounded in individual moral responsibility and his use of that pattern to comment upon the failure of the eighteenth century rebellion already imply that all historical events stamped upon the same landscape have a kind of simultaneous presence to the adverting mind. Like retold versions of traditional narratives, though fragmented rather than sedimented, these half-volcanic, half-granite mountains, as if new-made from some "primeval earthquake's sway," still exist for us. Outlasting both Bruce's new nation and the last Stuart's exile, they can make these reciprocal histories present to Scott's readers who can travel to their shore, though inland far they be. If the minstrel's oral art bows before their stark silence, it eventually uses their emptiness and silence as the space—and the moment made permanent—for its cautiously-expressed surmise of the poet's control.

A nagging doubt cannot be silenced, however, in this conversion of Edith into a surrogate or symbol for Scott as modern, publishing poet. In her disguise on Skye, her silent presence may also be heard as a disruption or at least a questioning of the traditional Celtic role of the bard, which Scott describes as "patriarchal," in the midst of a society Johnson describes as having once been patriarchal.[43] The apparently silent and apparently mute minstrel who might speak as a female suggests another agency or power for transmitting traditional Celtic culture, but an agency that, if recognized, becomes revolutionary. Virginia Woolf wryly speculates that the ballad singers recorded in written collections as "Anon" were often women, and Scott's own border ballad raids confirmed this.[44] With Edith's miraculous outcry at Bannockburn and her subsequent return to a woman's clothing and identity, the problem of interpreting the minstrel becomes even more acute. This miraculous speech is in one way the full assertion of the more active male role that Edith's disguise as a minstrel page had promised her. Yet because that speech is effective only in the context of its earlier denial, its miraculousness seems an elegant fraud that has in reality defrauded Edith—and all other women—of audible speech. Women's speech, women's abilities, women's leadership—like Edith's leadership of the camp followers—will seem miraculous when freed from the apparently voluntary constraints society has placed upon their exercise. Or further, once we consider the "miracle" of the page regaining his voice a false miracle, then the articulate speech and the leadership may themselves be seen as only fictional possibilities, not real, if belatedly recognized, accomplishments. As mediating symbolic object in and of the landscape, the green-clad silent minstrel takes on great power for the development of the male figures in the poem. As a woman in her own right, she subsides into a domestic silence, relinquishing her rights in marriage, and becomes identified with the silence of the land she no longer holds in her own name. A poem that Scott first called *The Nameless Glen*, an appropriate metaphor for the unappropriated and silent woman as well as for Loch Corriskin, he finally inscribes as *The Lord of the Isles*, to preserve that and other patriarchal titles.

SEVEN

Harold the Dauntless

PLUNDERING A NAME

APPROPRIATE ENOUGH for the hero of Scott's last long narrative poem, "dauntless" seems all too appropriate an epithet for the poem itself. Although begun as a playful experiment, this relatively short poem became a burden that he labored to complete. To conclude a study of Scott's major narrative poems by discussing it may seem to show the same dauntless but misguided persistence. *Harold* all too easily falls victim to Scott's own shifting attitudes toward the problem of how seriously we should take his poetry. Instead of finding release from the responsibilities of cultural and national definition in the anonymity of a brief and wittily-focused poem, he seems almost to engage in a clumsy parody of those responsibilities by suggesting and then blurring the clash between Christianized Saxons and pagan Danes. Yet this very problem in evaluating *Harold*—its shifts in tone from burlesque berserkery to high-romantic introspection—points toward the possibility of reading it as a review of Scott's earlier quest for poetic identity, as a reassessment of the uncertainties expressed in the *Marmion* epistles.

Although that quest takes shape in several ways, all of them involve naming. First, as stated in the *Triermain* chapter, that poem and *Harold* form a symmetrical pair of anonymous experiments and should be evaluated from that viewpoint. Second, like its immediate predecessor *The Lord of the Isles*, *Harold* includes the role of a disguised and pseudonymous female minstrel. Finally, in contrast to these two, the name of the poem's hero is overdetermined. With the publication of canto 3 of *Childe Harold*, no name could be more burdened with the ambivalence of a proclaimed and yet denied autobiography. Not naming himself, Scott names his rival's most personal protagonist and work.[1] Even more than the "landmarks of history" that nearly silenced Scott's portrayal of the historical Bruce, the complex mixture of actuality and fictionality that make up Byron's Harold test Scott's self-definition as a poet.

In taking seriously this mixture of anonymity, pseudonymity, and egregious naming, I do not wish simply to agree with Lockhart's assertion that Byron's success drove Scott out of poetry. Instead, I believe that Scott sympathetically, yet critically, analyzed Byron's poetic imagination and advised Byron in *Harold the Dauntless* not to give up poetry but to temper an emotional excess that emerges from and turns upon the self. As he urges Byron to temper his imagination, moreover, Scott tempers his own. Byron's self-correction, whether based on Scott's advice or not, was to complete *Manfred* and then in his ottava rima satires "turn what was once romantic to burlesque." Scott's self-correction may have been to combine the two: to write more prose, and in that prose to enhance the satire and humor already present in the poems.

By the time he published *Harold* in January 1817, Scott had of course already written a great deal of prose—most remarkably, the five novels published since 1814: *Waverley, Guy Mannering, The Antiquary, Old Mortality,* and *The Black Dwarf*. Like *The Bridal* and *Harold*, those novels were published anonymously. Because the novels could confront in far more detail than could his poems the historical challenges and qualifications to his romance plots, the two volumes of *The Bridal of Triermain* published in 1817 stand in a different relationship to Scott as announced, named author than did the single volume in 1813. He seems to take refuge in two different kinds of anonymity, one increasingly realistic in its development of history and one increasingly fantastic in its use of romance.[2]

In *Rokeby* and *The Lord of the Isles*, the two realistic longer poems that alternate with the two fantastic ones during the years between 1813 and 1817, Scott names himself as the author and thus an authority over their nearly epic dealings with history. His skillful use of romance to write resolutions for their history suggests a masterful, transforming gramarye. Yet his problematic portrayals of the minstrels in these poems point to the problems and stresses in such claims. In *Rokeby* Wilfrid's intense, aeolian sensibility and Edmund's rhetorical power alike escape prudent control and require the balance of Redmond's more active character. The almost feminine sensibility of *Rokeby's* Wilfrid seems in *The Lord of the Isles* to find emblematic, though not lyrical, expression through Edith of Lorn's disguise of the silent, nearly passive minstrel. Even more sharply than in *Marmion*, this criticism of the minstrel's transformative powers seems associated with limitations upon the woman's powers, as if the woman's threatened reduction to the pawnlike status of their land also imprisons or at least inhibits the minstrel. To the extent that Edith participates in the mediating power of the minstrel and of the lady of the lake, she recalls a transformative power; but that recalling is almost ironic in its limitation. In *The Lay* and *The Lady of the Lake*, the enchantresses may end in domestication, but the male minstrels seem to gain power by usurping, reparenting that of the women; their alien power of a supernaturalized nature must first be realized, then uncovered.

In the two briefer, anonymous poems, not surprisingly, this struggle to convert witch to muse becomes even less veiled. Confrontations with witchlike enchantresses shape both of these romantic plots. If the role of the enchantress is less displaced in these poems, does the role of the minstrel also gain power and clarity, sheltered by the anonymity of their publication? The interdependence of these two roles—enchantress and minstrel—works quite differently in the two anonymous poems, however, and some of that difference grows from the increased challenge of Byron's intertwined reputation and art between early 1813 and early 1817.

As I suggested in discussing *The Bridal of Triermain*, the publication of these two poems as two volumes by the same, if unnamed, author points toward their mirroring of one another. Set in symmetrical northern English locations—*Triermain* in Cumberland, *Harold* in Durham—the poems are symmetrical, playful imitations of the two great native sources of English-language narrative, Celtic romance and Scandinavian saga. The rollicking and swashbuckling action of *Harold*, especially apparent in the first two cantos, also suggests that Scott intended it to complement the much-praised delicacy of *The Bridal*.[3] Finally, although their border locations, ballad rhythms, and romance motifs immediately gained for both poems the label of Scott imitations,[4] I suggested that his private delight in the self-parody of the first poem may have led Scott to consider the second volume not only as a continued self-parody like the concurrent *Antiquary*, but also as a parody of Byron.

A strikingly similar topos in both of Scott's poems—that of the witch's enchanted castle—gives grounds for developing further than before the complex pattern of relationship between these two poets and their works. This pattern would be perceptible even if we were reading the two volumes of *Triermain* without knowing their author, but it becomes far clearer in connection with the other works of both poets, and especially in connection with Scott's anonymous review of *Childe Harold* III.

In both poems the quest for a mysterious castle begins with an enclosed narrative recounting its ambiguous mixture of desirability and danger, a mixture attributable to its presiding women. The search thus attempts to confirm that magical or visionary narrative and to fulfill the desire for those women. In *The Bridal* Sir Roland learns the identity of his dream woman through Lyulph's five hundred-year-old story of King Arthur's encounter first with the castle and then with its presiding enchantress. Roland's quest for the enchanted, sleeping daughter of their union must first locate the castle that has withdrawn into merely natural rock. In *Harold* the romance quest for a magical castle interrupts the saga motifs in mid-poem. A minstrel's ballad describes the mysterious Castle of the Seven Shields and the bizarre liebestods of the witches who built it two hundred years earlier. Yet patrimony, not matrimony, is the object of Harold's quest. Far from pursuing a witch or enchantress, Harold hopes to occupy the enchanted castle for a night without encountering any of its earlier, unremittingly hostile, women. The bishop of Durham, on the other hand, hopes Harold will fail to return and press the claim for his father's lands, now repossessed by the church. Although it comes oddly from a bishop, this arbitrary task—endurance of hazards in an enchanted place—is a familiar one in folklore.

Sharply different from Roland's paradigmatic romance quest for a visionary woman, Harold's journey follows another, more Elizabethan, pattern of romance—a pattern Scott employs in *Marmion* and in *The Lord of the Isles*, and that Byron too repeatedly uses, as contemporary reviewers of *Harold* were quick to point out.[5] The minstrel-page who accompanies Harold to the castle is revealed there to be a woman. Her patient and anonymous quest for his love now fulfilled, at the very end of the poem she briefly takes on the romance role of the quest object.

Familiar as this motif of the disguised page had become in Byron's life and art, it poses particular problems when Scott turns to it in *Harold*. In all three of Scott's poems that use the motif, the disguised woman adopts the role of minstrel and thus intensifies the problem of poetic identity for the male writer. In *Harold*, the problem of that identity, already raised by Scott's now seemingly borrowed plot devices and his publishing conditions of anonymity, is intensified still further by two elements. First, in *Harold*, as in *The Lord of the Isles*, the main narrator is far less characterized than in Scott's earlier poems. Second, as noted above, the minstrel-inspired quest for the alien enchantress's castle and the revelation of the familiar minstrel companion as more foreign than expected converge in the precincts of the ambiguous castle: minstrel and castle must be reinterpreted together.

Like the castle of St. John in *The Bridal of Triermain*, the Castle of the Seven Shields in *Harold the Dauntless* is associated both with witchcraft and with the redemption of the heroine from its threat. Thus it too represents a nightmarish form both of the female body and of the female imagination. Ruth Eller has suggested that in recognizing his page's female identity, Harold must also struggle to recognize the female aspects of his own psyche.[6] Such an interpretation should not lead us to ignore the problem of the female minstrel's place as actual, socialized woman. Yet its linking of certain kinds of imagination to gender intensifies the problem of the relationship between Scott and Byron.

During the writing of *Harold the Dauntless*, Scott twice uses a strikingly similar metaphor of a ruined, haunted castle to describe Byron's mind. In late 1816 he wrote Morritt,

> I have just received *Childe Harold*, part 3rd. Lord Byron has more avowedly identified himself with his personage than on former occasions. . . . It is wilder and less sweet . . . than the first part, but contains even darker and more powerful pourings forth of the spirit which boils within him. . . . We gaze on the powerful and ruined mind which he presents us, as on a shattered castle, within whose walls, once intended for nobler guests, sorcerers and wild demons are supposed to hold their Sabbaths. [*Letters*, 4:296-97; 22 November 1816]

The metaphor may well have arisen from Scott's playful attempt to conclude *Harold the Dauntless*—or the figure in the letter may have inspired the conclusion of the poem. In his own poem, Scott's Harold experiences a similar, if far more lightly handled, confrontation both with his own "spirit which boils within him" and with the wreckage of a witchcraft that images that dark emotional power. Letters written while Scott worked on *Harold* change from an early delight in its playful supernaturalism to a later sense of disappointment and staleness. He wrote Morritt on 2 November 1815 about "an odd sort of tale which I have taken into my fancy to write, for indulgence of a certain propensity to the marvelous. . . . I have written it rather roughly but *con amore*" (*Letters*, 4:112). The same day he wrote to Lady Louisa Stuart, "It is a tale of errantry and magic which, entre nous, I am very fond of, though ashamed to avow my frailty" (*Letters*, 4:114). Yet when the poem was complete he wrote to the same two correspondents of his changed attitude (*Letters*, 4:380, 383; 31 January 1817). That shift coincides with his reading of canto 3 of Byron's *Childe Harold*. Even if his own poem becomes more puzzling in its tone, however, it also becomes more profound in its magic.

As J.T. Hillhouse has shown, the dating of Scott's work on *Harold the Dauntless* has been difficult because of his anxiety to dissociate the work from *Childe Harold*.[7] In the same January 1817 letter to Morritt that voiced his disappointment, Scott claimed, "Among other misfortunes of Harold is his name but the thing was partly printed before *Childe Harold* was in question" (*Letters*, 4:383). Quoting this letter, Hillhouse then goes on to quote his later admission in the 1830 introduction to *The Lord of the Isles*: "I am still astonished at my having committed the gross error of selecting the very name which Lord Byron had made so famous" (*PW*, 475). Because the manuscript of canto 1 is watermarked 1814 and carries what Hillhouse conjectures are printer's notes dated 28 October 1815, and because the last five cantos are written on paper watermarked 1815, Hillhouse concludes that Scott is being honest with

Morritt but refers only to canto 1 of his own poem and to canto 3 of *Childe Harold*; that is, his canto 1 was sent to press before the publication of Byron's canto 3. Once in press, however, all six cantos of the first edition were printed on paper watermarked 1812, possibly from the *Triermain* stock. Although the 1812 date in fact only shows that the poem could not have been printed any earlier than that, it implies almost by association the poem's claim to priority over *Childe Harold*.

Supporting the hypothesis of a long break in composition between canto 1 and canto 2, Hillhouse argues, is the change from "Harold the Hardy," used through canto 2, stanza 12, to "Harold the Dauntless," first used in canto 4, stanza 3. The earlier epithet, making his hero sound like the historical Harold Hardradi and therefore more Scandinavian, would support Scott's claim that when he began he was thinking not of Byron but of the sagas. He had already used Harold as the name of an Orkneyan "bard" in canto 6 of the *Lay*. Furthermore, if we consider genre alone, a saga imitation has far more claim to the name than does Byron's neo-Spenserian "romaunt."[8]

Nevertheless, the first two cantos of *Childe Harold* were not only themselves renowned in 1815, they marked the beginning of Byron's whole series of melancholy, wildly popular narrative poems before 1816. Thus claiming the name of a poet is precisely the problem. As earlier chapters have noted, Scott's relationship to Byron had been a complex and highly conscious one over a number of years. Byron's attack upon the publishing arrangements for *Marmion* in *English Bards and Scotch Reviewers* (1809) intensified Scott's own conflict between the medieval roles of chivalric minstrel or chieftain and the modern one of commercial writer. In 1812, as he worked on the *Marmion*-like *Rokeby* and its portrayal of the minstrel "brib'd by bandits' base applause," Scott was also reading and praising the first two cantos of *Childe Harold*. On 3 July, when Lord Byron had relayed to him some praise from the Prince Regent, he accepted the olive branch, taking the opportunity both to praise Byron and to clear himself of Byron's charges: "I may be well excused for a wish to clear my personal character from any tinge of mercenary or sordid feeling in the eyes of a contemporary of genius" (*Letters*, 3 July 1812; 3:138). On 6 November 1813 he wrote to Byron again, to praise *The Giaour* and defend Byron's "condensing of the narrative" against charges of obscurity. The defense becomes strangely ambiguous, however, as he goes on to say, "It requires most uncommon powers to support a direct and downright narrative; nor can I remember many instances of its being successfully maintained even by our greatest bards." Byron, meanwhile, had sent Scott a copy of *The Giaour*, inscribed "To the Monarch of Parnassus from one of his subjects."[9] The compliment must have arisen, in part, from Scott's joking in his letter about a "bard" who asked Scott not only for "his due station on Parnassus" but also for "a post in the Edinburgh Custom House." Soon after he read *The Giaour*, Scott reports to Murray his "great delight" in *The Bride of Abydos* (*Letters*, 6 January 1814; 3:396).[10]

During the summer of 1815 Scott visited London and finally met Byron; they continued to meet on the former's return from Waterloo in September.[11] Although these cordial meetings almost completely - erased the hostility of *English Bards*, it also intensified Scott's sense of the closeness of Byron himself to his haunted, driven heroes. Thus, even if Scott had written canto 1 of his *Harold* before this, his decision to send it to the printer in October is startling. Scott's conscious belief, one assumes, was a light-hearted conviction that his contribution to a series of "Harold" poems of Norse or neo-Norse origin was so totally different from Byron's that the identity of name was irrelevant.[12] Yet underlying this, whether consciously or unconsciously, seems to be a stubborn defiance of Byron's now notorious claim on the name "Harold."

Between the fall of 1815 and the fall of 1816, Scott's progress on his *Harold* is erratic. He writes Morritt on 22 December 1815 (*Letters*, 4:145), "The second volume of Triermain . . . is nearly finished . . . [and] I shall then set myself seriously to the Antiquary." Instead he first finished the novel, which appeared on 4 May 1816. A week or so later he wrote to Morritt (*Letters*, 4:233), "Another Incognito proposes immediatly [sic] to resume the 2nd Volume of Triermain which is at present in the state of the Bear and Fiddle." His allusion to *Hudibras* reveals that he is still in the middle of the poem; it also suggests a partial model for the rough, satirical humor of *Harold*.[13] Again his novel writing has delayed the poem. Finishing *The Black Dwarf* in early October and *Old Mortality* in early November, he publishes them together at the end of November.[14] On 14 November 1816, he writes to Lady Louisa Stuart, "As for Harold the Dauntless I hope soon to finish him & have him out so as to charge horse and foot in the same month" (*Letters*, 4:294). Before he finishes it, though, he receives the review copy of *Childe Harold* III from the *Quarterly Review*, as indicated in the late November letter to Morritt quoted above. To judge from the letters, he writes the review and finishes the poem almost at the same time. On 10 January 1817 he writes Murray he is sending the review that day (*Letters*, 4:363). Though that issue of the *Quarterly Review* was dated October 1816, it finally appeared on 11 February (*Letters*, 4:363n); *Harold*, on or just before 31 January (*Letters*, 4:380, 383).

Not until his review of *Childe Harold* III does Scott mention having read more of Byron's Eastern romances than *The Giaour* and *The Bride of Abydos*. In that review he describes the closeness of Byron to Childe Harold by drawing upon the repeated variants of the Byronic hero.

There he quotes the passages from *The Corsair* and *Lara* that describe the hero most powerfully.[15] In broad terms his own *Harold* resembles both of these two poems, as the reviewers noted, in its plot device of the woman disguised as a page. Looking as far back as *Marmion*, we can see the two writers exchanging this motif. *Harold*'s further resemblance to *Lara*, the semisequel to *The Corsair*, suggests Byron's influence on Scott. In each poem the misanthropic exile returns from eastern exile to claim his estates. Yet another aspect of the relationship between Harold and the disguised page Gunnar (revealed in the haunted castle as the woman Eivir) suggests that in Scott's last poem the motif has a Byronic shape. As in *The Bride of Abydos*, the two main characters have been brought up as foster siblings. In *The Bride* their love begins almost as incest; in *Harold* the hero is so totally ignorant of Eivir's sexual identity that he shares none of the Byronic fatal attraction to the forbidden. Because Scott treats Harold's puzzling blindness to Gunnar-Eivir's sex far more like a parody of literary convention than as a serious psychological event, looking for parallels to Byron's relationship with Augusta seems on the surface of it to take his silliness far too seriously. Scott's review of *Childe Harold* III shows that the problems of Byron's personal life were very much on his mind as he finished his own *Harold*, but to relate the profound seriousness of Scott's review to the erratic playfulness of his poem requires a tact almost as great as Scott employed in the review.

His tact in the review begins with its premise, a defense of genius. The spontaneous outpourings of imaginative art, even if unpolished or obscure, demand our awed respect when genius is at its peak. In words he surely applied to himself and his own often delayed and increasingly less spontaneous poem, Scott also warns against the mechanical repetition of formula when that genius or imaginative energy slackens. Modifying the earlier Morritt letter's powerful image of Byron's mind as a ruined castle haunted by "sorcerers and wild demons," he makes its quest romance plot more universal in order to describe the restless dissatisfaction of such a mind. In "the man of quick and exalted powers of imagination," he writes in the review, "His fancy overestimates the object of his wishes, and pleasure, fame, distinction, are alternately pursued, attained, and despised when in his power. Like the enchanted fruit in the palace of a sorcerer, the objects of his admiration lose their attraction and value as soon as they are grasped by the adventurer's hand." Although this description attributes Byron's tortured melancholy, both personal and literary, to a fundamental characteristic of all imagination, Scott goes on to consider first what personal circumstances might have made Byron's melancholy worse and, second, what remedy might emerge from greater control—not of poetry making, but of the temperament that tortures the maker. Scott suggests that Byron's discovery of his own gift for writing about sublime emotional agony led him to adopt this pose in life as well as art.[16]

Dismissing the most serious charges against Byron by naming them rumors, Scott names nothing else about them: "Though his youth may have shared somewhat too largely in the indiscretions of those left too early masters of their own actions and fortunes, falsehood and malice alone can impute to him any real cause for hopeless remorse or gloomy misanthropy."[17] With a powerful and sympathetic indirection, Scott replaces the privacy of "those scenes, ever most painful" to Byron personally, with "the scene" of "the multitude, idly or maliciously inquisitive, [who] rush[ed] from place to place, gathering gossip, which they mangled and exaggerated." The result is a brilliant defense accomplished without "pleading a cause" in any detail. Given this strategic unwillingness to discuss the rumor of incest, one might interpret the love between foster siblings in *Harold the Dauntless* as a further disarming of rumor through archetype or literary convention. By pointing to the artificial, literary nature of this motif in the resolution of his comic fiction, Scott implies that Byron's use of the motif has similar literary roots; yet he also wittily explores, as he will not explore in the serious prose of the review, its thematic significance.

His concluding advice to Byron in the review, however, corresponds closely to one of the most serious parts of his poem, the disguised Eivir's appeal to Harold to leave berserking for Christianity. In the review he writes:

A powerful and unbridled imagination is . . . the author and architect of its own disappointments. . . . The Giver of all talents . . . has endowed the owner with the power of purifying and refining them. But, as if to moderate the arrogance of genius, [the owner] . . . must regulate and tame the fire of his fancy, and descend from the heights to which she exalts him, in order to obtain ease of mind and tranquillity . . . to bridle those irritable feelings, which ungoverned are sure to become governors; to show that intensity of galling and self-wounding reflection. . . . Such seem the most obvious and certain means of keeping or regaining mental tranquillity.

He concludes more specifically:

Let the patient submit to the discipline of the soul enjoined by religion, and recommended by philosophy, and the scar will become speedily insensible to [the] stings [of the over-inquisitive crowd]. . . . many . . . have their thoughts fixed on Lord Byron, with the anxious wish and eager hope that he will bring his powerful understanding to combat with his irritated feelings.[18]

The scald Eivir's ministering, as we shall see, closely resembles Scott's sympathetic and tactfully-phrased advice in the review.

Byron received Scott's review of *Childe Harold* III on 1 March.[19] Though I can find no reference to his having received the second *Triermain* volume, Samuel Rogers refers to it in an 8 February 1818 letter to Byron: "Of *Rob Roy* the opinions are numberless; but I am sure it is Scott's, as well as *Harold the Dauntless*, which nobody reads."[20] Answering a hostile review of *Don Juan* in *Blackwood's*, Byron describes *Harold the Dauntless* more positively: "None of his imitators did much honour to the original, except Hogg, . . . until the appearance of The Bridal of Triermain, and Harold the Dauntless, which in the opinion of some equalled and surpassed him; and lo! after three or four years they turned out to be the Master's own compositions."[21] In March 1817 Byron complained repeatedly to Murray that he had not yet received *The Black Dwarf* and *Old Mortality*; Murray, this time, was their publisher. He had already read *The Antiquary*. One further reason for his interest in *Tales of My Landlord* may have been that Augusta thought he himself had written of the misanthropic, physically-impaired dwarf. Review, poem, and novels were all anonymous, though the novels had established their own fame, and Murray told Byron the author of the review by 10 March.[22] By his praise of Byron as "The Champion of the English Parnassos,"[23] a returning of the compliment Byron had inscribed in his copy of *The Giaour*, Scott also signals for the other writer his authorship of the review.

Because the end of Scott's *Harold* may have influenced the end of *Manfred*, Byron's reading of Scott should be pursued a step or two further. Byron had mailed the first act of *Manfred* to Murray on 28 February 1817, having begun work on it the preceding late summer and fall; he sent the early version of act 3, with its ridiculing of the abbot, on 9 March. Not until 9 May did he send the "reformed 3rd Act" of *Manfred* to England;[24] in one of his cover letters to Murray, he mentions having read *Tales of My Landlord*. Given these dates there is no possibility of *Manfred* having influenced *Harold the Dauntless*. If he had received the anonymous and small second volume of *Triermain* along with the review or with Murray's *Tales of My Landlord* during the spring, there is some possibility that Byron might have read Scott's poem before completing his final version of the third act. A comparison with the conclusion of *Manfred* would thus possibly illuminate the conclusion of Scott's *Harold*.

To see how the comic berserker Harold can be read as an analogue for the tragic and sublime figure Byron had made himself, we should now turn to Scott's poem itself and to its revisions of the mysterious romance castle as a place for psychological confrontation.

Looking at the poem directly is more difficult than might at first appear, for its representation of Norse culture stands at a watershed between the late eighteenth century's fondness for the bloodsoaked sublime and the nineteenth century's more balanced and historically-based interest in that early culture. As Margaret Omberg has shown, British acquaintance with Scandinavian culture developed in three stages. The first, prompted by a tracing of British constitutional liberties to Germanic and Scandinavian origins, was based on Saxo Grammaticus and on the Latin translations of the sagas made in the seventeenth century by Wormius, Bartholinus, Olaus Magnus, and Torfaeus.[25] The second, more literary stage, developed from Paul Henri Mallet's *Northern Antiquities* (1760), especially in the version translated from Mallet's original French by Percy and published in 1770. This new literary interest was inspired by fascination with the Ossianic material. Correcting Mallet's confusion of the Celts and the Scandinavians, Percy sought to define the cultural heritage of the latter as a separate Northern strain yet, like the Ossianic poems, free of classical rules. Yet when Gray, Percy, and others began to produce Norse translations or imitations, they were working from Mallet and from his seventeenth-century Danish predecessors writing in Latin, not directly from Old Norse.[26] From this mixed, mediated background develop the motifs of supernatural horror and the acceptance of violent revenge or violent death as the defining of heroism. Acquainted with all of this material from the early 1790s, Scott had taught himself a little Old Norse, enough to review William Herbert's direct translations from that language in 1806. With Herbert's translation a new and more scholarly exploration of Norse poetry begins.[27]

Many of the elements in *Harold the Dauntless* that seem most unlike Scott's usual balanced, skeptical narrative technique may emerge from the somewhat synthetic modern myth of the ancient Scandinavians developed in this middle stage and only gradually modified by the impact of more accurate scholarship. One such element is the poem's recurrent supernatural intervention. Another is Harold's mindless, violent response to cultural threat, a response defined more through its violence than through details of the real cultural conflicts involved. Even *Harold*'s curious mixture of saga and romance elements can be partially explained by the speculation Scott advances in his review of Herbert's translations from the Icelandic. Sagas, he says, are "northern romance." Further, "the popular poetry of Scandinavia . . . we cannot help thinking is the real source of many of the tales of our minstrels."[28] The clunking humor of the first several cantos seems drawn, on the other hand, directly from such Old Norse narratives as "Thrym," translated by Herbert and quoted by Scott in the review. Scott's abstract of the Erbyggi-Saga, completed for a new edition of the Mallet-Percy *Northern Antiquities* in fall 1813,[29] also leads toward a less fantastic, more varied and balanced view of Norse culture.

In *The Antiquary*, one of the novels that breaks into his composition of *Harold*, Scott also casts a critical eye on those late eighteenth-century cliches of Scandinavia. As Oldbuck and his nephew Hector MacIntyre walk along the beach, the antiquary praises Norse over Celtic culture. First quoting Gray's Norse poems and asserting authoritatively, "They're not so fine as the original," he turns to a fragment of something resembling the death song of Ragnar Lodbrog, "who smiled in death," one of the songs first published in translation by Percy, translated by Herbert, and noted by Scott in his review.[30] Oldbuck then turns to a consideration of Scandinavian funeral rites and Runic monuments. His enthrallment with past culture has already led him to lose his breakfast toast to MacIntyre's marauding dog; but Hector, too, is foiled by an animal. After the highlander defends his childhood memories of Ossianic poetry and seriously quotes a far more earthy quarrel between Ossian and Patrick than Macpherson ventures on, he attacks a seal and finds his own heroic high seriousness even more badly damaged than was Ossian's in the passages he claims to remember. The scene is no clear victory for the Scandinavian faction, however. Not only does the seal head off to sea with Oldbuck's walking stick, but Hector's fiery, violent behavior seems all too suitable for both Norse and Celtic heroic traditions as the opponents have defined them. There is a good deal of Harold in him.[31]

The novel's interplay of comically-developed yet humane characters suggests, on external grounds, Scott's critical perspective toward Scandinavian sources. Some internal measure of his control over the narrative material in *Harold the Dauntless* emerges from a close look at its structure. Like most of his poems, it works through a series of contrasting locations: here, castles, cathedral, and wilderness. After a brisk and bloody summary of the Danish Witikind's Viking career, canto 1 focuses upon his conversion in Durham Cathedral—a conversion, the narrator points out, "less for the faith than the lands he wan" (*H*, 1:6). When the celebratory procession, led by the cross, returns to his Tyneside fortress, it meets a counter tableau beneath the "darksome strength" of the castle. Holding a bloody club above a dead she-wolf and her cubs, Witikind's son Harold epitomizes in an almost cartoonlike pose the eighteenth century's popular vision of Scandinavian violence. Repudiating his father's sell-out of that Scandinavian heritage for Christianity and castle, Harold goes into exile. At the very end of canto 6 he successfully claims his formal and territorial patrimony—yet after he, too, has abandoned his far older patrimony of

Scandinavian culture and religion for Christianity and has gone to Durham to confirm that change.

Scott shows the ambiguity of that change in the middle cantos, as Harold confronts the church and saga confronts romance. Both canto 3 and canto 4 open with the narrator's present meditations on the cathedral, borrowing metaphors of "spoils" and "ransacking" to describe his and his friend's scholarly antiquarianism.[32] In canto 3 Harold, like the narrator, sees the cathedral from the outside and from a distance. In canto 4 he invades "Saint Cuthbert's Hall," temporarily terrifying the Bishop's conclave with his destructiveness as he demands the castle and lands of his now-dead father. Yet from within the massive and historical presence of the cathedral, strongly evoked even as Harold batters at it, a minstrel's ballad describes the mysterious Castle of the Seven Shields as if it exists in a world of romance fiction or vision. When the wise prior of Jarrow first suggests delaying Harold's demand by shaping "for the giant gigantic task" (H, 4:11), he proposes the task as one suitable for the traditional heroes of popular romance. "Were Guy to return, or Sir Bevis the Strong," he suggests, "our wilds" with their demonic castle "might cumber them long" as they attempted to prove their chivalry.

Both its inhabitants and its fantasylike, or nightmarelike, origins connect the castle to Arthurian romance. The seven daughters of the "Druid Urien," aided by "the Arch-fiend," spin their seven towers from demonic spindles. In Malory, Urien is married to Morgan le Fay, the most consistently malevolent of the Arthurian enchantresses.[33] To house their new husbands,

> Beneath the pale moonlight they sat on the wold,
> And the rhymes which they chanted must never be told;
> And as the black wool from the distaff they sped,
> With blood from their bosom they moisten'd the thread.   [H, 4:14]

Though this part of the gruesome scene owes much to Gray's Norse-inspired "Fatal Sisters," the result is the creation of a magic castle like Camelot, spun from the imagination: "As light danced the spindles beneath the cold gleam, / The castle arose like the birth of a dream; / The seven towers ascended like mist from the ground."

Though imaginary or magical in origin, the castle houses a violent, misogynist reality. Like the Greek daughters of Danaus in Aeschylus' *The Suppliants*, all but one of these daughters murder their husbands on their wedding night. Desired by all of the sisters, the seventh husband survives to kill all of them, then seals the silent castle. Now, two hundred years later, Harold belongs to the world of epic saga and is undeterred by the prospect of enduring a night in such silence: "And is this my probation? . . . Within a lone castle to press a lone bed?" (*H*, 4:15). The narrator points up his hero's literal-mindedness by teasingly saying, in the introductions to cantos 5 and 6, how "fantasy with pencil wild" blends "what seems and is in the rapt muser's gaze." Moreover, he goes on in canto 6, no modern tourist can find this castle as they have found other locations made famous by historical poetry, for "no towers are seen / On the wild heath, but those that fancy builds." Echoing *The Antiquary* he refers to "grave authors, with the no small waste / Of their grave time," who have claimed that they see in the remains of a fosse a Roman fortress. In an anti-antiquarian stance, yet one far more concerned with the desire for fantasy than is Edie Ochiltree's debunking realism in *The Antiquary*, he says he will ignore Hutchinson, Horsley, and Camden, and

> . . . rather choose the theory less civil
> Of boors, who, origin of things forgot,
> Refer still to the origin of evil,
> And for their master-mason choose that master-fiend the Devil.
> [*H*, 6:1]

By the end of canto 6, after Harold has gone through his trial, he will recognize not only the internalized nature of this romance setting but also its psychological significance. The genre of the poem, which begins to change as he listens to Gunnar's apparently-traditional Norse songs in canto 2, will then become as converted as Harold himself from action to psychological insight.

In contrast to cantos 1, 3, 4, and 6, which are organized through the structures of cathedral and castles, cantos 2 and 5 are set largely in the wilderness. Canto 2 chronicles Harold's clumsy courtship of Metelill, the woodman's daughter, and canto 5 his response to its failure. Before pursuing the psychological development involved in this failed courtship, a skeletal version of the Williamina Belsches love plot found in *Waverley* and *The Lord of the Isles* (noted by Adolphus, *Letters*, 206), we should note the skill with which Scott balances these two "wilderness" cantos. In the first, Metelill and her family fear Harold's size and rudeness as though he were some primeval giant. Yet the supernatural claims of Metelill's mother Jutta dominate the canto and attempt to control Harold. In the second (canto 5), another supernatural force—a Christian one—successfully controls his desire for revenge.

Jutta's husband taunts that her witchcraft is good for nothing "but to slay some peasant's kine, / . . . Or thorough fog and fen to sweep, / And hag-ride some poor rustic's sleep" (*H*, 2:14),—in short, only to play lower-class tricks and not to bring off their daughter's upwardly mobile marriage to the wealthy baron's heir, Lord William. Driven by those taunts, Jutta crosses "sable fell," "moss," and "cataract," to a "deep dell and rocking stone" (*H*, 2:16) where she invokes a "God of heathen days."

Paul Leider suggests that Scott was misreading Mallet's *Northern Antiquities* when he names Jutta's god Zernebock. Mallet, he argues, correctly points out the god's Baltic origins, but Scott thought Zernebock a Norse god.[34] Yet Jutta begins her invocation with a very correct geographical setting:

> From thy Pomeranian throne,
> Hewn in rock of living stone,
> Where, to thy godhead faithful yet,
> Bend Esthonian, Finn, and Lett. . . .   [*H*, 2:17]

She goes on, however, to recall his worship "here" by "hundred tribes," of whom she is "the last, the feeblest of thy flock," seen as a witch in her Christian culture. If her allusion to runes in this passage suggests a Scandinavian culture, the rocking stone suggests an even earlier one. Adolphus (*Letters*, 171) calls them Druid monuments.

Since Jutta seems unfamiliar with Harold's mores, it is not surprising that all references to Odin, and thus to a more clearly Scandinavian cultural pattern, are delayed until Harold's major confrontation at the end of the poem. Here the narrator seems less concerned with cultural conflict than with a naively allegorical, ultimately Christian struggle between good and evil, since he refers to Zernebock as "The Evil Deity." Jutta too refers to Zernebock's "master" as one that her spell can "wake from his trance, / Shake his red mansion-house of pain, / And burst his seven-times-twisted chain!" Astonishingly, even Zernebock, as he "rocked on the base that massive stone," sees himself as a hellish demon struggling against the good:

> Daughter of dust! Not mine the power
> Thou seek'st on Harold's fatal hour.
> 'Twixt heaven and hell there is a strife
> Waged for his soul and for his life,
> And fain would we the combat win,
> And snatch him in his hour of sin.

In words that increasingly resemble both the diction and the obscure cosmological dualism of *Manfred*, he continues: "There is a star now rising red, / That threats him with an influence dread . . ." (*H*, 2:18). In spite of its gloomy fatalism, however, the mysterious voice goes on to make a practical, nonmagical recommendation that Jutta eventually follows: "Involve him with the Church in strife, / Push on adventurous chance his life." Her immediate response, however, is indignation. As

Jutta's wand strikes the altar, the inscribed stone rolls from its "balanced base" and is swallowed up in a "moonlight tarn." Thus Scott, if not the simpler narrator, neatly disposes of the lack of evidence for Zernebock cults in northern England.

A similar "Deep Voice" and a similar nudged boulder appear in canto 5 to help influence Harold's next encounter with Metelill and her witch mother (noted by Adolphus, *Letter*, 280). Yet this deep voice has a message very different from Zernebock's. It belongs to a visionary palmer, visionary enough to be unseen by Harold's page Gunnar. When Harold defends his violence as his culturally determined heritage, the palmer warns, "If thou yieldest to thy fury, how tempted soever, / The gate of repentance shall ope for thee never." Though made uneasy by this apparition, Harold turns to drink instead of analysis. About to open the poisoned vial supplied in canto 3 by Durham's holy apothecary—in another attempt to retain Witikind's lands for the church—he is saved only by the opportune arrival of Metelill's and William's wedding-procession. The scene, and to some extent the cultural conflict, resembles that in Gray's *Bard*. While the wedding-procession winds below, Harold stands "high on a rock" and shouts "like the doom of death . . . o'er their heads." In his berserker's rage, he anticipates the woodman Wulfstane's bowshot and crushes him with a fragment (*H*, 5:14). Before he can kill the bridegroom, however, Gunnar intervenes to reinforce the words of the "visionary seer," and Harold's frenzy subsides. As he crosses himself, he begins to join the now-dominant culture. Meanwhile, in a nice comic irony, Jutta samples the poisoned elixir—and her dying screams, like her night-journey in canto 2, again make the wilderness echo. Metelill (her name, oddly enough, drawn from Herbert's Icelandic poetry) and her William, the narrator assures us, go on to live happily ever after.

This symmetrical development suggests that Scott's control of large structural elements has not weakened. If the wild variations in tone and action among the sublime, the bloody, and the comic reflect Scott's models in Norse literature and especially in its late eighteenth-century imitations of Norse literature and Norse heroism, they also reflect Scott's satire of those models. The sublimely death-defying laughter of Ragnar, hero of an often-translated Old Norse poem, reappears in the audience's laughter at Harold.[35] In canto 3, however, the cultural conflict becomes simultaneously more overt and more internalized. When Harold asks Gunnar, "offspring of prophetess and bard," to inspire him "with some high strain of Runic rhyme," the minstrel-page sings three songs in answer. As is often the case in Scott's narrative poems, the apparently objective folk lyric turns into a subjective, individual expression—or, rather, into a means of provoking such commentary. It becomes a code through which broadly-sketched characters can find themselves described and can then react in individual self-definition. Although the process is not completed until the fifth and sixth cantos, Harold is converted not only to Christianity but to a more developed self.

If in those later cantos his conversion is abetted by a series of supernatural encounters, it is surely significant that Gunnar does not see the visionary palmer in canto 5, but only an oak tree. For Gunnar's motives, beginning to emerge in canto 3 but not fully clear until the revelation of her sexual identity as Eivir at the end of canto 6, are thoroughly human. Just as the Lord of the Isles is drawn into Bruce's camp partly by his infatuation with the king's sister, so Eivir works to change Harold's allegiances for personal reasons and thus forms part of a larger change in historical and cultural development. Even though Harold is far more comic a figure than MacDonald, his individuality is more developed. True, Lady Louisa Stuart writes Scott upon first reading the poem that Eivir herself may not have known she was a woman until the last canto.[36] Surely, too, Byron's use of greater narrative distance enables him to avoid a similar problem of cross dressing in *Lara* with far greater finesse. Yet Scott both parodies the traditional disguise and uses it to develop Harold's character in realistic and symbolic ways. On rereading we see Gunnar, an actual person, work to change him. Symbolically, we recognize as Eller argues that his discovery of Eivir is not only a Renaissance or Greek romance happy ending but the discovery of his gentler, more humane self beneath the fatalistic bear shirt of his Norse heritage.

In the songs and dialogue of canto 3, Gunnar begins as traditional scald and Harold as the chieftain who calls upon that public voice to define himself in relation to his ancestors. Harold recalls how "Heymar the Scald" inspired his grandfather and fellow chieftains so that they "rush'd in emulation forth / To enhance the glories of the North" (*H*, 3.5). In a sign of the wandering life led by the Vikings, he does not even know where his grandfather is buried or whether his afterlife is in Valhalla or in a Christian heaven. Yet although he seems to want a patrimonial reassurance that "to thee are known . . . / Our wars, our wanderings, and our woes," he interrupts Gunnar's answering song when it suggests that Eric's spirit is made restless by his grandson's exploits in defense of Christianity. In lyrics closely following both Norse elegies and eighteenth-century translations of them, Gunnar describes how the almost totemic birds of prey "scream'd for joy / O'er the beetling cliffs of Hoy," and how on this bloodstained battlefield in the Orkneys "Dane and Northman piled the stone" as a cairn for the slain Eric. In the second stanza, figure merges with landscape in an Ossianic mood of nostalgia: "Where eddying currents foam and boil,

... The seamen sees a martial form / Half-mingled with the mist and storm." As the singer asks rhetorically what funeral rite may have been neglected to cause this restlessness, the song returns to Norse models like Hervor's incantation.[37] Then, in the fourth stanza, Gunnar evokes other bloodstained battle scenes, the ones that have caused Eric's ghostwalking. These scenes, much further to the east, include Harold's own heroic deeds "on Carmel's cliffs and Jordan's strand." Apparently Scott's Harold, like his namesake Harold Hardradi in the mid-eleventh century, has been fighting for the Byzantine Christians and against the Saracens or Turks. Historically, this mercenary service had begun even before the Vikings who joined the Varangian guard had become Christians,[38] but the fictional ghost of the pagan Eric may have anticipated that conversion through military allegiance and may have felt deserted by his grandson as well as by his son.

Instead of justifying himself against this implication of betrayal, Harold instead accuses Gunnar of a similar betrayal: "The noble Scald," he reminds Gunnar, "our warlike father's deeds recall'd," but his "harp ne'er stoop'd to flattery." His next comment, however, opens the more personal discussion Gunnar had signaled with her song. When he praises the scald "whose daring lay / Hath dared unwelcome truths to say," he correctly "construe[s Gunnar's] doubtful smile," both urging the page to "say on" and warning against "the rude / And wild distemper of my blood." Two motifs for that wild distemper dominate the rest of this brief canto. In the first of these, Gunnar develops a psychomachia like the one Scott uses to describe Byron: "Oft seems as of my master's breast / Some demon were the sudden guest. . . . From her firm seat his wisdom driven" (*H*, 3:7). In the second, his berserker's rage is compared to a storm-driven ocean. Through both metaphors Harold claims a fatalistic lack of control that is the very essence of his strength: "The spirit of our line," he argues, is "the bold Berserker's rage divine . . . When full upon his gloomy soul / The champion feels the influence roll." Fighting "unshielded, mail-less," he can perform deeds. . . . Past human strength and human thought."[39] Arising in part from his "gloomy soul," this sublime ecstasy is almost a prophetic trance.

In the midst of this sharp definition of Norse culture, we should note how Scott blurs—in playful irony or in deliberate synthesis—the historical context. After rooting this psychology in Scandinavian culture, Harold goes on to say that Gunnar may at other times "speak boldly out whate'er / Is fitting that a knight should hear" (*H*, 3:8). Though all of this poem should have been set before the Norman invasion, as suggested by its primary conflict between Saxon church and Danish warrior, the institution of knighthood reached the area far later.[40] Equally anachronistic are several Norman names: that of the

Durham minstrel and of "Lord William." The Durham minstrel's ballad also sounds Norman in its affinities with Arthurian romance. Even if the British sources for such romance precede the Normans, they are scarcely Saxon.

Yet even though Harold's criterion of fitness for a knight's ear is jarring in its anachronism, his turn from mindless violence to chivalric decorum signals a larger shift in the poem. Here the assumptions of cultural development seem sketched in as if to support psychological development, instead of the reverse. As the narrator compares Gunnar to a "watchful pilot" steering cautiously among the shoals and depths of Harold's temperament, the "Page"—yet another anachronism—begins a second song with a related metaphor, that of a storm-tossed ship with a traitor at the helm. Gunnar's second and third warning stanzas also warn of betrayal by bad advisors; the third, describing a knight betrayed by listening to a woman's advice, Harold immediately takes as a literal attack upon Metelill—which it is. As we later realize, Gunnar is also a woman giving advice, and her advice here is fidelity to Harold's Norse heritage through fidelity to "a Danish maid":

> Were I a Danish knight in arms,
>   As one day I may be,
> My heart should own no foreign charms;
>   A Danish maid for me!

So often associated in romance and in Scott's novels with calm domesticity, blond beauty is associated here with the Danish woman's almost Amazonian freedom of action:

> 'Tis hers the manly sports to love
>   That southern maidens fear,
> To bend the bow by stream and grove,
>   And lift the hunter's spear.

Retrospectively, this cultural role makes Eivir's transsexual disguise slightly more plausible. Yet all of this analysis must go on after the end of the poem. At this point only Gunnar's slightly excessive hostility to Metelill is a clue. We can see, however, that Gunnar attempts to revise Harold's allegiance, within the Danish culture, from rule by a demonic "rage divine" to guidance by a Danish woman.

At the end of canto 3 and in canto 4, we realize more clearly the violence Metelill's witch-mother Jutta has reinforced in Harold, a violence Gunnar is already aware of. All the time Harold and the page have been sitting on the hill analyzing his berserker psychology, the sack beside Harold has held a head and a hand once belonging to the church's tenants on his father's former lands. When he throws them before the monks, his swaggering, their cowering, and the exuberant rhythm all recall the first canto and seem to deny the greater introspection of canto 3. This episode might be compared to one in the Heimskringla, when Hakon brings to the Danish King Svein's feast the head of the king's beloved but unruly friend. Yet Snorri's understated depiction of the participants' tense confrontation is markedly different from the treatment in this poem.[41] Without being fully defined as a character himself, Scott's narrator seems at such points to see both cultures—Christian Saxon and pagan Danish—externally, viewing each through the cliches and cultural prejudices of the other.

Though Harold's "language," "look," and "laugh" make him seem an "arch-fiend incarnate," the task the monks propose for this energetic giant form leads instead to his confrontation with the demons who seemed to house themselves in his own breast. In canto 5, as we have already seen, Harold encounters a visionary palmer who reinforces Gunnar's warnings against berserker violence. Both in his appearance as a pilgrim and in his threats of damnation the palmer is a spokesman for Christianity. When Gunnar urges Harold to make the sign of the cross instead of swinging his mace at Lord William (*H*, 5.17), the disguised page is of course trying to be sure her rival Metelill is married off—though until the end of canto 6 we see only her more altruistic motive of attacking Harold's internal "fiend" (*H*, 17, line 22). Neither motive involves a direct and positive affirmation of the Christian faith, but only a pragmatic use of its sign as a psychological device. Yet its success becomes clear with the repetition of the word "sign" in this stanza. First Harold "with arm uprais'd" waits like a "headsman. . . . That pauses for the sign" to kill; second, he "sign'd the cross divine"; and third, the narrator interprets his choice as "one sign" of a new forbearance.

In canto 6 Harold and Gunnar must similarly learn to interpret cultural signs first as symbols beyond themselves and then as symbols of their inner selves. Ruined for two hundred years, the Castle of the Seven Shields might have dated from a Celtic kingdom in the era of a Celtic Arthur, as the name Urien suggests. Yet Scott's treatment is no more historical than elsewhere in the poem. Instead, he draws on later medieval or even Renaissance allegorical romance, as in the third section of *The Bridal of Triermain*. In spite of the seven shields' "marks" and "signs," however, interpretation here is far more difficult than in the earlier poem, both for characters and for readers. In fact the whole episode might be seen as a comedy or even a parody of interpreting the symbolic castle, just as the ballad seemed to parody Arthurian characters such as Lot and Urien, were it not for the two major recognitions that emerge in this process of interpretation. These recognitions are, first, Harold's coming to terms with the cultural inheritance, in fact the patrimony, of his personality, and, second, his acknowledgment of what we might describe as a female vision of the world. Not only are the two recognitions dramatically and symbolically interdependent, they also draw equally upon, and reshape, the Byronic motifs so present to Scott as he completed the poem.

Harold's and Gunnar's exploration of the castle develops in three stages. The first, their passage through its skeleton-strewn court and their somewhat anticlimactic bivouac for the night raises more acutely than elsewhere in the poem the problem of woman's status. Second, after their emergence from the castle the next morning, Harold tells of a dream experienced during their stay, a nightmare that intensifies Harold's conflict between pagan and Christian beliefs. The third, climactic stage develops as Gunnar runs back into the castle to retrieve Harold's glove. When a giant figure of Odin seizes the page and reveals her identity as a woman, the two problems become one and must be resolved together. The first of these stages is a static tableau of violent death that Harold interprets as emblem; the second, the dream, spells out its own interpretation as it unfolds; and the third stage is a startlingly direct confrontation that reevaluates, even confounds, the first two.

Harold's emblematic interpretation of the scene they witness at the witches' castle is anticipated by the narrator's introduction. With his assertion that Harold gazes on "fiend-built towers," the narrator recalls medieval romance accounts of Merlin's exploits. When Harold and Gunnar enter the castle, both the narrator's double Spenserian stanzas and his use of allegorical personifications suggest a more psychological, internalized, and self-conscious use of romance:

> More strong than armed warders in array,
> ....
> Sate in the portal Terror and Dismay,
> While Superstition, who forbade to war
> With foes of other mould than mortal clay,
> Cast spells across the gate, and barr'd the onward way. [H, 6:3]

This more analytical, yet pictorially static mode distances slightly the Gothic horror of the scene within the castle and prepares for Harold's facile emblem making at the end of the scene.

Most important, though, this Spenserian frame of allusion recalls the Renaissance witches that inhabit its fairyland, the Duessas that haunt every Una. Empty halls and bowers, "frail" tapestries, tarnished vessels, and "barbaric ornaments" all lead to the seventh chamber with "each skeleton" of the "witch-brides" in the posture of its moment of death. The scene evokes no pity in the narrator. Two hundred years frozen not precisely in that realized moment of vengeance but in its grotesque, flesh-deprived aftermath punishes these witches both for their magic and for their aggression (and finally, perhaps, for their bodies): "One bony hand held knife, as if to smite; / One bent on fleshless knees, as mercy crying; / One lay across the door, as kill'd in act of flying" (*H*, 6:6).

In the second half of this, the last of the normally introductory Spenserian stanzas, Harold "smiled this charnel-house to see, / For his chafed thought return'd to Metelill." Rankling from her rejection, he condemns not the specific witchcraft of these brides, but what he now suddenly claims is a betrayal by all women:

> . . .'Well,' he said, 'hath woman's perfidy,
> Empty as air, as water volatile,
> Been here avenged. The origin of ill
> Through women rose, the Christian doctrine saith:
> Nor deem I, Gunnar, that thy minstrel skill
> Can show example where a woman's breath
> Hath made a true-love vow, and, tempted, kept her faith.'

Even before his acceptance of Christian faith, Harold seems to have accepted Christian misogyny. The magical powers of these witches in building their seven towers seem far less important to him than their "perfidy" in betraying and murdering the six grooms; or, rather, that magical tower building becomes a prior affirmation of their violent, deadly usurpation of male power. Harold suggests that the surviving groom's vengeance is every Adam's retaliation against Eve.

By turning to Gunnar and challenging his "minstrel-skill" to show a woman faithful to her vows, Harold places Gunnar in a dilemma: to lead Harold away from berserking violence to greater humanity, must this new misogyny be the price? Gunnar seems to suggest a middle ground. To offset Harold's universal accusation against women, he (not yet revealed as she) alludes to a story "of woman's faith," but says he could do justice to the full story only if "it were my dying song," since "our scalds have said, in dying hour / The Northern harp has treble power." Like Gunnar's retelling this story of "a love unknown, . . . unrequited," and faithful "from clime to clime, from place to place" is to become known only at the woman's death, upon her burial stone. "Eivir," concludes Gunnar, could accomplish such faithfulness because she "was a Danish maid." This double dependence upon death, along with the parallel of similar journeys, is meant to raise Harold's—and our—suspicions. Like Gunnar's song in canto 3, this one recalls Harold to his own culture, but to a woman's fidelity, not a berserker's violence. It also points toward the later revelation that Gunnar is Eivir. Because that hint is lost on Harold, he offers to share his mantle with the page; thus, their closeness, the woman's fidelity, and the scald's possible story, all seem dependent upon disguise and ignorance, not upon any fuller revision of Scandinavian or Christian cultures. A fuller reinterpretation of the witch-brides' tableau, to renounce its male horror story of female creativity, must await the dispelling of Gunnar's disguise.

Before this recognition Harold must come to terms with the relationship of his own male fantasy of behavior to Christianity's quite different ideals. In the second stage of their visit to the "fiend-built" castle, this confrontation will lead to further exploration of the Christian values—or, at least, the antiberserker values—that Gunnar also advocates. After a night anticlimactic in its lack of outward incident, Harold awakes distraught from a nightmare vision. Pulling Gunnar quickly out of the castle, he then explains how this dream or waking vision has convinced him to reject his older patrimony for a newer one, his grandfather's berserking for his father's Christianity. In his dream the "cavern'd gulfs" of Mount Hecla, the Icelandic volcano that holds a central place in Norse legend, reveal not a pagan underworld, far less a Valhalla, but instead a "hell."

Standing on Hecla he sees its "cavern'd gulfs" as a "central place of doom," to which "fiends" in "elvish train" draw "souls of the dead." Then, like a ballad of the Shee or of the Erl-King, a train of ghost riders leads a black horse for him to mount. Accompanied by Jutta and Wulfstan, the parents of Metelill, these black riders declare that his powers have come from them and thus from Zernebock. In his vision, as in Zernebock's own speech in canto 2, they no longer retain the integrity of a pagan culture but see themselves as devils:

> From us, O Harold, were thy powers,
> Thy strength, thy dauntlessness, are ours;
> Nor think, a vassal thou of hell,
> With hell can strive. [H, 6:10]

Even though these figures are now placed on the fringes of another, dominant culture, Harold feels the old berserker fatality draw him toward their procession, until he is saved by his good angel—or, more correctly, his guardian spirit—the palmer. When the palmer reveals himself as Harold's "father Witikind! / Doom'd . . . A wanderer upon earth to pine / Until his son shall turn to grace" (H, 6:11), Gunnar's song about the restless dweller of the cairn (H, 3:6) becomes ironically complete. If the ghost of Harold's grandfather Eric haunts the Orkneys because his grandson fights for Christian causes, his father haunts those Christian battlefields and the neighborhood of Durham because his son is not Christian enough. Recognizing now the demonic nature of his berserker abilities and recognizing that they need not be a part of his patrimony—or, rather, that he has a choice of fathers and of father cultures—Harold chooses grace. Yet what he chooses is not so much a Christian revelation as a domestic or psychological balance: "I'll tame my wilful heart to live / In peace, to pity and forgive."

The rest of the palmer's message, as Harold tells it, leads toward the comically slow revelation of Gunnar's identity. Yet it also shapes the role of Gunnar in Harold's recognition of a more peace-loving and humane self, even as a projection of that self that must be recognized and claimed. Reporting the palmer's hints of a disguise arranged by Gunnar's mother to make closer "the fatal textures which knit thy thread of life with mine," Harold makes a gesture that reveals both the difficulty of his new role and the difficulty of leaving the old one behind. When "his hand . . . sought his thoughtful brow," he discovers that he has left his mailed glove, a symbol of his violence, in the castle. To hide a blush "like an opening rose" (*H*, 6:12), Gunnar retreats in embarrassment to find it, but then becomes hostage to the last—and most central—image of Scandinavian culture in the poem: an apparently direct, not dreamlike confrontation with "Odin in living form" (6:13). As several critics suggest about the gloves and hands in *The Fair Maid of Perth*, however, the hand is also the writer's hand, as the berserker's "powers" seem those of an uncontrolled imagination.[42] Further, if Gunnar is a pawn in Harold's struggles for cultural identity, the scald must also struggle with the fate of artistic power in Eivir's new sexual identity. Scott's complex awareness of Byron, shown earlier in his metaphors of the other poet's mind as a ruined, haunted castle, gives this struggle for the artistic identity particular force.

The narrator identifies Odin as "the semblance of the Evil Power," and his physical description has a sort of satanic sublimity: "For plumy crest a meteor shed / Its gloomy radiance o'er his head, / Yet veil'd its haggard majesty / To the wild lightnings of his eye." Yet unlike the demonic ghost riders in Harold's night vision, Odin does not identify himself as a messenger of hell. Instead, he reminds Harold in lines of some dignity that he is "thy Warrior-God," focus of "the worship of thy line," and dispenser of "the joys for which the valiant live, / Victory and vengeance." Though cloaked in a polar bear's skin and thus dressed as the ultimate shape-changing berserker, he does not appeal directly to berserker rage but to the culture that values it. Yet Harold recognizes the implicit appeal. He also, interestingly enough, recognizes the ambiguity of that "living form" in a moment of conversion:

> 'Tempter,' said Harold, firm of heart,
> 'I charge thee, hence! What e'er thou art,

> I do defy thee, and resist
> The kindling frenzy of my breast,
> Waked by thy words. . . .
> . . . .
> . . . God or Demon, part in peace.' [H, 6:15]

Although unsure whether he addresses an actual, independent god, or whether this "semblance" of Odin is, like Zernebock in his vision, a demon subordinate to the Christian God, Harold like Odin achieves a great dignity in his ability to deal with that intellectual uncertainty. Because of this his firmness of heart is all the more remarkable; he can resist not only the glory of the berserker, but also the total certainty of its mindless "kindling frenzy."

As a contemporary reviewer noted with puzzlement, at this point Harold closely resembles Byron's Manfred. Discussing *Harold the Dauntless* for *The Monthly Review*, this critic writes: "In the rencontre with the *deep voice*, and in Harold's *defiance* of the spectre who claims an authority over him, we recognize a most extraordinary similarity to several passages in the late dramatic poem of Lord Byron; where Manfred, the hero, behaves in a manner unaccountably resembling that of Harold in the occasion above-mentioned; and which occasion is also the same in both works. Every circumstance forbids plagiarism in the noble author." Yet the reviewer goes on to note that *Manfred* was "written . . . at or about the time *Harold the Dauntless* was first published in England," and thus "it is still more out of the question that he [the author of *Harold the Dauntless*] should have been the plagiarist than Lord B ———.”[43] It is possible that Byron received a copy of Scott's poem along with the *Tales of My Landlord* he had requested so urgently from Murray, or along with the review of *Childe Harold* that appeared in the *Quarterly Review*. Because Scott's poem was anonymous, Byron might have read and absorbed it without making any conscious note of its supernatural confrontation —and may have drawn upon it for his own poem. Yet if the resemblances are puzzling in origin, they are ultimately more interesting for the way in which they show Byron's and Scott's differences. *Harold the Dauntless* is clearly part of Scott's response to *Childe Harold* III; for that reason we can also read it as a response or corrective to *Manfred*, though the chronological evidence for the latter suggests that if there is direct influence, it moves from Scott to Byron.

In act 3 of Byron's play, Manfred faces death and after it a total uncertainty about what follows death. First rejecting the abbot's appeal to repent and accept Christianity, he then also rejects the claim of "a dusk and awful figure . . . robed as with angry clouds" (3:4.62). As the figure advances toward Manfred, the abbot's description intensifies the spirit's relationship to Satan: "On his brow / The thunder-scars are graven: from his eye / Glares forth the immortality of hell—" (76-78). Yet much of the power in Byron's conclusion comes from the uncertainty not only of this figure's identity but also of his exernality. Repeating "I do defy ye," (99-100, 120), Manfred first denies that he has made any compact "with thy crew"; his Faustian powers were his own. Then he explains, echoing both Marlowe's Mephistophilis and Milton's Satan, that his punishment is also his own: "I bear within / A torture which could nothing gain from thine: / The Mind which is immortal makes itself / Requital for its good or evil thoughts, / Is its own origin of ill and end— / And its own place and time."[44] Manfred's Faustian quest for ultimate knowledge is of course far more metaphysically serious and treated with more consistent tonal seriousness than Harold's quest for his material, cultural, and spiritual patrimony. Further, Manfred's claim that he is his own Satan, needing no external demon to torture him, undercuts the external cosmology or spirit personae of the play more completely than does Harold's theological skepticism about the figure of Odin. Manfred's radical, suffering subjectivity, like Harold's berserker frenzy, is both a self-indulgent and self-relinquishing state of mind that usurps the more humane, balanced responsibility Scott recommends to Byron in his anonymous *Childe Harold* review.

In *Manfred* the Faustian quest for knowledge of the universe is so tangled with the quest for knowledge of the mirrored self through incest that the reader has great difficulty interpreting Astarte's role. Is she a symbolic projection of Manfred, an objective person, or both? This issue is far too complex to discuss here, but it points toward a similar difficulty in *Harold the Dauntless*. In *Harold* the difficulty of interpreting Gunnar's role is equally tied to the central problems faced by the hero: his search for his patrimony and his redefinition of a self. Scott's Harold, of course, rejects his more conservative patrimony and psychological disposition for one he and Scott see as revolutionary within a ninth- or tenth-century context. For Byron and his Manfred, rebellion against the patrimony of Christianity is part of a rebellion against all laws or structures beyond the self. The tone and resolution are of course far more comic in Scott's poem than in the final version of Byron's, and any critic with a sense of humor and of proportion might well note Scott's own witty self-mockery and retreat from further interpretation. Yet because Scott makes Gunnar Harold's foster sibling, he parallels not only Manfred's relation to his half sister Astarte and Byron's to his half sister Augusta, but also that fundamental pattern in romantic poetry of the sister who is epipsyche or emanation, an immanent, not a transcendent, muse. Harold's direct struggle with Odin in canto 6 is prompted by the god's seizing his page and claiming

Gunnar as Eivir and as his priestess. On one level of interpretation, Harold must recognize Eivir as the female, peace-loving side of himself in order to complete his rejection of Norse culture. Such a reading redefines imagination from a violent, aggressive egotism—though redefined by Harold as a transcendent possession—to a greater perceptiveness. It also follows a Spenserian psychology of reading romance as projected, internal allegory.

If we acknowledge a further independence in Gunnar-Eivir, and if we recall how closely her advice to Harold corresponds to Scott's advice to Byron in the *Quarterly Review*, then we seem faced with an anticipation of that curious letter Byron writes to Scott in 1822, comparing his "tremulous anxiety" before the older poet to an accomplished housemaid-seducer's embarrassment before a "beautiful woman of our own degree with whom one is [in love] enamoured in good earnest."[45] Cited almost without comment by John Clubbe, this letter with its sexual power games has recently been analyzed by Sonia Hofkosh as typifying Byron's competitive need to dominate Scott.[46] Yet in *Harold the Dauntless* Scott seems to balance or soften his own aggression in using the name "Harold" by offering his own advice through what we might call a disempowered speaker. Like Edith in *The Lord of the Isles*, Eivir counsels a rein on violence, but neither counsels—either directly or symbolically—a rein on imagination. Rather, a feminized imagination need not be fully disempowered but, within a less-than-primitive culture, empowering. In spite of the misogyny shown through the witches of both woodland and castle, moreover, Eivir can claim an inheritance as a prophetess from her mother, not—like the enchantresses in earlier poems—from her father. Both from culture and from her specific circumstances, her origins show more independence than theirs.[47]

In contrast to these readings of the romance as an internalized, almost Spenserian allegory, a more dramatic reading of Eivir as an independent person leaves her, paradoxically, less independent. All along she has been an advocate not of that Norse culture but of her version of it: though against Harold's berserker spirit, she nevertheless has spoken for the independent and warlike, if devoted, role of an ideal "Danish maid." From a twentieth-century woman's point of view, these elements of her revised Norse culture do not appear inconsistent. Nor do they seem totally inconsistent with her role as scald and even as prophetess, though disguise seems to have made her role as scald more easily acceptable.[48] Her independent, imaginative synthesis breaks down, however, under the combined pressures of cultural conflict and of romance convention—not to mention the patriarchy inherent in both cultures, if less strong in the Norse one. As Frye points out, romance as a genre tends to represent a conflict between eschatological extremes, and the medieval Christianity that Harold is drawn into and that the narrator reinforces divides imaginative or supernatural visions into extremes of good and evil.[49] In order for Eivir to win release from the father-god of Harold's and her own forefathers, she gives up her role as Norse scald for a medieval romance role as passive lady rescued from castle—a role foreshadowing that of passive Christian wife. As symbol of a crucial imaginative force or civilizing element within Harold's newly-balanced psyche, she is victorious and makes Harold so as well; but as a poet and as a creative individual, she is a victim. She has already heard and seen the fate and the monks' evaluation of the other creative women in the poem, the seven daughters of Urien who spun their castle towers from their own visions. Husband murderers and witches, their remembered images will hold her captive long after Harold wins her release from Odin. Their magical control is condemned as demonic just as Eivir's Norse minstrelsy is condemned. Her individuality is subdued by the romance genre because it offers a psychological way of interpreting her as an aspect of Harold and because its social norms, reinforced by Christianity, allow her even as a realistic individual far less latitude for creative behavior than did her Norse world.

If we view Eivir realistically, the turn from a romantically-portrayed version of living as a Norse scald to an even more romantically-portrayed happy ending ends her wandering in a vision of historical progress, of a more moderate, balanced civilization. For that she sacrifices her own freedom. For Harold and for Eivir, this entry into a more moderate culture does not occur with the apocalyptic severity signaled by the Scots' defeat at Flodden in *Marmion* nor with the Lady of Buccleuch's hooding of her Merlin and submission to the *Dies Irae* in *The Lay*. Their confrontation with Odin comes close to suggesting such an apocalypse. Yet Scott seems to suggest here, as he does in the "Essay on Chivalry," that respect for women emerges from Norse and Germanic culture and develops further in medieval Christian culture.[50] Thus the differences between those two cultures emerge only indirectly through Eivir's confronting of Christian misogyny and her conversion to passivity.

Harold, of course, has also made sacrifices for his new stability: his physical ecstasy in violence, accompanied by an uncontrollable mood of sublime superiority, of the self expanding without constraint to control the world. When they emerge from that doubly haunted castle, Harold and Eivir emerge not only from confronting dangerous sources of social disharmony, but also from dangerous and individuating sources of power within the human mind. If Scott compares Byron's mind to a "shattered castle," he also acknowledges the powerful creativity within that castle, even though he calls those creative forces demons or sorcerers. Scott's decision to turn fully to novels after *Harold the Dauntless* is not, I believe, an acknowledgment of Byron's greater skill as a poet. Instead it is an acknowledgment of Byron's willingness to stay within the castle's precincts and anatomize the tortured self, instead of subduing it, like Scott, within a society whose conventions are only mildly satirized and whose beliefs are ultimately seen as beneficial to a balanced self. Scott, of course, does not abandon the romance form, but he continues to develop a social and critical context for it. After *Manfred* and the fourth canto of *Childe Harold*, Byron too turns from an inward quest, symbolized in Scott's thinking by the mysterious haunted castles of romance, to develop the complex and comic social satire of *Don Juan*. *Harold the Dauntless*, along with its companion piece in *The Bridal of Triermain* volumes, remains as an awkward, yet humorous and fascinating, exploration of romance as a genre nearly freed from the particular textures of historical context and from a framing, distancing narrative voice. Yet, given its undaunted choice of name, it is not free from the pressures of authorial identity. The very name of Scott's final narrative poem heralds his continued commitment to "the quick and exalted powers of imagination" he praises in Byron and in himself as well.

CONCLUSION

> An elf-queene wol I love, ywis,
> For in this world no womman is
> Worthy to be my make
> In towne;
> Alle othere wommen I forsake,
> And to an elf-queene I me take
> By dale and eek by downe.¹

Gillian Beer quotes this passage from Chaucer's Tale of Sir Thopas to show how self-conscious criticism and satire accompany quest romance even at the height of its medieval development. Scott, too, knows and uses the passage. Because Chaucer's narrator reels off the names of the same romance heroes whose adventures are gathered in the Auchinleck Manuscript, scholars have argued that he probably used that manuscript or a version of it for his comical fragment of a quest romance. This manuscript provided Scott with the basis for his 1804 edition of *Sir Tristrem* and for his belief that its redactor's reported oral source "Thomas" was the Thomas of Ercildoune who travelled with the elf queen.² Though the presence of Chaucer's passage has vanished, like the Castle of St. John, from modern editions, it appears as an epigraph on the title page of the anonymous *Bridal of Triermain* in 1813.³ Not only does it point to Sir Roland's quest for the visionary Gyneth, who haunts his dreams and makes him dissatisfied with ordinary women, but like the ballad *Thomas the Rhymer* it epitomizes the quest-romance pattern Scott adapts and then displaces in all of his poems. More than the ballad, however, the passage also points to the complex and often comic self-displacement in which Scott also follows Chaucer. Telling a stereotypical romance, the apparently bumbling dramatic narrator of the *Canterbury Tales* almost distracts us from the sophisticated counterpoint of realism in the actual poet's other tales and prefaces. Among Scott's poems *Harold the Dauntless* is closest to *Sir Thopas* in the awkward ambiguity of stereotypes that do not always sharpen to irony. Yet the modern Arthur who plots to elope by narrating Roland's and King Arthur's quests, the last minstrel who counters his own sense of loss with an acute sense of his audience's responses, the lady of the lake who teases both her minstrel and her king about the supernatural powers she herself symbolizes—all of these reflect what

Scott's perceptive contemporary Adolphus characterizes as "a kind of serious banter, a style hovering between affected gravity and satirical slyness" (*Letter*, 68).

Reaching beyond *Sir Thopas* to "true Thomas," however, each of Scott's narrative poems also affirms the value of romance, even if a value sheltered within a self-reflexive, ironic commentary. This longing to explore an alien, visionary world, a world encountered through the figure of the elfin queen and communicated through her gifts of prophecy, is a fundamental impulse of medieval high romance. It is also one of the central narrative patterns for the early nineteenth-century's high romanticism. The nostalgia for a vanished mythic fusion of being, an unfallen or unfragmented consciousness, has defined romanticism since Schiller and the Schlegels; Geoffrey Hartman's 1962 essay, "Romanticism and Anti-Self-Consciousness" is a more recent example of such definition.[4] Discussions of romanticism that make central the modes or figures of myth and symbol but exclude the recognition of ironic, tragic, even comic responses or frames to such modes or figures might then be said to participate unwittingly in a kind of naively sentimental nostalgia.[5] Without necessarily deconstructing the belief in wholeness or vitality expressed through such narrative myths or symbols, we can recognize the way in which the frames or contexts radically qualify them. Those frames increase the tension between such visionary power that dodges time and our everyday steps toward a mortality that completes it.

For the romantics the form of the goal, the ideal model of wholeness posited by Schiller, by the Schlegels, by Keats, and in a more radically skeptical way by Shelley, is most often Greek classical sculpture. That art served as an analogy for the lost perfection of a culture so in harmony with nature that its divinities seemed immanent and human. Keats's *Hyperion* most magnificently defines the aesthetic and natural wholeness of this image; his *Fall of Hyperion* recognizes more explicitly—as *Hyperion*'s Apollo begins to do—the lostness, the absence of this model, and the need to search for it. Such a longing for an infinitely receding or lost goal, a longing typified by the analogy of painting, defines the romantic or modern era for the German thinkers read by Keats and Shelley. Although formulations of its time span varied, that era extended from the medieval period to the present. In the earlier *Alastor* and *Endymion* the quest for a visionary ideal, though borrowing from classical myth, seems closer to the medieval romance model of the Rhymer and the elfin queen. In Keats's *La Belle Dame* that medieval model becomes explicit but fails to carry—or perhaps enigmatically transcends—the cultural and historical tension of the German formulation and of Keats's and Shelley's uses of the Titan-Olympian struggle.

Scott's ambivalent fascination with historical differences is obviously very strong. Because of its basis in gradual, progressive change and because the changes he describes fall within the continuum from medieval to early nineteenth-century eras, Scott does not make use of the dialectical contrast between classical and romantic cultures. Nor does a longing for the vanished classical era take root in his thinking. Yet within the gradualist continuum of the history he works with runs the persistent opposition between impulses toward documented, empirical narrative and toward a more visionary, more fantastic narrative. Beginning with his categories for the ballads of the *Minstrelsy*, this opposition manifests itself in the alternating models of riding ballad and of romance that he adopts for his own narrative poems. Though dominated by one of those models, each of his narratives also contains elements of the opposing model. Thus the mysterious, elusive center of the elf queen's realm, the realm toward which the wanderings and errings of the romance model tend, becomes equivalent, in both groups of Scott's poems, to the mysterious, elusive wholeness of the classical ideal in Keats's *Hyperion* or in Schiller's and Schlegel's prose versions.

Because the continuum of historical development seems so inevitable to Scott, yet seems to come at such a cost of cultural tradition as well as of "fine fabling," it is this very continuum—or, rather, the sudden recognition of its continuous progress—that becomes apocalyptic for his romance narratives. That inevitability of ongoing time and changing, apparently improving, culture may find expression in a single historical event that seems apocalyptic in a more conventional sense as it completes one era and signals the beginning of a new one. Growing from the riding ballads, this is the pattern that works with variations in *Marmion, Rokeby,* and *The Lord of the Isles*.

Though not a raid but an embassy, Marmion's journey into Scotland is a kind of riding ballad, the more especially since both Marmion and the king of Scotland are equally corrupt and equally courageous: one side of the border seems to mirror the other, and the historical tragedy of Flodden, finally, is all the more ironic for its analogy to an ordinary border raid. Because Marmion's circular journey into a politically alien realm makes his own corruption evident, the romance pattern modifies that of the riding ballad to suggest a complex mixture of playful delay before the judgment of his criminality and the less playful delay before Flodden's judgment of James's IV's chivalric aspirations. Marmion's forgery, the unusual and ungentlemanly means for his attempt at claiming land and woman, can be read as an ambiguous comment on the fictive art of the poet to transform the apocalyptic moment of Flodden.

Conclusion

Rokeby varies this pattern of delay before a sharp recognition of historical change so thoroughly that it seems to invert it. Signaled by Marston Moor, the Puritan kingdom of the saints is bracketed or set aside by the power of romance to project a regenerated—and landed—community that reconciles political and religious differences. At first the younger characters see themselves as part of a chivalric romance, but one whose plot seems to have stalled, then turned on them and played them for fools. Like the manor house of Rokeby itself, their romantic visions seem to go up in the flames fanned by enemies who try to exploit their nostalgia. This exploitation is prompted by Oswald Wycliffe's desire for the property of the Rokeby estate. Yet the territorial reorganization he plans is in turn thwarted by a Spenserian interweaving of narrative plots that links the three great houses and the wilder-than-apparent woods between. This interweaving employs the Alexandrian and the Elizabethan romance patterns of the rediscovery of a lost heir; Scott evokes a larger, offstage geography as the wilderness, or various wildernesses, from which the lost parents and children return from death. More like *Daphnis and Chloe* or *The Winter's Tale* than like Thomas the Rhymer's visit to Elfland, this circular pattern for romance becomes a prophetic myth of return. Through it the progressive, ongoing course of actual history appears not only to leap over the interregnum, but to move almost beyond the very real accommodations and compromises of the eighteenth century into an idealized vision of community. Though aristocratic and conservative, this vision seems more broadly tolerant than would be a simple restoration of prerevolutionary society.

In *The Lord of the Isles* Scott's organization of Bruce's campaign supplements history to provide a spatially isolated romance world on the Isle of Skye and a changeling or a limited lady of the lake—Edith in disguise—to signal the larger changes in the course of personal and public careers. Here the characters do not recognize and play with the genre of romance as they do in *The Lady of the Lake*. Scott himself plays, but with a profound anxiety about his ability—and the morality—of supplementing history with perfectly fictional forms. The concluding, actual battle of Bannockburn promises a newly legitimate, newly independent realm of Scotland after the guerilla struggle of Bruce's forces as well as a renovated domesticity after MacDonald's broken loyalty to Edith of Lorn. Yet its celebration of those loyalties, personal and national, is shadowed by the analogy of 1745 and by continued adjustment to the emotional and cultural consequences of the Union. If Bannockburn celebrates the beginning of a new era, the poem's supplementing of that pattern by the journey to Skye gives the narrative both an elegiac and a prophetic resonance.

Flodden, Bannockburn, and Marston Moor are only the most obvious harbingers of historical change. Because these battles mark confrontations that actually happened, they do not seem at first as subject to interpretation as the Titanic battles Keats and Shelley borrow from mythology. Their particularity seems to bar the possibility of fictional control, just as the women in these poems seem barred from control even of their own property. Yet Scott's gramarye of fictional narratives that supplement with their free play the undefined spaces before battles, or within the gaps of a documented social shift, leads not only to a revelation of that shift's significance, but to the sense that a rhymer's imagination, whether seen as forgery or as free play, might in part control that change.

Such Blakean or Shelleyan hubris toward the transforming of historical event and historical pattern is only suggested, never fully claimed. Instead, even in Scott's poems that present a romance world and an elfin enchantress most directly, their shaping of ongoing time through a radical gramarye is repudiated or deferred, only to be accepted in milder and more domestic forms. Even if the elf queen does not explicitly grant Thomas the gift of prophecy in Scott's version of the ballad, she does lead him to the vision of a fairy world, a realm of play and possibility between the absolute places and absolute judgments of heaven and hell. Challenged by her demand of silence in that timeless world, he is driven to assert his own claims for the rhetoric of fiction—in flattering the courtiers who hold power. In Scott's own poems that develop the elf queen's role most directly—*The Lay*, *The Lady of the Lake*, and *The Bridal of Triermain*—the woman who is literally or figuratively an enchantress repeatedly manifests an illicit power of transformation, a power associated either with the natural energy of the wilderness or with a bower or castle isolated from conventional society and its ongoing history. Each time she manifests that power, she must relinquish it—and yet the power itself, safely domesticated, remains.

In *The Lay of the Last Minstrel* the enchantress seeks to preserve the spatial realm of her family's estate, but the only space she controls is her own isolated tower study. As cause or result of this failure to achieve sufficient isolation, the spatial structure organizing the plot of the *Lay* is basically that of an historical riding ballad, not a romance of entry into magical space. The reputed witch must relinquish her magic, not least because it attempts to block an almost paradisal pause in border warfare that anticipates the end of her family's cultural pattern. The wizard Michael Scott's magic usurps hers, then itself gives way to the song of the minstrel, then to the writing and publishing modern poet. In *The Lady of the Lake* the title points toward the role of Ellen Douglas as enchantress and presider over the fertility of nature. Yet if the Perthshire highlands and Loch Katrine seem to the wandering

James V a romance realm of enchantment, both enchantress and her spatial realm are a fictional overlay or veil concealing the actual political and geographical world he—and not she—must learn to rule. If he and Ellen use romance clearsightedly to negotiate their own relationship, a part of Ellen's clear sight is her recognition of the wilderness's dangers for her; a civilized domesticity will limit her playfully assumed power but preserve her safety. In *Triermain* interruptions of the present by past narratives allow witchcraft or enchantment to manifest itself, then to be chastised by narratives successively closer to the present. *Harold the Dauntless* contains as a climactic episode the venturing into a witches' castle, but the real confrontation there turns out to be a struggle over—and between—fathers. The witches wither away, and the woman who is the romantic lead must relinquish claims to their positive, as well as negative, powers as she also gives up her role of Norse scald for the apparently more progressive one of Christian lady.

In each poem a more limited version of the woman's transformative power, once manifested, can be claimed by male rivals to the woman's witchcraft. Other magicians, like Michael Scott and Merlin, assume control; or male minstrels voice the powers of their incantatory words in ways that seem less threatening than the women's spells; or the witches' power is attributed not to their own sexuality, but to their fathers'. Even the near-outcast Brian the Hermit in *The Lady of the Lake* has found an acceptable role for his prophecy. Finally, these male figures do not simply reclaim power or restore the old order; they develop it, Scott suggests, to reconcile opposing factions.

Significantly, if the enchantress's powers are taken away, the women themselves are domesticated once they relinquish that power. Their alien otherness recedes with their power; they remain, hooded and chained with a silken twist like the Lady of Buccleuch's merlin. Yet their domestication and the marriages that celebrate it both in *The Lay* and *The Lady of the Lake*, like the concluding marriages in *Rokeby* and *The Lord of the Isles*, reconcile opposing factions in an image, if an idealized one, of an ameliorating civilization. In this respect the women in Scott's narratives differ sharply from the ladies of the lake in Arthurian romance, from the Renaissance witches in Ariosto, Tasso, and Spenser, from Blake's woman in "The Crystal Cabinet," and from Keats's Belle Dame. All of these women, in contrast to Scott's, remain elusive, alien, and magical. Scott's female figures also differ from the not explicitly magical but nevertheless romancelike figures that tease the *Alastor* visionary and Manfred. It would be tempting to take these examples of nineteenth-century visionary women who vanish, like their medieval and Renaissance predecessors, into their transcendent promise of power, as markers of high romanticism, and thus firmly to exclude Scott. This contrast is too sharp, however, for we would also be forced to exclude Keats's *Endymion*, Shelley's *Prometheus Unbound*, and Blake's *Milton* and *Jerusalem*, high romantic poems in which the women symbolize in part a commitment to earth and to human relationships. Scott's domesticated enchantresses symbolize that commitment and represent it more realistically; but in that realism they represent the cost to and the dangers of a visionary imagination.

Scott's exceptions to this conversion of visionary to domestic occur in two poems that escape this category of the quest for the elfin queen: in *Marmion* and in *Harold the Dauntless*. In *Marmion* the minstrel forger whose creative powers seem woven in a tangled web with her sexuality does not escape into an infinite wilderness but is violently suppressed early in the poem. Buried alive by the structures and executors of the dominant society, she leaves the field clear for the already domesticated Clare. Forced into the dungeons of Lindisfarne, she is a mirror image to the Guendolen of *Triermain* whose own castle disappears, and at her own wish, into "fragments of rock and rifted stone." In *Harold* the minstrel who tries to work out her identity through disguise faces two different, but equally negative models of witchcraft. The witches who spin out their seven towers also act out a grotesquely violent parody of the evils of woman's free emotional choice in marriage—they all choose the same groom, become killers, and are themselves killed. Thus the narrative savagely condemns both creativity and individual emotional choice for promoting savagery.

It seems significant, moreover, that both of these anomalous plots (though *Marmion* on the whole fits the plot of the riding ballad with the woman as pawn in the raids) involve female minstrels. If the elfin queen or enchantress is a threatening counterforce to the male minstrel's control, she may also be a muse: the otherness of her mode of existence can become a province or colony, a projection, of his own mind.[6] Even if the female minstrel exists within a fiction at one remove from the male minstrel, her challenge is more direct because less convertible to allegory. Thus Constance's songs are heard only after her death, and Eivir leaves her scaldic role behind in the bone-strewn castle, sacrificing her creativity to control Harold's berserking ecstasies.

With the exception of Constance in *Marmion*, the women in the three more realistic narratives do not directly threaten the minstrel's control. Given their roles as pawns in the maneuvering for landed estates, they are far more threatened than threatening. Yet their situation oddly resembles that of the enchantresses. The land they possess is the source of great power, but they have gained it by inheritance from male power, not by their own skills or intelligence. More important, to participate in society, they must relinquish that power, or most of it, when they marry. A marriage settlement would be based on the dowry brought; a marriage without that contract would guarantee no control at all, as Scott shows later in *The Fortunes of Nigel*. Thus the domesticity of marriage for Clare, Matilda, and Edith will also lead to a loss of power, or, more clearly, a loss of unlimited potentiality. Moreover, they cannot like Guendolen retreat into any mysterious otherness—their land is bounded and contracted, and their castles do not instantly disappear. The towers that marked the territories of Edith of Lorn still stand, if in ruins, above the sublimely empty sea lochs of the west coast.

This irony of relinquishing power is explicit only in *The Lord of the Isles*; in the two earlier poems, the emotional completion of the happy ending closes off such questions. Yet the legal, contractual status of this land—clearly reflected in the forgeries of *Marmion* and the multiple scrolls and tablets that eventually untangle *Rokeby*—also associates these women and the narratives that turn around them with the documentation of history.

We cannot associate the ambiguities of writing only with the ambiguous status of these women as pawns, and the performative power of song only with the magical, incantatory powers of the enchantresses in the group of Scott's poems that most closely follow the quest romance. A first objection rises from the frequent association of writing with gramarye: forgery and written fictions, as well as songs, all escape from, and transform, the documents of history. Marmion's written forgeries as well as Constance's songs and forgeries, the Lady of Buccleuch's book as well as the last minstrel's lay, all work such transformations. Scott's anxiety about the passing temporality of the minstrel's voice can be assuaged in the written forgeries of Marmion, but the freedom of written texts from public morality as well as from the ravages of time brings its own instabilities and anxieties. Gilpin Horner, that imp of uncontrolled reading, never quite disappears.

A second qualification of this broad parallel emerges from the conditions of oral performance, still represented even in the last minstrel's visit to Newark. When minstrels sing directly for their present audience, both minstrel and audience reinforce the controlling values of that group. For the riding or raiding ballads of the oral tradition and thus also, to some extent, for the group of more realistic, historical narratives that Scott models after them, this situation of group reinforcement reflects their primary narrative action, which is itself public and physical. Scott's quarto volumes still preserve a process of communal, public performance, celebrating through their print-minstrelsy the border past of the Scotts of Buccleuch far beyond the range of their original raids. Disinterring their violence—and their tight communal identity—from the treaties and law courts of later, more effective civilization, these volumes offer a momentary reversibility of historical change, framed in the acknowledgment of its difference from the present. Yet that escape from "progress" is not an escape from, but an affirmation of, the communal values held by performer and audience. For the romances and the romantic ballads of the oral tradition, the tension between individual fantasy and public, social values is far more acute than in the riding ballads; yet as we have seen in some of Scott's poems based on the romantic ballads, that communal context almost seems necessary to support or sustain the mysterious venturing into an alien world.

Yet even with these qualifications to the broad parallels suggested above, the alien nature of the enchantresses, their mysterious power that is too dangerous for them to keep and thus that must be reclaimed for male prophets and minstrels, and even their sexuality, an extreme form of intimacy, all have affinities with the presentness of speech and song in an oral tradition. Like the enchantresses, that presence is elusive; it seems to vanish from the increasingly documented world of a print culture. In spite of their apparent presence, both enchantress and song seem closer to the evasive, elusive fantasies of the private writer and reader. Paradoxically, then, they also point back toward the timeless play and release of the enchantress's romance world before its visitors return to the judgments of an ongoing, progressive history.

Thus Scott plays off the opposition between oral and written against that between quest romance and riding ballad, to define the ambivalent allure of license and law, of a chaotic ferment of origins and progressive change, of imagination and of civilization; but he never quite allows us to accept these oppositions as neatly parallel to one another. Moreover, because their ironic differences are more often reconciled in compromise and comedy than preserved in isolation and tragedy, his enclosures of the visionary sources of imaginative energy within a present awareness of its loss or at least of its limitation may seem less compelling to advocates of high romanticism than the Promethean struggles to reconstruct a golden world enacted in Blake's, Keats's, and Shelley's poems.

For in all of these poems, we see a movement toward the center, from the extreme stereotypes of witch or pawn, and from the extreme models of riding ballad and quest romance. The pawns gain some power through the virtues of domestic morality, and the witches must lose their power in order to share the same domesticity, whether they want it or not. This center of domestic morality, moreover, is the realm toward which the novel had been developing, especially in the hands of the women novelists writing in the genre from the 1790s through the following twenty years.[7]

In some sense Scott's turn toward the female minstrel, if a disguised minstrel, may reflect his own role as a male writer anonymously taking on the female role of novel writing, and along with it some of the female values of domestic morality. The banned figures not reconciled to domesticity—Constance and Urien's daughters—may reflect some of the tensions in that turn. No wonder Jane Austen, when she heard the strong rumor that Scott had turned from his best-selling poems to novel writing, said, "Walter Scott has no business to write novels, especially good ones. It is not fair. He has fame and profit enough as a poet, and should not be taking the bread out of other people's mouths."[8] Yet it is fair to say that even in his poems Scott employs the patterns of witch and pawn, not simply for fame and profit, but in order to criticize and to modify them. If that modification costs his more interesting women too much independence, and especially too much power over "mighty words and signs," he at least seems more sensitive to the cost than one might at first have suspected.

Much of that sensitivity emerges, as we have seen, through his exploration of the genres he moves between, the riding ballad that confronts an apocalyptic moment of irreversible history in which an era ends, and the quest romance that explores more fully the errant transformations before such a moment. Shaping and shaped by the gender roles within them, those genres seem to define two opposing poles. Yet because each echoes the other, often through allusion and irony, they define one another. Further, they define an unresolved field of play before the more fully gradualist synthesis of his novels. Given the definition of apocalypse I have been using, his own novels, not Byron's poems, mark the apocalyptic end of his poetry.

Finally, Scott transforms his own self-image. True Thomas, proud of his own courtly, political fictions yet also graced—or haunted—by the more visionary powers of the alien elf queen, yields to another model. We might describe this new image of the poet as a minstrel who hides beneath his professional garments a woman's sense of what it is to choose, or to be driven back and forth between, the roles of elf queen and pawn—and to preserve the ambiguity in that wavering. Yet such an image, though partially true, assumes too great an appropriation or internalization. It would be more apt to say that the minstrel recognizes and delineates the constraints of both roles and thus understands their implications for the quester. This pairing, like the verse of the rhymer Scott, begins with familiar, even conventional oppositions. Yet, like the other oppositions explored here, it gains a sophisticated resonance through the complex awareness of the singer who makes his fortune as a writer but always recognizes the cost in that final gramarye of becoming modern.

NOTES

Introduction

1. [Sir] Walter Scott, *Minstrelsy of the Scottish Border*, 2 vols. (Kelso: James Ballantyne, 1802), 2:283. I have also consulted the second edition, in three volumes (Edinburgh: James Ballantyne for Longman and Rees, London, 1803). See also the standard modern edition with notes and introduction by Sir Walter Scott, rev. and ed. T.F. Henderson, 4 vols. (Edinburgh: Oliver and Boyd, 1932), 4:79-85, 98. For a discussion of Scott's reluctance to consider evidence that there were prior German and French versions of the romance, see Arthur Johnston, *Enchanted Ground: The Study of Medieval Romance in the Eighteenth Century* (London: Athlone Press, 1964), 183-84.

2. See Ruth Elizabeth Eller, "'Enchanted Land': Scott's View of the Nature and Function of Poetry and Poetic Romance" (Ph.D. diss., University of California, 1980), 3; and Judith Wilt, *Secret Leaves: the Novels of Walter Scott* (Chicago: University of Chicago Press, 1986), 106, 216 n. 14. For his early self-identification with the Rhymer, see Scott's letter to Jessie ——— (1787-89) in *The Letters of Sir Walter Scott*, ed. H.J.C. Grierson, 12 vols. (London: Constable, 1932), 1:9.

3. Fredric Jameson, *The Political Unconscious: Narrative as a Socially Symbolic Act* (1981; rpt. Ithaca: Cornell University Press, 1982), 112.

4. See Earl Wasserman, *The Finer Tone: Keats's Major Poems* (1953; rpt. Baltimore: Johns Hopkins University Press, 1967), 68. Wasserman notes that Keats used Robert Jamieson, *Popular Ballads* (1806), and not Scott.

5. See M.H. Abrams, "English Romanticism: The Spirit of the Age," in *Romanticism Reconsidered*, ed. Northrop Frye (1963; rpt. New York: Columbia University Press, 1968), 26-72; M.H. Abrams, *Natural Supernaturalism* (New York: Norton, 1971); Northrop Frye, "The Drunken Boat," in *Romanticism Reconsidered*, ed. Frye, 1-25; Northrop Frye, *A Study of English Romanticism* (New York: Random House, 1968), chap. 1; René Wellek, *Concepts of Criticism* (New Haven: Yale University Press, 1963), 128-221; and Harold Bloom, *The Visionary Company*, rev., enl. ed. (Ithaca: Cornell University Press, 1971).

6. See Jerome J. McGann, *Romanticism and Ideology* (Chicago: University of Chicago Press, 1983), pt. 2; and Marilyn Butler, *Romantics, Rebels and Reactionaries: English Literature and Its Background, 1760-1830* (Cambridge: Cambridge University Press, 1981). In an MLA talk several years ago, McGann included Byron, Austen, and Scott (the novelist) as the anomalous authors; here he mentions Scott only briefly. On pp. 77-80 he compares Scott's *Thomas the Rhymer* to Keats's *La Belle Dame*, arguing curiously that Keats's ballad is more self-conscious than Scott's because Scott interposes editorial apparatus on a naive medieval ballad. His more extended discussion of the Keats poem in "Keats and the Historical Method in Literary Criticism" (*MLN* 94, no. 5 [Dec. 1979]:988-1032) clarifies his view of Keats

but not the parallel to Scott, and thus not the basis of his sharp division between the Enlightenment Scott and the romantic Keats—a sharp division I do not accept. For further discussion of this debate, see Frank Jordan's introductory chapter in *The English Romantic Poets: A Review of Research and Criticism*, ed. Jordan (New York: MLA, 1985).

7. See George Lukacs, *The Historical Novel*, trans. Hannah and Stanley Mitchell (1962; rpt. Boston: Beacon, 1963), pt. 1: The Classical Form of the Historical Novel, esp. pp. 30-63. Its first publication was in Russian (1937), then in German (1955; 1961 in West Germany). For work on Scott's novels from 1932 through 1977, see Jill Rubenstein, *Sir Walter Scott: A Reference Guide* (Boston: G.K. Hall, 1978); her bibliography also includes writings on the poetry and other works. Since 1977, at least eight book-length studies either totally or largely devoted to Scott have appeared; see n. 9 below for those most useful in pointing to poetic elements.

8. Only recently has criticism of Scott's poetry moved beyond perfunctory preludes to discussions of the novels, or praise for the brief lyrics within the longer poems or novels. See Thomas Crawford, "Scott as a Poet," *Etudes Anglaises* 24 (Oct.-Dec. 1971):478-80, for a concise account of the beginning of this change. Two other relatively early landmarks in the poetry criticism are Donald Davie, "The Poetry of Sir Walter Scott," *Proceedings of the British Academy* 47 (1961):61-75, though his last-page defense of Scott as a Hemingway-like "masculine" artist of action in contrast to the "sedentary" high romantics is an argument I find unappealing; and Karl Kroeber's chapter, "The Narrative Pattern of Scott," in *Romantic Narrative Art* (1960; rpt. Madison: University of Wisconsin Press, 1966). The structure of his book reflects a division similar to Davie's, between "visionary" and "realistic adventures"; Scott falls into the latter category, with Byron. Edgar Johnson's massive critical biography *Sir Walter Scott: The Great Unknown*, 2 vols. (New York: Macmillan, 1970), is certainly not perfunctory in its discussions of the poetry and has repetedly provided a jumping-off point for further criticism. More recent criticism of the poetry that I have found useful will be cited in the notes following; the work of Jill Rubenstein, J.H. Alexander, and Ruth Eller has contributed especially strongly to my own. Stuart Curran, *Poetic Form and British Romanticism* (New York: Oxford, 1986), which appeared after this manuscript was completed, discusses Scott's poems in his chapter on romance and recognizes their often ironic critiques of their own genre. See esp. pp. 135-40.

9. See Alexander Welsh, *The Hero of the Waverley Novels* (1963; rpt. New York: Atheneum, 1968), esp. chap. 3; Francis R. Hart, *Scott's Novels: The Plotting of Historic Survival* (Charlottesville: University of Virginia Press, 1966), 9-11; Robert C. Gordon, *Under Which King? A Study of the Scottish Waverley Novels* (Edinburgh: Oliver and Boyd, 1969), chap. 1; Graham McMaster, *Scott and Society* (Cambridge: Cambridge University Press, 1981), 3-4, 142, 150; Jane Millgate, *Walter Scott: The Making of the Novelist* (Toronto: University of Toronto Press, 1984), esp. chaps. 1, 2; Daniel Cottom, *The Civilized Imagination: A Study of Ann Radcliffe, Jane Austen, and Sir Walter Scott* (Cambridge: Cambridge University Press, 1985); and Wilt, *Secret Leaves*, intro. and chap. 1.

10. Wilt, *Secret Leaves*, 27.

11. See Janice A. Radway, *Reading the Romance: Women, Patriarchy, and Popular Literature* (Chapel Hill: University of North Carolina Press, 1984), for an analysis of

readers of popular romance. For narrative theory, see Claude Levi-Strauss, *Structural Anthropology* (New York: Anchor, 1967); Vladimir Propp, *The Morphology of the Folktale* (1928), trans. Laurence Scott, 2d ed., rev., ed. Louis A. Wagner, intro. Alan Dundes (Austin: University of Texas Press, 1968); Northrop Frye, *The Anatomy of Criticism* (Princeton: Princeton University Press, 1957); Northrop Frye, *The Secular Scripture: A Study of the Structure of Romance* (Cambridge: Harvard University Press, 1976); Frank Kermode, *The Sense of an Ending: Studies in the Theory of Fiction* (New York: Oxford University Press, 1967); Frank Kermode, *The Genesis of Secrecy: On the Interpretation of Narrative* (Cambridge: Harvard University Press, 1979); Tzvetan Todorov, *The Poetics of Prose* (1971), trans. Richard Howard (Ithaca: Cornell University Press, 1977); Roland Barthes, *S/Z: An Essay* (1970), trans. Richard Miller (New York: Farrar, Straus and Giroux, 1974); Gerard Genette, *Narrative Discourse: An Essay in Method*, trans. Jane E. Lewin (Ithaca: Cornell University Press, 1983); Paul Ricoeur, *Time and Narrative*, trans. Kathleen McLaughlin and David Pellaver, vol. 1, 1983; vol. 2, 1985 (Chicago: University of Chicago Press); Peter Brooks, *Reading for the Plot: Design and Intention in Narrative* (1984; rpt. New York: Vintage, 1985); and Patricia A. Parker, *Inescapable Romance: Studies in the Poetics of a Mode* (Princeton: Princeton University Press, 1979), 219. For analysis of these theories and others, see Wallace Martin, *Recent Theories of Narrative* (Ithaca: Cornell University Press, 1986).

12. Graham McMaster, "Levi-Strauss in the Scottish Highlands: A Structuralist Account of Scott's *The Lady of the Lake*," *Studies in English Literature* [Tokyo: The English Literary Society of Japan], 61, no. 1 (Sept. 1984):3-25.

13. See Gina Luria and Irene Tayler, "Gender and Genre: Women in British Romantic Literature," in Marlene Springer, ed., *What Manner of Women: Essays on English and American Life and Literature* (New York: New York University Press, 1977), 98-123. See also the introductory chapter of Sandra Gilbert and Susan Gubar, *The Madwoman in the Attic* (New Haven: Yale University Press, 1979). Two papers on this poem at the December 1985 MLA exemplify the diversity of approaches even within feminist criticism: the first, "Harassing the Muse," by Karen Swann, took as an experimental hypothesis the point of view of the enchantress; the second, "From Honey to Ashes in Keats's 'La Belle Dame sans Merci,' " by Theresa M. Kelley, showed the fetishizing of the representation of an enchantress by essentially patriarchal literary conventions. A problem more specific to Scott's uses of historical settings is that of discriminating or not between his analysis of women's roles in, for example, the time of Robert the Bruce and in his own time. Two helpful works in beginning to make some of these distinctions are Rosalind K. Marshall, *Virgins and Viragos: A History of Women in Scotland from 1080-1980* (Chicago: Academy Press, 1983) and, for more general social history, T.C. Smout, *A History of the Scottish People, 1560-1839* (1969; rpt. London: Collins/Fontana, 1981).

14. See Brooks, *Reading for the Plot*, chaps. 1 and 4.

15. Gilbert and Gubar, *Madwoman in the Attic*.

16. Millgate, *Walter Scott*, 8-10.

17. In the first and second editions of the *Minstrelsy*, all three parts of *Thomas the Rhymer* are in vol. 2: Romantic Ballads. In a separate final section of this volume are four "Imitations of the Ancient Ballad." In both editions he notes that the third part of *The Rhymer*, "being entirely modern, would have been placed with greater

propriety among the class of modern ballads, had it not been for its immediate connection with the first and second parts of the same story" (1802, 2:285; 1803, 2:310). The third volume of the 1803 edition contains additional ballads for each of his original three categories. In Henderson's modern edition, all three parts of *Thomas the Rhymer* are placed in the third category, that of modern imitations. See also *Scott's Poetical Works*, with the Author's Introduction and Notes, ed. J. Logie Robertson, Oxford Standard Authors (1904; rpt. London: Oxford University Press, 1967). Because there is no modern scholarly edition of Scott's poetry and because this edition is complete and accessible, I will use it, abbreviated *PW*, for all quotations from Scott's poetry unless otherwise noted. In a paper at the Edmonton Scott conference (August 1987) Jane Millgate pointed out that the 1833-34 edition of the poems, the basis for Robertson's text, was supervised by J.G. Lockhart after Scott's death; the last edition supervised by Scott was the 1830 edition. Lockhart's changes in the text itself seem to be mostly punctuations, but his arrangement of text, notes, and variants, Millgate argues, changes Scott as poet and editor into a museum piece. For a somewhat different use of *Thomas the Rhymer* as a paradigm of Scott's relation to the popular tradition, see Thomas Crawford, Introduction to *Sir Walter Scott: Selected Poems*, Oxford Paperback English Texts (Oxford: Clarendon Press, 1972), ix.

18. See Kroeber, *Romantic Narrative Art*, 33.

19. See Charles G. Zug, Jr., "The Ballad and History: The Case for Scott," *Folklore* 89, no. 2 (1978):231.

20. See Charles G. Zug, Jr., "Scott's 'Jock of Hazeldean': The Re-Creation of a Traditional Ballad," *Journal of American Folklore* 86, no. 340 (April-June 1973):156, 237. See also James Reed, *The Border Ballads* (London: Athlone Press, 1973), for a study of the ballads' historical and sociological milieu. See also Scott's 1802 introduction to the *Minstrelsy*, Henderson, 1:118-19.

21. J.H. Alexander, *"The Lay of the Last Minstrel": Three Essays*, Romantic Reassessment 77 (Salzburg: Institut für Englische Sprache und Literatur, 1978), 77-78.

22. Scott's introduction to "Kempion" points out a parallel in Boiardo's *Orlando Innamorato* (*Minstrelsy*, 1802, 2:84-85). See also Northrop Frye, *Anatomy*, 189; and Eleanor Terry Lincoln, Introduction, *Pastoral and Romance: Modern Essays in Criticism* (Englewood Cliffs, New Jersey: Prentice-Hall, 1969), 4-5.

23. The standard edition for the romance of Thomas the Rhymer is *The Romance and Prophecies of Thomas of Erceldoune, Printed from Five Manuscripts; with Illustrations from the Prophetic Literature of the Fifteenth and Sixteenth Centuries*, ed., intro., notes by James A.H. Murray, Early English Text Society, vol. 61 (London: N. Trubner, 1875). See also Francis James Child, ed., *The English and Scottish Ballads*, 5 vols. (1888; rpt. New York: Folklore Press, 1956), 1:317-29, 4:454-55; he prints the Thornton MS. version of the romance and four ballad variants. Murray thought that Mrs. Brown of Aberdeen, the source for both Scott's and Jamieson's versions of the ballad, wrote it; Child finds another, independent source and other roots in a long oral tradition.

24. Frye, *Secular Scripture*, 94; idem, *Anatomy*, 190, 203-6; Jameson, *Political Unconscious*, 130.

25. *Inescapable Romance*, 4-5; *Secular Scripture*, 53.

26. See Parker, *Inescapable Romance*, 4-5, 70, 102. On p. 74 she notes Scott's

half-critical recognition that Spenser's story in all but his first book led "'him astray from his moral' " (*Quarterly Review* 43 [Sept. 1830]:486). For Roland Barthes's linguistic description of narrative delays as a function of his "hermeneutic code," see *S/Z*, 75-76.

27. John Pikoulis, "Scott and 'Marmion': The Discovery of Identity," *Modern Language Review* 66 (Oct. 1971):738-39; Frye, *Anatomy*, 193; Gillian Beer, *The Romance*, Critical Idiom Series (London: Methuen, 1970), 9; "Scott and 'Marmion,' " 738.

28. Peter Brooks's argument that reading is itself the circuitous, delaying process of discovery makes the reader the hero but continues a similar psychological—or psychosexual—reading of the temporal drive toward narrative closure (*Plot*, 101-2). For Brooks, however, the process seems less anxious than for James, Frye, and Pikoulis, perhaps because he is talking more generally about narrative than about the specific, often starkly extreme, manifestations of "obsessive themes and motifs" that must be confronted and contained in the forests of romance.

29. See Lowry C. Wimberly, *Folklore in the English and Scottish Ballads* (1928; rpt. New York: Ungar, 1959), chap. 3, esp. pp. 109, 117, 122, 147; and Child, *Ballads*, 1:319-23.

30. Child, *Ballads*, 1:322-23; see also Lucy Allen Paton, *Studies in the Fairy Mythology of Arthurian Romance*, 2d ed., with bibliography by Roger Sherman Loomis (New York: Burt Franklin, 1960), 77.

31. *Inescapable Romance*, 225.

32. Frye, *Secular Scripture*, 17.

33. Child argues that these stanzas are modern and thus implies they are Scott's own additions (*Ballads*, 1:321). They also focus upon speech *in* the otherworld, not speech in the real world *about* the otherworld.

34. *Walter Scott*, 8-10; *Political Unconscious*, 110-17, 130-31, 141.

35. For an analysis of the "interplay of innovation and sedimentation" in defining genres, an analysis that comes from a very different philosophical perspective than Jameson's, see Ricoeur, *Time and Narrative*, 1:68-70. Jameson's attempt to demonstrate the moments of historical change from "decentered, magic-oriented" and "pre-individualized narratives" to the greater individualism of the narratives of "nascent capitalism" slips uneasily from the Renaissance to the early nineteenth century.

36. William Hazlitt, *Complete Works*, ed. P.P. Howe, 21 vols. (London: J.M. Dent, 1932), 11:57.

37. Paul Ricoeur's sustained discussion of relationships between fictional narrative and history in *Time and Narrative* raises the problem of an "interweaving reference between history and narrative fiction," and will be extremely useful for Scott criticism (1:82), as will his complete discussion, "History and Narrative," in part 2 of the first volume.

38. See Annette Kolodny, *The Lay of the Land: Metaphor as Experience and History in American Life and Letters* (1975; rpt. Chapel Hill: University of North Carolina Press, 1984); Sherry Ortner, "Is Female to Male as Nature Is to Culture?" in *Woman, Culture, and Society*, ed. Michelle Zimbalist Rosaldo and Louise Lamphere (Stanford: Stanford University Press, 1974), 67-87; and Gilbert and Gubar, *Madwoman in the Attic*, 17-19.

39. See Jonathan Culler, *Structuralist Poetics: Structuralism, Linguistics, and the Study of Literature* (Ithaca: Cornell University Press, 1975), 134; he is discussing Barthes's arguments for conventions of reading and interpretation as an answer to Derrida's "infinite play of differences" that would erode even the differences between speech and writing.

40. See McMaster, *Scott and Society*, 51-59; he cites *the Cambridge Journal* (April 1954). See also Jill Rubenstein, "Scott's Historical Poetry," (Ph.D. diss., Johns Hopkins University, 1969), chap. 1; and Peter Garside, "Scott and the 'Philosophical' Historians," *Journal of the History of Ideas* 36, no. 3 (July 1975):497-512.

41. See Cottom, *Civilized Imagination*, 138, 179.

42. Parker, *Inescapable Romance*, 52-53, 126.

43. J.H. Alexander, *The Reception of Scott's Poetry by his Correspondents: 1798-1817*, Romantic Reassessment 84, 2 vols. (Salzburg: Institute für Anglistik und Amerikanistik, 1979), 1:3-8.

44. See Davie, "The Poetry of Sir Walter Scott," 63-65, and Thomas Crawford, *Scott*, 2d ed., Writers and Critics Series (Edinburgh: Scottish Academic Press, 1982), 37-38.

Chapter One: *The Lay of the Last Minstrel*

1. See Crawford, Introduction, *Scott: Selected Poems*, x; and Charles Zug, "'Jock of Hazeldean,'" 157.

2. See entry for "metonymy" in *The Princeton Handbook of Poetic Terms*, ed. Frank J. Warnke and O.B. Hardison, Jr. (Princeton, N.J.: Princeton University Press, 1986). The handbook, however, warns against the equation I make here, following Roman Jakobson, "The Metaphoric and Metonyonic Poles," in Hazard Adams, ed., *Critical Theory since Plato* (New York: Harcourt Brace Jovanovich, 1971), 1113-6. See Christine Larner, *Enemies of God: The Witch-hunt in Scotland* (London: Chatto and Windus, 1981), 7, 97-100, 136, 139-42; and Alan Macfarlane, *Witchcraft in Tudor and Stuart England: A Regional and Comparative Study* (New York: Harper, 1970), 170-72. Although both writers emphasize the distinction between English and Scottish beliefs in witchcraft, they both also emphasize the importance of incantation and cursing. Wimberly, *Folklore in the Ballads*, 219, notes that witches in the ballads were almost always women and that male conjurers acted "under instructions from the women." See also Wilt, *Secret Leaves*, 17. For a discussion of gramarye see Graham Tulloch, *The Language of Walter Scott: A Study of his Scottish and Period Language* (London: Andre Deutsch, 1980), 27-28, 233-34, 236.

3. For a slightly different interpretation, see Wilt, *Secret Leaves*, 190; and Ruth Elizabeth Eller, "The Poetic Theme in Scott's Novels," in *Scott and His Influence: The Papers of the Aberdeen Scott Conference, 1982*, ed. J.H. Alexander and David Hewitt (Aberdeen: Association for Scottish Literary Studies, 1983), 79-80.

4. See J.H. Alexander, *Two Studies in Romantic Reviewing*, vol. 2: *The Reviewing of Walter Scott's Poetry, 1805-1817*, Romantic Reassessment, 49 (Salzburg: Institut für Englische Sprache und Literatur, 1976), chap. 1. Reviewers debated between calling it a "neatened-up" medieval metrical romance and an

expanded ballad; they also acknowledged that it had ambitions worthy, at times, of a Miltonic epic seriousness.

5. Charles Zug, "The Ballad Editor as Antiquary: Scott and *The Minstrelsy*," *Journal of the Folklore Institute* 13, no. 1 (1976):59-60, suggests that Scott's pessimism about the erosion of the ballad tradition was based on his experience with the riding ballads of the border, and that if he had spent more time in Aberdeen collecting romantic ballads, he might have recognized the elliptical style of the ballads as intrinsic to the oral tradition, not the result of an erosion of that tradition.

6. *Narrative Discourse*, 228-34.

7. See Scott to Anna Seward, 30 Nov. 1802 (*Letters*, 1:166), in which he announces for the *Minstrelsy*'s third volume "a sort of Romance of Border chivalry and inchantment which will extend to some length" and to George Ellis, 30 Jan. 1803 (1:174-75), in which he announces the persona of the minstrel. By sometime in December, however, he had received the countess's fragmentary story of Gilpin Horner; see Johnson, *Sir Walter Scott*, 1:197-98 and note 61 (1:xx). As early as 21 March 1805 he wrote Anna Seward that the "dwarf page is . . . an excrescence," but that he was charmed into using him by the countess. His laughing claim, "if she had asked me to write a ballad on a broom stick, I would have done it," is perhaps a tribute to her bewitching of him (*Letters*, 1:242-43; Johnson quotes it, *Sir Walter Scott*, 1:227). Millgate suggests that Scott in 1830 has in his "fable of composition" fused this inspiration with the encouragement he received from Lady Anne Hamilton for "Cadyow Castle" (*Walter Scott*, 16-17).

8. See Mary Lascelles, *The Story-Teller Retrieves the Past: Historical Fiction and Fictitious History in the Art of Scott, Stevenson, Kipling, and Some Others* (Oxford: Clarendon Press, 1980), 44.

9. *The Poetical Works of Sir Walter Scott, Bart.* Complete in one volume. with all his introductions, notes, variant readings, and notes by J.G. Lockhart, Esq. (Edinburgh: Adam and Charles Black, 1857), 8.

10. In contrast to the duchess, the lady in *Launfal* is in deshabille, perhaps suitable for her pavilion in a meadow on a warm day. See *Launfal* by Thomas Chestre in *Ancient English Metrical Romances*, sel. and published by Joseph Ritson, rev. Edmund Goldsmid, 3 vols. bound in one (Edinburgh: E. and G. Goldsmid, 1885), 2:11-12, 28-33. Original publication London, 1802. Sir Launfal first is found by the ladies in a meadow and invited to their mistress's fairy castle; later, they arrive in contingents at Arthur's castle to save Launfal from Guinevere's slander. Scott reviewed Ritson's edition along with Ellis's *Specimens of Early English Metrical Romances* in the *Edinburgh Review* 7 (1806):387-413. See also Johnston, *Enchanted Ground*, chaps. 5-7, for Scott's knowledge of medieval romances.

11. Lascelles, *Story-Teller*, 5.

12. See *Encyclopedia Britannica*, 11th ed., entries for Buccleuch and Monmouth, Duke of; and *The Dictionary of National Biography* (hereafter cited as *DNB*), entry for James Scott, Duke of Monmouth. The duchess had remarried in 1688, but Scott ignores this fact.

13. Alexander, "*Lay*," 35, 50.

14. Ruth Eller, "Themes of Time and Art in *The Lay of the Last Minstrel*," *Studies in Scottish Literature* 13 (1978):47.

15. See Bishop Thomas Percy, *Reliques of Ancient English Poetry*, ed. Henry B. Wheatley (London: Unwin and Allen, 1885), app. 1: An Essay on the Ancient Minstrels in England. Percy's first version of this essay appeared in 1765, his final one in 1794. Percy argued that English minstrels composed their own romances; Ritson said they merely recited French romances and badly at that. See also Joseph Ritson, *Ancient Songs and Ballads, from the Reign of King Henry the Second to the Revolution*, 2 vols. (1792; rpt. London: for Payne and Foss, by Thomas Davison, 1829), Intro. For Scott's views, see his *Edinburgh Review* essay, 14 (Jan. 1806), 387-413, and his late "Essay on Romance" (1824) in *Miscellaneous Works: Chivalry, Romance, and the Drama* (Edinburgh: Adam and Black, 1861), 154-64. See also Johnston, *Enchanted Ground*, 95-97, and "Introductory Remarks on Popular Poetry," added to the *Minstrelsy* in 1830.

16. See Johnson, *Sir Walter Scott*, 1:56-57 for Scott's resistance to Greek. For a more general British resistance to Plato, see James Notopoulos, *The Platonism of Shelley: A Study of Platonism and the Literary Mind* (Durham, N.C.: Duke University Press, 1949); and Timothy Webb, *The Violet in the Crucible: Shelley and Translation* (Oxford: Clarendon Press, 1976).

17. See Crawford, *Scott*, 40-42; he cites J.L. Adolphus, *Letters to Richard Heber, M. P. Containing Critical Remarks on the Series of Novels Beginning with 'Waverley' and an Attempt to Ascertain their Author* (London: Rodwell and Martin, 1821), 136-37.

18. Eller, *Time*, 54.

19. "Lay," 194-96.

20. For Derrida's focus on Rousseau and the late eighteenth century as a turning point in the recognition that "what threatens . . . [logocentrism] is writing," see *Of Grammatology*, trans. Gayatri Chakravorty Spivak (Baltimore: Johns Hopkins University Press, 1976), 99.

21. For a concise statement of Derrida's sense of the absent writer, see *Marges de la Philosophie*, 376, quoted by Jonathan Culler in *Structuralist Poetics*, 132. A recent essay by Donald Wesling, "Difficulties of the Bardic: Literature and the Human Voice," *Critical Inquiry* 8, no. 1 (Autumn 1981), briefly considers the revival of interest in the bardic oral tradition during the late eighteenth century by setting Derrida's undoing of the privileging of speech against Walter Ong's argument for its priority. "The bardic," he concludes, is "print culture's nostalgia for oral culture" (p. 73).

22. See chap. 1, n. 40.

23. In *Christabel*, the narrator prays for Christabel's protection against the apparent witch Geraldine: "Jesu Maria, shield her well!" For Scott's explanation of the echo, and of the larger echo of the verse form, see his Introduction to the Edition of 1830, *PW*, 52-53.

24. Carol Gilligan, *In a Different Voice: Psychological Theory and Women's Development* (Cambridge: Harvard University Press, 1982).

25. Modern studies of witchcraft, particularly those of Macfarlane and Larner cited in n. 2, have challenged the earlier twentieth-century theory of Margaret Murray, which argued that witches were members of ancient fertility

cults still practicing their old religion. Nevertheless, the literary mythology of the Circe figures and the Arthurian enchantresses reaffirms such a connection. For the hypothesis of the persistence of pagan beliefs about land and about witches, though not about the connection between the two, see Scott, *Letters on Demonology and Witchcraft*, intro. Henry Morley, 3d ed. (London: George Routledge, 1887), 76-80, 85-88; and 111 ff. for a description of the Rhymer's elf queen as a "goddess of the woods," though rather a Diana than a Venus or Circe. He goes on in the following chapters to describe how testimony in trials for witchcraft often involved reports of dealing with fairies.

26. See J.H. Alexander, *The Reviewing of Walter Scott's Poetry*, 345-52.

27. See Eller, "Enchanted Land," 85-86, 127; Alexander, in *"Lay,"* 71, focuses upon the echoes of violence in the imagery of blood.

28. Alexander, *"Lay,"* 77-78.

29. See Kermode, *Genesis of Secrecy*, 88, for the suggestion that "the Jews, . . . whose prophecies of a Messiah were unfulfilled, kept the roll, but the Christians, having the desire to establish consonance between the end of the book and the beginning, needed the codex." Scott's fascination with scrolls in this and later poems might then reflect not simply references to the Old Testament and to the Apocalypse, but to a prophetic openness apparently closed by the book in which he publishes such images.

Chapter Two. *Marmion*

1. Scott, Introduction to 1830 edition, *PW*, 173. For stronger language, see Jeffrey's review in the April 1808 *Edinburgh Review*, rpt. in John O. Hayden, ed., *Scott: The Critical Heritage* (New York: Barnes and Noble, 1970), 38, 40-41. Zug, in "Scott and Ballad Forgery," quotes Joseph Ritson, *Scottish Songs* (Glasgow 1869): "The history of Scottish poetry exhibits a series of fraud, forgery, and imposture, practised with impunity and success" (p. 55).

2. See William Croft Dickinson, *Scotland: From the Earliest Times to 1603* (Edinburgh and London: Thomas Nelson, 1961), 289, and R.L. Mackie, *King James IV of Scotland: A Brief Survey of His Life and Times* (Edinburgh: Oliver and Boyd, 1958), 261: "No account [of Flodden] by a Scottish soldier is known to exist. So we must be content to watch the struggle from the English side."

3. See Eller, "Enchanted Land," 114, 130, and Crawford, *Scott*, 47-48. J.H. Alexander, *"Marmion": Studies in Interpretation and Composition*, Romantic Reassessment 30 (Salzburg: Institut für Anglistik und Amerikanistik, 1981), 20, argues that the epistles "establish . . . a set of moral positives against which the characters in the narrative can be judged." Alexander also suggests (p. 106) that "a complex plot is a consequence of the operation of sin"; I disagree.

4. Introduction to the First Edition, *PW*, 171. In "Scott and 'Marmion': The Discovery of Identity," 738, 742, John Pikoulis suggests that the narrative expresses Scott's search for historical identity.

5. Scott alludes to this in the 1830 Introduction (*PW*, 172); see also Johnson, *Sir Walter Scott*, 1:261, and N.T. Phillipson's discussion of the 1808 Ashestiel Memoir in "Scott as Story-Teller: An Essay in Psychobiography," *Scott*

Bicentenary Essays, ed. Alan Bell (Edinburgh: Scottish Academic Press, 1973), esp. p. 99.

6. See Pikoulis, "Identity"; J.D. McClatchy, "The Ravages of Time: The Function of the *Marmion* Epistles," *Studies in Scottish Literature* 9 (1972):256-63; Eller, "Enchanted Land," 106-30; Alexander, "*Marmion*," chap. 1; and Kathryn Sutherland, "Defining the Self in the Poetry of Scott and Wordsworth," in *Scott and His Influence*, 51-62.

7. Alexander, "Marmion," 17.

8. Eller, "Enchanted Land," 112, emphasizes Dryden's problems in equaling Spenser and Milton; Alexander points out the parallel between Lancelot's "disabling guilt" and Marmion's "impotence at Flodden" ("Marmion," 222), a parallel emphasized in Scott's first two notes.

9. Ibid., 18.

10. For a different view, see Eller, "Enchanted Land," 128-29.

11. Alexander, "Marmion," 17.

12. Ibid., 54.

13. Scott's 1827 "Essay on Chivalry," in *Essays on Chivalry, Romance, and the Drama* (London: Frederick Warne, 1887), praises the civilizing force of a devotion to women approaching "idolatry" (p. 10), and Alexander ("*Marmion*") argues that Marmion's villainy represents a specific falling-away from that ideal. I would argue that Marmion's attitude is an extreme form of a more pervasive cultural attitude not corrected by such idolatry.

14. The manuscript of *Marmion*, 1:16, originally suggested that the disguised page (Constance) "was erst, in Wilton's lordly bower, / Sir Ralph de Wilton's bride" (Lockhart's note to 1833 *Poetical Works*, 83; also noted by Alexander, 124.) Clare and Constance seem hardly separable here.

15. The fragment of a border ballad that Marmion hears is, ironically, a kind of literal forgery, because Scott's friend Surtees had passed it on as an authentic ballad but had in fact written it himself; see Johnson, *Sir Walter Scott*, 1:263-64. His deception is an extreme example of the problem Scott and other "editors" faced in recording, publishing, and re-using traditional songs. See Scott's discussion of 14 October 1808 in *Letters*, 2:95.

16. See Introduction, n. 20. In the first edition of the *Minstrelsy*, "The Laird of Laminton" was placed in the "historical" section; Scott then received other versions and published "a more perfect version" as "Katherine Janfarie." In Henderson it appears as a "romantic" ballad.

17. See Pikoulis, "Identity," 744.

18. See Ann B. Tracy, *The Gothic Novel, 1790-1830: Plot Summaries and Index to Motifs* (Lexington: University Press of Kentucky, 1981), entries no. 29, 33, 74, 75, 99, 129, 132, 198, 206. See also Sister Mary Muriel Tarr, *Catholicism in Gothic Fiction* (Washington, D.C.: Catholic University of America Press, 1946), 46, 48, 60-63. Tracy also lists thirty-five entries for cross-gender dressing.

19. Alexander, "Marmion," p. 32, n. 12.

20. See Norman Holland and Leona Sherman, "Gothic Possibilities," *New Literary History* 8 (1976-77):279-94; Mary Poovey, "Ideology and *The Mysteries of Udolpho*," *Criticism* 21, no. 4 (Fall 1979):307-23, though her opposition between the heroine of sensibility and an avaricious villain describes Clare's character

more than that of Constance; Claire Kahane, "Gothic Mirrors and Feminine Identity," *Centennial Review* 24, no. 1 (Winter 1980):43-64; *The Female Gothic*, ed. Juliann E. Fleenor (Montreal and London: Eden Press, 1983), esp. Cynthia Griffin Wolff, "The Radcliffean Gothic Model: a Form for Feminine Sexuality," 203-23; Judith Wilt, *Ghosts of the Gothic: Austen, Eliot, & Lawrence* (Princeton: Princeton University Press, 1980).

21. The clearest literary examples for this are the release of mother and daughter from convent prisons and threats of live burial in *The Italian*, and *Jane Eyre*. Blake's Thel, on plate 4 of that poem, rejects this "developmental" pattern.

22. Alexander, "Marmion," 4.

23. See Mackie, *James IV*, 230 ff. See also Sister Rose Marie Grady, "The Sources of Scott's Eight Long Narrative Poems," (Ph.D. diss., University of Illinois, 1933), 139; she points out that Sir Ralph Sadler, whose papers Scott was editing, was one of Henry VIII's ambassadors, was met by Lindesay, and stayed at Tantallon.

24. See Jeffrey's review in *Scott: The Critical Heritage*, 38, and for a pre-publication criticism, Johnson, *Sir Walter Scott*, 1:273-74. Alexander, in "To Visit or Not to Visit? The Yarrow Question in the 'Lay' and 'Marmion,' " in *Scott and his Influence*, p. 33, suggests that Scott should not have conceded that his motives were merely scenic.

25. See Scott's note 76 (*PW*, 148), and also Mackie, *James IV*, 248. But see Anna Seward's acerbic annotation to this passage: "This pageant is insinuated to have been a human contrivance and all believed de Wilton dead—why therefore is he cited to the awful Tribunal? No purpose whatever is answered by this appearance. . . ." Her copy of *Marmion*, later owned by Amy Lowell, is now in the Houghton Library, Harvard; listed in William Ruff, *A Bibliography of the Poetical Works of Sir Walter Scott 1796-1832* (Edinburgh: Edinburgh Bibliographical Society, 1938), no. 59.

26. For Lindesay's own view of vision, see Coleman O. Parsons, *Witchcraft and Demonology in Scott's Fiction* (Edinburgh: Oliver and Boyd, 1964), 24.

27. See Eller, "Enchanted Land," 132, for an argument that de Wilton is associated with the poet's powers.

28. The "if . . . then" form of the Linlithgow prophecy is closer to the biblical tradition of these writers than are the absolute predictions of the vision at the cross and Constance's predictions. The encounter with de Wilton as elfin knight can be seen as a version of the wrestling with supernatural figures for knowledge that we see in the Proteus episode of *The Odyssey*, in Jacob's wrestling, and in Blake's wrestling with Milton in his illuminated book *Milton*.

29. See Sir Walter Scott, *Tales of a Grandfather: History of Scotland*, 6 vols. in 3 (Boston: Houghton, Mifflin, 1861), first series, 2:7; and Mackie, *James IV*, 201, 249, 253. Rubenstein, "Historical Poetry," comments on similarities between James and Marmion, but does not note James's fascination with chivalric ceremony (p. 149). By making Norham and not Ford Castle the scene of the dalliance with Lady Heron, Scott makes clear the ironic complementarity between Marmion's journey north and James's south. Finally, both Mackie and Dickinson (pp. 287 ff.) emphasize James's physical engagement in battle, not his command of it.

30. See F.A. Pottle, "The Power of Memory in Boswell and Scott," 1945, rpt. in *Scott's Mind and Art*, ed. A. Norman Jeffares (1969; rpt. New York: Barnes and Noble, 1970), 236, 250.

Chapter Three. *The Lady of the Lake*

1. Jill Rubenstein, "Symbolic Characterization in *The Lady of the Lake*," *Dalhousie Review* 51 (Autumn 1971):370.
2. For a discussion of romance elements in Scott's poetry, which has stimulated my own reading of this poem, see Kroeber, "Narrative Pattern of Scott." Several perceptive readings of Scott's novels in addition to those cited earlier have demonstrated his skillful handling of romance and history; see A.O.J. Cockshut, *The Achievement of Walter Scott* (London: Collins, 1969); and S. Stewart Gordon, "*Waverley* and the 'Unified Design,' " in *Walter Scott: Modern Judgements*, ed. D.D. Devlin (1969; rpt. Nashville: Aurora Publishers, 1970), 81.
3. Erich Auerbach, "The Knight Sets Forth," in *Mimesis: The Representation of Reality in Western Literature* (1946; rpt. New York: Doubleday Anchor, 1957). For the social bias of the English Arthurian romance, see Helaine Newstead, "Malory and Romance," in *Four Essays on Romance*, ed. Herschel Baker (Cambridge: Harvard University Press, 1971), 4 ff. Increasing this bias in his sources is Scott's own interest in reading medieval romances as social history (see *Letters*, 2:55).
4. Thus it fits the earlier end of the long period Jameson argues is productive of romance as a genre (*Political Unconscious*, 148).
5. See *The Mabinogion*, trans., intro. Gwyn Jones and Thomas Jones (1949; rpt. London: Dent, 1968), 229-41; and Chretien de Troyes, *Arthurian Romances*, trans. W.W. Comfort, intro. and notes D.D.R. Owen (1914; rpt. London: Dent, 1975), 1-4. See also Geoffrey Hartman, "False Themes and Gentle Minds," in *Beyond Formalism: Literary Essays 1958-1970* (New Haven: Yale University Press, 1972), 293. He also cites D.C. Allen's very detailed discussion of the visionary hunt in *Image and Meaning*, enlarged ed. (Baltimore: Johns Hopkins University Press, 1968), 169 ff. See also "The Hunt as Literary Structure" in Marcelle Thiebaux, *The Stag of Love: The Chase in Medieval Literature* (Ithaca and London: Cornell University Press, 1974), 47-58; and Paton, *Fairy Mythology*, p. 16. For Scott's general acquaintance with earlier Arthurian material, see Johnston, *Enchanted Ground*, 40, 153, 159.
6. For Scott's immersion in Malory during this period, see *Letters*, 1:390, 2:236. Since he owned a copy of Stansby's 1643 edition of Malory and was unable to work directly from Caxton until late 1810, my citations will be drawn from *The most ancient and famous history of the renowned Prince Arthur* . . . (London: William Stansby, 1634). "W" in the text refers to Eugene Vinaver, ed., *The Works of Sir Thomas Malory*, 2d ed., 3 vols., (Oxford: Clarendon Press, 1967), taken from the Winchester MS., 1:52. For a fuller discussion of Scott's work with Malory, see Johnston, *Enchanted Ground*, 190 ff.; and Barry Gaines, "The Editions of Malory in the Early Nineteenth Century," *Papers of the Biographical Society of America* 68 (1974):1-17.

7. See Eugene Vinaver, *The Rise of Romance* (Oxford: Clarendon Press, 1971), 103-4. See also Rubenstein, "Characterization in *The Lady of the Lake*," p. 372: "Like Malory's Lady of the Lake, who offers Excalibur to Arthur not as an outright gift but as an opportunity to be pursued, she teaches the sovereign a lesson in kingship; or, more accurately, she provides him with an opportunity to teach himself."

8. Vinaver, *Rise*, 46-47 n., and Beer, *Romance*, 20-21.

9. See Richard Hurd, *Letters on Chivalry and Romance*, cited in John Arthos, *On the Poetry of Spenser and the Form of Romance* (London: Allen and Unwin, 1956), 189. See also Johnston, *Enchanted Ground*, 8 ff., 33-34, 168, where he analyzes the attitude of Scott's friend George Ellis in his *Specimens of Early English Metrical Romances*. See also Robert Southey's introduction to Malory, *The Byrth, lyf, and Actes of Kyng Arthure*, printed from Caxton's edition, 1485 (London: T. Davison, 1817), xxi-xxxi.

10. Henderson, *Minstrelsy*, 4:91-92. Scott's modern editor Henderson compounds the amusement by noting drily, "The . . . hypothesis [of modern editing] is not improbable." His comment, however, does not take into account the discovery of an independent version B of the ballad (Campbell MSS 2:83; Child, *Ballads*, 1:317).

11. *Prose Works* (Edinburgh: A. and C. Black, 1861), 17:51-52.

12. See Johnson, *Sir Walter Scott*, 1:398, for William Erskine's shared authorship of the preface.

13. Scott, *Prose Works*, 6:137-38. In romance, too, he now comments, "The supernatural and the extraordinary are relied upon exclusively as the supports of the interest."

14. See *Letters*, 1:324, and 2:240, 261, 274, and 277.

15. The two other queens reign over places: Northgalis and, evocatively, "The Wast lands" (Stansby, chap. 169; Sig. Nn3).

16. McMaster, "Levi-Strauss in the Highlands," 13.

17. See Wimberly, *Folklore in the Ballads*, 367-71.

18. For the parallels between Ellen and Blanche, see McMaster, "Levi-Strauss in the Highlands," pp. 20, 23.

19. Ibid., 18.

20. Eller, "Enchanted Land," 177.

21. See McMaster's criticism of Johnson's and my earlier readings of the poem, "Levi-Strauss in the Highlands," p. 10, also pp. 19, 24-25. Since Scott would soon discover that he had the Prince Regent as a reader, however, educating princes about their northern subjects would not have been an entirely anachronistic theme. See chap. 7, p. 182.

22. See *Observations*, 3d ed. (London: Dutton and Ostell, 1807), 45. Though Scott apparently did not own a copy of Thomas Warton's *Observations*, his familiarity with the *History of Poetry* appears as early as his 1806 review of Ellis's and Ritson's collection of medieval romances in *Edinburgh Review* cited above in n. 11. Both Beer, *Romance*, 34; and Johnston, *Enchanted Ground*, 103, mention Warton's analysis of Elizabethan interest in the romances. See also Ronald S. Crane, *The Vogue of Medieval Chivalric Romance during the English Renaissance*, abstract of Ph.D. diss. for the University of Pennsylvania (Menasha, Wis.: Collegiate Press, 1919). In Jonson's masque, "The Speeches at

Prince Henry's Barriers," *Ben Jonson*, ed. C.H. Herford and Percy and Evelyn Simpson (Oxford: Clarendon Press, 1941), 7:323, the Lady of the Lake presents the framework of an Arthurian kingdom revived through the kind of sovereignty exercised by James I and his son.

23. *Minstrelsy of the Scottish Border*, 2d ed. (1803), 3:271; in *Minstrelsy*, ed. Henderson, 3:29. The ballad is "The Broomfield Hill." In the note Scott cites William Dugdale's *The Antiquities of Warwickshire*, in which the pageantry at Kenilworth—and one of the appearances of the Lady of the Lake—is briefly described (London: Thomas Warren, 1656), 166; but in mentioning Lane (Laneham) and Captain Cox, he goes well beyond Dugdale. Scott's friend and fellow-medievalist Joseph Ritson, in *A Dissertation on Romance and Minstrelsy* (1802; rpt. Edinburgh: E. and A. Goldsmid, 1891), 111, cites a long passage from Laneham as part of his attack on the status of minstrels. Writing Constable in 1820 that he is deep in John Nichols's *Progresses and Public Processions of Queen Elizabeth*, Scott warns, "Please not to say a word about Kenilworth. The very name anticipates so much, that some knowing fellow might anticipate the subject" (*Letters* 6: [1934], 266). A 1788 copy of Nichols is listed in the *Catalogue of the Library at Abbotsford* (1838; rpt. New York: AMS Press, 1971). The library does not list dates of acquisition; in his note to the letter, Grierson suggests that Constable had sent it for Scott's work on the novel, though no earlier letter records a specific request for it. Nichols's *Progresses* contains both Laneham's *Letter* and Gascoigne's *Princely Pleasures*.

24. Richard Goode, "Spenser's Festive Poem: Elizabeth and Royal Pageantry and *The Faerie Queene*" (Ph.D. diss., University of Texas 1973), 162. See also Beer, *Romance*, 34.

25. *Captain Cox, His Ballads and Books; or Robert Laneham's Letter*, re-ed. Frederick J. Furnivall for the Ballad Society, no. 7 (London: Taylor, 1871), 6.

26. For a variant of this view, based in the early nineteenth century, see McMaster, "Levi-Strauss in the Highlands," pp. 16, 25.

27. George Gascoigne, "The Princely Pleasures at Kenilworth Castle," in *The Complete Works of George Gascoigne*, ed. John W. Cunliffe, Cambridge English Classics, 2 vols. (Cambridge: Cambridge University Press, 1910), 2:102.

28. *The Works of Edmund Spenser, A Variorum Edition*, Vol. 7: *The Minor Poems, Part One*, ed. Charles Grosvenor Osgood and Henry Gibbs Lotspeich, asst. Dorothy E. Mason (Baltimore: Johns Hopkins University Press, 1943), 44.

29. For a fuller discussion of these patterns, see Frye, *Anatomy*, 182-84, 186-206; "The Argument of Comedy," *English Institute Essays*, 1948, ed. E.A. Robertson (New York: Columbia University Press, 1949), 58-73; rpt. in *Shakespeare: Modern Essays in Criticism*, ed. Leonard F. Dean (1957; rpt. New York: Oxford Galaxy, 1961), 78-89; and *A Natural Perspective: The Development of Shakespearean Comedy and Romance* (New York: Harcourt, Brace, 1965); C.L. Barber, *Shakespeare's Festive Comedy: A Study of Dramatic Form and Its Relation to Social Custom* (1959; rpt. Cleveland: Meridian World, 1963); David P. Young, *"A Midsummer Night's Dream*: Structure," from *Something of Great Constancy: The Art of "A Midsummer Night's Dream"* (New Haven: Yale University Press, 1966), rpt. in *Modern Shakespeare Criticism*, ed. Alvin B. Kernan (New York: Harcourt, Brace, and World, 1970), 174-89; and Beer, *Romance*, 38. The quoted terms are from Frye's *Anatomy*. His discussion of the structure of romance in these works

owes, I would argue, as much to Renaissance as to medieval forms. Renaissance narrative romance, particularly Ariosto, Tasso, and Spenser, clearly influenced Scott as well, as both Scott and his critics have pointed out. See Johnson, *Sir Walter Scott*, 1:334, and Scott, *Letters*, 2:66. For Ariosto's use of an artful confusion, beautifully resolved, see Vinaver, *Rise*, 94; Scott, *Prose Works*, 6:195, and Patricia Parker's chapter on Ariosto in *Inescapable Romance*.

30. R.L. Mackie discusses that king's need to buy timber on the continent, "all the woods in Fife [having been] laid low," to build even a few ships (*King James IV*, 202). This gives little evidence, however, about the amount or accessibility of lumber in the Perthshire highlands.

31. M.C. Bradbrook, *The Growth and Structure of Elizabethan Comedy* (1955; rpt. London: Peregrine, 1963), 95, 101; see also p. 32, n. 16. Crawford notes the way the plot of *The Lady of the Lake* resembles traditional folk and ballad art (*Scott*, 45).

32. See Hartman, "False Themes and Gentle Minds," 290-94. Though Hartman does not consider *The Lady of the Lake* in this essay, his comparison of "The Wild Huntsman" to Wordsworth's "Heartleap Well" places in a new context Coleridge's remarks that *The Lady of the Lake* "commences with the poorest Paraphrase-Parody of The Hart Leap Well—" (Coleridge's letter to Wordsworth of October 1810, from E.L. Griggs, ed., *Collected Letters of Samuel Taylor Coleridge* [Oxford: Oxford University Press, 1959], in *Scott: The Critical Heritage*, ed. Hayden, p. 59).

33. See Scott, *Tales of a Grandfather*, first series, cont'd., 2:48-50.

34. Rubenstein, "Characterization in *The Lady of the Lake*," 371-72, builds her reading of the hunt upon its nature as a civilized game; although an excellent point, this does not consider sufficiently the tone of the manhunt. In her dissertation, "Scott's Historical Poetry," she points out James's "increased powers of empathy" as a result of this reversal (p. 101).

35. See Johnson, *Sir Walter Scott*, 1:351.

36. Ibid., 1:353.

37. See Rubenstein, "Characterization," 369; and Johnson, *Sir Walter Scott*, 1:354. Both of these critics emphasize throughout their discussions the need for this "steady skill" to control the violence of highland culture without rejecting its virtues.

38. Millgate, *Walter Scott*, 27-28, suggests that this stylization is so intense as to become static; we agree on the domination of Scott's artistry through that of the king.

39. Although this resolution may satisfy both romance allusion and Renaissance romance-comedy plot, it did not occur historically; see *The Works of William Robertson, D. D.*, vol. 1: *The History of Scotland*, 1759 (London: T. Cadell, 1840), 53 ff.; Scott, *Tales of a Grandfather*, 2:43, as well as a long discussion of the Douglasses in his original Introduction to the *Minstrelsy* (Henderson, 1:53-73).

40. For a different analysis of the king's dramatic impulse in this scene, see Rubenstein, "Historical Poetry," 118. In "Characterization," p. 383, she sees Ellen as intermediary; a fuller discussion in the dissertation emphasizes Douglas's role, as does Alice Chandler in *A Dream of Order: the Medieval Ideal in Nineteenth Century English Literature* (Lincoln: University of Nebraska Press, 1970), 34.

41. Rubenstein, "Historical Poetry," 98; and Rubenstein, "Characterization," 372-73.

42. For the suggestion that she is a "Sphinx figure" behind a tendency to idealize the "Stuart-Jacobite past," see Wilt, *Secret Leaves*, p. 154.

43. In "Historical Poetry," 68, while discussing *The Lay*, Rubenstein describes Scott's "customary pattern" of using the framing minstrel as mediator between "primitive vitality" and "progressive order and restraint," thus allowing him a vital, not an anachronistic, role.

44. Harold Bloom, "The Internalization of the Quest Romance," in *Yale Review* 58 (Summer 1969), rpt. in *Romanticism and Consciousness*, ed. Bloom (New York: Norton, 1970), 5-6.

45. Several recent readings even of these high romantic poets have argued that society and history are the displaced referents for much discussion of nature; see, for example, Marjorie Levinson, *Wordsworth's Great Period Poems* (Cambridge: Cambridge University Press, 1986).

46. See *Minstrelsy*, ed. Henderson, 4:155-56, a note to his *Glenfinlas*.

47. For a different view of these portraits, see Rubenstein, "Historical Poetry," 114 ff.

48. For an example of theories linking primitive culture and imagination, see Giambattista Vico, from "The New Science," in *Critical Theory since Plato*, ed. Hazard Adams (New York: Harcourt Brace Jovanovich, 1971), 293-301. See also M.H. Abrams, *The Mirror and the Lamp: Romantic Theory and the Critical Tradition* (New York: Oxford University Press, 1953), 78 ff.

49. *The History of the Kings of Britain*, trans. Lewis Thorpe (Baltimore: Penguin, 1966), 167-68. Scott's note to this passage is more overtly skeptical. See pp. 289-90, note 30.

50. Again, see Rubenstein, "Historical Poetry," 120-21, for a different view.

Chapter Four. *Rokeby*

1. Lord Byron, *The Complete Poetical Works*, ed. Jerome J. McGann, 1 (Oxford: Clarendon Press, 1980): 234-35, ll. 153-54, 157, 172-82 *passim*.

2. See Scott, *Letters*, 3:138 (3 July 1812) and Lord Byron, *Letters and Journals*, ed. Leslie A. Marchand, 11 vols., *Volume 2: 1810-1812* (Cambridge: Harvard University Press, 1973), 182-83 (6 July 1812). Although each volume has a separate subtitle and publication date (1973-82), I will cite only volume and page in succeeding references.

3. Kroeber, *Narrative Art*, 177; see also Johnson, *Sir Walter Scott*, 1:472-76. For contemporary reviews discussing the complexity of Scott's plot, see *British Review* 4 (May 1813):278-79, rpt. in J.H. Alexander, *Romantic Reviewing*, 2:325; *Eclectic Review* 9 (June 1813):588; *Monthly Review* (March 1813):232; *Port Folio* 3, 1 (1813):562 ff., and Ellis's review in the *Quarterly Review* 8 (December 1812):507.

4. See Alexander, *Reception of Scott's Poetry*, 2:385.

5. Kroeber, *Narrative Art*, 176-77.

6. Aylmer, *A Short History of Seventeenth-Century England: 1603-1689* (1963; rpt New York: Mentor, 1963), 129.

7. See McMaster, *Scott and Society*, 127, 130-31. Hume, Ferguson and others, he notes, compared the English civil war to the French revolution.

8. For the fate of this "outlaw's image" after the publication of Scott's poem and the tramplings of tourists over the owner's land, see *Letters*, 4:271 (to Morritt, 26 August 1816).

9. See Scott, *Letters*, 3:188 for an explicit reference to Robin Hood; see also Wilt, *Secret Leaves*, Intro. and chap. 1. Henderson's index to the *Minstrelsy* is "Robin Hood, mentioned *passim*." For "Dacre," see *The Lay*, canto 4; a Dacre Castle stood in Cumberland (*Blue Guide: England*, ed. L. Russell Muirhead and Stuart Rossiter, 7th ed. [London: Benn, 1965], 455). Ravensworth Castle is near Gateshead, Durham; see James C. Corson, *Notes and Index to Grierson's Edition of the Letters of Sir Walter Scott* (Oxford: Clarendon Press, 1979), 607.

10. Goethe's *Götz von Berlichingen* and Schiller's *Die Räuber* are early examples; Scott translated Goethe's play in 1799. See Peter L. Thorslev, Jr., *The Byronic Hero: Types and Prototypes* (Minneapolis: University of Minnesota Press, 1962), chap. 5.

11. Johnson calls Mortham the Byronic hero, though noting Scott's prior claim to the type (R, 1:469). See also Thorslev, *Byronic Hero*, 80-82.

12. See *The Borderers*, ed. Robert Osborn (Ithaca: Cornell University Press, 1982), 243; ll. 1862-73 in 1842 version. Given the border location, it is possible that Wordsworth or Coleridge read or recited some of its passages to Scott before 1812; more likely they share a similar interest in a haunted psychology. Wordsworth's villain is not named Oswald until an 1841 draft.

13. See Alexander, *Reception*, 2:385

14. Alexander, *Reception*, 1:82; and Corson, *Notes and Index*, 384.

15. See David Beers Quinn, *The Elizabethans and the Irish* (Ithaca: published for the Folger Shakespeare Library by Cornell University Press, 1966), 17.

16. See J.C. Beckett, *The Making of Modern Ireland, 1603-1923* (London: Faber and Faber, 1966), 42-44; and Sean O'Faolain, *The Great O'Neill: A Biography of Hugh O'Neill, Earl of Tyrone, 1550-1616* (New York: Duell, Sloane, and Pearce, 1942).

17. Quinn, *Elizabethans and the Irish*, 16: R, n. 43.

18. See Quinn, *Elizabethans and the Irish*, p. 16; *Dictionary of National Biography*, 14:1085; and Richard Bagwell, *Ireland under the Stuarts and during the Interregnum*, vol. 1: *1603-1642* (London: Longmans, Green, 1909), 38.

19. Beckett, *Modern Ireland*, 80.

20. *A View of the Present State of Ireland*, ed. R.L. Renwick (London: Scholastic Press, 1934), 95. See also Quinn, *Elizabethans and the Irish*, 17-20 and Scott, *Letters*, 3:213-22.

21. Joseph Cooper Walker, *Historical Memoirs of the Irish Bards* (Dublin, 1786; facsim. rpt. New York: Garland, 1971), 139-41.

22. Carryl Nelson Thurber, editor's introduction to Sir Robert Howard, *The Committee*, in University of Illinois Studies in Language and Literature, no. 7 (1921), 45; from *Dryden's Works*, ed. Walter Scott (Edinburgh: Constable, 1808), 2:225.

23. Scott, *Letters*, 3:103-4; see also *The Works of Jonathan Swift, D. D. with Notes and a Life of the Author*, ed. Walter Scott, 19 vols. (Edinburgh: Constable, 1814), 1:318, 474 n.

24. See Ita Margaret Hogan, *Anglo-Irish Music, 1780-1830* (Cork: Cork University Press, 1966), 6, 91-93.

25. *Reliques of Irish Poetry* (1798); and *A Memoir of Miss Brooke* (1816) by Aaron Crossley Hobart Seymour, ed. Leonard R.N. Ashley (Gainesville, Fla.: Scholars' Facsimiles and Reprints, 1970), vii-viii. See also *Catalogue of the Library at Abbotsford*, 196.

26. Sydney Owenson, Lady Morgan, *The Wild Irish Girl*, intro. Robert Lee Wolff, 3 vols. (New York: Garland, 1979), 3:258.

27. Charles Maturin, *The Milesian Chief*, Introduction by Robert Lee Wolff, 4 vols. (New York: Garland, 1979). See *The Correspondence of Sir Walter Scott and Charles Robert Maturin* (Austin: University of Texas Press, 1937; xerox facsim. Ann Arbor: University Microfilms, 1970), 7. When Scott answers Maturin's first letter in December 1812, he tells Maturin that he has read "the House of Montorio and the Irish tale"; Fannie Ratchford and William McCarthy, Jr., footnote the latter as *The Wild Irish Boy* (1808; rpt New York: Garland, 1979). Scott had probably not yet read *The Milesian Chief*, nor can I find reference to it in his correspondence with Maturin in the several years immediately following *Rokeby*. In spite of its title, *The Wild Irish Boy* does not correspond as closely to Owenson's metaphor of cross-cultural love as does *The Milesian Chief*; it does, however, contain a long speech from its hero (3:134-39) censuring the negative effects of Catholicism in Ireland but arguing that emancipation would lessen these effects. See Charles Maturin, *The Wild Irish Boy*, Introduction by Robert Lee Wolff, 3 vols (1808; rpt. New York: Garland, 1979), 3:134-39.

28. See R.L. Edgeworth, *Memoirs*, 2 vols. (London: Baldwin, Cradock, and Joy, 1820), 2:207 ff., 239; Oliver MacDonough, *Ireland: The Union and its Aftermath*, rev. and enl. (London: Allen and Unwin, 1977); R.B. McDowell, *Irish Public Opinion, 1750-1800* (London: Faber and Faber, 1944), 139-216; and Patrick O'Farrell, *England and Ireland since 1800* (Oxford: Oxford University Press, 1975). See also, for typical articles, *Quarterly Review* 3 (1810):114-15 and *Edinburgh Review* 12 (1808):336 ff.; according to O'Farrell, the latter is written by Malthus.

29. One must of course keep in mind his close connections during this period not only to the conservative *Quarterly* but also to Southey's anti-Emancipation discussions in *The Edinburgh Annual Register*. See Kenneth Curry, *Sir Walter Scott's Annual Register* (Knoxville: University of Tennessee Press, 1977), 21.

30. See [John Roby], *Jokeby: A Burlesque on Rokeby, a Poem, in Six Cantos, by an Amateur of Fashion*, 5th ed. (London: Thomas Tegg, 1813), 3:7 and 4:8.

31. See Thomas Pakenham, *The Year of Liberty: The Story of the Great Irish Rebellion of 1798* (Englewood Cliffs, N.J.: Prentice-Hall, 1970), 57 ff. and *Jokeby* 4:6, 204 n. *Jokeby* contains a reference to the 1641 Irish rebellion when it changes one of the robber minstrels' songs from naming "Allan-a-Dale" to "Phelim O'Neill" in canto 3. See Bagwell, 3:336-37, 356-57.

32. See Johnson, *Sir Walter Scott*, 1:108 n. (notes, p. ix).

33. See Johnson, *Sir Walter Scott*, 1:179 and 197 for Scott's early hearing of *Christabel* in 1802; in 1809 Scott and Coleridge were reciting their own and each other's poems at a literary party (1:313), so there is a possibility of Scott's having heard "Kubla Khan," too, before its publication.

34. See Millgate, *Scott: The Making of the Novelist*, 29-33.
35. See Introduction, n. 44, above.
36. See Scott's own Note 34 to *Rokeby*, which points out that he has adapted the song from a Jacobite farewell.
37. See Alexander, "To Visit or Not to Visit," 39-40.
38. See Johnson, *Sir Walter Scott*, 1:471; for narrative patterns in history, see Hayden White, *Metahistory: The Historical Imagination in Nineteenth-Century Europe* (1973; Baltimore: Johns Hopkins University Press, 1983).
39. See my chap. 1, n. 29.
40. In meter and image, these lines echo the magnificently apocalyptic final chorus of Dryden's "Song for St. Cecilia's Day."
41. The reformer was supposedly born not in but near the ancestral family holdings of the Wycliffe family, very much in the neighborhood of Barnard Castle and Rokeby (*DNB*).
42. Ruth Eller pointed out, in hearing a version of this chapter at the Aberdeen conference, the recurrent association of poetic characters with names beginning with "E"; Redmond, she observes, includes Edmund.

Chapter Five. *The Bridal of Triermain*

1. See Ruff, *A Bibliography*. I have examined the first editions of both poems at the Houghton Library of Harvard University.
2. J.G. Lockhart, *Memoirs of the Life of Sir Walter Scott, Bart.* (Edinburgh: Adam and Charles Black, 1862), 5:107.
3. J.T. Hillhouse, "Sir Walter's Last Long Poem," *HLQ* 16 (1952-53):53-73.
4. See *Scots Magazine* 75 (April 1813):283 and Johnson, *Sir Walter Scott*, 1:476 on *Triermain*. Hillhouse, "Poem," 53-56, surveys contemporary criticism on *Harold*.
5. See, for example, *Quarterly Review* 9 (July 1813):491; *Critical Review*, 4th ser., 3 (May 1813):474; and for reviews of the two-volume 1817 edition, *Blackwood's Edinburgh Magazine* 1 (April 1817):76-78, cited by Lockhart in his notes to *Scott's Poetical Works*, 401 n., 402 n.
6. See Ruff, *A Bibliography*, no. 155 and no. 161.
7. *Edinburgh Annual Register*, 1809, part 2, pp. 596-99. This fragment, "The Vision of Triermain," and the other two are introduced by a comic pseudo-contributor as having been recalled from his dream-vision visit to hell. He is awakened from his dream by his landlady, who must somehow be related to Coleridge's man from Porlock.
8. See J.H. Alexander, "To Visit or Not to Visit," in *Scott and his Influence*, 39.
9. The passage does not appear in the manuscript (Morgan MS. 44351, Ruff, *A Bibliography*, no. 131), but does appear in the first edition.
10. Jill Rubenstein, "The Dilemma of History: A Reading of Scott's *Bridal of Triermain*," *SEL* 12, no. 4 (Autumn 1972):725.
11. Ibid., 723, 729, 726.
12. *Mansfield Park* presents these consequences most seriously; see also *Pride and Prejudice*, and Marshall, *Virgins and Viragos*, 182-85.

13. See Alexander, *Reception*, 2:412, for Morritt's response to the satire; and Johnson, *Sir Walter Scott*, 1:410, 476, for Lady Louisa Stuart's and others'. George Ellis, in *Quarterly Review* 9 (July 1813): 486-91, praises the poem's delicacy, as do several acquaintances of Morritt (also in Alexander, *Reception*, 2:414).

14. See Scott's note 2 (*PW*, 587).

15. See Jameson, *Political Unconscious*, 140; and Ricoeur, *Time and Narrative*, 1:76. See also Kurt Gamerschlag, " 'The Bridal of Triermain' and Its Adaptations," *Influence*, 504-5 for a discussion of picturesque and sublime landscape in the poem.

16. See E.K. Chambers, *Arthur of Britain* (1927; rpt. New York: October House, 1967), 146. Another exception to this motif of the *roi fainéant* occurs in Joseph Ritson's *Life of King Arthur: From Ancient Historians and Authentic Documents* (London: Payne and Foss, 1825), 146. Ritson is trying to ignore the courtly-romance elements of the tradition. This work, completed before Ritson's death in 1803, was probably known to George Ellis (Scott, *Letters*, 1:113 n. [Grierson quotes from an Ellis letter], cited by Johnston, *Enchanted Ground*, 167). See Paton, *Fairy Mythology*, chaps. 1-3, 10, 11, for a theory about this displacement.

17. See *Launfal* in *Romances*, ed. Ritson, 1:11-12, 28-33.

18. See the Morgan MS. 44351.

19. See Richard Robinson, *A Learned and True Assertion of the original, Life, Actes, and death of the most Noble Valiant, and Renowned Prince Arthure, King of great Brittaine*, . . . Collected and written of late yeares in Lattin, by . . . John Leland (London 1582), ed. William Edward Mead for E.E.T.S. (Oxford University Press, 1925), 62-65; Cap. xiii.

20. Johnson points out the fairy-tale parallel but does not explore it (*Sir Walter Scott*, 1:478). See Bettelheim, *The Uses of Enchantment: The Meaning and Importance of Fairy Tales* (1975; rpt. New York: Vintage, 1977), 232-33. For a criticism of Bettelheim that resembles my protest of Gyneth's punishment, see Nina Auerbach, *Woman and the Demon: The Life of a Victorian Myth* (Cambridge: Harvard University Press, 1982), 41-43.

21. Bettelheim, *Uses of Enchantment*, 232-33.

22. See Thomas Gray's *Journal in the Lakes*, in *The Works of Thomas Gray in Prose and Verse*, ed. Edmund Gosse, 4 vols. (1884; rpt. New York: AMS Press, 1968), 1:253; Ritson's *King Arthur*, 93-94, refers to "an old castle that once stood near" a lake, supposedly "swallowed up by the lake."

23. See Philip Hobsbawm, "Scott's Apoplectic Novels," in *Scott and his Influence*, 150-51.

24. Although the parallels between enslaved women and exploited land are not as extreme as in Blake's *Visions of the Daughters of Albion*, Scott's poem may draw upon some of the same discussions of American agriculture and the slave trade. See David Erdman's discussion of the Blake poem in *Blake: Prophet against Empire*, rev. ed. (New York: Doubleday Anchor, 1969), chap. 10.

25. For Scott's knowledge of the two Italian writers, see R.D.S. Jack, *The Italian Influence on Scottish Literature* (Edinburgh: Edinburgh University Press, 1972), 214; and Johnson, *Sir Walter Scott*, 1:48, 60.

26. See *Ariosto's Orlando Furioso, Selections from the Translation of Sir John*

Harington, ed. Rudolf Gottfried (Bloomington: Indiana University Press, 1963), 147 (canto 6), 159 (canto 7); Torquato Tasso, *Jerusalem Delivered,* trans. Edward Fairfax, intro. John Charles Nelson (New York: Capricorn, 1963), 314-16 (Book 15, 58-66), 318-25 (Book 16, 1-30); and *The Works of Edmund Spenser: A Variorum Edition,* ed. Edwin Greenlaw, Charles Grosvenor Osgood, and Frederick Morgan Padelford: *The Fairie Queene, Book Two,* ed. Edwin Greenlaw (Baltimore: Johns Hopkins University Press, 1933), 174-76 (2:12.60-68).

27. See Johnson, *Sir Walter Scott,* 1:479. Gottfried notes that even Queen Elizabeth felt obliged to censure Harington a little for his translating and circulating a particularly wanton section of Ariosto (Intro., *Orlando Furioso,* 10). Eller notes the shift to Spenserian allegory as a deliberate moralizing of the imagination ("Enchanted Land," 207).

28. The motif of the underworld fairy castle, reached by passing through a rock, is more widespread than that of its sudden disappearance. The romance of *Thomas off Ersseldoune* (Murray, Thornton MS.) preserves it, as the elfin queen "ledde hym in at Eldone hill, / Undir-nethe a derne lee" (stanza 33, Child, *Ballads,* 1:327), but the ballad versions do not. The romance version published by Scott has only the second of the two lines above. In the romance version of *Sir Orpheo* published by Ritson in *Ancient English Metrical Romances* (3:12), Orpheo follows the fairy procession "into the roche," and finds a fairyland and a castle. A similar pattern appears in "The Wee Wee Man," 1802 *Minstrelsy,* 2:234; and Child, *Ballads,* 38; Scott's version ends with the sudden disappearance of the wee man, the fairy queen, and her twenty-four green-dressed ladies. Only Child's versions B, D, and G, however, specifically describe the scene—hall and meadow—vanishing as well. Stith Thompson's *Motif Index of Folk Literature,* rev., enl. (Bloomington: Indiana University Press, 1958), is unhelpful in proving such disappearances; F 222.1 is the closest parallel. In the Grail literature, I can find it only in the first continuation of Chretien's *Perceval;* see *The Continuations of the Old French Perceval of Chretien de Troyes,* Volume I: The First Continuation, ed. William Roach (Philadelphia: University of Pennsylvania Press, 1949), 40 (MS. T, lines 1486-1509). Paton includes a listing of other examples (*Fairy Mythology,* 86-87 and 87 n.3); see also J. Curtin, "Oisin in Tir na n-Og," *Myths and Folk Tales of Ireland* (New York: Dover, 1975), 230-41, rpt. in Kerry Cardell and Trevor Code, eds., *From the Celtic Oral Tradition,* Deakin University publication, 1987.

Chapter Six. *The Lord of the Isles*

1. See particularly *British Review* 6 (Aug. 1815): 89, 97, 132; *Critical Review,* 5th ser., 2 (July 1815):59, cited by Alexander in *The Reviewing of Scott's Poetry,* 399; Jeffrey in *Edinburgh Review* 24 (Feb. 1815):274; *Quarterly Review* 13 (July 1815):307. See also Johnson, *Sir Walter Scott,* 1:486.

2. David Dalrymple, Lord Hailes, *The Annals of Scotland from the Accession of Malcolm III to the Accession of the House of Stewart.* A new ed., 3 vols. (Edinburgh: William Creech, and London: T. Cadell and W. Davies, 1797), 1:324.

3. See *Barbour's Bruce,* ed. Malcolm P. McDiarmid and James A.C. Stevenson, 3 vols. (Edinburgh: The Scottish Text Society, 1985); Books 3 and 4

cover this time period, in 2:46-104. I have also consulted *The Bruce* . . . , compiled by Master John Barbour, 1375, ed. W.W. Skeat (London: E.E.T.S., 1870, 1874), in vols. 11, 21, 29, 55. See *Barbour's Bruce*, 1:38, for McDiarmid's evaluation of Barbour's sources and literary shaping. See also G.W.S. Barrow, *Robert Bruce and the Community of the Realm of Scotland*, 2d ed. (Edinburgh: Edinburgh University Press, 1976), 231-37; his mixed review of Barbour as historian and as constructor of a chivalrous "hero of a work of art" is on p. 431. The "violation of history" in Scott's sending Bruce to Skye is pointed out by Sister Rose Marie Grady, "Sources of Scott's Poems," 331.

4. See *The Letters of John Keats, 1814-1821*, ed. Hyder Edward Rollins, 2 vols. (Cambridge: Harvard University Press, 1958), 1:403 (24 October 1818).

5. Wilt, *Secret Leaves*, 30.

6. See Hailes, *Annals*, 1:321 and Barrow, *Robert Bruce*, 243.

7. See Scott's note 42; he cites Pennant's *Scotland* (1790); and Barbour, *Bruce*, from Book 10. See also Barrow, *Robert Bruce*, 409.

8. See Barbour (Book 3, 1. 659; 2:69) for a reference to Angus, Lord of the Isles, giving hospitality to Bruce at Dunaverty on the Kintyre peninsula as Bruce left for Rachlin the autumn before; see Barrow, *Robert Bruce*, 231, 237 for Bruce's support by Angus Oig and Donald MacDonald of Islay. Scott's 1814 journal (in Lockhart, *Memoirs*, 4:339), describes Ardtornish as the site of parliaments called by the Lords of the Isles. See also Iaian Thornber, *The Castles of Morvern Argyll: Their History, Antiquities, and Architecture* (Fort William: Nevisprint, 1975), 6, who says that the castle came to the MacDonalds in 1309 after the forfeiture of Lorn.

9. For the complaints, see *British Critic*, n.s. 3 (Feb. 1815):144; *British Review* 6 (Aug. 1815):98; *Edinburgh Review* 24 (Feb. 1815):272; and *Theatrical Inquisitor* 6 (January 1815):59, cited in Alexander, *The Reviewing of Scott's Poetry*, 330. Earlier guidebooks include Thomas Pennant, *A Tour of Scotland*, in *Beyond the Highland Line: Three Journals of Travel in Eighteenth Century Scotland: Burt, Pennant, Thornton*, ed., intro. A.J. Youngson (London: Collins, 1974); Martin Martin, *A Description of the Western Islands of Scotland* (London: Andrew Bell, 1703); and John Knox, *A Tour through the Highlands of Scotland and the Hebride Isles, in 1786* (London: J. Walter, 1787).

10. See Lockhart, *Memoirs*, 4:306 n., citing Scott's remembering later his sleeping in a haunted chamber at Dunvegan; see also *Letters*, 2:357 (3 July 1810) for an earlier awareness of Johnson's route; and Scott's note in [James] *Boswell's Journal of a Tour to the Hebrides with Samuel Johnson, L.L.D.* with notes of Scott, Croker, Chambers, and others, 2 vols. (1831; rpt. Westminster: Constable, 1898), 1:159, where he recalls all of his party landing on Skye in 1814 thinking of Johnson's composing a Latin ode in response to an evening of Gaelic.

11. Samuel Johnson, *A Journey to the Western Islands of Scotland*, ed. Mary Lascelles (New Haven: Yale University Press, 1971), 39-41, and editor's introduction, p. xix.

12. See David Daiches, *The Last Stuart: The Life and Times of Bonnie Prince Charlie* (New York: Putnam, 1973), plate 26 and pp. 107, 248-59.

13. See for example the title of A. Shields and Andrew Lang's biography of the Old Pretender, *The King over the Water* (London: Longmans, Green 1907).

14. See Johnson, *Sir Walter Scott*, 1:417, 419, 438, 460.

15. See *Waverley*, ed. Claire Lamont (Oxford: Clarendon Press, 198), 293 (3:16) and 299 (3:17).

16. James Boswell, *The Journal of a Tour to the Hebrides with Samuel Johnson, L.L.D. . . .* (London: Henry Baldwin for Charles Dilley, 1785), title page.

17. *Boswell's Journal of a Tour to the Hebrides with Samuel Johnson, L.L.D., 1773*, ed. Frederick A. Pottle and Charles H. Bennett, new ed. with supplementary notes by Pottle (New York: McGraw-Hill, 1961), 105 n. ; the quotation is from the 1785 *Journal*, p. 218.

18. Pottle, *Boswell's Journal*, xxi, 150n.

19. 1785 *Journal*, 236.

20. Sandra M. Gilbert, "Costumes of the Mind: Transvestism as Metaphor in Modern Literature," *Critical Inquiry* 7 no. 2 (Winter 1980):391-417.

21. 1785 *Journal*, 220.

22. See *Eclectic Review*, n.s. 3 (May 1815):473.

23. Especially by Jeffrey in the *Edinburgh Review*, 275; the *British Critic*, however (n.s.3 [Feb. 1815]:146), praises its "dignity of versification."

24. See Marshall, *Virgins and Viragos*, chaps. 1 and 8.

25. See Mary Poovey, *The Proper Lady and the Woman Writer: Ideology as Style in the Works of Mary Wollstonecraft, Mary Shelley, and Jane Austen* (Chicago: University of Chicago Press, 1984), chap. 1; Jane Austen, *Northanger Abbey* in particular; and Marshall, *Virgins and Viragos*, chap. 8.

26. See C.I. Rothery, "Scott's Narrative Poetry and the Classical Form of the Historical Novel," in *Scott and his Influence*, 70. In arguing that Scott moves toward Lukacs's definition of history through a private, ordinary, yet influential person, Rothery would presumably support Mary Lascelles's distinction between "fictitious history and historical fiction" (*Story-Teller*, 112-14) and argue for Scott's using "historical fiction" here. I would argue that Scott uses both techniques, the latter applicable to Ronald, the former to the Bruce.

27. Barbour, *Bruce*, Book 7; 2:162-88.

28. Pottle, *Boswell's Journal*, 163.

29. Hailes, *Annals*, 1:271, 281n, 303-5.

30. See Barrow's account; his analysis (p. 208) cautiously follows Hailes and Scott (though he doesn't cite Scott).

31. Bruce's relationship with the church hierarchy was more complex and less dramatically antagonistic than Scott's depiction here. For example, Wishart, the Bishop of Glasgow, did not excommunicate Bruce even though the killing of Comyn took place in his diocese, but instead supported him (Barrow, *Robert Bruce*, 210-13).

32. See Barrow, *Robert Bruce*, 78, 237 ff.; and also Scott himself in his Hebridean journal (Lockhart, *Memoirs*, 4:348).

33. See *The British Critic* in Alexander, *Reviewing of Scott's Poetry*, 401; Jeffrey, *Edinburgh Review* 24 (Feb. 1815):294; and *Quarterly Review* 13 (July 1815):306.

34. Barrow, *Robert Bruce*, 80, 200, 230.

35. Scott, *Tales of a Grandfather*, 1:92.

36. Johnson, *Journey to the Western Islands*, 111, 112, 116, 117-18.

37. [Walter Scott,] review of *Report of the Committee of the Highland Society*, appointed to inquire into the Nature and Authenticity of the Poems of Ossian,

and of *The Poems of Ossian*, etc., Containing the Poetical Works of James Macpherson, Esq., in Prose and Rhyme . . . in *Edinburgh Review* 6 (1805):431. See also Scott's late notes in *Boswell's Journal* (1831), esp. 1:227 n., 1:167 n., 1:248 n.

38. Scott, *Ossian* review, 430.

39. Barrow suggests that Barbour had used eye-witness reports in his 1375-77 *Bruce*, though he would have been unable to participate in those events himself (pp. 322, 324). See also McDiarmid's introduction in *Barbour's Bruce* and the editors' argument that some of those sources, and possibly Barbour himself, were Gaelic-speaking (1:72-73), commenting upon this episode (from Book 3, 2:48).

40. In a paper at the 1982 American Society of Eighteenth-Century Studies convention, John Sitter suggested that such a natural limit gives the Ossian poems their power. See also Turner's illustrations to this section of the poem, in Gerald Finley, *Landscapes of Memory: Turner as an Illustrator to Scott* (Berkeley: University of California Press, 1980).

41. See Barbour, *Bruce*, Books 11-13 (3:1-78); and Barrow, *Robert Bruce*, 326-27.

42. See Percy, "An Essay on the Ancient Minstrels," in *Reliques*, 367, who is challenged by Ritson in *Ancient Songs and Ballads*, xi ff.

43. Johnson, *Journey to the Western Islands*, 57.

44. See Virginia Woolf, *A Room of One's Own* (1929; rpt. New York: Harcourt, Brace, Jovanovich, 1957), 51; she credits Edward Fitzgerald with an earlier version of the suggestion.

Chapter Seven. *Harold the Dauntless*

1. See *Byron's Letters and Journals*, ed. Marchand, 4:107; to Murray, 26 April 1814.

2. See Adolphus, *Letters*, 9; Frank Jordan, "Scott, Chatterton, Byron, and the Wearing of Masks," in *Scott and his Influence*, 279-89, where he cites earlier studies of this topic; and Scott's review of Chatterton, *Edinburgh Review* 4 (April 1804):221.

3. See chap. 5, n. 13.

4. See chap. 5, n. 5; see also *Letters*, 3:241.

5. See *Blackwood's Edinburgh Magazine* 1 (April 1817):78; and *Literary Gazette* (March 15, 1817):118. Both also describe it as a Scott imitation, *Blackwood's* because of its humor and the *Gazette* because of its verse form.

6. Eller, "Enchanted Land," 225.

7. See chap. 5, n. 3.

8. The closest verbal parallel is the name Harald Hardradi, "Harald the Ruthless," the king of Norway who attacks northern England as William of Normandy attacks the Saxon Harold in the south. See *King Harald's Saga*, . . . from Snorri Sturlason's Heimskringla, trans. and intro. Magnus Magnusson and Hermann Palsson (Harmondsworth: Penguin, 1966), 9. See also Scott's letter to Morritt of 22 Dec. 1815 (4:145).

9. Johnson, *Sir Walter Scott*, 1:374, 392, 462.

10. The metaphor of the monarch runs through Byron's journal refer-

ences to Scott; see for example his entry for 17 November 1813 (Marchand, 3:208-9.) For accounts of the Scott-Byron relationship that cover a broader period than this discussion, see John Clubbe, "Scott and Byron," *Texas Studies in Language and Literature* 15 (1973):67-91; and Andrew Rutherford, "Byron, Scott, and Scotland," in *Lord Byron and His Contemporaries: Essays from the Sixth International Byron Seminar*, ed. Charles E. Robinson (Newark: University of Delaware Press, 1982), 43-65.

11. Johnson, *Sir Walter Scott*, 1:492, 505.

12. See Sister Rose Marie Grady, "Sources," 365; and Margaret Omberg, *Scandinavian Themes in English Poetry, 1760-1800* (Uppsala: Studia Anglistica Upsaliensia 29, 1976), app. A.

13. Canto 1, argument, ll. 5-6; cited by Corson, *Index*, 121.

14. See Johnson, *Sir Walter Scott*, 1:557; *Letters*, 4:276.

15. *Quarterly Review* 16 (Oct. 1816): 180, 184-85.

16. Ibid., 173, 180, 184-85.

17. Ibid., 185.

18. Ibid., 207-8.

19. Marchand, *Letters and Journals*, 5:178 n, 183, 185, 192.

20. *The Works of Lord Byron*. A new, rev., enl. ed. *Letters and Journals*, ed. Rowland E. Prothero, 5 vols (1898-1901; rpt. New York: Octogon, 1966), 4:207.

21. *Letters*, Prothero, 5:514; reply dated 15 March 1820.

22. Marchand, *Letters and Journals*, 5:182, 185, 186, 109, 170-71, 185.

23. *Quarterly Review* 16 (Oct. 1816):186.

24. Marchand, *Letters and Journals*, 5:183, 211, 219-20.

25. See Paul Lieder, "Scott and Scandinavian Literature," *Smith College Studies in Modern Language* 2 (Oct. 1920):10-21; Edith Batho, "Sir Walter Scott and the Sagas," *MLR* 24 (1929):409; Sister Rose Marie Grady, "Sources," pp. 368 ff.; and Omberg, *Scandinavian Themes*, 18ff.

26. See Omberg, *Scandinavian Themes*, 25-28, 37-38.

27. See Lockhart, *Memoirs*, 1:38, 272-75, and 461; 2:112. See also Lieder, "Scandinavian Literature," 9-11; Batho, "Sagas," 410; and Omberg, *Scandinavian Themes*, 135-38.

28. Review of *Miscellaneous Poetry*, by the Honorable W. Herbert, in *Edinburgh Review* 9 (Oct. 1806):220.

29. See Batho, "Sagas," 410, and *Northern Antiquities . . .* trans. from the French of M. Mallet by Bishop Percy, new ed., enl. rev. by I.A. Blackwell; to which is added an abstract of the Eyrbyggi Saga by Sir Walter Scott (London: Henry G. Bohn, 1847); see p. 525 for Scott's discussion of the berserkers. The abstract was first published in Henry Weber and John Jamieson, *Illustrations of Northern Antiquities* (Edinburgh: 1814); Omberg, *Scandinavian Themes*, 138 n.

30. See his review, p. 212. Omberg reprints Percy's version of this song from *Five Pieces of Runic Poetry* (1763); see pp. 155-58. This episode in *The Antiquary* occurs in chap. 30 of the Harper and Row edition of the Waverley Novels (New York: n.d.), 6:124, but bound in vol. 3, because 48 vols. are bound as 24.

31. For the difficulty of interpreting the past reliably as a theme of *The Antiquary*, see David Brown, *Walter Scott and the Historical Imagination* (London: Routledge and Kegan Paul, 1979), 60-63.

32. See Robert Surtees, *The History and Antiquities of the County Palatine of Durham*, 4 vols. (London: Nichols, Son, and Bentley; Durham, G. Andrews, 1816). This volume has disappointingly little information about the period before the Norman invasion.

33. See Joseph Ritson's *Ancient English Metrical Romances*, introduction to Ywaine and Gawin (1:115-116). Ewaine in Malory intervenes to keep Morgan from killing Urien in his sleep. Ritson then cites a Welsh variant claiming to be more historical or "what the literary Welsh idiots publish, in the eighteenth century, as authentic history."

34. Leider, "Scott and Scandinavian Literature," 30.

35. See Omberg, *Scandinavian Themes*, 155-58, for the text of the poem.

36. Alexander, "Reception," 2:436.

37. Omberg, *Scandinavian Themes*, 70-72.

38. See *King Harald's Saga*, 48 n. and 50-51.

39. The OED says "berserker" is "of disputed etymology," though modern scholars argue for "bear-sark," or bear-skin wearing in battle. Their first entry is from *The Pirate*, Note B, in which Scott writes, "The berserkars were so called from fighting without armour."

40. For an early objection to this anachronism, see *Critical Review*, 5th ser., 5 (April 1817):380: "At least this effect," the reviewer notes, "is not an imitation of Mr. Scott, who being a skillful antiquary, is extremely careful as to niceties of this sort."

41. See *King Harald's Saga*, 98-100.

42. See chap. 5, n.23; Hobsbawm draws on F.L. Hart's earlier point. See also McMaster, *Scott and Society*, 201-2.

43. *Monthly Review*, n.s., 84 (Sept. 1817):15, 17.

44. *The Works of Lord Byron*, a new, rev., enl. ed., *Poetry*, ed. Ernest Hartley Coleridge, 8 vols. (1898-1904; rpt. New York: Octagon, 1966), 4:134-35.

45. Marchand, *Letters and Journals*, 9:85; 12 January 1822.

46. See Clubbe in "Byron and Scott," 81; Sylvia Hofkosh, "Women, Authorship, Romanticism," Session 404, MLA, Chicago, December 1985.

47. On the other hand, one might read the Palmer as Scott's voice and hence as Harold's—and Byron's—father.

48. See Omberg, *Scandinavian Themes*, 54, commenting on Percy's translation of Mallet's *Northern Antiquities* (1:316-17).

49. Frye, *Secular Scripture*.

50. See Scott, *Essays on Chivalry, Romance, and the Drama*, 10-13. This essay agreed upon for the Encyclopedia Britannica in April 1814, was still underway in October 1817; see *Letters*, 3:433, 4:480, 506, 533, 537.

Conclusion

1. Geoffrey Chaucer, "Tale of Sir Thopas," in *The Complete Poetry and Prose of Geoffrey Chaucer*, ed. John H. Fisher (New York: Holt, Rinehart, Winston, 1977), 249, ll. 790-96.

2. See Johnston, *Enchanted Ground*, 179; *Sir Thopas*, Fit 2, stanza 2 (Fisher, p. 251), ll. 897-900, and Fisher's headnote, p. 233.

3. See Kurt Gamerschlag's suggestion that the original stanzas of *Triermain* published in *The Edinburgh Annual Register* represent a *Sir Thopas* to the *Knight's Tale* of *Don Roderick*, appearing in the same volume (" 'Triermain,' " *Influence*, 502).

4. *Centennial Review* 6 (Autumn 1962):533-65, rpt. in Hartman, *Beyond Formalism*, 298-310.

5. See Tilottama Rajan, *Dark Interpreter: The Discourse of Romanticism* (Ithaca: Cornell University Press, 1980), Introduction, and my *Uriel's Eye: Miltonic Stationing and Statuary in Blake, Keats, and Shelley* (University, Ala.: University of Alabama Press, 1985), Introduction.

6. Alan Richardson, "Romanticism and the Colonization of the Feminine," paper read in Session 404, MLA, Chicago, December 1985.

7. See Margaret Kirkham, *Jane Austen, Feminism, and Fiction* (Sussex: Harvester Press, 1983), Introduction. See also Scott's review of *Emma*, *Quarterly Review* 14, no. 27 (Oct. 1816):189.

8. To Anna Austen, 28 Sept. 1814, in *Scott: The Critical Heritage*, ed. Hayden, 74.

INDEX

Abrams, M.H.: definitions of high romanticism in, 2, 32
Adolphus [John Leycester], 190; on rocking stones, 191; similarity of *Manfred* to *H*, 192; satire in Scott, 207
Aeschylus: *The Suppliants*, 189
Alexander, J.H., 44, 103
Alexander III of Scotland, 12, 62
allegory: in *BT*, 134
Annual Register for 1809: early draft of *BT* published in, 131
anonymity: in *BT* and *H*, 131; in Scott's poetry and fiction, 178
apocalypse: and Bannockburn, 175; and castle's location, 146; and disappearing castle, 153; and enlightenment gradualism, 16; and waking from enchantment, 141; in historical narrative poems, 208, 215; in *L*, 39, 204; in *M*, 63, 101, 204; in romance, 8, 9; in Spenser and Milton, 15; mild version of, 85
Ardtornish Castle, 158-59; and false minstrels, 165; Bruce's arrival at, 168
Ariosto, Ludovico: *Orlando Furioso*, 56, 148-50
Aristotle: *hamartia* in, 124
Arran, Isle of, 158
Arthur, King: in *BT*, 133. *See also* romances: Arthurian
Auchinleck: and end of Hebrides tour, 160
Auerbach, Eric: and definition of courtly romance, 69
Augustine, St.: and temporality, 9, 10
Austen, Jane: and challenge to definitions of romanticism, 2; and elopement, 134; and protest at Scott's novel-writing, 215

Aylmer, G.E.: on civil-war conflicts, 99

ballad: and romance structure, 73; and style of, in *BT*, 144; "Childe Roland" in *BT*, 132, 144; gender roles in, 6
—historical: "Chevy Chase," 5; "in *M*, 6; Katherine Janfarie," 5; "Otterburn," 5; "Sir Patrick Spens," 5
—riding or raiding, 13; and communal context of, 214; historical model of, 5; genre in *L*, 21, 68; model for Scott's historical narratives, 208
—romantic: "Alice Brand" in *LL*, 74, 90, 166; and oral tradition, 214; "Clerk Saunders," 6; "The Douglas Tragedy," 6; "Kempion," 6; in *BT*, 135; "Lord Thomas and Fair Annie," 6; "The Wild Huntsman," Scott's version of, 81; "Young Lochinvar" in *M*, 52-53
Balliol, John, 157
Bannockburn, 174, 176; and new beginning, 155-56; and prophecy of nationalism, 209; harbinger of historical change, 210; minstrel redeemer at, 167
Barbour, William: *Bruce*, 156; and Celtic allegiances, 173; Ossianic references in, 172; romance elements in, 165; Scott's revisions of, 166
bard: Celtic traditions of, 174-76; hireling, 95, 96, 119, 165; Irish, 107-9; naming places by, 174; prophetic, 81. *See also* minstrels: as prophets
Barnard Castle, 99, 111, 124

Barrow, J.M., 160
Barthes, Roland: and hermeneutic code, 27; and narrative structures, 8
Beer, Gillian: on psychology of romance, 9; on satire in romance, 206
Ben Cruach, 143
berserker: and burlesque, 177; and Byronic excess, 185-86; and conflict with Christian values, 199; and ecstasy, 212; and fatality, 199; frenzy similar to subjectivity, 202; in Norse culture, 203; psychology of, 194; rage of, 192; shape-changing of, 200; violence of, 198
Bettelheim, Bruno: and sleeping beauty, 142
Blackwater, battle of, 107
Blake, William: and bard's power, 96; "Crystal Cabinet," 211; giant forms in, 126; prophecy in, 63; roles of women in, 4; woman as earthly in *Milton* and *Jerusalem*, 212
Bloom, Harold: and high romanticism, 2, 32; and internalization of quest-romance, 86
book: as magical, 36-37, 105; as metaphor, 18
Boswell, James: and attitudes toward Prince Charles Edward Stuart, 161-62; and prince's escape on Skye, 167; in Hebrides, 159; on Skye, 160
Bowhill: Dalkieth estate at, 22
Boyd, Henry: and Irish theme, 106
Bradbrook, M.C.: on disguise in romance, ballad, and comedy, 81
Branksome Castle, 26, 36, 37
Brooke, Charlotte: and English-Irish links, 110
Bruce, Isabel (historical figure), 169
Bruce, Robert the. *See* Robert the Bruce, king of Scotland
Buccleuch, Duchess of (seventeenth century), 22
building: by magic words, 146-47
burial, live, 51, 55, 58

Butler, Marilyn: and attack on high romanticism, 2
Butler, Samuel: *Hudibras*, 183
Byron, George Gordon, Lord: and incest, 184; and Scott's shift to prose, 215; challenge of, 179; challenge to definitions of romanticism, 2; change from *Manfred* to *Don Juan*, 205; criticism of L and M, 95, motifs in H from, 197; reading Scott's novels, 186; response to H, 186; Scott's advice to, 178; Scott's relationship with, 182-84
—*Bride of Abydos*, 183-84
—*Childe Harold* 1-2, 129, 182
—*Childe Harold* 3: and dating of H, 182; publication of, 177; Scott's reading of, 181; Scott's review of, 179, 183
—*Corsair*, 184
—*English Bards and Scotch Reviewers*, 95, 182-83
—*The Giaour*, 182-83, 186
—*Lara*, 184, 193
—*Manfred*: and change of mood, 178; and resemblance to H, 191, 201-2; and Scott's influence, 186
Byzantium: Viking guards at, 194

Caledonia, 30-31
Carlisle: King Arthur's return to, 141; site of executions in *Waverly*, 161
Carrick, 157-58; minstrel redeemer at, 167, 170; seizure, in Barbour, 166
castle, magical: 137-39; and abrupt scene-change, 32; and charnel-house, 198; and Renaissance epic analogues, 148-49; and Scott-Byron relationship, 179, 181, 184; and surrounding lake, 151; and temptations, 147-48; as prison, 140; as womb, 142; built by witches, 197; described in ballad, 187; disappearing, 139, 150, 152, 212; in *BT* and *H*, compared, 132; in *LL*, 69, 71; in saga, 180; in Scott's narrative poems, 21; in Spenser,

132; linked to Arthurian romance, 189, 196; search for sleeping beauty in, 145; symbolic interpretations of, 132
Caxton, William, 48
Charles II, Scottish and English king, 24
Chaucer, Geoffrey: "Tale of Sir Thopas," 206
Chretien de Troyes: and magic stag-hunt, 70
civil war: as choice of subject, 98; personal conflicts in, 99; religious conflicts in, 100
Clandeboy, 117
Clifton, 161
Clubbe, John, 203
Coleridge, Samuel Taylor: and roles of women, 4; building through poet's art, 122, 147; opiates in, 113
composing process: for LL, 73
Comyn: murder of, 157-58, 169, 171, 174
convent, 54, 56, 58; and roles of women, 56-57
Cottom, Daniel: and romance in *Waverly* novels, 3
Cromwell, Oliver: and Marston Moor, 99
cross, burning of, 77
cross, sign of: and disenchantment, 76-77
cross-dressing: and absence of enchantress's power, 166; and freedom of action, 195; and morality in M, 163; as minstrel, 155, 165, 176-77, 180; as scald, 189; in Elizabethan comedy, 57, 165; in *Lara*, 193; in LL, 19; in M, 56; in *Orlando Furioso*, 56; of Prince Charles Edward, 162-63, 165; useful to spy, 170
Culloden, 161
Cumberland: location of BT, 131, 179

Dalkieth, Harriet, Countess of: influence on L, 22-23
Derrida, Jacques, 32

documents: and biblical interpretation, 126; and enlightenment scepticism, 33; and fictions in M, 41; and interpretive judgments, 44; and structure of R, 92, 111; in literate culture, 20; in interpreting past, 96, 120; legal, 16, 43, 213; letters, forged, 64, 68; letters, Irish, 106; magical, 93; redemptive, 105, 111; scrolls, 123-25; signs, 146-47; symbolic functions of, 12; tablets, 125; versus oral tradition, 128. *See also* forgery; scrolls
domesticity: and rise of novel, 214; not for muse or enchantress, 89; women's role in, 195, 215. *See also* women, roles of
double: character as, 170-71
Douglas family: in LL, 67-94 *passim*; in *Minstrelsy*, 13
Dryden, John: and ethics of poetry, 54; definitions of romance, 45
Dumfries: Comyn murdered at, 157, 168
Dunfermline: and escape from fairyland, 76; civilized realm of, 79
Dunvegan: visited by Johnson, 159
Durham: bishop of, 180; cathedral, 188-89; county as location of H, 131, 179; haunted by ghost, 179; Norman minstrel at, 195

Edgeworth, R.L.: and Irish theme, 106
Edinburgh, 37, 53; compared to Britomart unarmed, 46; Marmion's journey to, 42, 48, 59-60; start of Boswell's and Johnson's journey, 160
Edward I, English king, 62, 157
Edward II, English king, 174
Egliston Abbey, 111, 122, 127
Eildon Hills, 1, 35, 57
elf-queen, 51; absence of, in R, 96; and circular journey, 74; and gift of prophecy, 210; and silencing of minstrel, 10-11; contrasted with

historical situation of women, 42;
Edith analogous to, 159;
Guendolen weaker than, 138; guide
to otherworld for Thomas the
Rhymer, 1, 2, 58, 208; Lady Heron
as, 52; Lady in *L* compared to, 68;
minstrel's love for, 6-7; model for
enchantresses in Scott's poems, 14;
power of, 4; quest for, 212; replaced
by elf-king, 90
Elizabeth I, English queen, 79, 82
Eller, Ruth: and female aspects of self,
180, 193; and naming of poet-
surrogates, 127; and sibling love in
LL, 79; on Thomas the Rhymer, 1
Ellis, George, 47, 72, 98
elopement: and narrative persuasion,
143; complexities of, 153; in Austen,
134; in *BT*, 134
enchantresses, 159, 166; and absence
of writer's anxiety, 68; and
performative language, 213; and
private fantasy, 214; as natural
other, 135; demythologized, 93;
domesticity of, 94, 178; guilt
attributable to, 69; heroine
mimicking, 74, 89; in *L*, 68; in
magical castle, 21; in Scott's
narrative poems, 4, 14, 210;
intellectual women as, 20;
knowledge from sexual encounter
with, 139; Lady Heron as, 59;
power allied to otherworld, 76;
singer as, 52. *See also* witches;
women, roles of
Erskine, William, 46-47, 55, 130
Ettrick: peasant from, misburied, 55,
65

fathering: of imagination, 15, 88,
90-91, 93, 178, 211; of magic, 39,
138, 140
feminist theory, 3
Flodden, 46; and grounding of
romance, 66; and judgment of
dalliances, 59; and judgment of
fictions, 44; and non-heroic events,
42; and private trial by combat, 50;
61; and Scottish suppression of
memory, 41; as apocalyptic
turning-point, 63, 155; battle
analyzed, 63-64; compared to
Marston Moor, 100; harbinger of
historical change, 210; prophecies
of death at, 61; song prophesying
fate at, 55
forgery: and conflicts of loyalty, 44;
and deceptive plots; 41; and
fictions of treason, 49; and
opportunism in use of romance, 43;
and Scott's fictions as, 52, 64; as
crime of writing, 42; exposed to
public censure, 62; to acquire
property, 43. *See also* documents.
frame narratives: in 1830 edition, 22
Frye, Northrop: *Anatomy of Criticism*,
8; and high romanticism, 2; and
popular narrative forms, 3; and
romance, 3, 15, 203

Gascoigne, George: and ladies of the
lake, 79
Genette, Gerard, 20-21
Geoffrey of Monmouth: and King
Arthur's career, 139; and Merlin, 91
Gifford: hill fort at, 50, 54; prophecy
gained at, 60-62
Gilbert, Sandra: and cross-dressing,
163
Gilligan, Carol: and reconciliation, 33
glamour: as shape-changing, 19; in
BT and *H*, 130; in fairyland, 75; in
illusion of peace, 38; interpretation
of, 77; practiced by goblin, 36
Gordon, Robert C.: and romance in
Waverley novels, 3
gothic architecture: cathedral as
model for romance structure, 47.
See also Egliston Abbey; Melrose
Abbey
gothic friar, 119; in *The Monk* and *The
Italian*, 120
gothic novels: and female
imprisonment as sexual metaphor,
58; roles of women in, 56

gramarye: absence of, in *LL*, 68; and poet's supplementing of history, 210; as written performative language, 19; historical resolution through, 178; in *H* and *BT*, 130; in romance, 42; in wizard's books, 36; practiced by benevolent people, 21, 37; practiced by goblin, 75; thematic, in minstrel's lay, 32
Grasmere, 144
Gray, Thomas: "The Bard," 192; Norse culture described by, 187-89
green clothes, 115, 163, 166, 176; worn by James V, 80; worn in "Alice Brand," 75, 80
Greta River, 95, 98; confluence with Tees, 101-2; woods near, 114
guilt: of artist-minstrel, 121; of Marmion, analogous to Scott's, 65

Hailes, Lord (David Dalrymple), 156; on murder of Comyn, 157, 168
hand: as symbol, 147
Harold Hardradi: model for Scott's Harold, 182, 194
harp: and alienation, 118; and estate-building, 97; and poet's success, 93; and primitivism, 52; and prophecy, 89-90; and traditions of minstrels, 42; as enchantress, 87; Irish, revival of, 109; magical, 135; narrator's inadequacy before, 86; opposed to words, 29
Hart, Francis, 3
Hartman, Geoffrey: and definitions of romanticism, 207; and magical stag-hunt, 70
Hartsonge, Matthew Weld, 109
Hazlitt, William: and prophecy, 13
Hebrides Islands, 155, 158, 160-61; landmarks of, 156; visited by Johnson and Boswell, 175
Hecla (Icelandic volcano), 199
Helvellyn, 135
Herbert, William: and Norse poetry, 187, 192
Hermitage Castle, 135

hero: ambiguous, 103, 123; Byronic, 104, 183-84; redeemed, 127; Satanic, 105; Wordsworthian, 105
hero, romance: split in *LI*, 156
Heber, Richard, 47
Henry VIII, English king, 42, 59
Hillhouse, James, 129, 181
Hofkosh, Sonia: and Byron-Scott relationship, 203
Holyrood, 24; and ballad-singing, 52; as bower of bliss, 53; Marmion's mission to, 59
Hortus conclusus, 132
Howard, Robert: *The Committee*, 109
Hurd, Bishop: and gothic structure in literature, 71
hunt, magical, 135

implication: in romance structures, 16
incest, 185, 202
Iona, 158
Ireland, 105-6; conflicts under Elizabeth I, 101; conflicts under George III, 99; emancipation debate, 110, 161; in *Jokeby*, 117; origin of Mortham's wife, 124; primitive culture in, 102, 107

James IV, king of Scotland, 42, 49, 51, 53, 60-61; and belief in romance, 63; as romance hero, 64; audience for "Lochinvar," 53; judged at Flodden, 208; redeemed at Flodden, 101
James V, king of Scotland, 67, 81; and belief in romance realm, 69, 211; as romance quester, 88; paralleled in *BT*, 136; romance and history in characterization of, 101
James VI, king of Scotland (James I of England), 12
Jameson, Fredric: and pre-individual self, 32; negative hermeneutics in, 8, 11, 27; romance, origins of, 14; romance, temporal structures in, 7-8
Jeffrey, Francis, 32
Johnson, Edgar, 67, 122, 148

248   Index

Johnson, Samuel: and Hebrides, 159; and Ossian, 172; and patriarchal culture, 176
Johnston, Arthur, 15
Jonson, Ben, 38
judgment: and deferral, 59-60; divine, 62

Keats, John, 4, 119; *Endymion*, 207, 212; *Hyperion* poems, 207-8;
—*La Belle Dame Sans Merci*, 207; and disappearing castle, 153; and elfin queen, 2; and elusive woman, 211; and enchantresses, 14, 76; and feminist theory, 3; and ladies of the lake, 78; and liminality, 75; and role-playing, 82
Kenilworth, 79-80
Killiecrankie, 26-27, 37
Kintyre, 158-59
Kroeber, Karl, 97, 99

Lady of the Lake: and playful uses of romance, 82, 209; as border figure, 166; boon granted to, 84; in Arthurian romances, 74; king's confrontation with, 67, 88; replaced by elf-king, 93; symbol for imagination, 94
lake, magical, 70, 148
Lake Country, 144
Laneham, Robert, 78-79
Lascelles, Mary, 22
Launfal, 23
Leider, Paul, 191
letters: forged, 49; prefatory, 43-44; revealing forgery, 50
Levi-Strauss, Claude, 3
Lindesay, David, 60
Lindisfarne Abbey, 51, 57, 60, 64-65, 212
Linlithgow, 61, 63
Loch Corriskin, 155, 173, 176
Loch Katrine, 67, 74, 79, 83, 210-11
Loch Lomond, 80
Lockhart, J.G., 129, 177-78
Lovejoy, Arthur, 2

Lukacs, Georg, 2
Luria, Gina, 3

Mabinogion, 70
MacDonald, Angus Oig, 169
MacDonald, Flora, 162, 167
MacDougal of Lorn, 169
McGann, Jerome, 2
McMaster, Graham, 3, 74
Macpherson, James, 172
magic: and breaking of wand, 152; and expectations for narrative, 42; and fear of narrating it, 38; as expression of individual, 37; as other, 11; as revelation, 87; book of, 18-19, 21, 68; heroine's authority in use of, 74, 86; in architecture, 35; in minstrel's power, 113; James V's use of, 83-85; natural versus civilized, 77; performative codes of, 12; relinquished by women, 16; used by enchantresses, 14, 133; written, 33, 58
Mallet, Paul Henry, 187, 191
Malory, Thomas: and enchantresses, 14; and judgments of women, 50, 76; and medieval romance, 69-71; in prefatory letters, 45; and stag-hunt, 71, 79
marriage, arranged, 164
Marston Moor, 99, 107; and bracketing of era, 209; and characters' ages, 108; banners lost at, 117; battle described, 100-101; harbinger of historical change, 210; location of, 98; murder attempted at, 127
Marvell, Andrew, 128
Maturin, Charles, 110
Mayburgh: stones of, 135
Melrose Abbey, 18, 34, 39
Merlin (hawk), 39
Millgate, Jane, 3, 4, 11
Milton, John: and writer as prophet, 43; *Comus*, 138, 142, 151-52; in prefatory letters, 45; *Paradise Lost*, 121, 147, 202

Index 249

minstrels: and oral tradition, 39; as prophets, 88-90; as surrogate for poet, 42, 88; interpreter of romances, 122-23; manipulation by, 113-20; mute, 171, 174; narrator of lay, 22-32; powerlessness in historical poems, 178; structure shaped through, 97; weakness of, 112-13; woman as, 178, 180, 212, 214

Minstrelsy of the Scottish Border, 1; and genre of *L*, 20; and magic hand, 87; and raiding ballad structure, 42; and songs in *M*, 53; and structure of *R*, 111; classification of ballads in, 4; Kenilworth in, 78; models for narrative poems in, 208; romantic ballads in, 2, 6; *Thomas the Rhymer* in, 4, 13

Monmouth, Duke of, 23
Morritt, John, 97, 134, 181
mothering: and domesticity, 39; and imagination, 37; of Scott as writer, 40
Mull, Isle of, 158
Mull, Sound of, 158
muses: absence of, 96; mute minstrel as, 160; woman as, 4, 52, 86-87, 171, 203

Napoleon, 46
narrative structure in: *BT*, 133
narrative theory, 3
nature-goddess, 51, 88, 90
Newark Castle, 22-23, 27, 31, 87, 213
Nine-stane Hill, 135
Norham, 42, 52-54, 59
Norse culture: Scott's knowledge of language, 187; translations of poetry, 188; views of, 187-88

Omberg, Margaret, 187
O'Neill, Hugh, 107
O'Neill, Owen Roe, 108
oral tradition, 171-72, 213; and kinds of truth, 21; and knight's illiteracy, 35; and conditions of performance, 30; and shift to writing, 1; in *L*, 32; in *LL*, 68; intimacy of, 214; minstrels in, 1; Samuel Johnson's attacks on, 160, 175; used in Scott's narrative poems, 16; versus documents, 112

Orkney Islands, 193, 199
Ossian, 108-9, 189
Otherworld, 7, 34-35, 58
Otterburn, 102
Owenson, Sidney, Lady Morgan, 110

Parker, Patricia, 7-8, 16, 27, 146
patriotism, 30
pawn, woman as: in *BT*, 143; in historical narratives, 14, 42, 51, 58-59, 69, 96, 159, 164, 170, 178, 214; romantic elements of, 68
Penrith, 139, 142
Percy, Bishop, 24, 187
picturesque: ruins as, 60
Pikoulis, John, 9
Plato: *Ion*, 28, 62, 89
primitivism: generic models of in *BT* and *H*, 131
Prometheus, 2, 76, 96, 122, 158
prophecy: and history, 11, 12, 43, 59-60; and liminality, 91; and poetic fiction, 41, 88; and primitivism, 83; and psychology of trance, 62; and narrative design, 61; as heuristic model, 92; as retrospective, 60; as superstition, 61; by scald, 203; in song, 64; manipulation by, 61-63; of reversed hunt, 81; produced by alienation, 91-92; through letters, 91
Propp, Vladimir, 3
publication format for *BT* and *H*, 129

Redesdale, 36, 102
Richmond, 103
Ritson, Joseph, 24
Risingham, 102
Robert the Bruce, king of Scotland: 156; and problems of loyalty, 168;

Boswell's view of, 167; red-handed, 157, 168
Roby, John, 110
Rogers, Samuel, 186
Rokeby estate, 111; and idealized community, 209; burning of, 121; Gothic architecture of, 117; location of, 96; minstrel's art at, 120
Roland, Chanson de, 145
romances: behavioral ideal in, 43; Celtic origins of, 131; contrasted to epic, 85, 131; definitions in prefatory letters, 44; hermeneutics of, 67; in Scott's narrative poems, 16; political control through, 89; practiced by British poets, 42, 45; psychology in, 9; rebirth in, 97; songs as enthrallment in, 43; sources of, in Border, 42; sources of, in childhood, 46; structure of, 7-8, 15, 72; wish-fulfillment in, 49
—Arthurian: in *LL*, 68; in *H*, 195
—medieval, 74-77
—Renaissance, 78; and allegory, 153; and matter of Charlemagne, 144; formal and social unity in, 80; in Elizabethan comedies, 78, 86, 106; ladies of the lake in, 78-80; models, 7
romanticism: definitions of, 214; high, 32
Rose, Stewart, 45
Rubenstein, Jill, 67, 133

sagas: as model for *H*, 131, 179; *Harold Hardradi*, 194; Scott's abstract of *Erbyggi-Saga*, 188; Snorri, *Heimskringla*, 196; translations of, in seventeenth century, 187
St. Mary's Loch: wizard at, 45-46
salvation-history: and quest-romance, 86
Saxo Grammaticus, 187
scald: and cross-dressing, 199
Schiller, Friedrich von, 32, 207
Schlegel, A.W., 208
Schlegel, Friedrich, 207-8

Scott, Walter: advice to Byron, 203; and journal-entry on Skye, 162; narrative poems, romantic and historical, 13; on Ossianic poems, 172; views of medieval romance structure, 71
—miscellaneous works: "Essay on Chivalry," 204; "Essay on Romance," 73; *Life of Dryden*, 109; *Life of Swift*, 109; review of Byron's *Childe Harold 3*, 179, 183, 184, 186, 201; review of Ellis's *Metrical Romances*, 72; review of Herbert's translations of Old Norse, 187; *Sir Tristrem*, edition of, 206
—novels: *The Antiquary*, 178, 179, 183, 188, 190; *The Black Dwarf*, 178, 183; *The Bride of Lammermoor*, 50; *The Fair Maid of Perth*, 147, 200; *The Fortunes of Nigel*, 213; *Guy Mannering*, 178; *Kenilworth*, 78; *Old Mortality*, 178, 183; *Redgauntlet*, 16, 157; *Rob Roy*, 186; *Tales of My Landlord*, 201; *Waverley*, 161, 171, 173, 178, 190
scrolls: and prophecy, 91; in *Dies Irae*, 10, 39; stone ornaments as, 34; symbolic image, 12. See also documents.
sedimentation: in interpreting romance, 12, 136, 150
Senachi: in oral tradition, 172
settings, geographical: and structure of *R*, 111; choice of Yorkshire, 98; confluence, 101; in *BT* and *H*, 131; piracy, 103; primitive, 102
Shakespeare, William: *King Lear*, 132; *Othello*, 122, 125; romantic comedies, 15; *The Winter's Tale*, 122, 209
Shelley, Percy Bysshe: *Alastor*, 138, 207; and bard's power, 97; and prophecy, 63; and roles of women, 4; and sculptural ideal, 207; *Prometheus Unbound*, 212
signs: in nature, 135; interpretation of, 136
Skiddaw, 135

Skye, 155, 157-58, 169, 173; and historical analogy, 159; disguised minstrel on, 165; growth of relationships on, 170; locations described in *LI*, 162, 175; minstrel as redeemer on, 167
songs: and ethical ambiguity, 56; and fiction in *M*, 41; and minstrel's control of battle, 83; and role of women, 52; feudalism in, 117-18. *See also* minstrel; oral tradition
speech: as performative, 16; in otherworld, 10-11
Spenser, Edmund: and judgments of romance women, 50; and structure of *R*, 111; and writer as prophet, 43; Bower of Bliss, model of, 53; Britomart and cross-dressing, 56; Britomart as Edinburgh, 46; hortus conclusus in, 132; in prefatory letters, 45; magical castles in, 148-50; on Ireland, 108; *Shepheardes Calender*, 78-79
Staffa, 158
stag-hunt: and source in Barbour, 166; as means to vision, 88; by James V, 69, 80; magical, 70, 79, 81, 166; realism and magic fused in, 71; reversal of, 82; song about, 85; song warning of, 92
Stanmore, 102-3, 105
Stirling, 69, 74, 77, 79, 82-84, 92, 158
Stuart, House of, 167, 175
Stuart, Lady Louisa, 134, 181, 183, 193
Stuart, Mary, 85
Stuart, Prince Charles Edward, 157, 160, 167
sword, magical, 70, 84, 166

Tantallon, 49, 63
Tasso, Torquato, 56, 148-50
Tayler, Irene, 3
Tees River, 98
Teviot River, 26
Thomas of Ercildoun, 1, 206

Thomas the Rhymer ballad, 1, 73, 206; and fictional additions, 13; and *Mintrelsy* classifications, 5; model for Scott's narratives, 68; prophecy in, 12; romantic elements in, 6-7
Thorslev, Peter, 103
Tone, Wolfe, 109
Tonkin, Humphrey, 8
treasure, buried, 48, 101, 105, 123
Tyrone, 108

Ulster, 108
Union, Act of, 44

Valley of St. John: Castle Rock in, 146; isolation in, 141; magic castle in, 137, 140, 180, 207

Walker, Joseph Cooper, 109
Wallace, William, 46, 169
Warton, Thomas, 6, 78, 80
Welsh, Alexander, 3
William III, king of England, 27
Wilt, Judith, 1, 3, 157
Winston, 102
witches, 150; and choice, 212; and fertility goddesses, 34; and performative language, 19; and relinquishing of magic, 210; as brides, 198-99; as castle-builders, 180; domestication of, 151; in castle, 210; in *H*, 191, 195; in *M*, 42; in quest-romance, 214; in Renaissance, 197; muse as, 179; not exiled to attic, 4; spell-bound and -binding, 46, 50
wizards, 35, 45-46, 48, 93
women, roles of: as fiction-writers, 54; as objects of quest-romance, 4; differing in romance and history, 2; disguised as warriors, 56; generational split in, 151; illicit sexuality in, 55; in Gothic novel, 56-57; vanishing, 138. *See also* domesticity; enchantresses; muses; pawn; witches
Wordsworth, William, 30, 116, 144

Woolf, Virginia, 153, 176
writing, 40, *See also* documents; scrolls
Wycliffe, John, 126

Yarrow River, 31

Zernebock, cults of, 191-92

www.ingramcontent.com/pod-product-compliance
Lightning Source LLC
Chambersburg PA
CBHW022055160426
43198CB00008B/241